BLOOD

and

DARING

BLOOD

and

DARING

HOW

CANADA FOUGHT

THE AMERICAN

CIVIL WAR

AND FORGED

A NATION

JOHN BOYKO

ALFRED A. KNOPF CANADA

Library and Archives Canada Cataloguing in Publication

Boyko, John, 1957–
Blood and daring : How Canada fought the American Civil War and forged a nation / John Boyko.

Includes bibliographical references and index.
Issued also in electronic format.
ISBN 978-0-307-36144-8

1. United States—History—Civil War, 1861–1865—Participation, Canadian.
2. United States—History—Civil War, 1861–1865—Influence. 3. Canada—History—1841–1867. 4. Canada—History—Confederation, 1867. 5. Canada—Politics and government—1841–1867. 6. Canada—Relations—United States—History. 7. United States—Relations—Canada—History. I. Title.

E540.C25B69 2013   973.70971   C2012-905614-6

Text and cover design by CS Richardson

Cover images: *Abraham Lincoln, three-quarter length portrait* by Anthony Berger, Prints and Photographs Division, Library of Congress, LC-DIG-ppmsca-19305; *Battle of Nashville* by Howard Pyle © Minnesota Historical Society / CORBIS; *Hon. Sir John A. MacDonald* from the Brady-Handy Collection, Prints and Photographs Division, Library of Congress, LC-DIG-cwpbh-00412

Printed and bound in the United States of America

2 4 6 8 9 7 5 3 1

This book is dedicated to Kenzie McIntyre, in the perhaps naive but still worthwhile hope that when she grows up, wars will have become merely sad stories of human failing, known only in dusty old books.

UNITED STATES,
CONFEDERATE STATES AND
BRITISH NORTH AMERICA

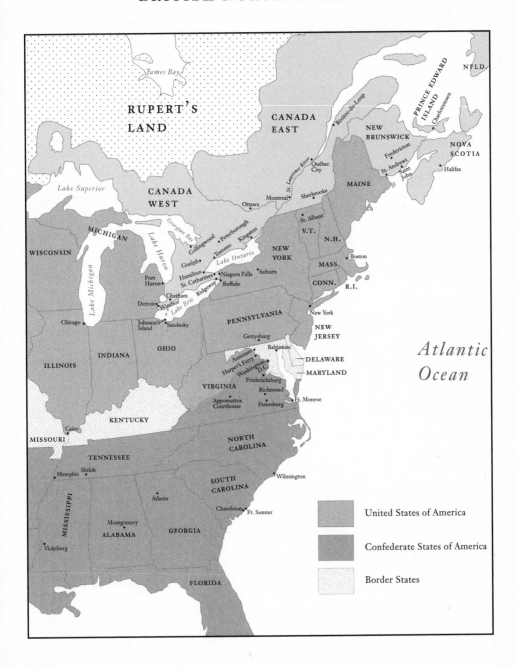

CONTENTS

BAD NEIGHBOURS IN
A DANGEROUS NEIGHBOURHOOD

T HE GHOSTS REMAIN ACTIVE. Even after the passage of more than a century and a half, the American Civil War's ideas, promise and pain still resonate. An understanding of the war is crucial to all who wish to comprehend America's civic conversation—to comprehend America itself. Similarly, no one can fully understand Canada without appreciating that the war was an essential factor in the country's birth, when and how it came about, as well as shaping the fundamental ideas upon which it is based. While saving itself by creating itself, Canada was intricately involved in the war's cause and course. Despite the efforts of America's wartime leaders, Canada's actions during and after the conflict kept Canada from becoming American. We owe it to ourselves to understand the Civil War—to heed its whispering ghosts.

Before embarking on our journey of understanding, we must know and accept a few things. First, throughout the Civil War and the years shouldering it, the vast and ruggedly beautiful land north of the American border was home to members of proud First Nations and communities of British,

French and other Europeans, some of whom were recent arrivals while others had roots going back several generations. Britain had claimed jurisdiction over it all, except for a broad swath surrounding James and Hudson Bays called Rupert's Land, which was owned and governed by the Hudson's Bay Company. There were small British communities gathered around Victoria and Vancouver, hugging Newfoundland's craggy shore and on Prince Edward Island. The Maritime colonies of Nova Scotia and New Brunswick were more populous and prosperous. Bigger and richer still was Canada, united under a single government but composed of Canada East and West and occupying what is now the southern portions of Ontario and Quebec.

We must accept a world where the air was empty and the sky silent. The trans-Atlantic cable had been laid but did not yet work, and the marvel of the telegraph was new but unreliable. Messages often took weeks to bounce back across the Atlantic and days even within North America. A momentous battle such as Gettysburg could have been won by Confederate General Lee, not with a thousand more troops, but rather if he'd had a couple of cell phones. While railways were used to great effect, Lee's army got to Gettysburg largely by walking from Virginia to Pennsylvania—it was not quick. Canadian political leaders could meet with British authorities only after a long ocean journey and were often gone for months at a time, grinding political progress to a halt.

We must also disenthrall ourselves of current myths, including that of the undefended border. Those struggling through the Civil War years bore memories not of Canadian-American friendship and economic and cultural integration but of more than a century of suspicion, hatred and bloodshed. Canada and the United States were bad neighbours in a dangerous neighbourhood.

At the outset of the Civil War, collective memories remained alive of the French and Indian War when, in the late 1750s and early 1760s, New York State, the Ohio Valley, Nova Scotia, Montreal and Quebec City were battlefields.* Britain's myopic handling of the war's aftermath bred

---

* *In Britain and Canada, it was called the Seven Years War.*

resentments and misunderstandings that grew to rebellion. In an attempt to keep Quebec loyal, Britain instituted the 1774 Quebec Act. Quebecers saw it as protecting their French/Catholic rights within a system of government they understood. American rebels, on the other hand, considered the Quebec Act as among what they called the Coercive or Intolerable Acts, because it was yet another example of Britain denying democracy to its colonies and, consequently, another precursor to revolution. Quebecers were invited to send delegates to join those representing the thirteen colonies who were defining the new America at the First and Second Continental Congresses in Philadelphia. Both invitations were ignored. With those rebuffs, patriot and later America's second president, John Adams, explained to his fellow delegates that, in order to defend the northern flank, Quebec would need to be attacked and liberated Quebecers should be persuaded to join the revolution.[1] In November 1775, Montreal fell to American troops, and Benedict Arnold's men tried but could not take Quebec City.

Congress dispatched three delegates, one of whom was Benjamin Franklin, to woo Quebecers to the rebel cause. They failed. The Québécois had little interest in joining a ragtag group of rebellious colonies, only two of which allowed the practice of their religion, and whose army mistreated civilians, and stole property and food.[2] Spring brought a British fleet to the St. Lawrence and the Americans scurried away. Adams, undaunted by the military and diplomatic failures, proclaimed, "The Unanimous Voice of the Continent is 'Canada must be ours.'"[3]

The Declaration of Independence made direct mention of the Quebec Act as one of the grievances levelled against the British king. As the Revolutionary War progressed, the Articles of Confederation were developed to serve as a constitution for the Continental Congress, which had become a government. Article 16 made it easy for Canada to join: "Canada acceding to this Confederation, and entirely joining in the measures of the United States, shall be admitted into and entitled to all the advantages of this Union."[4] The document was translated into French and sent north. Three years later, Congress passed a resolution stating,

"Every favorable incident [will] be embraced with alacrity to facilitate and hasten the freedom and independence of Canada and her union with these states."[5] Despite the appeal, neither the Quebecers, the Quebec government nor the Catholic Church, which was enormously powerful in the colony, had any interest in becoming American.

The Revolution was America's first civil war. About a third of the American colonists wanted nothing to do with what Adams, Jefferson and the others were selling. With every British military defeat, more of those loyal to the Crown left or were driven out. Some fled to Britain while others went south, but most escaped to what remained of British North America. Eventually, about thirty thousand moved to Nova Scotia and ten thousand to Quebec.[6] A number of freed Blacks emigrated.

Britain had lost thirteen of its North American colonies and did not fancy losing the others. Wary of allowing demographic and economic growth to create a new powerhouse such as wealthy and populous Virginia, it split Nova Scotia to create New Brunswick. It divided Quebec into Upper Canada (Ontario) and Lower Canada (Quebec). A new political system was installed that afforded a semblance of self-rule with British-appointed governors in charge. A border was loosely drawn, and American fishers were granted inland rights. Those long established in the suddenly growing British colonies shared with the revolution's refugees and the newcomers from the British Isles a deep respect for British political values and an abhorrence of the ideals and aspirations upon which the American Revolution had been based. They were determined to remain separate from the United States.

That determination was tested a generation later in the War of 1812. Relentless American expansion had led to Native resistance and then to uprisings inspired and led by Shawnee chief, Tecumseh, and his brother, known as the Prophet. So-called War Hawks in Congress convinced themselves that Britain was behind the Native unrest and was supporting piracy and the impressment of Americans into British naval service. The United States could only be safe and prosperous, they argued, if Britain was pushed out of North America.[7]

Americans saw the struggle as a war of liberation; Canadians believed it was a war of survival. It was a cousins' war—and it was horrible. The battles were savagely fought. Cities and towns on both sides of the border were burned and civilians were killed. Toronto, called York at the time, was taken by Americans and torched. Washington was captured and the president fled. The capitol was ransacked and the White House set on fire.

When the war finally ended, Britain's flag was still there—Canada remained. Border tensions eased as the 1817 Rush-Bagot Agreement led to the demilitarization of the Great Lakes. The war had given Americans a national anthem and the symbol of Uncle Sam. It afforded Canadians the pride born of having defended their land and the un-American ideals in which they believed. A new, unifying and unique nationalism was taking root.[8]

In 1837, rebellions erupted in Upper and Lower Canada. Gunfire echoed and blood stained the streets of Toronto and French Canadian towns. Britain sent Lord Durham to see what the fuss had been about, and his recommendations led to the creation of a more responsible and representative government in a unified colony called Canada. He hoped that Canada East (Quebec) would soon be subsumed by Canada West (Ontario). Nova Scotia and New Brunswick remained separate. Britain appointed a governor general to oversee all of its North American colonies. The Canadian government was ostensibly subservient to him, as were the Maritime governments to their lieutenant-governors who reported to him. It was with this political structure and its deep-seated suspicion of the United States that Canada and the Maritimes faced an increasingly belligerent America that was tearing itself apart.

THE CIVIL WAR

The tensions that led to the Civil War were complex and are still hotly debated. One point of view emphasizes the growing differences in outlook and needs between the urban, industrial North and the rural, agrarian South. This thinking examines banking, tax and tariff policies as significant points of conflict. Another argument paints Confederate leaders as either patriotic heroes or misguided villains attempting to protect the South's economic and social fabric and slavery, which was inextricably woven into it. Yet another school of thought contends that the Constitution was a compact created by the states and based on the Jeffersonian-Lockean premise that a government exists to protect rights, and that when it fails to do so, people have the duty to replace it; states' rights and property rights were seen to be under attack by Northern lawmakers and abolitionists, and so a new government needed to be created. Still others contend that the war was about right and wrong, morality versus wickedness and constitutionality versus lawlessness. To them, slavery was the cause and its abolition the justifiable value of the war.

Each point of view offers persuasive arguments and claims enthusiastic adherents. In the end, though, they all end up arguing over the degree to which slavery was a factor in causing the war. While other viewpoints exist and variants within these schools can be teased out, one always returns to slavery. It was a cancer present within the United States before there was a United States and was not removed by the wise men who wrote the Constitution. Racial bondage was allowed to grow and eventually it nearly ended the young country's life.

Shortly after the war began in April 1861, Britain declared itself neutral. The Canadian and Maritime governments dutifully echoed that official line and informed their citizens that it was against the law to support North or South, and for individuals to join in the fight. One would expect that Canadians and Maritimers would abide by their government's wishes and that public opinion would overwhelmingly support the North. After all, they were by and large law-abiding folks, loyal to Britain and nearly unanimous in their abhorrence of slavery, which had been banned in British North America a generation earlier. Further, Canadians and Maritimers were geographically closer to the North and for years thousands more had travelled to those Northern states for work than to the distant South. Business people enjoyed more commerce with Northern than Southern industry. Canadians travelling to Britain often went by way of New York and Boston. Despite such familiarity, however, public and popular opinion of the North and South was divided, volatile and multi-dimensional. It was coloured by class, ethnicity, religion, ideology and region.

Many factors led Canadians to sympathize with the Confederacy. In Canada East, the Catholic Church enjoyed enormous power, but considered itself under attack by popular democratic ideas on the separation of church and state.[9] In this fight, American republicanism was anathema. Montreal's *Gazette* called America the most "immoral" country in the world.[10] The destruction of the United States through civil war and the Confederacy itself was, consequently, seen as a good thing by the Church hierarchy. Priests often equated Southerners with the Québécois—a beleaguered minority, fighting to preserve a unique way of life threatened by a more politically and economically powerful enemy with no shared cultural values.

In New Brunswick, Fredericton was home to a Protestant majority that was unmoved by anti-Catholic threats. Its physical location in the centre of the province left it somewhat isolated. That it was the capital perhaps made its people more sympathetic to the exhortations of the government and the lieutenant-governor, who were resolutely neutral. The city's *New Brunswick Reporter* was staunchly pro-North throughout the war.

However, a few miles southeast, on the Fundy Bay, lay the much different Saint John. It was a blatantly pro-South city that recognized the potential of winning business for its port if the United States permanently split. Its Irish-Catholic majority empathized with Southern nationalism and with fighting a distant government. Confederate ships were encouraged to use its harbour, and its spies and recruiters made to feel at home in the city's hotels and bars. Many rich Southerners who had for years summered nearby moved their families to the fine cottages to escape the ravages of war. They were openly welcomed in the city. In June 1862, hundreds of folks gathered to enjoy a large and boisterous parade celebrating a Confederate victory. Confederate flags flew and a band played "Dixie." A Maine sea captain was roughed up by the crowd as police watched but did nothing. A similar parade was held in the border town of St. Andrews.

Halifax, Nova Scotia, was a garrison town that served as Britain's primary North American port for its enormous and peerless navy. An entrepreneurial spirit pulsed throughout the colony, with its ship manufacturers creating internationally respected wooden vessels and Halifax's magnificent natural harbour bustling with international trade. The city's business people enjoyed the profit earned by magnanimously welcoming both Northern ships seeking Confederate blockade runners and the elusive Southerners themselves. In allowing Southern ships free access to Halifax, the city served as an important link in the communication network between the Confederacy and European capitals.

A major factor that shaped, shifted and divided Canadian and Maritime public opinion was Lincoln's attitude toward that most irrepressible subject: slavery. Abolitionist Canadians and Maritimers suffered widespread disappointment when Lincoln said in his 1861 inaugural address that he would not immediately emancipate American slaves.[11] Even Toronto's pro-North *Globe* reflected disillusion in an editorial: "At first the sympathies of the British people were unmistakably with the North. They imagined that Mr. Lincoln had determined to wage a war against slavery, and in heart and soul they were with him."[12] The Emancipation Proclamation that followed in September 1862 came after the opinions of many had hardened against the president.

Another factor that gave rise to Confederate sympathies was the unmistakable anti-Canadian and anti-British sentiment that swept up from the North. Lincoln had appointed notorious anglophobe and enemy of Canada, William Seward, to his cabinet. Seward had issued numerous threats of annexation before and during the war, and then a crisis involving the taking of Confederate agents from a British ship called the *Trent* nearly brought war. Many Northern newspapers published damning stories and editorials that openly promoted a hatred of Canada and Canadians, while frequently advocating invasion.[13] Many of the anti-Canadian rants were reprinted in Canadian papers. The barrage of threats and disparagement led to worries that perhaps the Civil War would afford Americans such as Seward, who had for so long dreamt of taking Canada, an opportunity to turn dreams into plans.

The divided sympathies within Canada and the Maritimes were evident in its newspapers and public debates. The *Toronto Leader* was pro-South, while the *Toronto Globe* was pro-North. The *Montreal Gazette* was pro-South, while the *Montreal Witness* was pro-North. The reporting and editorial stances of eighty-four Canadian papers revealed themselves to be obviously pro-South, with only thirty-three pro-North and eight neutral.[14] A report of the Confederate victory in the war's first battle elicited a spontaneous cheer in Canada's legislature.

In the face of political authorities demanding neutrality and non-participation in the war, and despite the complexity of public opinion and the widespread sympathy for the South, many young Canadians and Maritimers left home to fight. Those who did fought overwhelmingly in Union ranks. A letter home from a young man stationed in the trenches facing the Confederate capital of Richmond, Virginia, in 1864 spoke with surprise of how many of his French-speaking countrymen he had met: "You have no idea . . . of the number of Canadians who are in different army corp. They may be counted not in the hundreds but in the thousands."[15] About forty thousand Canadians and Maritimers joined the fight, and the ratio was approximately fifty Canadians in Union regiments for every one in a Confederate regiment.[16]

The service of so many Canadians in America's duelling armies further split Canadian and Maritime public opinion. It also divided communities and, as in America, fractured families. Nova Scotia's Norman Wade, for instance, enlisted to serve on Union ships enforcing the blockade. In letters home he told of the many compatriots he had encountered and the divided loyalties they suffered together.[17] In November 1861, he wrote to his sister: "A schooner was seen working in towards the mouth of the river . . . the Captain told me to pitch a shot across her course . . . she proved to be a schooner from Lunenburg, Nova Scotia . . . some of our officers had the joke on me for firing on my own countrymen."[18]

Wade's family, like so many others, carried on a polite but sometimes terse debate through his correspondence. During the 1861 *Trent* crisis he wrote to his brother wondering why he and so many Nova Scotians supported the South: "I was not surprised to hear that your sympathies were wholly with the south, and do not see how it is possible, considering the relations we bear the northern people. You say if these million people want freedom they ought to have it, but is it freedom they are fighting for, or are they dupes of designing politicians."[19]

OUR GUIDES

The beliefs, struggles and dreams of six fascinating people will guide us on our journey of understanding. The highlights of their respective lives, and what they represent in the Civil War era, will offer insight into the most important and overlapping events and ideas that propelled Canada and the United States through the most dangerous period of their histories.

Our first guide is John Anderson. He was a courageous Missouri slave who escaped to freedom in Canada only to find his relentless pursuers unwilling to surrender their prey. His struggle to remain free came to involve international intrigue that angered Northerners, infuriated Southerners and frustrated British leaders. It inspired Canadians to stand up to both British and American pressure. The Anderson case helps us to see the extent to which Canada and the Maritimes played a part in the development of the Southern resentment toward abolitionists. Those iron resentments helped lead to secession and war. Meanwhile, the case sparked nascent Canadian and Maritime notions of greater independence.

William Seward was a rapaciously ambitious, cigar-chomping New York political leader and secretary of state to presidents Lincoln and Johnson. He was also an avowed expansionist. Before and during the early months of the war, he expressed an eagerness to instigate a war with Britain that he believed would lead to the capture of its Canadian colonies and a reunited America. His desire to bomb, buy or barter for territory never abated. Canadians and Maritimers were justifiably afraid and began polishing their weapons. With Britain's help, the borders were reinforced and preparations made for invasion. Seward enables us to recognize the growing desire on the part of British North American colonies to unify as a means to better defend themselves against American military threats, aggression and aspirations, and shows just how close the Civil War came to bursting its borders.

The mysterious Sarah Emma Edmonds invites us to comprehend why approximately forty thousand Canadians and Maritimers donned the blue or grey, and to appreciate the contributions they made. Many rest in Civil War cemeteries throughout the United States. Twenty-nine won the Congressional Medal of Honor. Some stood with Grant when Lee surrendered. Another captured Lincoln's assassin. Whereas Edmonds volunteered to serve as a nurse and spy, many Canadians and Maritimers, including children, were tricked into enlisting or even kidnapped by American agents. Meanwhile, British and American deserters passed each other as they crossed the border. The whole time, Edmonds hid a captivating secret.

Another of our guides is wily Mississippi politician and former federal cabinet secretary Jacob Thompson. When the Confederacy was awash in military, economic and diplomatic bad news, the decision was made to send agitators to Canada. They were to organize the large number of Southerners already there into a potent force that could harass the North from the north. Thompson led the mission. He and his agents worked openly in Niagara Falls, Toronto and Montreal. Thompson's efforts led to missions to burn Manhattan, spring Confederate prisoners of war, and support Lincoln's opposition in ways that could have split the North and guaranteed the South's survival. His Confederates killed Americans on raids launched from Canada. Thompson's exploits further illustrate how Canada's implicit participation brought the war dangerously close to involving Britain and the military subjugation of what would become Canada.

George Brown, our next guide, owned Toronto's *Globe*, Canada's most widely read, unabashedly partisan and influential newspaper. In the years leading up to and through the Civil War, he was a member of the

legislature, Reform Party leader and, for a very brief period, prime minister. When Canada needed concerted action to address American threats,
its political structure was a shambles. No one expected the taciturn Brown
to summon the courage needed to put political advantage and personal
ambition aside and bring squabbling factions together to seek a solution.
Similarly, few expected the Maritime colonies to warm to his vision of a
broad union. The ideas proposed by Brown and those he drew to him
became the basis for a new state, decidedly different from its neighbour.
Brown's work enables us to understand how the United States provided
both the alarming incentive to invent a new country and the negative
example that informed the nature of that invention. After all, the war
was startling proof to Canada's founding fathers that the American
political system was an abject failure.

While Brown began the nation-building process, it took our final
guide, the hard-drinking and effervescently convivial John A. Macdonald,
to get it done. Macdonald was the indispensable man in the nation-
building years beginning in 1864. But even after the war ended in 1865,
it appeared that his vision and political genius might not be sufficient to
allow Canada to survive long enough to be born. Canada and the Maritime
colonies were blamed for playing a role in starting the war and then in prolonging it. Montreal was identified as the site where the plot to assassinate
Lincoln was hatched, and Canadians were castigated for harbouring
the conspirators. American invaders crossed the border and blood was
spilled. The war was not really over. Macdonald needed to fight a renewal
of annexation plans by Seward and then-president Grant, who were
determined to use postwar compensation they demanded from Britain to
see the stars and stripes hoisted north of the border.

While enjoying the story of Canada and the Civil War through the
lens of our six guides' lives, we will also investigate the roles played by
many others. Americans Frederick Douglass, John Brown and John
Wilkes Booth advanced their goals while in Canada. Jefferson Davis and
many of his generals sought postwar refuge in Canada. Canadian and
Maritime politicians Thomas D'Arcy McGee, Alexander Galt and George

Étienne Cartier and soldiers George Denison, Charles Riggins and the four Wolverton brothers play important roles. Also significant are British lords Palmerston, Russell, Lyons, Head, Monck and Thornton. At different times and for various reasons, some British leaders irked America to the verge of war, while others pushed Canadians to save themselves and still others offered to give the young country away.

Throughout our journey, the political wiles, characters and visions of two men will tower over all the rest: Abraham Lincoln and John A. Macdonald. At a time when so much could have gone so wrong, Canada and the United States were blessed with wise, transformational leaders. Our stable and independent nations, which share a continent in peace, freedom and understanding, are their gifts to us and the Civil War's legacy.

Yours truly
John Anderson

———◆———

JOHN ANDERSON AND THE
RAILROAD TO FREEDOM AND WAR

J OHN ANDERSON WAS A SLIGHT MAN, about five foot six, with dark, intelligent eyes. Although only thirty years of age, his heavily lined face betrayed a lifetime of hardship. He wore a new suit purchased by his supporters, many of whom were there, watching him sit stoically behind a polished oak table in the main courtroom of Toronto's Osgoode Hall. The building was designed to intimidate. It demanded respect. The commanding façade greeted visitors and then, once they were inside, its dark oak and mahogany, rich leather and high ceilings whispered that this was a place for serious people conducting serious business. And today's proceedings were serious indeed.

Outside on that chilly morning of December 15, 1860, stood fifty Toronto police officers. At Government House, only five minutes away, a hastily assembled company of soldiers from the Royal Canadian Rifles had muskets at the ready with bayonets menacingly attached. All were prepared for the demonstration promised and the riot expected, should the court decision go as the two hundred or so people in the crowd feared. Stretchers were piled against a wall, ready to haul away casualties.

More heavily armed policemen were inside Osgoode, nervously eyeing the onlookers who were crammed into every nook and cranny. Toronto sheriff Fred Jarvis had tried a ticketing scheme to control access to the courtroom, but it had failed, and so the place was packed by the well-connected and the curious and by many of Anderson's staunchest supporters. Reporters from a number of Canadian and American newspapers were also in attendance.

All hushed and rose when the elderly and deeply respected Chief Justice John Beverley Robinson, flanked by justices Robert Easton Burns and Archibald McLean, entered the room. Anderson stood with his lawyers. With a nod from Robinson, the three justices sat and adjusted their robes. The spectators took their seats. Robinson looked up and cleared his throat.

There was a great deal at stake—far more than the life of an African American ex-slave. For months, the Anderson case had been discussed in the halls of power in colonial Canada, Britain and the United States. Political leaders such as George Brown, John A. Macdonald, Thomas D'Arcy McGee and others who would soon play crucial roles in the founding of an independant Canada concerned themselves with the case. Options for Canada's future as a British colony, an independent country or perhaps even new northern American states, were being openly debated on both sides of the border. The case had influenced a growing consensus among Canadians and those in the Maritime colonies that a new political structure—more independent of Britain and better able to defend itself against American threats, yet reflecting British values—was needed.

In Britain, the case brought to a head a confluence of issues that were forcing a re-evaluation of the country's relationship with its colonies and the United States. A growing number of influential leaders, including Chancellor of the Exchequer William Gladstone, were openly advocating cutting ties with increasingly expensive and bothersome colonies such as Canada. The Anderson case helped bolster their argument.

Others contended that the case was a moral issue, and that it necessitated intervention regardless of the consequences for Canada's growing independence or Anglo-American relations, even if such intervention might mean war.

In the United States, many hoped the Anderson decision would finally settle an issue that had been tearing the American North and South apart and straining relations between Canada, Britain and the United States for decades. It would once and for all either open Canada's doors to fleeing African Americans or slam those doors shut. It could destroy the Underground Railroad by allowing American slave catchers to capture their prey on the streets of Toronto, as in Boston or New York, or it could heighten tensions with the many Southerners who found the Underground Railroad, and the Northern and Canadian abolitionists who made it work, insulting to Southern beliefs. With that, it could also provide secessionists with one more reason to dissolve the fragile Union.

Anderson sat in silence. He had never sought notoriety. He had not wished to be at the centre of an international crisis. He had wanted only to live a quiet life. He had wanted only to be free.

THE ESCAPE

To comprehend the events that had brought Anderson and international attention to Osgoode Hall that cool December morning, we must understand slavery in America. Slavery meant suffering the wrenching, piercing pain of being deprived of home, family, health, name, language and religion; being denied options, opportunity, dignity and one's fundamental humanity. It inflicted the rage of powerlessness while witnessing one's husband emasculated and bloodied by the lash, or one's wife and children raped, beaten, and bought and sold as chattel by men protected by their status, wealth and race, and by the policies, practices and laws of the land. Slavery meant that even if one saved pennies and purchased one's liberty, life as a freeman remained beset by discrimination, violence and the constant threat of kidnapping by those more concerned with bounty than justice. Slavery was the contradiction at the heart of the American ethos.

The first American slaves arrived in Virginia in 1619 at the hands of Portuguese traders. They were referred to as *negro*, which is the Portuguese word for "black." By 1750, 44 percent of Virginia's population and 61 percent of the population of South Carolina were African slaves. Slaves carried the burgeoning colonies on their whipped backs. Slave labour built roads, farms and towns, and would later help construct the White House and the Capitol Building. An economist has called slavery "the first principle and foundation of all the rest, the mainspring of the machine which sets every wheel in motion."[1]

Slavery was not mentioned in the American Constitution but its presence was clear. In tallying Americans to determine Congressional representation, the Constitution's first article prescribed that slaves would count as three-fifths of a person. Article 4 stated that a person "held to service or labour" who escaped to another state would "be delivered up on claim of the part to whom such service or labour shall be due."

Southern states went further. All passed laws called Black or Slave codes meant to determine not just behaviour but thought. Slaves were legally obliged to show all white people deference, and whites were given the statutory right to determine if even a slave's eye contact, facial expression or body language represented a transgression of the law. Slaves could not carry firearms or ride horses without written permission, and it was illegal to teach a slave to read.

In 1777, Vermont banned slavery. By the turn of the century many other states had followed its lead. Abolitionist leagues grew in all northern cities. Northern states did not need slavery for economic reasons and could not abide it on moral grounds. As the United States developed south and west, the struggle to maintain a balance in Congress between those representing slave and free states tore at the fabric of the nation and the state.

While white America argued, increasing numbers of enslaved Americans demonstrated the fundamental human desire to be free. There were rebellions that saw whites killed. There were many sad but heroic acts of resistance, such as men who acted dumb to slow or sabotage work, and slave women and girls who underwent abortions after being raped by white owners.

Thousands of slaves risked their lives and ran. As early as 1793, run-aways were such a problem that Congress passed the first of many fugitive slave laws. Each afforded owners more freedom to hire slave catchers and their agents more power to chase, catch and return their prey. By the 1850s, about 50,000 runaway slaves were hiding somewhere in the United States.[2] Others ran south to Mexico or Spanish-held Florida. Canada had abolished slavery in the 1830s and so was seen by many slaves as the great beacon of freedom to be won by following the northern star. Escape to Canada meant leaving both bondage and the slave catchers behind. By 1860 an estimated 100,000 slaves had escaped to freedom and about 30,000 of those had found it in Canada.[3]

In December 1860, sitting in silent dignity, John Anderson had become a symbol in the overlapping waves of international moral, legal, political debates that were coming to a head and would soon bring war. Anderson had come to know the indignity of slavery when he was born to a Missouri slave in 1831. At seven he saw his mother reach her breaking point and lash out at her mistress. She managed to knock the woman down and rip a handful of hair from her head before being pulled away and, as John watched, savagely beaten. Shortly thereafter, as was the prac-tice for all slaves with the audacity to stand up for themselves or their children, she was sold to a Louisiana plantation where conditions were even more brutal and the chances for another such outburst remote. Young John had not known his father, for he had escaped years before, and now his mother had been "sold down the river," as the saying went.

Owned by Moses Burton, Anderson was raised by the white mistress of the house. He had been renamed Jack Burton according to convention at the time whereby slaves were given the surnames of their owners in order to assist with identification. He played with the Burtons' children, ate reasonably well, and was healthy and relatively well-clothed. At fif-teen, he was sent to the tobacco fields to work the sun-up to sun-down hours of the adults. His intelligence and work ethic soon earned him the position of overseer, supervising the work of other slaves. Mrs. Burton was so taken with young Anderson that she arranged for him to be given an acre and a half of land to raise his own crops and earn a meagre living when the tobacco work was done.

One Sunday Anderson attended one of the many religious revival meetings that owners allowed slaves to organize, where drink and fellowship were offered along with the spirituals and evangelical preaching. He was smitten by a young slave named Marie Tomlin, and the two were married in December of 1850. As was typical of slave weddings, the two vowed to be together until split by death or involuntary separation.

The couple were not allowed to live together; they were owned by different people and had work to do. Anderson walked two miles to visit Marie every Saturday afternoon and returned each Sunday night. Marie had two children from a previous marriage and the couple soon welcomed a third. Anderson began creeping out nearly every evening to be with his family. Early one morning, Moses Burton caught him sneaking back, and threatened to tie and flog him. Only the intervention of one of the Burton daughters, with whom Anderson had played as child, saved him.

The incident, and the death of Burton's wife, led to Anderson's sale to Saline County's Colonel Reuben McDaniel for one thousand dollars. McDaniel told Anderson that he had been purchased as breeding stock and that he should pick himself some slave girls and forget his wife and baby. An old slave named Jacob told his young friend about slaves who had fled and never returned, and of a place called Canada where slaves could live in freedom. Anderson became excited and was soon making escape plans.

On a cool morning on September 25, 1853, Anderson took a large knife, steeled himself, and then slowly walked away, leaving the indignity of the McDaniel farm behind. He crept into Marie's small shack and whispered goodbye to her and their child. He promised to find Canada and then return or send for her. Moments later, he vanished into the night. In fleeing, Anderson had become a thief. According to American custom and laws, Anderson was not a man but rather a piece of property, and so in running, he was robbing Colonel McDaniel by stealing himself.

Anderson had inadvertently fled when Missouri was aflame with a season of violence, crime and intrigue. F.H. Moss, a Canadian abolitionist, had travelled to Missouri and had been sneaking onto a number of farms to talk to slaves about joining him on an adventure back north. His work led to a number of escapes. Meanwhile, communities were shaken by two reports of escaping slaves raping white women. In both cases, suspects were caught and hanged without trial. The state had become so concerned about slaves escaping and running wild that a bounty was offered to anyone who caught a slave.

On the third day of his flight, Anderson accidently stumbled upon a farmer named Seneca Digges and four of his slaves. Anderson explained that he was travelling with the permission of Colonel McDaniel to see if he could have himself sold to a farm closer to his wife. Digges did not believe the tale, but he played for time by inviting Anderson to stay for dinner with his slaves. Anderson initially agreed, but then bolted for the woods. Digges shouted to his slaves that he would pay for Anderson's capture and with that, the chase was on. For thirty minutes they ran through woods and fields until Digges's slaves finally had Anderson surrounded. He pulled the long knife from his waistband and escaped, but almost immediately ran into Digges. Digges raised a tree branch, but before he could swing it the two men fell together. Anderson's knife plunged into Digges's chest. Two more thrusts to the back dropped Digges, and Anderson fled. Eight-year-old Ben Digges, who had been there throughout the violent encounter, was left staring at his wounded and bleeding father while the slaves gave chase.

With Digges dying of his wounds, local newspapers reported this latest attack on a law-abiding white man by a rampaging slave. At a hastily called meeting, Howard County residents expressed shock and anger. A vigilante committee was formed and a number of men eager to collect a reward headed out. Twice Anderson was nearly caught, but he managed to slip away before he was seen.

Dirty, exhausted, starving, and wearing shredded clothing, Anderson slowly struggled northward. He happened upon a white man whose reaction to seeing him was such that Anderson decided to risk trusting him. The gentleman offered a meal and bed for the night. He told Anderson of the quickest way to Chicago and of certain individuals he should find there who would help get him to Canada. With suspicion in his heart, but anguished desperation in his mind, he left the next morning, his pockets bulging with apples and bread. After weeks on his own, Anderson had boarded the Underground Railroad.

The Underground Railroad was at the time and would forever be shrouded in mystery and myth. Most slaves were on their own when running, but many were helped by sympathetic white people who offered them food, homes, wagons and courage.[4] Helping a slave to escape was akin to abetting theft and punishable with fines and imprisonment that became increasingly severe. Brave whites nonetheless persisted and their numbers increased. The Underground Railroad's name came from code words; safe houses were called stations and those offering help were dubbed conductors. In the harsh cruelty of all that slavery entailed, the Underground Railroad offered a spark of decency. Influential abolitionist Levi Coffin, a North Carolina Quaker, said with a sentiment that reflected the beliefs of all conductors, "The dictates of humanity came in opposition to the law and we ignored the law."[5]

After a few more days of hardship and terror, Anderson arrived in Chicago and he quickly found the people who had been recommended to him. They bought him clothes, found him lodging and gave him food. For three weeks, he lay hidden in a small room above a barbershop. Finally, train tickets were provided for him to travel to Detroit. Within days he was over the Detroit River and in Windsor. It was late November 1853, and John Anderson had made it to Canada. He was free.

CANADA

Following directions given to him by his Detroit contacts, Anderson found a safe house in Windsor owned by Henry Bibb, an escaped slave who dedicated himself to helping other fugitive slaves and the Canadian abolitionist movement. His efforts included the creation of an institute designed to help recent arrivals learn to read and master the vocational skills needed to begin their new lives. Bibb enrolled Anderson, who worked hard and did well. Soon, Anderson had a job working as a labourer with the Great Western Railway. He saved his money, and devoted his days off to doing maintenance work and his free time to learning to read, write and do sums.

The Canada in which Anderson found himself was idyllic compared to Missouri, but it still struggled with racism and segregation. Canada was not a stranger to slavery. Early French settlers had enslaved Aboriginal people, and then, in the late seventeenth century, African slaves arrived in Quebec. The capitulation agreement that ceded Quebec to Britain after the 1759 conquest guaranteed the continuation of slavery. In 1763, Quebec governor James Murray had sent an urgent request to New York for a shipment of slaves to meet a labour shortage.[6] Slavery was also common in the British colony of Nova Scotia. About five hundred slaves were brought to the Maritimes by loyalists fleeing the American Revolution.

Slaves were also a common sight in Upper Canada. Again, most had been brought north by American loyalists. As in Lower Canada and the Maritime colonies, slaves worked predominantly on docks and as domestic servants. But Upper Canada found its great emancipator when British army officer John Graves Simcoe was appointed the first governor of the colony of Upper Canada. He was a visionary under whose leadership the colony grew quickly. Simcoe was also an abolitionist. While he wanted complete emancipation, in 1793 he settled for the passage of an act that rendered illegal the further introduction of slaves into Upper Canada and the freedom of all children born to slaves.

Simcoe's gradual emancipation law reflected the growth of abolitionist sentiment in both Canada and Britain. In 1807, Britain had abolished the Atlantic slave trade, and in August 1834, it abolished slavery throughout its empire. British-Canadian abolitionist laws had thus created a haven for slaves and freemen. With numbers that started slowly but grew each year, American slaves began moving to what many called Canaan, a land where they could be human.

Partnerships between American and Canadian abolitionists were developed to assist the growing number of racial refugees. An important element in their co-operative efforts was the construction of dispersed and diverse Black communities.[7] Some small Black communities developed in Nova Scotia and New Brunswick, but most—about forty—were established in Canada West.

Canadian and War of 1812 veteran Richard Pierpoint founded Garafrax in the 1820s. The community struggled but eventually did well and grew to become the town of Fergus. In 1831, Wilberforce was formed by American freemen James Charles Brown and Benjamin Lundy, who had been inspired by their attendance at a Philadelphia abolitionist conference the year before. While well-intentioned, that community failed because of inadequate capitalization and faulty management.[8] Escaped slave Josiah Henson established the Dawn Settlement in 1842. It began as a school to teach basic vocational skills and grew to become a small village. It helped a good number of people, but like Wilberforce, quickly fell into trouble. Henson had literally and heroically carried his children on his back to escape slavery and was later both the inspiration for Harriet Beecher Stowe's Uncle Tom and an influential leader in the Canadian abolitionist movement. Nevertheless, he was a poor administrator. The most successful of the many communities began with a fundraising effort that saw the purchase of 9,000 acres of farmland in Elgin County's Raleigh Township. The Buxton Mission, named after British abolitionist Thomas Fowell Buxton, became a thriving town.

THE FUGITIVE SLAVE LAW

While all southern American states and most municipalities had laws that segregated the races and rendered life miserable for slaves and freemen alike, in 1850 things got worse. In September, the American Congress passed, and weak president Millard Fillmore signed, an omnibus bill that included a new and strengthened version of the Fugitive Slave Law. The law went further than previous laws by making it obligatory for all whites to help apprehend fugitive slaves. More severe penalties than ever before were imposed on runaways, and their right to a trial was removed. The law changed everything. Issues that had been distant and subject to somewhat philosophical discussion for northern Americans suddenly became real, practical, urgent and local because it was now their legal responsibility to involve themselves in capturing escaped slaves. Wilful blindness was no longer possible. All were suddenly involved.

The Fugitive Slave Law and the new generation of slave catchers it spawned sent a wave of fear through northern cities, where many African-Americans had been living peaceful lives in their first or second generation of freedom.[9] The law enraged and inspired northern abolitionists. In rapidly increasing numbers, they reacted by bringing the Underground Railroad above ground. Public meetings and support, along with overt defiance of the Fugitive Slave Law, became commonplace. The federal government's inability to effectively enforce the law pleased and encouraged abolitionists.

Many national leaders spoke out against the law. Powerful New York Republican senator William Seward spoke against it and Massachusetts Democratic senator Charles Sumner forced a doomed vote on the law's repeal. The nationally known, splendidly articulate, and politically efficacious ex-slave Frederick Douglass was more incendiary in his reaction, stating: "The only way to make the Fugitive Slave Law a dead letter [is] to make a dozen or more dead kidnappers."[10]

Many heeded Douglass's call. In Detroit, a federal agent taking a runaway slave to jail was pelted with paving stones by white citizens enraged by what they perceived as injustice. The prisoner was freed and sent across the Detroit River to Windsor. An abolitionist mob descended upon a Boston courthouse in which the ownership of a fugitive slave was being decided, and a man was killed in the riot that ensued. The president threatened to send federal troops to northern cities to protect the slave catchers.

All at once, the slow but steady migration across the Canadian border became a flood. Within weeks of the law's passage the city of Baltimore reported a problem in staffing hotels: all the Black waiters and porters had gone to Canada. Black churches in Buffalo and Rochester complained that their congregations had nearly all fled.[11] In the first three months after the Fugitive Slave Law was passed, about three thousand African-Americans crossed into Canada.[12]

As more and more slaves and freemen traded their shackles and low-paying insecure jobs for Canadian freedom, even more elaborate campaigns were waged to capture and dissuade them. Additional state and local laws were passed, bounties were raised, more slave catchers were hired, and the punishments for escape attempts and abetting became increasingly violent and draconian. Many people who risked all to help runaway slaves were heavily fined or imprisoned for up to year. Kentucky's Reverend Calvin Fairbank, for instance, was convicted of helping slaves to escape and handed a sentence of fifteen years' hard labour. Those caught helping escaping slaves or freemen were often beaten and banished, and many had "SS" branded onto their left palm—slave stealer.

Propaganda was also spread—that Canada is always frigidly cold; slavery existed in Canada with conditions worse than in the south; all runaways were imprisoned upon crossing the border.[13] But nothing worked. The lure of freedom remained stronger than frantic lies and desperate power. Canadian governor general Lord Elgin wrote to the British colonial secretary that Canada West was "flooded with blackies who are rushing across the frontier to escape from the bloodhounds whom the Fugitive Slave Bill has let loose on their track."[14]

Many American slaves and freemen who fled to Canada had by that time come to play prominent roles in the country's development. Wilson Abbott, for example, had been born a freeman in Richmond, Virginia, and run a successful grocery business in Mobile, Alabama. In 1834, he was warned that his store was about to be attacked and just in time escaped with his family first to New Orleans and then, in 1836, to Toronto. He operated a number of successful businesses and ploughed profits into real estate speculation, and soon found himself a leader among the city's small but powerful Black elite. His son Anderson was the first Black graduate of Toronto's King's College and the first African-Canadian doctor. He later served as a surgeon in the Civil War.

Thornton Blackburn and his wife had escaped from slavery in Kentucky and eventually found their way to Detroit but, in 1833, were tracked down by slave catchers. A daring jail break led to a riot when abolitionists turned on the police and slave catchers. Blackburn and his wife, Lucie, made their escape and soon settled in Toronto. He tried his hand at a number of jobs before forming the city's first taxi company.* Blackburn retired a wealthy man.

Abbott and Blackburn were two success stories among many. Thousands of other Black farmers, teachers, priests and business owners were enriching the growing Canadian nation while pursuing their dreams. And all the while, the personal was political. Every intelligent, successful, law-abiding African-American in Canada was one more arrow flung into the heart of the Southern idea that Blacks were unworthy, unable and unwilling to lead such lives.

William Lyon Mackenzie understood the danger that the success of former slaves in Canada posed for the future of the South. Mackenzie was Toronto's first mayor and leader of the ill-fated 1837 Upper Canada Rebellion. On a visit to the United States, the former newspaperman wrote an article that was widely published south of the border. He spoke glowingly of Blacks and whites living and working together in Toronto and of some ex-slaves doing so well in business that they kept domestic servants in their impressive homes. Mackenzie wrote, "This is turning the table on the Sothrons [sic], and fairly balancing accounts with the ebony-hearted slave-holders."[15]

Among those who echoed the point was George Brown. The tall, handsome, and always fastidiously tailored Brown had emigrated to America from Scotland and worked in the New York City newspaper business with his father. An intelligent, ambitious and articulate man, he moved to Toronto and founded the *Globe*. By 1850 it had become Canada's most widely read and influential newspaper. Brown was also an important

---

* Until the 1980s, the Toronto Transit Commission used the burgundy and gold colours on their vehicles, the colours Thornton had chosen for his cabs.

politician who became the Reform Party leader and later played an essential role as one of Canada's Fathers of Confederation.

In the early spring of 1851, Brown helped form the Anti-Slavery Society
of Canada. His brother-in-law Thomas Henning, who also served on the
Globe's editorial staff, was its secretary. The Anti-Slavery Society made connections with other like-minded associations in Canada; in addition, on a
rather regular basis, Henning exchanged letters with the British and Foreign
Anti-Slavery Society and the American and Foreign Anti-Slavery Society.

The Canadian abolitionist movement ultimately weakened itself
through schisms born of politics, religion and ego, but the Anti-Slavery
Society remained an important voice for the cause. Its drawing power and
the popularity of its beliefs and goals were seen when a convention was
held in Toronto's St. Lawrence Hall in March 1851. Twelve hundred
people applauded speaker after speaker, including Brown, who attacked
the Fugitive Slave Law, the institution of slavery, and the Southern interests that defended both. Brown promised to urge the Canadian government to do all that could be done to end slavery in the United States.[16]

The Anti-Slavery Society's connections led to visits to Canada by
influential abolitionists. In April 1851, Frederick Douglass was the keynote speaker before a crowd of two thousand at St. Lawrence Hall. British
abolitionist George Thompson and American abolitionist Samuel May
also spoke. May brought the crowd to its feet when he exclaimed, "I ask
you, members of another nation, to assist in our over throwing one of the
institutions of my country."[17]

Many important Americans were already in Canada doing what May
advocated. Harriet Tubman, for instance, had been born a Maryland slave,
but in 1849 had fled to freedom in Canada. In 1850, she had begun a courageous campaign of risking her life to travel back over the border again and
again, eventually rescuing about seventy people.* In 1851, Tubman took up
residence in St. Catharines, where she continued her efforts until moving

---

* *Earlier estimates suggested that Tubman had helped about three hundred people over the border,
but recent scholarship has settled on about seventy. The lower number does nothing to decrease
Tubman's importance as a person or symbol of courage.*

back to the United States to serve in the Civil War. In 1850, Henry Bibb founded a paper called the *Voice of the Fugitive* and became an important member of the Canadian abolitionist movement. Mary Ann Shadd was born a freewoman and was running a successful school for freed Blacks in Wilmington, Delaware, when the fallout from the Fugitive Slave Law led her and her brother Isaac to move to Canada. She also took a home in Windsor. With her founding of the *Provincial Freeman* in March 1853, she became North America's first female newspaper publisher. While neither Bibb's nor Shadd's paper was as influential as the *Globe*, they, along with others who came and went, added voice to the abolitionist cause and, in so doing, added to the friction dividing the American North and South.

The growing links between the American and Canadian abolitionist movements were demonstrated in September 1851, when fifty-three delegates from the United States and Canada gathered at Toronto's St. Lawrence Hall for the inauguration of the North American Convention of Colored Freemen. While Boston had been considered as a site for the first meeting, members determined that Toronto was safer. The three goals established were that American Blacks should continue to be encouraged to escape to Canada, that Canada must continue to be a comfortable asylum for those fleeing slavery or threats of kidnapping, and that assistance in resettlement must be offered to all who came. It was also determined that Toronto would be headquarters for the cross-border abolitionist efforts, with branch offices in major American cities. This effort and others resulted in even more correspondence between Canadian and American abolitionists, and more influential Americans such as William Lloyd Garrison, Gerrit Smith, and Arthur and Lewis Tappan began Canadian speaking and fundraising tours.

JOHN BROWN'S RAID

In October 1859, passionate and perhaps unstable American white abolitionist John Brown shook the movement on both sides of the border and sent tremors through the American body politic with a raid on the federal armoury and arsenal at Harper's Ferry, fifty miles northwest of Washington. His goal was to capture weapons and ammunition as the first step in instigating a widespread slave insurrection, which he believed would lead to the creation of an African-American state for freed slaves in western Virginia. The year before the raid, John Brown had come to Canada.

In the spring of 1858, Brown spoke at a number of towns in Canada West. In April he took a room in Chatham at the home of Isaac Shadd, Mary Ann's brother. He organized a convention that was held in Chatham on May 8 and 10, designed to further publicize his bold plan while raising money and recruits. Twelve white and thirty-three Black men attended. The convention wrote a constitution and appointed people to positions that created the trappings of a provisional government, with Brown as commander-in-chief. In the end, only one former slave, Osborne Anderson, accompanied Brown back across the border.

The Harper's Ferry Raid turned to fiasco, as Brown and many of his compatriots were captured by marines led by a young colonel named Robert E. Lee. Three of Brown's men escaped to Canada. One of them, physician Samuel Gridley Howe, summarized the role he believed Canada would play in the fight against slavery in a letter to a fellow American abolitionist: "I look with the more interest upon Canada, because it seems to me she is to be the great and reliable ally of the Northern States, in the coming struggle with slavery."[18]

Meanwhile, Brown's case intrigued both Canadians and Americans. The documents created in Chatham the year before played a significant role in his trial and his conviction for treason, conspiracy with slaves to rebel, and murder in the first degree.[19] When Brown was hanged on December 2, 1859, a martyr was created. While vilified in the American south, Brown was celebrated in many Canadian quarters. The *Globe* called Brown "the hero of Harper's Ferry."[20] In another article it posited that Brown would be fondly remembered "as a brave man who periled property, family, life itself for an alien race."[21] On the day of his funeral, bells tolled in many Windsor, Chatham, Hamilton, Montreal and Toronto churches, and many held memorial services and collected money for his widow.

Southern leaders knew of the raid's Canadian connection and that association further poisoned thoughts about Canada, its abolitionist movement, and its opposition to Southern beliefs and goals. Virginia's governor Henry Wise, for instance, addressed his legislature shortly after Brown's hanging and spoke stingingly of Canada's role in the raid. Wise reported: "It was an extraordinary and actual invasion, by a sectional organization specially upon slaveholders and upon their property in negro slaves . . . a provisional government was attempted in a British province, by our own countrymen, united to us in the faith of confederacy, combined with Canadians to invade the slave holding states."[22]

The *New York Herald*, always ready to stir up trouble between the United States, Britain and its North American colonies, was among many newspapers that spoke of the Canadian connection to the raid, and noted the widespread popular ire directed toward Canadians who were now apparently not only hurting and insulting the South by providing refuge to runaway slaves, but also serving as a base for invasion and insurrection. A *Herald* editorial that was reprinted in the December 28, 1859, edition of the *Globe* demanded that the president take action to end Canada's ability to serve as a sanctuary for fugitive slaves and headquarters for those plotting treason. It quoted Governor Wise as suggesting that Canada's role in condoning the Harper's Ferry raid was sufficient to provoke war with Britain and promising, "The war will be carried into Canada."[23]

Perhaps most vehement in its opinion of Canada was the *Southern Review*. It condemned Canada for its years of providing a terminus for the Underground Railroad, and now for its complicity in the Brown Raid, and spoke of "the vile, sensuous, animal, brutal, infidel, superstitious, Democracy of Canada."[24]

This was the charged environment—and the Canada—in which John Anderson found himself. Canada was the mystical Canaan of inspirational Negro spirituals, a place where slavery was but a memory. Yet it seethed with many of the same moral, political, economic and social debates concerning racial equality that for generations had divided America.

A HUNTED MAN

While happy with the beginnings of a new life as a free man, Anderson missed his wife terribly. One evening in the early spring of 1854, four months after arriving in Canada, he broke down in tears and told one of his sympathetic teachers, an American social reformer named Laura Haviland, of how separation from his wife and family was breaking his heart. With Haviland's help, he composed a letter to Marie telling proudly of his adventures. Guessing that Missouri authorities were likely still after him, Haviland offered to have the letter mailed from a friend in Michigan to Lewis Tomlin in Missouri, who would, in turn, forward it to Marie.

Within weeks it looked as if the letter had succeeded in reaching its destination, for a reply arrived saying that Tomlin had arranged to steal Marie away from her owner, and that he and a man named Warren would bring her and the children north. The family could be reunited in Detroit. It sounded good, but Anderson and Haviland were suspicious. It seemed too easy.

In late April, Haviland travelled to Michigan and met with Warren. She became wary of the man with the southern accent. After the meeting she immediately sent word to Anderson that Warren was most certainly a slave catcher. Anderson was instantly on the run again.

Swallowing the pain of dashed dreams, Anderson told friends he was going north to Sault Ste. Marie, but then he took the train to Chatham. He introduced himself as James Hamilton to the first African-Canadian men he saw and was immediately welcomed into the town's eight-hundred-member community of fugitive slaves and freemen.[25] In a couple of days a group of white men with southern accents arrived in town asking about a slave named Jack who had escaped from Missouri and killed a man. No one betrayed him. On the contrary, one evening a group of Black men cornered and surrounded a particularly aggressive slave catcher named Brown. They taunted the entrapped man, producing a rope and threatening to lynch him. Brown drew a pistol and barely escaped with his life.

Anderson had no way of knowing that Missouri authorities had posted a thousand-dollar bond for his return after his love-torn letter was intercepted by the Howard County police. Tomlin, to whom Haviland had forwarded the letter, was wrongfully convicted of having helped Anderson to escape. He had been ruthlessly whipped and banished from the county, and Warren and Brown had been hired to bring Anderson back to Missouri.

With reports of Anderson's new disappearance, the authorities of Howard County took the case to Missouri governor Robert Stewart. He wrote to Canada's governor general, Lord Elgin, asking for his assistance. Haviland later wrote that a New Orleans attorney told her that, by that point, Anderson had become known across the South. He had become the symbol of all that was wrong with the lenient Northerners and Canadians who attracted and harboured criminals. He had told her: "We are going to have Anderson by hook or by crook; we will have him by fair means or foul; the South is determined to have that man."[26]

Anderson fled again. He moved to Brantford and learned to be a mason and plasterer. With his work ethic, intelligence and new vocational skills, and ability to read, write and keep ledgers, he quickly set out on his own as a successful independent contractor. After four years, in 1858, he had saved enough to purchase a house. Those chasing him seemed to have forgotten him. But it would not last.

While Anderson was hiding in plain sight, American slave interests became even more convinced that abolitionists and their Canadian accomplices were dangerous threats to their way of life. As the abolitionist movement grew more powerful on both sides of the border, more incidents of violence were sparked by slave catchers attempting to capture and return alleged fugitive slaves. A Democratic Mississippi congressman summed up Southern rage at the increasingly frustrating situation in a speech to the House of Representatives:

Men cannot afford to own slaves when, by crossing an imaginary line, they fall into the hands of our enemies and friends who aid them in their flight. . . . Do you think, gentlemen, that we will remain quiet while this is being done? The south will never submit to that state of things. It matters not what evils come upon us; it matters not how deep we may have to wade through blood; we are bound to keep our slaves and their present condition.[27]

Letters from angry Southern governors demanding the return of slaves had been sent to Canadian political leaders as far back as the 1820s. Canadian replies were blunt. In an 1829 response to Illinois governor Ninian Edwards, for instance, Sir James Kemp of the Canadian Executive Council explained that the slave under discussion would not be returned: "The state of slavery is not recognized in the law of Canada nor does the law admit that any Man can be the proprietor of another."[28] The case was closed.

In 1833, the Canadian government had attempted to bring order to the cross-border problems with the passage of the Fugitive Offenders Act. It did little to placate Southern governors, however, for it stated in law what had long been common practice; that is, a person would be returned to the United States only if it was clear that he or she had committed a crime for which an arrest could be made in Canada. Stealing oneself was clearly not a Canadian crime, so the law promised that no escaped slaves would be returned simply because they had once been slaves in America.

Abraham Johnson escaped from a Virginia plantation on a stolen horse in 1834. He eventually found his way to Detroit and Windsor, but was captured by a slave catcher. Canadian authorities intervened and refused to allow Johnson to be returned to the United States. Michigan's territorial governor Stevens Mason involved himself in the case, arguing that he wanted Johnson back not because he was a slave but because he had committed a capital crime: horse theft. Mason was told that while Johnson had indeed stolen the horse, he had done so in order to escape slavery and so the crime was justifiable. A precedent was set. It appeared that anyone could do just about anything as long as it was part of an effort to escape slavery.

American authorities were not surprisingly displeased by the Canadian laws and the way they were being interpreted and enforced. In 1842, the

Webster-Ashburton Treaty had been negotiated between Britain's privy councillor Alexander Baring, First Baron of Ashburton, and American secretary of state Daniel Webster. Their primary goal was to settle the boundary disputes on the Maine–New Brunswick border and on Lake Superior's northwest shore. Tangential to the negotiations were questions arising from the *Creole* Affair. In 1841, a ship called the *Creole* was transporting 135 American slaves from Virginia to New Orleans when the slaves took control of the ship. Several of the nineteen crew members were killed. The ship was forced to shore at British-controlled Nassau, where authorities freed the slaves. Despite President Tyler's pleas and threats, the slaves were not returned. Eager to alleviate the tension that had developed from the incident and to avoid future misunderstandings, Ashburton and Webster wrote up extradition procedures and tacked them on to the agreement in a tenth article of the treaty. They would leave it to others to establish a more complete extradition agreement later.* By 1859, however, later had yet to arrive. Consequently, Anderson's life was to be decided by an interpretation of the treaty's hastily devised tenth article.

Anderson had a friend named Wynne, whom he had known for some time. The two had shared stories of escape and for years Wynne had known Anderson's true identity, of his having stabbed a man while fleeing, and of the Missouri officials probably still on his trail. As sometimes happens with friends, a trivial disagreement in the spring of 1860 turned into a falling out. But Wynne took it further. He reported Anderson to a local magistrate named William Matthews, who did as his duty implied. The next day, while Anderson was tapping a maple tree, a sheriff approached and without incident arrested him.

While Anderson languished in the Brantford jail, Matthews sent a message to police in Detroit. They dispatched Samuel Port with the original Missouri warrant for Anderson's arrest for having killed Digges. At a brief hearing, despite never having seen Anderson before, Port identified him as Digges's slayer. Matthews then informed Port that Anderson

---

* In 1855, Britain agreed to pay the United States $100,000 in compensation for the slaves.

would be held until the proper extradition papers were received. American detective James Gunning took charge of the case and directed cables to Missouri and Washington asking for help. American secretary of state Lewis Cass became personally involved in expediting the matter.

While waiting for the American response, Matthews interviewed Anderson, who was forthright about his escape and about having stabbed a man who was trying to stop him. Until that conversation, Anderson did not know Digges's name or the fact that he had died of his wounds.

Influential British abolitionist John Scoble, who in 1851 had moved to Canada and become involved in the Canadian abolitionist movement, understood the importance of the case and found a lawyer to represent Anderson. He hired successful Hamilton attorney Samuel Black Freeman who, eight years previously, had been a founding member of the Anti-Slavery Society of Canada. Freeman had read of the Anderson case and it had moved him.

Freeman met with Anderson, then Matthews. He argued that according to British and Canadian law, there was no Canadian charge pending against Anderson and so no reason to keep him jailed. The persuasive lawyer threatened that if Anderson were not immediately freed, he would take the case to a higher court.

While Matthews considered his options, Scoble saw to it that Canadian newspapers brought Anderson's story to the largely anti-slavery public. In an April 9 editorial, the *Globe*, like most others, took a protective stance: "Every care will be taken that he is not delivered to the United States authorities for such a crime."[29] Meanwhile, a number of abolitionist sympathizers and members of the Anti-Slavery Society sent letters to Canadian government officials, all demanding that Matthews free Anderson.

Detective Gunning finally arrived on April 30 with extradition papers, but he was too late. Anderson was gone. Matthews had ordered him released just two days earlier, and Freeman and Scoble had helped him disappear.

Anderson settled this time in the small town of Simcoe, where he found lodging within the town's community of fugitive ex-slaves. Undeterred, however, Gunning, a Detroit detective named Julius Blodgett, and a hired tracker set after their man. Anderson was protected and the hunters mis-directed, but they were pugnaciously persistent. On August 27 Anderson was discovered and after a brief struggle hauled to Simcoe's Norfolk County jail.

Having had an apparent change of heart, brought on, some said, by a promise to share in Missouri's thousand-dollar bounty, Magistrate Matthews petitioned to have Anderson returned to Brantford, and sent a group of police officers to carry out his orders. But Crown lawyers and Simcoe magistrates would not give him up. Meanwhile, newspapers told the tale of Anderson's arrest and the stories brought abolitionists and Simcoe's Black community out in force, demanding that the prisoner be set free.

Matthews eventually won the day and Anderson was returned to Brantford. He was accompanied along the entire route by white abolitionists and Black friends and supporters. They camped outside the Brantford jail to ensure that the Americans did not simply whisk their prisoner back over the border without Canadian due process. Inside, Anderson lay handcuffed and alone in a small cell. He was allowed to see only his lawyer.

The extradition hearing began with American and Canadian reporters joining Anderson's supporters, a contingent from Missouri, and others filling the small courtroom. Matthews would make the final decision without the advice of a jury. He had a background and reputation that impressed few. A former mayor of Brantford, he had harassed electors, been accused of fraud during his election and of having beaten a prisoner, and was widely believed to have found his way to the bench only because he was a friend of John A. Macdonald.[30]

Macdonald was Canada's most fascinating and influential political leader. Tall and gangly, with a quick smile, dancing eyes and an endless supply of jokes and funny stories, Macdonald was a hard drinker, a rascal and a charmer. His intelligence, political genius, and charisma would soon play an essential role in the birth of an independent Canada, and by 1860 Macdonald was already a successful corporate lawyer in Kingston and an experienced and skilful political strategist. His allies loved him and even enemies bore him grudging respect.

Since 1849, Canada's government had been split into three parts: the
Legislative Assembly (House of Commons), the Legislative Council
(Senate) and the Executive Council (Cabinet). The British-appointed governor oversaw it all. In the late 1850s, the governor general still held significant power, especially with respect to international matters. Internal
political power, however, rested in the elected Legislative Assembly, as it
controlled the purse and decided which party would form the government
(that party's leader became premier, or in modern parlance, the prime minister). Macdonald had been Canada's joint premier, with Étienne-Paschal
Taché and George Étienne Cartier, since 1856. He was also attorney general of Canada West, although everyone regarded him as representing the
entire colony in legal matters. The Anderson case was a complex challenge
that Macdonald needed to meet with consideration for its legal and domestic political ramifications, and its effect on Canada's dangerous and shifting
relationship with the United States and an increasingly truculent Britain.

Macdonald was torn by the case. His personal opinion sided with
Anderson and the abolitionists.[31] In April 1856, he had involved himself
in a similar case relating to a fugitive slave named Archy Lanton, whom
American authorities wanted returned. Macdonald wrote to the provincial secretary arguing that the local magistrates had badly mishandled the
case in allowing the Americans to retrieve Lanton without a hearing. He
said, "There is so much reason to fear that Lanton, a man of colour, fugitive from the United States, was a victim of a scheme to kidnap him."[32]
Macdonald ordered that the magistrates responsible for allowing Lanton
to be taken back to the United States be fired.

Macdonald's major political rival was Reformer George Brown. The
two had clashed for years and seen political rivalry escalate to personal
hatred. Macdonald concealed his feelings with barbed wit but Brown was
transparently contemptuous toward his Conservative enemy. Because
Brown was one of the abolitionist movement's chief spokesmen, it would
have been politically hazardous for Macdonald to enthusiastically support
Anderson. Macdonald sought to avoid political problems by ordering
Matthews to "require evidence of criminality sufficient to sustain a charge

according to the laws of the Province before extradition should follow."[33] In other words, stick to the law.

The court heard a deposition from one of Digges's slaves and then testimony from his son, both of whom had been present at the stabbing. It also heard an interpretation of the Fugitive Slave Law, which decreed that Digges had been legally obliged to try to stop anyone suspected of being a runaway slave. Finally it was Anderson's turn. He testified that it had not been his intention to kill Digges. He explained that he had needed to use force to escape from the situation and from the United States in order to be free.

Matthews took little time to come to a decision. He explained to the court that his interpretation of the Webster-Ashburton Treaty led him to rule that Anderson should be extradited to the United States. The final step would be for the Canadian government to approve of the court's decision. It would be up to Macdonald.

Missouri's governor, Robert Stewart, was in a political pickle as treacherous as Macdonald's. Should he remain quiet and allow the Canadians to decide a property issue involving one of his citizens? Should he use the power of his office to exert pressure on Canada and be seen by the people of his state, and indeed the people of the South, as doing so? Or should he do nothing? To do nothing would mean surrendering to the northern abolitionists and to Canadians, who had for some time been placing enormous pressure on slave states such as his and, in so doing, helping to make the secessionists' case.

Stewart decided to join Missouri senator James Green, who had also been carefully following the Anderson case, and the two wrote letters to Secretary of State Cass. They demanded that the federal government intervene through Britain or directly with Canada.[34] In his final speech upon leaving office in January 1861, Governor Stewart said that no state had suffered more as a result of what he called slave abductions. But, he continued, while he hoped his state would remain loyal to the Union, Missouri must continue to fight to retain its rights. And among them was the right to maintain slavery and do all that could be done to have runaway slaves returned from Canada.[35]

Cass responded to Stewart and Green's lobbying efforts and penned a formal request to Britain. Like the Canadian and American governments, the British government needed to balance a host of considerations in its response, and primary among them was the desire to avoid conflict with the United States. Westminster's instruction to Canadian Governor General Sir Edmund Head, who had succeeded Lord Elgin in December 1854, was clear. Canadian authorities were to take whatever actions were necessary according to Canadian law but then they were, according to British Foreign Secretary Lord John Russell, to "deliver up the person of the above named John Anderson to any person or persons duly authorized by the authorities of Missouri to receive the said fugitive and bring him back to the United States for trial."[36]

Freeman, the Hamilton attorney and founder of the Anti-Slavery Society of Canada, had petitioned the Canadian government on October 1, and on October 6 he began a fascinating correspondence with Macdonald. He wrote that the case rested entirely upon an interpretation of the Webster-Ashburton Treaty, and Macdonald agreed.

Freeman wrote to the attorney general explaining that he wished to present the argument that because Anderson and Digges had fallen into a scuffle while Anderson was attempting to flee, he was not guilty of murder but at most manslaughter.[37] Manslaughter was not included in the treaty's list of extraditable crimes. Furthermore, there was the precedent stating that any action taken in escaping slavery was justifiable. It was a broad moral argument, leaning more upon natural law than upon a narrow interpretation of Canadian law and the British treaty, but it might work.

During his long and storied political career Macdonald earned the nickname "Old Tomorrow," for he was a master at knowing when it was wise to postpone decisions. In this case, he opted to do just that. He wrote to Freeman stating, "I have come to the conclusion with great regret, but without any doubt existing in my mind that this party has committed the crime of murder: under which circumstances all I can do is to give you every assistance in testing the question before the Courts or a Judge by

Habeas Corpus."[38] Macdonald also secretly pledged to have the government pay all of Anderson's legal fees.

GATHERING POLITICAL STORM

On November 4, 1860, Anderson stood as three sombre men in black robes entered Toronto's Osgoode Hall courtroom. He could hear the sounds of the crowd in the packed and overheated hallways.

Freeman made the arguments he had carefully rehearsed. He concluded by quoting respected British statesman Lord Denman, who had once said that the Webster-Ashburton Treaty and related cases were based on the belief that "no nation is entitled to enforce a law of another country which was believed to be founded in injustice, such as the law of slavery."[39] Freeman then dramatically paused, slowly gathered his papers, carefully ordered them, and took his seat.

Henry Eccles led the Crown's case. He dismissed Freeman's moral arguments, saying that this was simply a narrow legal question. Furthermore, there was no exemption in the treaty for escaping slaves, and the court, he argued, could not invent one. He explained: "No doubt it is contrary to the spirit of every law of Great Britain and of this country, that anything savouring of slavery should be countenanced in the slightest degree, or that the least assistance should be lent towards forwarding the views or objects of such an institution, but we must be governed by the words of the treaty, which is to be construed as a contract, and we cannot add exceptions or provisions which it does not concede."[40] Eccles concluded with the point that, according to the Fugitive Slave Law, Digges had not an option, but a legal obligation, to stop Anderson.

Anderson was allowed to read from a prepared statement. He stood slowly and straightened himself. After three months in jail, often chained and with bad food and little exercise, Anderson had lost a considerable amount of weight. He cleared his throat and read carefully from a single sheet of paper. He concluded, "When I made up my mind no man should take me alive I was compelled to do what I did."[41] With that, Anderson sat and Chief Justice Robinson adjourned with the promise of a decision as quickly as possible.

Canadian newspaper reaction matched particular editorial bents. The *Globe* believed the case had been made for Anderson's immediate release. In a series of articles and editorials it attacked Macdonald—nothing new for Brown's paper—for shifting the political decision to the courts. The Conservative *Hamilton Daily Spectator*, on the other hand, attacked Brown and the *Globe* in an editorial that stated: "It is rather too much to accuse him [Macdonald] of being on the side of the slave catchers, and make people believe it, when it must be clear to everyone, that he could have no object of a personal or political nature in straining the law, as he is charged with having done."[42] On November 15, the *Globe* reprinted an editorial from the *Daily Spectator*'s cross-town rival, the *Hamilton Times*. It bristled with piqued nationalist-imperialist fury,

It is not alone the interests of the poor fugitive which are now involved. The sanctity of the refuge which the British flag has been supposed to provide to the unfortunate, is at stake; the honour and dignity of Canada is assailed; the safety of thousands of industrious, long suffering and loyal subjects of the Empire is threatened. It has come to this, that Canada is to be made the preserve of the slave hunter. . . . If the poor creature is left friendless and alone to battle with his hungry foes, he is lost and Canada is dishonoured; but if his interests are properly cared for, our glorious heritage—the laws of England—will hold him harmless.[43]

The decision was to come on November 29. Extra police were brought to Osgoode Hall and a large crowd mostly of Black men gathered outside. Chief Justice Robinson appeared just long enough to announce that the other two justices needed more time and so the decision would be delayed.

The delay allowed newspapers more time to stir flames of indignation. The *Globe*'s editorial the next day was scathing. It said that a decision to send Anderson back to the United States would in itself be tantamount to murder: "The universal heart and conscience of the people of Canada and of the British nation will say upon the facts of the case that [Anderson] is not a murderer in the sight of God, or under English law, and therefore, that to surrender him to the bloodthirsty slave catchers of Missouri is to make those who order that surrender guilty of the murder of [Anderson] with all its horrible accompaniments."[44]

The exploding notoriety of the case led a range of Canadian politicians to weigh in. Many new alliances were created and a number of old grudges forgotten. Reformers such as Michael Foley, for instance, who had previously been rather critical of Brown, swept into line behind him and attacked slavery, the Americans that hunted fugitive slaves in Canada, and Macdonald for his apparent support of their efforts.[45]

At the same time, Macdonald was being criticized for an embarrassing incident that took place during the Royal tour of Canada by Edward, the Prince of Wales. His Royal Highness and the British secretary of state for the colonies, the Duke of Newcastle, had to spend twenty-two uncomfortable hours aboard a ship in Kingston harbour to avoid dealing with displays by enthusiastic members of the anti-Catholic Orange Order, which in Canada was a powerful force but in England was illegal. The incident was hardly Macdonald's fault but the scandal wouldn't die, so he took his case directly to the people with something that had never been done in Canadian politics—a speaking tour.

On December 3, in a crowded St. Catharines hall, the air smudged with smoke and the 350 people in attendance plying themselves with food and liquor, the attorney general took his stand on the two issues of the day. He handled the Orange Lodge matter with deft humour. No one could charm like John A. He then turned to the Anderson case and for the first time addressed it in a public forum.

Macdonald defended the rule of law, the professionalism of the three presiding justices and all the decisions that had been made. He was greeted by rousing applause and cries of shame whenever Brown's name was mentioned. "Strange to say," he said, "Mr. Brown of the *Globe*, attempts to make it a matter of political capital against me, that instead of sending the man to be tried in the States . . . and I had to the power to send him at once to Missouri—I sent the matter to the judges, to have it fully decided whether a case was fully made out against him."[46] Macdonald concluded with the argument that he and his party, and not Brown's, were more avowedly anti-slavery.

Meanwhile, many American newspapers continued to raise concerns about the damage the Anderson case could do. The *Detroit Daily Advertiser*, for instance, published an editorial stating, "if this case is decided in favor of the claimants, it will virtually break up the underground railroad, and make Canada no longer a resort for runaways."[47] The *New York Times* reported extensively on the Anderson case and reflected an understanding of its importance in Canadian internal political struggles and in Canadian, British and American relations. One article spoke of the case potentially leading to war, arguing, "as to the relations between Great Britain and the United States . . . [t]he case could be a *casus belli* between the two countries."[48]

The *Baltimore American* joined many Southern papers in making public the argument that Missouri governor Stewart and others were making privately: the Anderson case was playing a role in the debates taking place in many Southern cities regarding secession. One article, for instance, stated bluntly that Anderson needed to be quickly extradited to stand trial in Missouri to help dissuade those in the state wishing to secede. It argued: "It is important to the south that assassins like Anderson be returned to face their justly deserved punishment. When such deeds go unpunished, who will say that the people of the South have no cause of complaint."[49]

Finally, the justices were ready. It was December 15 and the day had dawned cold. A large and restless crowd had assembled and armed police were again ready with a contingent of soldiers assembled nearby. Just after ten o'clock, Chief Justice Robinson led justices McLean and Burns to their spots. The judges would rule separately, so it would take two decisions in Anderson's favour to save his life.

Robinson began reading his carefully prepared statement. He presented the argument that it was not necessary to prove that the murder had been committed in order to extradite Anderson but only that there was sufficient evidence for there to be a trial. That he stabbed Digges in an attempt to escape slavery was, bluntly, irrelevant. He concluded that Anderson should be sent back to Missouri to stand trial for murder.

Next up was Justice Archibald McLean. He disagreed with Robinson and took a broad interpretation of existing law, echoing Freeman's moral argument. He said Anderson was "a fugitive from the adjoining republic [where] the evils and the curse of slavery are every day becoming more manifest and . . . in my judgement the prisoner was justified in using any degree of necessary force to prevent what to him must inevitably have proved a most fearful evil. . . . I can never feel bound to recognize any enactment which can convert into chattels a very large number of the human race."[50]

It would be up to Burns to break the tie. He argued that in order to interpret the treaty it was necessary to determine not just the words but the intentions of those who wrote and ratified it. "It is true," he said, "that the moment a slave puts his foot upon Canadian soil he is free, but the British government never contemplated that he should also be free from the charges of murder, piracy or arson, though the crime was committed in the endeavour to obtain freedom."[51] The audience gasped. Burns was agreeing with Robinson.

All eyes returned to Robinson. The chief justice ordered Anderson returned to jail in Brantford to await extradition to the United States. He then agreed to Freeman's request that the execution of the order be delayed a week to give time to deal with the question of an appeal.

Anderson was led out the front doors in handcuffs. Some in the crowd cheered him while others roared in anger to demonstrate their opinion of the decision. Freeman calmed the crowd and shouted out, "It is the law. We must obey it."[52] People rushed forward as Anderson was led to a waiting cab. There was confusion as to whether they were seeking simply to see him or wanting to spring him from the custody of the deputy sheriff. Police roughly pushed people away and cleared a path for the cab to leave. Within minutes Anderson was back in his small cell at the Toronto jail. The crowd dispersed without incident. But it was not over.

From the Kingston home he seldom saw, Macdonald sent a telegraph to Freeman offering to have the government pay expenses for an appeal.[53] A couple of days later, on December 22, Freeman was back in court before Chief Justice Robinson. Robinson made it clear that he saw little chance of the appeal being successful and ruled against allowing it. Anderson was placed on a train and returned to his cell in Brantford to await extradition to Missouri.

Newspapers across Canada reported the decisions. The *Quebec Mercury* was typical of its province's abolitionist, pro-Anderson consensus and demanded Chief Justice Robinson's impeachment.[54] Similarly, the *Globe* decried the decision as criminal and announced that it was organizing a public demonstration to allow people to parade their anger. It printed the text of inflammatory handbills that were plastered around Toronto spreading fear and reporting rumour as fact: "When the inhabitants of the Northern States are petitioning by Tens of Thousands to be united to Canada, this is not the time to succumb to the slave power and their invasion in Canada. Arouse then, Petition our Government, Petition our Beloved Queen, No surrender of a Freeman at the dictation of Slaveholders. Let Death or Liberty be Your Watchword."[55]

Toronto mayor Adam Wilson opened the December 23 rally in the St. Lawrence Hall. Several hundred people were there. He advised calm and came down on neither side of the issue. But every speaker who followed was clearly a supporter of Justice McLean's interpretation, and cheers rose whenever his name was mentioned. Professor Daniel Wilson made the point that all of Canada, and indeed the entire British Empire, was now watching to see if a blow might yet be struck against slavery.[56]

Among the speakers that night was John Scoble. He spoke in detail about the Webster-Ashburton Treaty and about the work he had done to bring pressure to bear on British politicians when the treaty was being negotiated. Scoble explained to the attentive crowd that Ashburton had personally assured him that Article 10 was not intended to be applied to the cases of fugitive slaves. He quoted Canadian governor general Lord Metcalf as having said that he agreed with Ashburton and would never be party to the treaty being used to bring harm to fugitive slaves.[57]

Rallies were also held in many other cities and towns. Montreal mayor Charles Seraphin Rodier painfully rose from his sick bed to attend the boisterous meeting at the James Street Mechanics' Hall. He and the other speakers were highly critical of the decision and all argued that if the treaty demanded that Anderson be returned to the United States then the treaty was wrong and should be amended or ignored. The rally's consensus view became that of Montreal's newspapers, which had been filled with editorials spewing various degrees of invective levelled against the decision, the justices, the power of the British treaty over Canadian domestic affairs, and the slave catchers and Southern interests that had led to Anderson's predicament in the first place.[58]

Before a large crowd at Montreal's St. Patrick's Literary Society, the powerful political leader, future Father of Confederation, and passionate spokesperson for Montreal's large Irish-Catholic minority Thomas D'Arcy McGee shouted, "The true voice and spirit of this province is that when the fleeing slave has once put the roar of Niagara between him and the bay of the bloodhounds of his master—from that hour, no man shall ever dream of recovering him as his chattel property."[59]

Freeman was running out of options. He wrote to Macdonald asking for advice. Macdonald recommended that he advance the case to the Court of Error and Appeal, which could hear it in February. Despite all the criticism that was being heaped upon Macdonald, he remained a strong advocate for Anderson, while recognizing the importance of adhering to the law and using the case to either establish a precedent or have the treaty amended so that no one else would be in Anderson's position in the future. Macdonald wrote, "I have the strongest hope that I shall be able to relieve you of the necessity of making an order for the surrender of 'the negro.'"[60]

The Anderson case had become both a window and a weapon. It allowed all to see the precarious nature of the Canadian political and legal systems labouring under Britain's imperial shadow, and the relationship between Canada and the United States that was tilting toward American dissolution and cross-border confrontation. Things could only get worse if complicated by a sudden intervention by Britain—and Britain moved.

THE EMPIRE STRIKES BACK

Thomas Henning, secretary of the Anti-Slavery Society of Canada, had maintained a regular correspondence with Louis Alexis Chamerovzow, his counterpart at the British and Foreign Anti-Slavery Society. In one letter Henning had written, "The cry here is throughout the land, Anderson is not a murderer but a hero and he must not be given up."[61] Chamerovzow had, in turn, been keeping British political and civil society leaders abreast of the Anderson case and stressing its importance.

The British law community had been aroused by the many issues the Anderson case raised. There were more law journal articles about the ramifications of the case than about any other in years. There was near unanimity that Anderson should not be surrendered to the Americans.[62]

The Robinson court's split decision on Anderson had led many British newspapers to dismiss the entire Canadian justice system as incompetent, inhuman or both. The *London Post*, for instance, posed the rhetorical question: "Are they [fugitive slaves] all to be relegated to the whip and the tortures of the planter because a majority of Canadian Judges think that the word 'murder' in the treaty is to be interpreted according to the laws of Missouri, and not in accordance with the enlightened and human principles of English freedom?"[63]

There had been further outrage when Robinson declined to hear an appeal. *The Times* suggested that if the law said Anderson and others like him should be returned to the United States, then the law should be ignored and a prison break should be arranged. Claiming wide support for its conservative point of view, the article said, "We suppose there will be hardly a man in England who will not hope for the success even of his forcible rescue, if things come to that."[64]

On January 4, 1861, the British and Foreign Anti-Slavery Society executive committee discussed the Anderson case at length. It was agreed that Anderson had become the symbol of all that was right with the abolitionist movement and all that was wrong with America.[65] Unwilling to wait any longer for the British government to intervene,

Chamerovzow prepared to take the Anderson case to the Court of Queen's Bench. He would argue that Anderson was being held without a charge, demand that a writ of *habeas corpus* be issued, and spring him from the possibility of extradition to America by bringing him to London. It was a bold gambit.

On January 15, Chamerovzow stood before Chief Justice Alexander Cockburn who, from beneath his outrageously large horse-hair wig, heard that Anderson was in imminent danger, as extradition would likely lead to his death. Chamerovzow cited precedents, reviewed the Webster-Ashburton Treaty, and argued that because the Canadian legal system had been created by Britain, it remained under its jurisdiction and so could be overruled.

Cockburn and his fellow justices came to a decision after only twenty minutes of deliberation: the Canadian courts were British courts and so the writ could be issued and Canadian law officers would be obliged to obey it. Anderson would be brought to England. The packed courtroom erupted in cheers. A writ of *habeas corpus* was prepared.

Cockburn's decision meant that the case was no longer just about slavery, or about British, Canadian and American relations, or about America's internal struggles. It was now, even more than before, about Canada's evolving independence and national pride. Cockburn was no fool. In rendering his decision he said: "We are sensible of the inconvenience which may result from the exercise of such a jurisdiction. We are also sensitive that it may be thought to be inconsistent with the higher degree of colonial independence, both in legislation and judicature, which has been carried into effect in modern times with happy results."[66]

The decision indeed seemed to be in contradiction to British policy, which for years had been granting Canada a fuller degree of sovereignty. A step toward political independence had been taken with the establishment of responsible governments following the 1837 Upper and Lower Canada rebellions. Subsequently, greater economic independence had evolved through the 1854 Canadian-American Reciprocity Treaty, which for the first time in British imperial history saw a colony establish a bilateral free trade agreement that did not involve or bring value to the mother country. In 1859, Canada became the first of Britain's colonies to place duties on the importation of a number of British products.

The Cockburn decision was debated at length at the British cabinet table and on the floor of the House of Commons. Concerns about British relations with the United States were balanced against precedents regarding colonial independence. Abolitionists, anti-Americans, and others who had for some time been advocating saving money by cutting the colonies loose, all weighed in.

Finally, Prime Minister Lord Palmerston announced to the House of Commons that his government supported the writ of *habeas corpus*, as it would ensure that Anderson would not be surrendered to American officials. He said Canadian authorities should do nothing with Anderson until his government issued instructions.[67] As secretary of state for the colonies, the Duke of Newcastle was blunt in his assessment: "The case of Anderson is one of the gravest possible importance, and Her Majesty's Government are not satisfied that the decision of the Court at Toronto is in conformity with the view of the treaty which has hitherto guided the authorities in this country."[68]

A number of issues were considered in the cabinet's decision. Henry John Temple, Third Viscount Lord Palmerton, was Britain's prime minister from 1855 to 1858 and he returned to office from 1859 to 1865. At the time of the Anderson decision he was seventy-six years old, with long, white hair and side-whiskers, but he remained a wily politician and, despite a half century in public life, one whom few wished to cross. Palmerston was an avowed abolitionist, who held America and Americans in rather low esteem.[69] But he was a clever player of *realpolitik*. He understood that Britain needed to maintain its supply of southern cotton if its textile mills were to keep operating and so he wanted to avoid unnecessarily provoking the United States. Then again, if an Anglo-American war would help the United States to break in two or shatter to shards, then the balance of global geopolitical power that had been teetering toward America might totter back to Britain.[70] A series of

Anglo-American spats in the mid-1850s had made clear that, just as there was a need for diplomatic calm and understanding, those elements of the relationship were demonstrably absent.

Palmerston also needed to keep his eye on Europe, where the growing unity of a new Prussian-German state was made more even troubling by the fact that Britain was still recovering from the Crimean War and a crisis in India. Those crises had necessitated the shifting of troops and resources from its colonies, including Canada, to engage in struggles that were expensive, divisive and inconclusive.

With respect to Canada, while Palmerston and Foreign Secretary Lord John Russell had never supported Canada's steady evolution toward political and economic independence, they were reluctant to impose British interference on colonial legislatures and courts.[71] Yet there was anger on the part of many British leaders that Canada's Militia Act of 1856 had demonstrated Canada's reluctance to muster the money and men to adequately defend itself against possible American threats, and that the 1859 Canadian tariff on British goods had served up a bit of economic pain with a large dollop of colonial temerity. Although Palmerston and Russell did not count themselves among their numbers, the so-called Little Englanders, who argued for a reduction or perhaps even a severing of colonial ties, were growing in power among Britain's political elite. And if all that was not enough, Palmerston's government was on unsteady political ground, with unreliable support in the caucus and the House and victory in the next election by no means assured.

The British government's Anderson decision told Americans that abolitionist sentiment would be a considerable factor in Britain's reaction to their growing sectional crisis. And for Canadians, Palmerston's decision made it clear that Britain had no compunction about overriding Canada's nascent sovereignty. The old lion had roared. Southern secessionists and Canadian nationalists took heed.

The *London Times* supported the decision and predicted criticism from the United States, but argued that morality and the law were on the side of the Cockburn court. It also noted that Canadians deserved to be shocked by the decision. "It may excite surprise, when we consider the ample powers of self-government possessed by Canada . . . to find the Court of Queen's Bench assuming to act directly on the rights of persons within her territories, just as if Toronto were situate on Windermere instead of Lake Ontario."[72] The *Liverpool Post* was also prescient in predicting the negative response of both Canadians and Americans: "While a quarrel between the United States and Great Britain is therefore possible a dispute between this country and Canada seems inevitable."[73] Canada's governor general, Sir Edmund Head, had seen the whirlwind coming too. He had warned his British superiors against intervention, saying, "Self Government, which is only to operate when its acts agree with the opinions of others, is a contradiction in terms."[74]

Canadian reaction was indeed hostile. Established enemies came together against a common threat: imperial overreach. The *Globe* called the writ an "arrogant claim" and demanded it be rescinded.[75] The *Globe*'s great rival, the conservative *Toronto Leader*, took the same stand. It wondered whether the infringement on the rights and powers of the Canadian judiciary might soon be followed by Britain's overriding decisions of the Canadian executive and legislatures as well.[76]

Thomas Chandler Haliburton, who had enjoyed a career as a legislator and judge in Nova Scotia before moving to England and becoming a Tory member of the British House of Commons, denounced the Cockburn decision and Palmerston's support for it. In Canada, he argued, the courts are as independent of Britain as the governor general, who is responsible to the government of Canada and not to the whims of Westminster.[77]

Macdonald kept his anger private. He wrote to the governor general, stating that what was at stake was the independence not just of the Canadian courts but of the Canadian people. Macdonald wrote: "In the case of Anderson the writ of *habeas corpus* was without doubt, sued out from praiseworthy motives, but it may hereafter be applied for . . . the withdrawal of Criminals from the control and jurisdiction of our Courts, and perhaps for the oppressive removal of individuals from their own country to a distant one."[78] He urged the governor general to press the British government to pass a law in the next session of its Parliament rendering it illegal for British courts to issue writs in Canada. The language was tough, perhaps treasonous, and perhaps revolutionary. America was inspiring Macdonald to become a little less British and a little more Canadian. The man who took such tremendous pride in being British, and had until that point largely rejected notions of Canadian independence, was being pushed by the Anderson case to rethink his most fundamental political beliefs.

American reaction to the British attack on Canadian sovereignty, and Britain's desire to save Anderson, betrayed a residue of the moral and ideological outrage from the American Revolution, as well as blatant self-interest. George Dallas, the American ambassador in London, had attended the Cockburn court and cabled his notes to Washington. He told President James Buchanan that the significant and widespread British opposition to slavery was at the heart of the case and was revealed by the positive public reaction to the decision to issue the writ.[79]

Britain's actions brought the Anderson case again to the front pages of a number of American newspapers. The *New York Times*, for instance, recognized that the case was accumulating attention throughout the American south and that Canadians were, from the Southern view, insultingly claiming the moral high ground in their refusal to release the fugitive slave. The case, the paper stated, had become a *cause célèbre* and an element of the struggle that was tearing the United States apart.[80] The *New York Herald* was among many papers that reprinted Canadian stories and supported them with interpretations that were sometimes wildly off-base. The *Herald*, for instance, predicted a Canadian revolution and the likelihood that Canadians would soon ask to join the United States. The gain of Canada, it argued, would more than compensate for the possible loss of any Southern states.[81]

More attention in American papers came when famed New York abolitionist Gerrit Smith spoke at Toronto's St. Lawrence Hall. Before a crowd of hundreds, he attacked the Canadian courts for the decision to return Anderson to certain death in Missouri and praised the British for their desire to save him. Many southern papers used their reports on the Smith speech to reassure their readers that Britain's need for southern cotton was such that, if the time came, it would quickly support the South's cause. Others saw things differently. The *New York Times*, for example, argued: "In this determination of Great Britain to protect the fugitive, and in the overwhelming popular sympathy that the fate of Anderson has excited, our Southern politicians may learn the monstrous absurdity of their hope that a Confederacy based upon Slavery will ever be recognized by the Government or the people of England."[82]

While the case was catching fire in Britain, Canada, and the United States, few paused to consider Anderson himself. An exception was Canada West's *Peterborough Examiner*, which in a front-page article mixed a little empathy with its anti-American sentiment: "The dread of a decision which will return him to the blood hounds of the South, will haunt his sleeping as well as his waking hours, and the fearful conviction that if given up, a cruel death, or a more cruel bondage awaits him, must weigh heavily upon his spirits."[83]

DECISIONS

Despite its growing notoriety, other events were overshadowing the Anderson case. In November 1860, Illinois Republican Abraham Lincoln had been elected president of the United States. His election was the final straw for Southerners. The campaign had seen Southern secessionists conflate Republicans with abolitionists, and warn that the election of any from that party was another nail in the coffin of slavery, states' rights, and the Southern way of life. Those believing the propaganda ignored the fact that, while Lincoln indeed personally found slavery reprehensible, he had advocated not its immediate eradication, but just a restriction of its growth. Emotion ran roughshod over reason.

With the slavery issue splintering political parties, there were three presidential candidates sympathetic to Southern causes opposing Lincoln. Demonstrating the importance that Americans placed on their selection of this president, 82.2 percent of eligible voters cast a ballot—the second highest of any election in American history. Lincoln won with only 39.9 percent of the popular vote. He had not taken a single Southern state. In many, he had not even been on the ballot. Lincoln said to newspapermen who came to his Springfield home the next day, "Well boys, your troubles are over now, mine have just begun."[84] He was right.

His victory was followed by secessionist rallies throughout the South. State legislatures began to debate not whether to secede, but how and when. The first to go, in December, was South Carolina. Within weeks, state after Southern state dropped the stars and stripes from flagpoles. President-elect Lincoln could do nothing for, according to the Constitution, he did not take office until March. No one could guess exactly what he would be president of by then.

Meanwhile, the British writ requiring that John Anderson be taken to London had been despatched, folded within a large envelope protected by a red wax seal. It had arrived in Canada on the first of February 1861. While it was on its way, John Macdonald had cabled Brantford and ordered that Anderson be brought to Toronto to appear before Chief Justice William Draper in the Court of Common Pleas. The court would consider the appeal that Justice Robinson had denied but which Freeman, tenaciously working through the system, had finally won the right to be heard. By the time Britain's order to send Anderson to London arrived, the Canadian court was already in session and so the case had to be heard first.

A large crowd had again gathered in and around Toronto's Osgoode Hall. American and British reporters joined their Canadian counterparts. The overcrowded room meant that Anderson had to sit in the box usually reserved for Queen's counsel. Arguments were presented and the justices parlayed with questions for nearly eight and a half hours. The justices finally adjourned to deliberate, and Anderson was taken to his cell to wait.

Events in the United States had been advancing quickly. On February 8, delegates from South Carolina, Mississippi, Florida, Alabama,

Georgia and Louisiana announced from Montgomery the founding of the Confederate States of America. Jefferson Davis, senator from Mississippi and long-time advocate of states' rights and the legality of secession, was proclaimed its president. There were tremendous celebrations throughout the South.

Days later, on a bright and cold February 16, a crowd had gathered again in Toronto. Anderson's time had come. Flanked by justices William Richards and John Hagarty, Chief Justice Draper began slowly and deliberately reading his decision to the packed but silent room. Richards and Hagarty followed. While each used different words, their points were the same. They ignored the international intrigue. They even ignored the Webster-Ashburton Treaty. All three stated that the initial warrant for Anderson's arrest had been for killing, not murdering Digges, and that as a result, it was too vague to be enforceable. Anderson was a free man. He was free on a technicality, but free nonetheless.

Anderson rose unsteadily to his feet and beamed a huge smile. He raised his arms over his head in silent jubilation. Those in attendance noted that his months of incarceration had left him thin and wan, and that he appeared more distracted than in previous appearances.[85] But months of wasting away in cold, damp cells with fear and boredom his only companions seemed to be forgotten for the moment. He said in a quiet voice, "Thank you, gentlemen—thank you, your lordships."[86] Draper's gavel fell and there was a roar of shouting and applause from those in the courtroom and from the crowd shivering outside. Sheriff Jarvis removed Anderson's handcuffs. The two shook hands and then Anderson shook the hands of his lawyers.

They led Anderson from the courtroom and to resounding cheers when he appeared at the grand building's portico. Well-wishers, including white abolitionists, and fellow fugitive slaves and freemen, joined in rapturous applause. Anderson was surrounded by back-patting, hand-shaking men, women and children. He was taken triumphantly away on a horse-drawn sleigh through Toronto's snow-packed streets, accompanied by John Scoble and Toronto alderman John Nasmith.

Canadian reaction was ecstatic for it was a three-way victory. Anderson was free. Canada had told the United States to forget its designs on Anderson and had warned Britain to respect the independence of the Canadian legal system. The *Peterborough Examiner* reflected a consensus among many papers as to which of the three aspects of the decision was most important: "We feel particular pleasure . . . for several reasons. Our chief one is that by the timely service of the Canadian writ of *habeas corpus*—the English one was superseded, and by the discharge of the prisoner it has become *nulla bona*."[87]

Despite his halting style and limited vocabulary, Canadian and American abolitionists quickly had Anderson giving public speeches to educate and raise funds to support their efforts to help more fugitive slaves. By June, Anderson had undertaken an ocean journey and was in London delivering more speeches. He addressed his largest audience at Exeter Hall, where the newly formed John Anderson Society welcomed six thousand to see him.

While Anderson was touring and taking classes in England, the United States suffered through its secession winter with president-elect Lincoln waiting to take office in March while Southern states solidified their new Confederacy. At the same time, an election was underway in Canada. Among the campaign's primary issues was how Canada should react to the growing storm south of the border, and Anderson's name was bandied about. The *Globe* joined papers in swing ridings that attacked Macdonald and his Liberal-Conservatives for their apparent support of southern slave owners, as evidenced by their willingness to send Anderson back to a certain death in Missouri. Conservative papers, meanwhile, praised Macdonald for allowing the legal system to work and ultimately saving Anderson. The Conservative *Hamilton Spectator* released letters showing that Macdonald had arranged to cover Anderson's legal fees. The election results showed that all attempts to smear Macdonald were ineffective. He took his Kingston riding in a hard-fought campaign and his Liberal-Conservative party won a majority government.

One of the first acts of the new government was to improve the Fugitive Offenders Act. Macdonald's amendment made it more difficult for slave catchers to extradite fugitive slaves. Macdonald also led the fight to pass the Canadian Extradition Act, which gave power to decide such matters to the superior rather than lower Magistrates' Courts. But it did not really matter anymore. Anderson was the last fugitive slave that Americans would fight to extradite from Canada.

Meanwhile, Macdonald's request relating to the independence of Canada's courts was taken to Westminster. In March 1862, the British government passed the *Habeas Corpus* Act, which rendered it illegal for Britain to issue writs in Canada. The Anderson case had thus led to the taking of major step toward Canadian nationhood.

John Anderson stayed in England and continued to live and attend classes in England. A year later, in 1862, the American Civil War was grinding into its second year, and Anderson's draw as a speaker, a role at which he was never especially adept, had waned. He was no longer needed to make a point or further a cause. Without consulting Anderson, British abolitionists arranged for him to be given land in and free passage to Liberia, the west-African nation created to provide a home for ex-slaves. Its capital, Monrovia, was named after the American president.

On December 22, 1862, Anderson delivered his last speech. As always, he ended with the mournful hope that he might again see his family. The next day he was aboard the steamer *Armenian*, bound for Cape Palmas. There are no records of him in Liberia; nor are there records of his wife, Marie, or their children in Missouri. They became as lost to history as they were to each other.

Found, however, was the South's determination to save its soul through fighting for its independence, while in the North a new president demanded more risk and sacrifice than the country had ever mustered to deny that independence. Also discovered in the shadow of that titanic struggle was Canada's soul—un-American, British; modestly but stubbornly Canadian. The question was whether, stuck between the angry giants, Britain and America, Canada could survive long enough to save that soul by bringing about its own creation. If William Seward had his way, it would not. He was just about to be given the power he needed to prevent it.

2

———— •◆• ————

WILLIAM SEWARD AND THE
POWER OF DIVIDED LOYALTIES

ABRAHAM LINCOLN WAS AN exceptionally skilled com-
municator who was often most lucid when saying nothing at
all. For weeks after becoming president-elect in November
1860, he was nearly silent. He remained at his modest home in Springfield,
Illinois. He granted a few interviews and spoke with many people who
were eager to offer advice or seek jobs, but said nothing on the main issues
of the day, most specifically on the fact that his country was falling apart.

Among the many decisions that Lincoln made in those first weeks after
his election was who would form his cabinet. He decided upon men who
would bring talent and experience to their jobs while reuniting the Republican Party. For secretary of state, Lincoln chose William Seward. Seward was
intelligent, well-read, well-travelled and widely respected for his knowledge
of international affairs, which had been developed and reflected in his service
as an influential member of the Senate Foreign Relations Committee. Despite
his many strengths, and even before Lincoln swore upon the Bible in March
1861, Seward became one of the most dangerous men in the world.

Seward was a fit and feisty man who enjoyed a hearty laugh and nothing more than long dinner parties that served raucous stories and juicy gossip along with eleven sumptuous courses and fine wines. He puffed a dozen Havana cigars a day, which he had imported two thousand at a time.

Seward had served in the New York legislature, as governor, and then as one of his state's senators in Washington. He was hard-working and a brilliant political strategist. Seward was also a staunch abolitionist who, in welcoming fugitive slaves to his Auburn, New York, mansion, was a conductor on the Underground Railroad. He narrowly missed being nominated as the Republican Party's presidential candidate in 1856. Four years later he won the party's first two ballots for that nomination before Lincoln surprised nearly everyone by taking it on the third.

Seward had toured Britain in 1833 and then Britain, Europe and the Near East for seven months in 1859. In 1857, he set out on a tour of Canada. With influential journalist Francis Blair and several political friends, he marvelled at the crashing cascades of Niagara Falls, spent time in Toronto and enjoyed fishing at Lake Ontario's picturesque Thousand Islands. Joined by his son Frederick and wife, Anna, Seward chartered a small boat for an invigorating stint to Labrador. While admiring Labrador's spectacular vistas, he was moved to record in his journal that Canada was "a region grand enough for the seat of a great empire."[1] But he was no friend of Canada. The empire he had in mind was American.

Seward was an unapologetic supporter of Manifest Destiny, the belief that the United States should and would someday own or control all of North America. He saw territorial expansion as an essential element of America's economic development. In line with that vision of peaceful, relentless, commercial growth, he believed that Canada should someday become part of the United States. He held no compunction about telling people in public and private that he would do all he could to see it happen.[2] But he was patient. In 1855, for instance, he helped shepherd the Reciprocity Treaty through the Senate, creating a free trade arrangement between the United States and Canada. He spoke of increased economic integration as the first step toward eventual annexation. He said: "I would not seize in haste, and force the fruit, which ripening in time, will fall of itself into our hands. . . . I have shown you then that a continent is to be peopled, and even distant islands to be colonized, by us."[3] His endgame made itself brazenly apparent in an 1860 speech at St. Paul, Minnesota, when he addressed Canadians directly: "It is very well you are building states to be hereafter admitted to the American union."[4]

A number of British political and civil society leaders had met Seward and were not impressed. On his 1859 trip to England he had insulted all those at a reception held in his honour by observing that absurdly high prices for art and books were probably a reflection of the willingness of upper-class English snobs to pay too much for just about anything. In a conversation with *London Times* journalist William Howard Russell, he had repeated his designs on Canada and blustered that Britain should not threaten the United States for, "A contest between Great Britain and the United States would wrap the world in fire, and at the end it would not be the United States which would have to lament the results of the conflict."[5]

In October 1860, the Duke of York and Britain's colonial secretary, the Duke of Newcastle, had visited Seward. It was part of the royal tour that had caused such embarrassment and political trouble for John A. Macdonald in Kingston. During the meeting, Seward announced boldly that he would make full use of insults to Britain to help the American domestic situation. The Duke of Newcastle reported the conversation to the British cabinet and also warned Canadian governor general, Sir Edmund Head.[6] Newcastle found Seward's comments and attitude distressing, but guessed that Seward would stop short of war. After Lincoln's election, Britain's secretary of war, Sir George Cornwall Lewis, offered what became the consensus opinion among Britain's political leaders who were suspicious of American democracy, the untested president and the belligerent Seward: "The Washington government is violent and unscrupulous but it is not insane."[7]

In February 1861, Seward invited Lord Richard Lyons, Britain's minister to the United States, to his home to discuss what he saw as an unacceptable threat. Lyons had served in a number of diplomatic posts with his father since 1839, and had been appointed to Washington in 1859. He had arrived in April knowing little about America yet firmly believing in the superiority of Britain, Britons, and the British parliamentary system. Like many of his contemporaries, he saw American democracy as beholden to the mob power of the uninformed majority, and most political leaders as lacking the education and breeding necessary to rule.[8]

Besides these philosophical differences, he and Seward could not have had more divergent personalities. Where Seward was effusive and extroverted, Lyons was shy, disdained displays of emotion, and seldom met people's eyes. He was a cold and officious man who disliked the social aspects of his job and later bragged about not having delivered a speech or sipped a drink the entire time he was in Washington. A non-smoker, Lyons suffered through meetings in rooms reeking of Seward's everpresent cigar smoke. His Victorian priggishness and unwillingness to establish personal contacts sometimes led to a failure to appreciate context. He seemed to confuse American patriotism for arrogance and confidence for aggression. Lyons's suspicion of Seward, at least at the beginning of their professional relationship, blinded him to the clever tactics the wily secretary of state was employing in the pursuit of a greater strategy. Lyons grew to like Seward, but he never really understood him.[9]

Seward told Lyons that Britain must stay out of American domestic affairs and, no matter what might happen, it could never recognize the Confederacy or meet with Southern commissioners. Seward stated bluntly that if Britain ignored these directives, then the United States would respond with a war that would involve an immediate invasion of Canada. The war would actually be helpful, he said, because all Americans, even those in rebellion, would rally around the flag and in a patriotic fervour directed against Europe, forget old grudges and reunite.[10]

Lyons had no way of knowing whether Seward was speaking for Lincoln, and believed that he was not bluffing. He wrote to British foreign secretary, Lord John Russell, on February 12 stating: "Some of the leaders of the party which is about to come into power are on the lookout for a foreign dispute in the hope that they should rekindle the fire of the patriotism both in the North and the South."[11] Britain and France began to work together, assuming that, while the United States might declare a diversionary war on one of them, it would not be so foolish as to initiate a conflict with both. Lyons was not so sure. He wrote a number of increasingly desperate notes to London, declaring Seward a dangerous demagogue with designs on Britain that ran through Canada.[12] He became convinced that Seward was spoiling for a diversionary war to end the Civil War or, failing that, that if the South were somehow lost, then the annexation of Canada might be apt compensation.[13]

Canada was a sitting duck. Its forts and harbour defences had been left in a sorrowful state since the War of 1812. There were not nearly enough soldiers to guard the long American border, let alone defend it should an attack come. Responding to tension with the United States in the mid-1850s and with troops freed up by the end of the Crimean War, Britain had increased its military presence in Canada a little, but by 1860 there were still only about 4,300 British regulars stationed mostly in Canada East and West and in Nova Scotia. Augmenting that meagre number were Canadian volunteer militia. Every male between sixteen and sixty was a member of a militia company and had to devote two weekends a year to military training. Intentions were often good, but absenteeism was widespread. The training was mostly useless if it happened at all. British soldiers scoffed at the Canadian Sedentary Militia in which many men drank more than drilled. In addition, about 8,500 paid Active Militia could be called on in a time of emergency. They met for two to three weeks a year, and their training was somewhat more strenuous but, like the militia units, their equipment was antiquated and their dedication questionable.

With the Americans heading toward war, the sad state of military preparedness in the Canadian and Maritime colonies worried the British government. Prime Minister Palmerston and Foreign Secretary Russell regarded North American events with the seriousness they deserved, but at the same time they were focused upon disturbing changes that were taking place in Europe. Prussian representative to the German Confederation, Otto von Bismarck, was building his personal power through his plans to unite Germanic states into a central-European powerhouse that could threaten the relative peace the continent had enjoyed since the 1815 Congress of Vienna. Palmerston and Russell were also dealing with France, and to a lesser extent with Spain, in their interventions in Mexico, which in October 1861 would lead to the Franco-Mexican War.

Palmerston and Russell both saw America and Americans in a negative light. Palmerston once said that Americans were, "totally unscrupulous and dishonest."[14] They were both attracted to the logic and romance of the Confederate experiment and agreed that Britain would be the beneficiary if the United States split into two or more republics. They also agreed on their assessment of Seward. In cabinet one day, Palmerston called him "a vapouring blustering ignorant man."[15]

Further complicating the British government's response to the Civil War and the dangers it posed to Canada were the growing divisions in political circles regarding the costs and benefits of maintaining such a far-flung empire. Palmerston's chancellor of the exchequer was the politically powerful William Gladstone, who counted himself among the so-called Little Englanders, who used every new military expense demanded for or by Canada as another excuse to argue that colonies should support themselves. The Duke of Newcastle, secretary of state for the colonies, shared Gladstone's concerns and publicly wondered whether Canada should not be asked to do more for its own defence before Britain offered another farthing.[16]

Palmerston wrote a long and thoughtful letter in an attempt to maintain Newcastle's support. In it, the prime minister reiterated his anti-Americanism and, despite Gladstone's objections, his support for Canada's defence: "Peace with men who have no Honour and are swayed by the passions of irresponsible masses, and by a reckless desire to hold their position by all and any means consists in being strong by sea on their coasts and respectable in our military force in our Provinces. . . . If in consequence of over hesitation, we should expose our Provinces to insult and disaster we should justly incur reproaches from which no defence could be pleaded."[17]

Palmerston and Russell believed that Canada's weakness was too tempting for Seward to resist, and so stood opposed to the Little Englanders and ordered a regiment of British regulars to be sent to Canada. Palmerston made clear that he wanted them fully armed with the most modern weapons, so as to demonstrate to the Americans the seriousness of British intentions. The British fleet in the Caribbean and along America's coast was also reinforced.

THE WAR BEGINS

It was April 12, 1861. With a thundering boom at four thirty in the morning, a shell tore into the dark sky above the Charleston harbour. It seemed to hang there—mysteriously suspended in time. In those few seconds, in that illusion of stillness, lay America's final moments of peace.

Lincoln had been elected president of the United States the previous November. In the three months that followed, South Carolina and then Mississippi, Florida, Alabama, Georgia, Louisiana and finally Texas had declared his election the final insult, secession their only option, and had left those United States. In selecting Mississippi senator Jefferson Davis as president, and with his forming a government in the temporary capital of Montgomery, Alabama, those states insisted that a new country had been born. The Confederate States of America then did as all countries do and sought to express its sovereignty by securing its borders and the land and property within them. It took possession of all federal property and military installations. The only exceptions were three Florida forts and, most significantly, the one at Charleston, South Carolina.

In December, six days after South Carolina seceded, that garrison's commander, Major Robert Anderson, grew concerned about the possibility of an attack on his eighty-two men and so moved them from Fort Moultrie to the much stronger Fort Sumter, a mile from shore. South Carolina Governor Francis Pickens ordered him gone, but he refused to leave. With access to the city denied, Anderson needed to be resupplied with men, ammunition, and food. Those provisions could come only from Washington. Upon Lincoln's decision to withdraw or support Fort Sumter would hang the future of the United States.

In his March inauguration speech, Lincoln had not mentioned the Confederacy. He never would. He was conveying his belief that, because the Constitution was silent on the issue, secession was illegal. There was no Confederate States of America; there were only American states in rebellion. There were no Confederates, only disloyal Americans. Lincoln said to the thousands gathered around the Capitol's sun-dappled east portico that he would do his sworn duty to uphold the Constitution by seeing that all the laws of the United States were carried out and, most provocatively given Major Anderson's precarious position, that all government property would be held, occupied, and possessed. In his high-pitched Midwestern twang, he addressed himself directly to the people of the South, saying, "The government will not assail you. You can have no conflict, without being yourselves the aggressor."[18] But to Southern minds, with Lincoln's determination to stop the expansion of slavery, his stubborn refusal to recognize their Confederacy, and now his promise to take back what they considered their property, they had already been assailed. To Southerners, Lincoln was promising not peace but to become the aggressor in what for them would be a defensive war.

Two weeks earlier, Jefferson Davis had delivered his own inaugural address, in which he had assumed the Confederate States of America to be an established fact. He had expressed the goals of the new country with clarity but summed it all up succinctly in a phrase that he would repeat many times—we wish to be left alone. But Davis clearly saw the fire storm on the horizon. The Confederate Congress passed the Army Act, asking that states provide one hundred thousand men to create an army all assumed would soon be needed.

The vexing question of what to do about Major Anderson and his men at Fort Sumter remained open and critical. As secretary of state, Seward needed to advise the president as to the answer. However, even though Seward would eventually concede Lincoln's strengths, at the moment he was finding it difficult to work as the president's subordinate. Seward sincerely believed that, with his much greater experience, he would be the real power behind a weak president. Even before he was officially appointed,

Seward had worked through his old friend and political advisor Thurlow Weed to have an article placed in the *Albany Evening Journal* stating that he would act, using British parlance, as Lincoln's "premier."[19]

Shortly after the president was sworn in, and with the decision about Sumter's resupply in the balance, Seward wrote a memo to Lincoln that he entitled "Some Thoughts for the President's Consideration." It was not done in an emotion-filled rush, for he had Weed look it over, his son rewrite it in a neater script, and then let a friend at the *New York Times* know that, after approval by the president, he would be forwarding a piece for publication.[20]

The memo was as insulting as it was inappropriate. It stated as fact that the administration had no domestic or foreign policies, and that the president was spending far too much time on trivial matters. He recommended the evacuation of Sumter and the reinforcement of the Florida forts. Further, Lincoln should immediately demand explanations from France and Spain as to recent activities in Mexico and the Caribbean, which had all the appearances of Europe's intention to return to the western hemisphere. Further, Russia and Britain should account for their mild reactions to the South's declaration of independence, which hinted at official recognition and perhaps even support. If any of the responses were unsatisfactory, the memo argued, Lincoln should ask Congress to declare war. He repeated the belief he had asserted to British officials that if the United States were to enter a foreign war then Southerners would rally to the flag, forget secession, and the country would be saved. Seward concluded that whatever policy was adopted, the president needed either to step up and carry it out or delegate responsibility for its execution to a member of his cabinet—supposedly Seward himself.

Demonstrating the patience, intellect and skill with people for which he would become known, Lincoln sat with his secretary of state. He asked for neither apology nor resignation. Seward left that April 1 meeting with the clear understanding that Lincoln was in command and would act as such with policies he had enunciated. The episode showed that Lincoln wanted no war with any foreign power. It also proved that Lincoln would play a bigger foreign policy role than many believed, even though Seward would still be its voice. However, at the time no one knew about the memo or the meeting, and so from the British and Canadian points of view the ambitious and aggressive secretary of state remained powerful and dangerous.

Despite the unfortunate memo and other bumps in the road, Lincoln and Seward actually became quite close. Seward moved to a spacious three-storey red brick house overlooking Lafayette Park, a short walk from the White House. Lincoln often strolled over and the two enjoyed intense political conversations and shared laughter over ribald stories. While disagreements over tactics sometimes led to tense conversations and even offers of resignation, he and Lincoln agreed on all the big matters and grand strategies. Other cabinet secretaries, in fact, expressed disdain that the two became so close that they often discussed issues fully before bringing them to cabinet.[21] When special meetings were necessary, it was nearly always Seward who summoned the others. The enormous influence of Seward's office, coupled with his special relationship with the president, meant that the man who dreamt of someday seeing Canada absorbed into the American republic was that republic's second most-powerful man.

Meanwhile, Seward, Lincoln and others had worked through every option regarding the resupply of Fort Sumter and a decision was finally made. On April 6, a message was sent to South Carolina's governor. It warned him that provisions would soon be sent to the fort. Six days later, in Charleston's cool early morning sky, the seconds ticked by with that shell seeming to hang there, suspended in time. And then it fell.

The shell dropped directly into the centre of the fort. More than four thousand shells then screamed back and forth until, two days later, on a bright Sunday afternoon, Major Anderson surrendered. He was permitted to fire a fifty-gun salute to his flag, lower it, and then bring it with him as his men were brought ashore. They were allowed to march proudly beneath their colours and with shouldered muskets to ships waiting to transport them home with Southern troops at attention in respectful silence. The ceremony was a nod to chivalrous ways of old at the outset of a new and thoroughly modern war.

On the afternoon of Sumter's fall, Lincoln sent a message to governors asking for 75,000 troops to be mustered and sent to Washington. The recruits were to volunteer for three months of service. He also announced that all southern ports would be immediately blockaded.

Tennessee, Arkansas, North Carolina and Virginia promptly seceded. But nothing was clearcut or clean. The northwest portion of Virginia broke away and formed its own state, which remained loyal to the Union. Missouri's governor declared for the Confederacy, but his legislature was not in session so the declaration was not ratified. Kentucky's governor also announced that his state would join the Confederacy but his legislature voted to remain in the Union.

Days after the thunder of Sumter's guns, the highly respected general Robert E. Lee refused an offer to lead the Northern armies. With Virginia's secession he sent a polite one-sentence letter of resignation to Secretary of War Simon Cameron. Lee packed a few belongings and left his Arlington estate with his wife, Mary Anna Custis Lee—the daughter of George Washington's adopted son—and headed south. He offered his services to Jefferson Davis, who accepted without hesitation. Lee later famously explained his decision to serve Virginia: "I did only what my duty demanded. I could have taken no other course without dishonor."[22]

Each of the approximately 16,000 officers and men who comprised the standing army of the United States had to make the same decision as Lee. Many felt the same way, being swayed by their passion and loyalty for their state rather than their country. Of the 1,108 officers in the army before the war began, 387 resigned to join the Confederacy.[23] In the border states of Delaware, Kentucky, Maryland and Missouri, Northern and Southern recruiters often worked side by side. In the summer of 1861, one Union regiment in Louisville was marching to catch an eastbound train while a Confederate regiment marched the opposite way down the other side of the street. Lincoln had brothers-in-law in the Confederate army, while Davis had a brother-in-law fighting for the Union.

The city of Washington sat defenceless. It was a southern city. It was surrounded by Virginia to the south and west, and slave-holding Maryland to the north with slave state Delaware not far beyond. Windows were boarded up and sandbags and flour sacks piled to protect entrance ways. People wearing yellow badges declaring themselves for the Confederacy walked the city's muddy streets. A worried president stared out White House windows and wondered aloud when his army would arrive.

The Massachusetts 6th Regiment had quickly heeded Lincoln's call and was making its way south. As the young soldiers were changing trains in Baltimore, a rock-throwing mob descended upon them. The raw Massachusetts boys formed a firing line. Shots rang out from both sides and left twelve civilians and four soldiers dead.* Baltimore's mayor called on the people of his city to do all they could to stop these and other Union troops. He demanded that the governor declare the state for the Confederacy. Rail lines were sabotaged, mail was stopped and telegraph cables were severed. For six days Washington was cut off from the world.

The Massachusetts men marched the rest of the way, often pelted with rocks and taunts. Lincoln was relieved to see them, but unnerved by the fact that no other troops followed. He stood on the roof of the White House and through a telescope saw Confederate tents amassing across the Potomac on the towering hills of Lee's Arlington estate. He gazed southward and could see Confederate flags snapping on Alexandria's rooftops. After a number of tense days and nights, regiments from New York and more from Massachusetts made it to Washington. Their arrival provided a welcome respite from his anxieties, but Lincoln still awaited his army.

As for Seward, although his enthusiasm and ambition often caused him to overstep his responsibilities, his primary job was to deal with foreign governments. Nonetheless, his most urgent task became stopping Jefferson Davis from achieving his ultimate goal—independence. If Davis's newly established country were to survive and thrive, he would need Lincoln to allow the Confederacy to stand; but with little hope of that, and with war coming, he needed official recognition from other countries, most importantly from Britain and France. He addressed the Confederate Congress on

---

* *Within the crowd watching the melée was a famous actor named John Wilkes Booth.*

April 29, two weeks after Fort Sumter's fall, and noted that he had sent commissioners to negotiate a process of peaceful separation with Seward and Lincoln but that they had been lied to and rebuffed. Davis then spoke of three commissioners who were at that point en route to negotiate with European leaders, seeking official recognition of the Confederacy. He said he expected recognition to come quickly, and concluded with his belief in the rightness of the South's cause: "With a firm reliance on that Divine Power which covers with its protection the just cause, we will continue to struggle for our inherent right to freedom, independence, and self-government."[24]

There were valid arguments for international recognition. The Confederacy had a functioning government, a constitution, an army, and about nine million people, if one included the approximately three and a half million slaves, all spread over 750,000 square miles of definable, defensible territory. If recognition came, the Confederacy could legally negotiate loans, buy arms from neutral countries, and put ships on the ocean with the right to search and seize enemy craft. Further, recognition would destroy Lincoln's insistence that there was no Confederacy and thereby weaken the foundation upon which he hoped first to fight and then to re-unify and rebuild. Davis had to have recognition, and Lincoln and Seward could not let it happen. It was in that struggle to stop the recognition of the Confederacy that Seward's desire to save the Union met his long-held beliefs in America's commercial expansionism, and at that intersection of dreams, goals and strategic planning lay Canada.

Davis could count. He realized that the North's vast superiority in population, gold, and industrial capacity meant that the Confederacy needed help. His bargaining chip was cotton. While France and others purchased southern cotton, fully one-sixth of Britain's working population was tied to the textile industry. By 1860, 85 percent of the cotton upon which that industry relied came from the American south.[25] The three-man commission that Jefferson had sent to Europe under the leadership of William Yancey focused on Britain, France and Russia, and offered an uninterrupted cotton supply in return for official recognition of the Confederate States of America.

Neither Seward nor Davis would learn until long after the war that Britain, and to a lesser extent other European powers, had taken actions to protect themselves from being cut off from supplies of southern cotton. Britain stockpiled it, rebuilt many of its looms to use a different type of fibre, bought cotton from other sources, and then during the war managed to sneak an estimated one- to one-and-a-half million bales of cotton through the Northern blockade, a good deal of it through Halifax.[26] While the British economy was hurt and thousands suffered unemployment and hardship as a result of the slowing and closure of many mills, it was not crushed. The British government was certainly influenced, but not blinded, by a desire to renew a steady flow of Southern cotton. So-called King Cotton was important, but not to the extent Davis hoped or Seward feared.

With his goals for the Confederacy and Britain set and his long-term designs on Canada still clear, Seward's bluffing, threatening, manipulating tactics came into play. At one moment he appeared to be a ruthless warmonger and at the next an inspired peacemaker. At his frequent dinner parties, no one quite knew when he was joking or stating policy. Through it all, he was Lincoln's most valuable asset in dealing with Britain, Europe and Canada.

On April 16, just days after Sumter's fall, Seward's fears were realized when a motion was introduced in the British House of Commons supporting the recognition of the Confederacy. Foreign Secretary Russell managed to have debate delayed. But he also met unofficially with Confederate agents. Days later Davis announced that he would issue letters of marque to any sailor with a vessel who applied, thereby affording legal sanction for a navy of privateers charged with the task of disrupting Northern trade and, more important, running Lincoln's porous blockade. Things were happening quickly and nothing was going as Seward had hoped. He needed to stop reacting and regain the initiative.

RISING TENSION ON THE BORDER

Seward knew about the military preparations in Canada and heard rumours of Canadians not only sympathizing with the Southern cause but acting to help it by harbouring ships and supplying arms. He needed to know more. At an April 12 cabinet meeting, Seward was given permission to appoint former Massachusetts congressman George Ashmun as a secret agent. For ten dollars a day plus expenses, Ashmun was asked to travel to Canada on a three-month mission to determine Canada's views on the war and to influence those views while also checking on material support for the South.

Ashmun was qualified for the job, as he knew Canada well and had just the month before visited Quebec City as a representative of the Grand Trunk Railway. While there, he had met with Governor General Sir Edmund Head. Having served as governor general for five years, Head was accustomed to dealing with the tangle of inoperable parts that was Canada's government and the coiled spring that was its neighbour. Head worried about Seward. He had written to London regarding his suspicion that Seward would seek to indemnify the United States by annexing Canada or by waiting to take Canada once the problems with the South were solved.[27] But Head was a cautious, professional man and so kept those suspicions to himself when meeting with Ashmun.

Ashmun had also met with a number of Canada East's business elite and with political leaders such as Montreal financier, railway man, Macdonald's minister of finance and future Father of Confederation, Alexander Galt. The two had spoken mostly about Canada's desire to protect the Reciprocity Treaty, which had made steps toward free trade between Canada and the United States.

Ashmun left for Quebec City in mid-April, but while he was en route the *New York Herald* heard what he was up to and in a front-page article characterized his activities as a propaganda mission.[28] Lyons, the British minister in Washington, went to Seward and insisted that his sending agents to Canada was an insult to Anglo-American relations, and demanded that Ashmun be recalled. Seward assured Lyons that there were no others like him in Canada and that Ashmun would indeed be asked to return home.[29] Communications were such, however, that Seward's note to Ashmun was a long time arriving. Even after receiving it, he remained in Canada as a private citizen doing much as he would have done had his intent not been discovered. He met again with Head and members of the cabinet, including Galt and the increasingly powerful leader of Canada East, George Étienne Cartier. Ashmun left shortly afterward with nothing of value to report to Seward, who had been embarrassed by the entire debacle.

Shortly after having seen Ashmun, Governor General Head learned of rumours regarding talk of Canada's annexation, complete with plans as to how it would come about and the work to be done once it was accomplished. According to reports, Seward was purchasing Canadian newspapers to promote the idea, believing that, once they were persuaded of the benefits of annexation, Canadians would ask to become Americans: Canadian businessman Hamilton Merritt would become the Canadian territorial governor in control of Canada, and New Brunswick's Israel Andrews would lead a Maritime territory.[30] The rumours were rubbish but nonetheless resulted in Head's requesting additional military support for the attack that he believed to be inevitable.[31]

From London, Palmerston responded with an order to send another three regiments to Canada armed with modern artillery. A garrison was moved from China to British Columbia, and Queen Victoria issued a rare statement noting, "it is of great importance that we should be strong in Canada."[32]

British Rear Admiral Sir Alexander Milne was told to bring an additional eight vessels to the American coast to prepare for possible engagement with the Americans in the defence of Canada. Milne reported that the British fleet was superior in both the quality of its ships and armaments, and in sheer numbers, to anything the Americans could throw at it. He developed a plan whereby the ships blockading Southern ports would be destroyed, and attacks on American commercial shipping would ensue.

Palmerston realized that the additional troops and naval preparations were still wholly inadequate should the United States invade, but these measures were meant to dissuade Lincoln and Seward while encouraging Canadians to increase their efforts at defending themselves.[33] There was also a feeling among most in the British cabinet that, should war actually come, it was the navy's to win. Either that or, if Canada ended up falling to American troops, it could be retaken or negotiated for after the war's end.[34]

While these preparations were being made, the British consul in Chicago informed Head that a group of men had entered Canada to buy weapons for Illinois regiments and noted that he hoped the weapons would be supplied. American consul J.E. Wilkins added that arms sales such as this would help Canada maintain good relations with the United States, and threatened that if the arms were not forthcoming the western states would reconsider their practice of shipping western grain through the St. Lawrence.[35] Head ignored the threat and on April 21 told local authorities that there must be no arms sales. The next day, a gentleman named Amaziah Jones arrived in Head's office at the behest of New York governor, E.D. Morgan, and politely asked to purchase fifty thousand Canadian rifles for use by New York regiments. The day afterward, the governor of Ohio asked to buy weapons. Head again refused to sell the arms, stating that it was against Canadian law to take arms meant for the Canadian militia out of the country and, besides, the militia barely had enough weapons as it was.[36]

Seward heard of the attempted purchases and wrote to Lyons demanding an explanation as to why they were not allowed. With a copy to Head, Lyons responded with a stern letter to Seward asking him again to keep agents out of Canada and repeated Head's insistence that no surplus weapons existed and that even if they did, none would be sold to either the North or South.[37] Attempts to procure arms from New Brunswick and Nova Scotia had met with similar rejections. Head's strong stance and the cooperation of Canadian businesses who could have turned a profit but, for the time being at least, refused to involve themselves in the American war, demonstrated to Seward and the Northern press that Canada would not simply do as America wished.

Meanwhile, Palmerston and his cabinet struggled to determine Britain's official position with respect to what had clearly become a civil war. The cabinet decision was finally announced on May 13, 1861, with Queen Victoria's Proclamation of Neutrality. Britain would stay out of the fight. Further, the proclamation brought the Foreign Enlistments Act of 1818 into effect, meaning that no British subject, including Canadians, could legally enlist in the Union or Confederate armies or navies, or help outfit either side with armaments of any kind. The proclamation also named the Confederate States of America as a belligerent. This designation was important. According to international law and precedent, a belligerent could arrange loans from foreign governments and get fuel and supplies from neutral ports, including those in Canada. France, Russia and Belgium quickly followed with their own similarly worded declarations of neutrality.

Seward was outraged and made no attempt to hide it. Massachusetts senator and chair of the Senate Foreign Relations Committee, Charles Sumner, later wrote that he had never seen Seward "more like a caged tiger, or more profuse of oaths in every form that the English language supplies, than when prancing about the room denouncing the Proclamation of Belligerency, which he swore he would send to hell."[38] The proclamation flew in the face of everything that Seward had been diplomatically demanding, and on which Lincoln had been politically insisting; for, in naming the Confederacy as a belligerent, Britain was stating that there was indeed a Confederate States of America with its own army and navy. The Proclamation was rightly interpreted as just short of official recognition.

Britain's action was doubly insulting to Seward in that Palmerston had not even waited for the new American minister to London, Charles Francis Adams, Jr. to arrive and present his credentials. As the son and grandson of presidents, and having spent his formative years in British schools, Adams was uniquely qualified for his job, but the timing of the announcement had not allowed him to do it. He had arrived in Liverpool on the morning the proclamation was released and found out about it through reading a newspaper while on a train to London.

Lincoln said nothing publicly about Britain's affront to everything he believed so vitally important, but there were heated debates in the White House and halls of Congress. Senator Sumner ensured that his many British contacts heard everything that was being discussed. Sumner hated

Seward. His personal disdain was darkened by professional jealousy. He shared Seward's goal of annexing Canada to bolster America's economic future, but the two seldom agreed on tactics. Sumner and others thought Seward was unnecessarily leading the United States into war with Britain in Canada and he relayed those opinions to a number of British correspondents as disparate as Queen Victoria's daughter Louise, the Duchess of Argyll, and *London Times* journalist William Russell. Sumner's frequent and gossipy letters derided Seward as reckless, sinister and dangerous.[39] A Sumner letter that ended up with Lord Lyons reported that at a dinner at Seward's home, the secretary of state had become enraged when speaking of Canada and Britain and at one point snapped, "God damn 'em. I'll give 'em hell."[40]

Lyons reported to Lord Russell that, according to Sumner, there was uncertainty as to whether Lincoln or the cabinet were willing to stand up to Seward and temper his aggressive tendencies. Seward's profane declaration might, Lyons speculated, be the final insult that could lead to war with America and the invasion of Canada.[41]

The preparations to meet that invasion continued. The first British regiment departed for Canada in May. In early June the other two were sent, this time aboard the *Great Eastern*, the fastest vessel in the British fleet. The use of that ship was designed to impress and possibly intimidate the Americans in that it crossed the Atlantic in only eight days. A large crowd at the Quebec City docks welcomed the red-coated soldiers with hearty cheers.

The British troops arrived amid new, swirling rumours of war. The always truculent *New York Herald* reported that a group calling itself the 69th Irish Reserve was assembling in Buffalo and preparing to attack Canada to promote independence for its beleaguered people. It then published gossip to the effect that an armistice between the American North and South was apparently imminent, with both sides agreeing to jointly attack Central America and Canada.[42] These and other rumours were soon dismissed, but because the *Herald* was widely read in Canada and Britain, they added to the already palpable tension. Palmerston had by this point already sent three thousand troops to Canada. He ordered more. He wanted at least ten thousand soldiers on the Canadian border, bolstered by modern artillery.[43]

While British troops were settling into their quarters and preparing to take on their new mission, the mistrust that had brought them across the ocean grew even greater. The steamer *Peerless* was resting in Toronto's harbour, having just been purchased from the Bank of Upper Canada by J.T. Wright of New York. Word leaked out that it was being outfitted with armaments and about to be sold to the South to be used as a blockade runner. Hearing those rumours, Massachusetts governor John Andrew wrote to Governor General Head demanding that he stop the purchase.[44] Seward met with Lyons on May 1 and supported that demand. Seward wanted Head to detain the ship, seize and search its papers, and then report to him regarding its ownership and mission. If the Canadians would not seize the ship, Seward threatened, then he would have Americans do it. Lyons told Seward that such actions could lead to war and telegraphed Head to warn him of coming trouble.[45] He also sent a message to Lord John Russell stating that Seward looked prepared to violate Canadian territory."[46] Seward carried through and issued commands to American warships to watch for the *Peerless* in the mouth of the St. Lawrence and to capture it regardless of which flag it might be flying.

On May 10, with the Union Jack crackling in the morning breeze, the *Peerless* left Toronto. Head had ordered Lt. General Sir William Fenwick Williams, the British commander of Canadian forces, to place armed guards along its route with special attention to the canals where the ship would be most vulnerable to American attempts to board her. It stopped in Montreal where its mast was temporarily removed to allow it to pass under the Victoria Bridge. It then sailed on to Quebec City, where Wright tried to secure registration as an American ship. The U.S. consul seized her and a bureaucratic stand-off ensued. American consular authorities were finally convinced to allow the *Peerless* to be on its way if captained by a Nova Scotian named McCarthy. American naval vessels allowed it to pass.

The Ashmun and *Peerless* episodes were blemishes on Seward's career.

He had gained only suspicion and derision, and afforded Head yet another reason to ask for British reinforcements and Palmerston another reason to send them. Seward's reputation as a hot-headed bully whose actions and attitudes might yet bring Britain and America to war was solidified in the minds of many.[47]

Throughout the gathering storm, American minister to London Charles Adams and his son Henry, working as his secretary, carried on regular correspondence with family back in America. Henry wrote to his brother in June 1861: "I believe that our Government means to have a war with England; I believe that England knows it and is preparing for it; and I believe it will come in the next two months. . . . Wait for a Canadian campaign."[48]

Like Adams, Head and Lyons remained convinced that the United States was moving inexorably toward an invasion of Canada, and that because the war against the rebellious South would be over quickly that invasion would be coming sooner rather than later.[49] Canadians, reading their newspapers and seeing the British soldiers gathering in their midst, could not help but share those fears.

FIRST MANASSAS AND THE STING OF REALITY

Bells jangled and jaunty carriage tassels swayed as freshly groomed horses trotted southwest from Washington on the Warrenton Pike. Hundreds of congressmen, bureaucrats and businessmen, joined by their wives and children, had their hearts set on adventure that gleaming Sunday morning of July 12, 1861. They were drawn by the widely held belief that the battle about to take place a mere twenty miles away could be the first and last with the rebel South. It was not to be missed. Picnics were laid out. They squinted to see the black smoke rising from the distant battlefield as Union troops advanced in ragged lines just a couple of miles away. They gasped at the echoing thunder of artillery and puffs of musket-fire. A British reporter heard a woman squeal: "This is splendid. Oh my! Is not that first rate? I feel we will be in Richmond this time to-morrow."[50] It did not work out that way.

Union troops had advanced toward Bull Run Creek at three in the morning. Their feints at two spots were immediately seen as such and Confederate troops shifted to stop the main assault coming on their left. Artillery roared from both sides. The Washington voyeurs cheered from the hill.

There was no questioning the courage of the men, but neither side had a consistency in vocabulary and so orders were often misunderstood—when orders came at all. More confusion was caused by the lack of unity in regiment and state flags and the wild mix of state-issued and home-made uniforms that saw many Southerners in blue and Northerners in grey. There was even a New York and an Alabama Fire Zouave unit, both decked out in bright red baggy pants and white turbans.

After a series of charges and counter-charges, the Union looked as if it was about to take the field, for its advance up the Henry House hill had broken the Confederate units—except for one. Confederate Colonel Thomas Jackson, dressed in his blue Virginia Military Institute uniform, ordered his troops to scream while attacking down the hill, firing first and then plying bayonets. For the first time, Union forces heard the blood-curdling rebel yell. And they ran. Jackson had held the line long enough for reinforcements to surge forward.

The Union lines broke, with soldiers turning to run and many dropping their muskets to run faster. In no time they became entangled with the civilians who had been frantically rolling blankets and gathering their children. Ohio Senator Benjamin Wade and Michigan Senator Zachariah Chandler grabbed up discarded weapons and, along with a handful of other steadfast men, tried to block the road, bellowing at panicking soldiers to return and fight. But there was no stopping them.

Jefferson Davis had ridden to Manassas Junction and arrived in time to see the Union troops in their mad flight back to Washington. He urged General Beauregard, the hero of Fort Sumter, to pursue them, but the general said his men needed rest and water. It was over.

Lincoln had heard the thundering artillery from the White House. Now he stood at the window watching bedraggled soldiers stumbling their way to safety. Darkness brought rain. Through heavily lidded eyes, the melancholy president glimpsed soldiers huddled beneath dirty, sodden blankets and curled in nightmare-filled sleep on the capital's rain-drenched lawns.

Reaction throughout the north was swift and harsh. The Democratic *New York Herald* blamed the administration and Lincoln in particular. The *New York Tribune* removed the masthead "Forward to Richmond," which for some time had festooned its front page. Its publisher, Horace Greeley, composed a letter to Lincoln urging the president to begin peace negotiations with Davis. The *New York Times* sought not to affix blame but rather to consider consequence. Its editorial stated, "It is pretty evident now that we have underrated the strength of the resources and the temper of the enemy."[51]

Lincoln did as he had always done and put his thoughts on paper. He made a nine-point list of things that needed to be done and then immediately set out to do them. He called for thirty-five-year-old George McClellan, who had done good work in Virginia, was well respected by the troops and was known as a crack military organizer, to take control of the Army of the Potomac. Lincoln ordered a more stringent military blockade. And he declared that all three-month recruitment agreements would now last for three years.

The battle that the North called Bull Run and the South called Manassas was only hours old but, like the *New York Times*—and like Davis—Lincoln understood its message. The war was real. It would be long and it would be bloody. Those who had believed the Union would easily defeat the Confederacy were cowed. Davis wrote to his governors asking for more men. Lincoln did the same.

Britain's reaction to Bull Run was captured by a long article in the *London Times* written by journalist William Russell, who had travelled throughout the South and, even before the battle, had concluded that the North could never win the war.[52] The battle served to prove the validity of his thesis. The article was so critical of the North's leadership and military that Lincoln denied his request to embed himself with McClellan's forces.

Palmerston agreed with Russell's assessment. He wrote to the Foreign Office: "It is in the highest degree likely that the North will not be able to subdue the South, and it is no doubt certain that if the Southern union is established as an independent State it would afford a valuable and extensive market for British Manufacturers, but the operations of the war have as yet been too indecisive to warrant an acknowledgement of the southern Union."[53] In other words, Britain's policies regarding the Civil War, including the paramount question of recognition for the South, would be ultimately determined not by the diplomats but by the soldiers.

THE ANTI-AMERICAN ELECTION OF 1861

The Canadian legislative assembly was in session when news of Bull Run arrived. Two government members burst into the chamber and, with no attempt to hide their glee, announced the Union defeat. Three cheers arose for the Confederacy.[54] Most of the government members joined in the hurrahs, while most of the opposition remained silent.

The fissures seen in the assembly reflected those of the nation. Class, race, ethnicity, region and religion were dividing Canadian loyalties well before decisions had to be made regarding support for the North or South. The various elements of Canada's nascent civil society were slowly coalescing into the complexity that would become its defining characteristic. The divisions came crashing to the fore in every election and, because of Canada's unstable political structure, there were plenty of them. But the election that took place in the summer of 1861 all but ignored the usual issues and focused on one—anti-Americanism.

Canadian elections were not for the faint-hearted. The secret ballot was deemed "unmanly," and so voters, all men, had to stand and publicly declare their choice. Voting took place over a number of days and voting lists were shabby at best, so it was common for wagonloads of those promising to vote for a particular candidate to be plied with liquor and then rushed from one polling place to another to exercise their franchise over and over again. Polling stations were often in bars.

The tenor of the 1861 campaign was seen in John A. Macdonald's Kingston riding. For many elections in a row Macdonald had grown used to winning by wide margins and with little effort. This time, however, George Brown's friend and fellow Reformer Oliver Mowat announced at the last minute that he was vying for the seat. Macdonald had once brought the young Mowat into his Kingston firm and helped start his law career, but those halcyon days were long gone. Just before the election call, Mowat had been on his feet in the House lambasting Macdonald and accusing him of all kinds of chicanery. In a rage perhaps fuelled by gin, Macdonald had crossed the floor, grabbed the much shorter, stouter Mowat, and shouted, "You damned pup, I'll slap your chops."[55] He would surely have done so if not pulled away. Now Mowat had local toughs attending Macdonald's meetings and yelling rude interruptions. Fights sometimes broke out, and more than once rocks were thrown at Macdonald and others on stage.

Elections were often a time for fights, and professions of love for anything as non-British as America or republicanism were fighting words. Thoughts of joining the United States had been a part of the Canadian civic conversation since the early days of the American Revolution. Every period of economic strife brought those thoughts back to the light, but it was always a small minority who seriously advocated annexation. In the late 1850s, new talk of annexation had been sparked by the dominant commercial adventure of the era: railway construction. Many of those who ran and financed the Grand Trunk were trying to woo investors to support the building of the intercolonial railway that the Montreal and Maritime business communities had both been talking about for years. Their efforts were being focused by John Poor, of Maine, who was negotiating to build a line from Saint John, New Brunswick, to Portland. If Poor was successful, Montreal would be hurt and the potential profits of an all-Canadian line to the Maritimes would be dashed.

Grand Trunk's Alexander Galt brought the railwaymen's concerns to Macdonald. Poor's scheme, according to Galt and those who supported him, was little more than a step toward the eventual annexation of Canada.[56] In the fog of fear and suspicion that the war had created, and which Seward's bluster and actions had exacerbated, annexation had become a bogey man that Canadians seeking political or commercial advantage could exploit.

Galt's warnings found an audience among Canadians increasingly worried by the prominence of the viperous Seward, the threats of invasion and intrigue filling the newspapers, and a war that was obviously going to be bigger and longer than anyone had expected. To a growing number of Canadians, the United States was a failed state, a dangerous place and one with foul intentions on their homes.

Adding to the anxiety that newspapers were stirring up were a number of pamphlets released in the spring and summer of 1861. The most persuasive—and because large portions were reprinted in the *Globe*, probably the most widely read—was entitled *Canada: Is She Prepared for War?* It was written by Toronto's Lieutenant Colonel George Taylor Denison, under the pseudonym "A Canadian Native." The pamphlet spoke of America's desire to either annex Canada or take it by force. It outlined Canada's woefully inadequate preparations for the invasion that it argued was sure to come.[57]

Macdonald had risen in the Canadian legislature shortly after Fort Sumter had fallen. He did not fan the fears of invasion, which he did not believe would likely occur; nor did he promote annexation, which to him was anathema. He had exploited America's troubles to promote the idea of a stronger, larger Canadian union that could include the Maritime colonies. The American war and threats on Canada demonstrated why a strong, united state was needed. He further argued that, with their Constitution, the Americans had committed the fatal mistake of making each state sovereign unto itself, a structure that had led to political collapse and war. This reality, he said, demonstrated why a strong state needed a foundation of British institutions. Canada, Macdonald said, must learn from America's mistakes and become "an immense confederation of free men, the greatest confederacy of civilized and intelligent men that had ever had an existence on the face of the globe."[58] These were the visionary words of a practical man ready to meet the people in an election in which the United States would be the primary issue. Macdonald fully understood the importance of the election and the grand Canadian vision he was articulating. He wrote to the polymath Egerton Ryerson: "We are on the eve of an election contest which may determine the future of Canada, and whether it will be a limited constitutional monarchy or a Yankee democracy."[59]

At that point, George Brown's Reform Party opposition was composed of a loose amalgam of strange bedfellows. Radicals, Reformers and a group calling themselves Clear Grits were divided on many issues but united in their belief that the current political structure was unfair. The constitutional imperative to split seats evenly between Canada East and West made no democratic sense, they argued, because there were more people in Canada West. Making that point had led to many of them, including George Brown, being labelled anti-French and anti-Catholic. Either the allocation of seats should be changed to reflect the populations of the two sides, the intrepid Reformers argued, or they should be split into two separate entities. Macdonald disagreed. His Liberal-Conservatives drew strength from a number of constituencies but depended upon support from English-speaking Montreal business people, and so he needed the current system to either grow much broader or remain as it was.

In 1861, census results demonstrating that the population gap between the two parts of Canada was actually growing gave credence to Brown's argument about unfair representation. An opposition motion was presented to adopt a system of representation by population. A number of the speeches on the motion reiterated points that had been made for years, but the war and energized talk of defence were injecting new elements into the old argument.

William McDougall was a member of the legislature, a lawyer and a journalist who had run his own paper and written for the *Globe*. He was instrumental in the creation of the radical Clear Grit movement that was part of the Reform opposition. The Clear Grits had long advocated greater democracy and spoken of an admiration for the American political system. McDougall's ideological orientation was in his newspaper's name — *The North American*. McDougall made an impassioned speech in favour of representation by population and then, appearing to be carried away by his own oratory, cried out that if the motion was not passed, Canadians should turn away from their current political structure, turn away from Britain, and look to Washington.

The motion was defeated and the election was soon called. The wily Macdonald recognized that with anti-Americanism growing in Canada's civil society, McDougall had handed him a political gift and a weapon too good to waste. In June, Macdonald wrote a letter to his Kingston constituents announcing his candidacy and his party's platform. He later used it as the basis of a stem-winding speech at a large and boisterous rally. Deploying his always effective conversational style of address, he spoke to many current issues, but hit his stride with what would be the crux of the summer campaign. He attacked McDougall directly on the matter of the American war and American threats and the need to create a broader, stronger union to respond to the danger and belligerence.

> The fratricidal conflict now unhappily raging in the United States shews us the superiority of our institutions and of the principle on which they are based. Long may that principle—the Monarchical principle—prevail in this land. Let there be no "looking to Washington" as was threatened by a leading member of the opposition last session; but let the cry, with the moderate party, be "Canada United as one Province, and under one sovereign."[60]

No matter how hard or how often Reform candidates tried to deal with other issues—and there were plenty—the question of American threats and Canada's alleged yearning for annexation returned. In Whitby, Macdonald supporters hung an effigy of McDougall at the site of a Reform rally. Its hands held signs that said "Look to Washington" and over its heart was a sign saying "annexation." Before the meeting, it was burned.

The July 1 election saw Macdonald take his riding and the Liberal-Conservatives win a majority. But it was a hollow victory because Macdonald's support in Canada West—always a problem—had nearly evaporated. Anti-Americanism had won the day, but the fissures within the Canadian nation were made deeper and more divisive than ever.

Throughout the campaign and in the following weeks, much of the American press had maintained a strong anti-British and anti-Canadian bias. Most hostile of all was the *New York Herald*. Macdonald read it and often commented on its articles. Typical of the *Herald*'s stance was a July 13 editorial that insulted Canadians as being unable to stand up for themselves against Britain. It concluded: "When they are annexed to the republic, which is only a question of time—a question which may receive its solution before the termination of the present year—we will show them the way to act an independent part, and to assert the dignity of freedom of the Anglo-Saxon race."[61]

In response to the American papers, many Canadian newspapers printed equally vituperative articles that reflected the tenor and tone of the election. The *London Free Press*, for instance, on September 11 published a front-page editorial stating, "At the present moment, the liberties and lives of the people in the United States are subject to the despotism of a mob government."[62] It went on to discuss the espionage taking place in Northern cities, where people expressing anti-government ideas or pro-Southern ideas were considered traitors, and where liberties such as the right of *habeas corpus* had been suspended. Lincoln and Seward were specifically named as villainous but the American system itself was said to be the culprit: "There is but a step between liberty and despotism under a Republican form of government. Let all British subjects ponder these things, and ask themselves what there is to be gained, after all, by living under a Republic."[63]

Back in April Alexander Galt had warned George Ashmun of the growing anti-Americanism among Canadians.[64] The election had proven the power and popularity of those sentiments, and in the fall Seward read reports from his consuls in Canadian and Maritime cities that included Canadian newspaper articles and stated that anti-American feelings were becoming more popular, openly expressed and intense.[65]

The rising tide of anti-Americanism, the increased number of British troops and the eleven British battleships in the Halifax harbour either worried Seward or inspired him to flex some muscle. On October 10 he wrote a circular to all Northern governors. He urged them to do all they could to prepare and protect their canals and harbours so that they would be ready to defend against attack from the Atlantic or across the Great Lakes. A second, more specific circular came days later. Perhaps the circulars were just more bluff and bluster aimed at Britain and Canada and border town insecurities. Regardless of their purpose, they indicated that if a war in Canada was to come, as many expected it would, America would be ready and willing to wage it. All that was needed was a spark to ignite the firestorm—and then it came.

THE *TRENT* CRISIS

On the warm, turquoise narrows off the Bahama Channel on November 8, 1861, the *Trent*, an unarmed British mail packet, was steaming from Havana unaware that it was being hunted. Its captain, James Moir, spied a large fifteen-gun sloop off his bow and hoisted the Union Jack. The *San Jacinto* raised the American flag, and then sent a shell crashing across the *Trent*'s bow. Moir sped up but was startled by a second, even closer blast. The ships came to and Moir allowed men from the *San Jacinto* boats to board his vessel. American Lieutenant MacNeill Fairfax announced that he was acting on behalf of Captain Charles Wilkes of the *San Jacinto*, who suspected the *Trent* of transporting Confederate agents James Mason and John Slidell, and contraband documents to Europe. He demanded the passenger list.

Mason and Slidell immediately stepped forward and identified themselves. Fairfax announced that they were under arrest. Moir protested as Slidell turned to his wife and daughter, bade them goodbye, and promised to see them soon in Paris. Slidell's wife was not so sanguine. She blasted Fairfax and called him a pirate with no authority to arrest people on a ship under the British flag. She mocked him, saying that she had enjoyed tea with Captain Wilkes just weeks earlier.

Fairfax was unmoved. He told Moir that when the two men and their personal secretaries had been removed, the ship, passengers and crew were free to go. As Mrs. Slidell fumed, her children burst into tears as they watched their father and Mason, and their two personal secretaries, being rowed to the *San Jacinto*, which then, slowly disappeared over the horizon.

Seven days later, the *San Jacinto* steamed into the Union naval base at Hampton Roads, Virginia. Telegrams tore across the country announcing the news of the capture. Wilkes was ordered to take his prisoners to Boston, where they joined other Confederates in Fort Warren.

Their fellow prisoners warmly welcomed Mason and Slidell, for they were both well-known. Slidell was a popular Louisiana senator who had led the fight to repeal the Missouri Compromise and had aggressively interviewed John Brown of Harper's Ferry fame in an attempt to link him to Northern abolitionists. Mason was a well-respected Virginia senator and former chair of the Senate Foreign Relations Committee who had been the principal author of the Fugitive Slave Law. Jefferson Davis had appointed Mason as his agent to England and Slidell to France with identical missions: to lobby for recognition and intervention. They were slated to serve as ambassadors when that happy day arrived.

Captain Wilkes, a renowned explorer and author, became an instant Northern hero. After having suffered months of humiliating battlefield defeats, at last the North could boast of a Union victory. He arrived at New York City to a brass-band welcome and a parade up Broadway. There was a grand reception and lavish dinner at City Hall and then another in Boston. Wilkes proudly told the story again and again of how he had learned of the two trying to run the blockade and had hunted them down. To those pondering the legality of his action, Wilkes explained that it was legal to capture contraband documents and since Mason and Slidell were, in effect, walking contraband, it had been legal to capture them. The *New York Times* concurred: "We do not believe the American heart ever thrilled with more genuine delight."[66] The *New York Herald*, always ready to push for a British-Canadian war, editorialized that it was "quite elated" with Wilkes's action. It was emphatic that the Confederates "should not be surrendered by this government, even if their detention should cause a war with Great Britain."[67] The *Philadelphia Sunday Transcript* went further: "In a word, while the British government has been playing the villain, we have been playing the fool. Let her now do something beyond driveling—let her fight . . . she will meet the American people on land and on the seas, as they long to meet her, once again, not only to lower the red banner of St. George . . . but to consolidate Canada with the union."[68]

Those wondering about the administration's stand were perhaps instructed by Navy Secretary Gideon Wells, who gushed to Wilkes: "Your conduct in seizing these public enemies was marked by intelligence, ability, decision and firmness and has the emphatic approval of this department."[69] Seward and Lincoln hold their tongues in public, worried about the legality of Wilkes's actions, but were nonetheless swept up in the euphoria of the rare victory.[70]

It was November 27 before the *Trent* finally made it across the Atlantic, conveying its captain and passengers to London. They were hailed and feted as heroes while Wilkes and the Americans were branded as pirates. Stories were told of "brutish American marines" rushing at a terrified Mrs. Slidell, and Yankee bayonets being thrust at women and children.

The *London Times* said of Captain Wilkes: "He is an ideal Yankee. Swagger and ferocity, built on a foundation of vulgarity and cowardice, these are his characteristics, and these are the most prominent marks by which his countrymen, generally speaking, are known throughout the world."[71] The *Halifax Morning Chronicle* was even harsher: "Abraham Lincoln . . . has proved himself a feeble, confused, and little-minded mediocrity. Mr. Seward, the firebrand at his elbow, is exerting himself to provoke a quarrel with all Europe, in that spirit of senseless egotism that induces the Americans, with their dwarf fleet and shapeless mass of incoherent squads they call an army."[72] These and other papers reflected the overwhelming British opinion that its honour had been insulted by an irresponsible captain on behalf of incompetent leaders of a disintegrating rogue state.

The next day, the *Times* joined other papers in placing blame for the insult to Britain and international law upon the shoulders of the man it loved to hate. Its November 28 editorial expressed no doubt that Seward had been behind the whole crisis, for he had been aching for a reason to go to war with Britain, in order to claim Canada in compensation for losing Southern states.[73]

Palmerston called his cabinet together. The discussion began with some members downplaying the incident. International law of the seas was still being written and so was open to broad interpretation, but the views brought to the table that day were presented as facts. It was agreed without reservation that Wilkes should have respected the British flag. If he had suspicions regarding the movement of contraband goods, then he should have escorted the *Trent* to a belligerent port where a tribunal would have ruled on his suspicions. Wilkes had broken international law and, if he had acted on the orders of the American government, then Britain had the legitimate right to demand the immediate release of Mason and Slidell. If the United States refused, then Britain had the right to declare war.

Palmerston listened to the discussion and then, according to a story that became popular and may have been true, finally thundered, "You may stand for this but damned if I will."[74] The decision was made to act with firmness. First came a limited trade sanction. In the fall of 1861, Seward had sent DuPont Company representatives to England to buy up all the saltpetre they could. It was an essential ingredient in gunpowder. Just as the British cabinet was debating the *Trent* Crisis, 2,300 tons of saltpetre were being loaded onto five ships. The loading was stopped. The cabinet office cabled to the shipyards that all saltpetre sales to the United States were henceforth banned, and the shipment was moved back into warehouses.[75]

There was more. A letter was composed to American minister Charles Adams, demanding that the two prisoners be released and that an official apology be issued from the American government to the British. If the men were not released and the apology announced within seven days, then all diplomatic relations would be severed and a state of war would exist. The letter went through several drafts and was finally sent to the Queen for her signature. At that point Prince Albert, Victoria's beloved consort, despite suffering from the typhoid fever that would take his life only two weeks later, suggested amendments that offered the Americans an honourable way out. Albert's softened draft expressed hope that Wilkes had acted without orders, confidence that the United States wanted to adhere to international law, and certainty that it had never intended to insult Britain or violate the security of British mails and transportation. The changes were accepted by cabinet and the letter sent aboard the ship *Europa* on the first of December.

Foreign Secretary Russell sent instructions to Lyons in Washington that reflected his belief that Seward had been directly involved in the *Trent* crisis from the outset. The best thing that could happen at that point, he wrote, would be for Seward to be fired.[76] Russell met unofficially with Benjamin Moran of the American legation on November 27 and told him to expect war. Moran recorded in his journal that Palmerston had something of a "boyish passion" about having been insulted by the Americans.[77] Russell also met with Adams, who then wrote of Britain's determination in a letter to his son: "This nation means to make war. Do not doubt it."[78]

Uncertain as to how the Americans would react to the sanctions and the ultimatum, Palmerston ordered more reinforcements to Canada. Eighteen hundred British regulars with artillery pieces and all the food, supplies and war *matériel* they would need were dispatched with orders to bolster border defences and prepare for invasion.

A new governor general had arrived in Canada just the week before. Charles Stanley, 4th Viscount Monck, would play a hugely positive role in the current crisis and in the turbulent years ahead. Like Head before him, he was in the delicate position of needing to liaise between Lyons in Washington, Russell in London, and Macdonald out his back door in Quebec City. As he was constitutionally responsible for military and defence matters, he and Macdonald spoke often, and seldom would one move without the other. He also oversaw often-troublesome and bull-headed lieutenant-governors in New Brunswick and Nova Scotia. Although he arrived with little experience, his intelligence, genial manner and stoicism in the face of difficulties served him exceptionally well.

Monck did not wait for instructions from London. Upon hearing the news of the *Trent*, he had sensed the seriousness of the event and its implication for Canada. He ordered Lt. General Williams to move men and *matériel* to the border. He asked that the preparations be done as quietly as possible, not to keep them secret from the Americans but rather to avoid creating panic among Canadians. Troops began securing the harbours and canals where the British military commander predicted an American attack was most likely. New batteries were still under construction in Montreal and Toronto, and Monck had the work expedited.

News of the military preparations along the border reached Washington. Seward then received a letter from Thurlow Weed, his old and trusted friend and political partner, who had been acting as his unofficial agent in Europe. Weed informed him that if it was discovered that Wilkes had acted under official orders, then it would be war. He reported that British dockyards were alive with war supplies being gathered and shipped to Canada and that ships were being specially outfitted with the goal of once and for all sweeping the American navy not only from the Confederate coast but from the Atlantic. He assured the secretary of state that there was a growing consensus both in the British press and in official circles that he had been behind it all and that Wilkes had been sent to provoke a war that would allow the United States to pivot and take Canada.[79]

In London, preparations for war continued. Palmerston created and chaired a special war council of cabinet that drew on the expertise of men who had served in Canada and knew it well. It was noted that from the Bay of Fundy to southwestern Canada the border was 1,500 miles long, and settlement patterns meant that it was only about 50 miles deep. It was suggested that a force of 10,000 British regulars supported by 10,000 Canadian militia would be needed to mount a credible defence. Even these numbers would not guarantee success, however. The Americans had more roads, canals and railroads that would allow a quick and easy shifting of troops to counter any British-Canadian tactical moves or to simply carry the American forces around any new Canadian fortification.[80]

Another major problem in defence planning was that with only one road running from the Maritimes to Canada—and that dangerously close to the Maine border—the only safe way to move troops and equipment was on water. That fact presented many problems. First, the Beauharnois Canal allowed transport down the St. Lawrence River to Canada West, but it was on the river's south shore, rendering it easy pickings for even a small American force. The canal's size also meant that only the smallest of British military craft could be moved to the Great Lakes. Second, after the War of 1812, the Rush-Bagot Agreement had dictated that each side could only have three armed ships on the Great Lakes and that they must weigh less than 100 tons and be armed with no more than an 18-pound cannon. The British and Canadians had adhered to the treaty but the Americans had not. The American *Michigan* was too heavy and too well armed, and another schooner that acted as a revenue ship was also rigged for military action. These ships and others that could be quickly gathered and prepared could easily make mischief for British troop movements on the lakes. The third problem with water transport was that from December to April the St. Lawrence and shorelines of the Great Lakes were frozen.

Macdonald considered these problems and more, and set out to do all he could to prepare for invasion. He called out existing militia units with a request that 2,000 more men be assembled and trained. The Active Militia Force had been bolstered so that it comprised 5,500 trained men. He ordered the reorganized of militia units into battalions and companies. Soon, 454 militia battalions reported to be ready to fight, but Macdonald found that 20 companies still had either antiquated smoothbore rifles or no weapons at all. Working with Lt. General Williams, he ordered new British-made Enfield rifles.[81]

The threat of American invasion, spoken of for so long but now looking imminent, united Canadians and Maritimers in common cause. Member of the Legislature Thomas D'Arcy McGee of Montreal made a number of speeches to Irish communities in Canada East and West. He exhorted them to forget old grievances and join in the defence of Canada. In a number of cities, benefit concerts and other fundraisers were held to gather money to purchase uniforms and weapons. Montreal businessmen agreed to close their establishments three afternoons a week so that their employees could drill. At the University of Toronto, students and faculty formed a rifle corps and took time from classes each day to prepare for war.

With talk of war everywhere, a Union officer visiting his wife in Toronto made the mistake of wearing his neat blue uniform into a tavern. He ordered a beer, but before it arrived the patrons served up a round of blistering insults and mocking laughter. Some broke into a coarse rendition of "Dixie." He fled through howls of laughter and a chant: "Bull Run! Bull Run!"

The vicious partisanship of newspaper editors seemed to evaporate as papers on both sides agreed that Britain was right to be outraged and that war with the United States was inevitable. The *Globe* called the *Trent* crisis unfortunate but supported efforts to prepare for war.[82] The *Toronto Leader* called directly for war but then couldn't resist the opportunity to call George Brown a spokesman for the Union.[83] Brown responded in kind with a *Globe* column calling the *Leader*'s editor, James Beatty, an agent for Jefferson Davis.[84]

Meanwhile, American papers entered the fray with the *New York Herald*, as usual, most inflammatory in its rhetoric. A December editorial predicted that Britain would be happy to be rid of Canada and that, if asked, would gladly hand it over.[85] In another editorial, the *Herald* called Canadians "a toothless pack of yelping dogs."[86] A *Buffalo Express* editorial was more measured but equally scathing: "Out of this Trent affair has come one permanent good . . . 'our Canadian brethren,' these suckling Britons to whom, like fools we have opened our ports . . . these reciprocal brethren of ours have been ready to fly at our throats from the moment when they felt it safe to be indolent."[87]

By mid-December Macdonald had 38,556 militia men armed, trained and ready. He ordered yet another 7,500, making just over 46,000 prepared to face the American invaders. He also approved $12,000 to augment defences at the Welland Canal. He was following the American press carefully and trying to discern what Lincoln and Seward would do. He was pleased to read that the *New York Herald* reported on December 23 that the administration was, in his words to a friend, "about to cave in."[88] But he did not stop his preparations. Anticipating the need for more men, he ordered 100,000 tunics, trousers, caps and great coats.[89]

After conferring with Monck, Macdonald dispatched Finance Minister Alexander Galt to Washington. Galt met with Seward's Canadian agent, George Ashmun, who could tell him little, and then with Seward, who would tell him nothing. Galt did not think much of Seward, writing to his wife, "he did not impress me much; seemed fidgety, and out of temper."[90] Galt had dinner with Lyons twice and met with several congressmen. He also attended Lincoln's State of the Union Address, during which the president deliberately ignored specifics related to the *Trent* crisis but mentioned his support for military preparations underway on the Atlantic coast and the Canadian border.

On December 4, Galt met with Lincoln at the White House. Ashmun was present. Galt began by telling the president that the current tension, coupled with Seward's belligerent circulars and other actions that put troops on the Canadian border, and the bellicose tone of much of the Northern press, was disconcerting for Canadians. Lincoln replied that Galt should never think that the press accurately reflected the views of his administration. He ducked the main issue, saying that he had supported increased military preparations at the border, but had expressed concern at the time that Canadians would react negatively. There lurked a dagger within his reassuring words, however, for he added that he had been disappointed when Britain had named the rebellious states as a belligerent.[91]

Ashmun raised the *Trent* crisis. Lincoln told Galt that for him the issue had both domestic and international ramifications. He said that he wanted to avoid war and did not want to invade Canada but, leaving the door open, continued, "We must do something to satisfy the people."[92] Galt pressed and asked what would be done with Mason and Slidell. Lincoln replied vaguely, "That will be got along with."[93]

Galt wrote to his wife that he was impressed by Lincoln: "He is very tall, thin, and with marked features, appears fond of anecdote, of which he has a fund. I liked him for his straight forward strong common sense."[94] In a memo to Macdonald, Galt indicated that Lincoln was as charming and reassuring as he was unconvincing: "The impression left on my mind is that the President has . . . no hostile designs upon Canada. . . . I cannot, however, divest my mind of the impression that the policy of the Govt is so subject to popular impulses that no assurance can be, or ought to be relied upon under present circumstances . . . the idea is universal that Canada is most desirable for the north, which its unprepared state would render it an easy prize."[95]

Lord Lyons and Governor General Monck were briefed on Galt's visit with Lincoln and shared his misgivings. Lyons maintained his hope that war would not come, but he urged both Monck and Foreign Secretary Russell to prepare for it. Lyons added that preparations for war concerned more than Canada; it was to be a global mobilization involving British ships from the Pacific and the West Indies.[96] Concerned, Monck wrote to Britain's secretary of state for the colonies Newcastle, "I am afraid however this dispute may end, we will have to fight them sooner or later."[97]

From Washington, Lyons set up a code with Monck. If the invasion was underway, or if he believed it to be imminent, Lyons would telegraph the following: "Is Mr. Charles Pelham still with you?" If it was received and understood, then Monck was to respond: "Mr. Charles Pelham started for England." If a particular point on the border was under attack or menaced, Lyons would write: "Forward these letters to (the place under threat)" and Monck would respond, "Unlikely your letters were forwarded to . . ."[98]

Jefferson Davis had seen Britain and the North talking themselves into war and, of course, recognized the opportunity for the Confederacy. He fanned the embers, hoping to turn them into flames. On November 18, Davis delivered a message to the Confederate Congress and, referring to Mason and Slidell, said: "These gentlemen were as much under the jurisdiction of the British Government upon that ship and beneath its flag as if they had been on its soil; and a claim on the part of the United States to seize them in the streets of London would have been as well founded as that to apprehend them where they were taken."[99]

Lincoln was balancing conflicting advice and reading the fiery newspaper editorials calling for war. He saw that the New York stock market had dropped 7 percent since the crisis began—a significant fluctuation in nineteenth-century terms. Ohio financier Jay Cooke, who had been successfully leading efforts to raise money for the North through the sale of government bonds in Europe, urged a quick solution to the crisis if he was to have any chance of raising additional capital.[100] Meanwhile, daily military reports brought no news of victories or even much activity from General McClellan, who seemed almost smug in reporting that all remained quiet along the Potomac day after infuriating day. Lincoln did not want quiet. He wanted action and victory, while his young general McClellan seemed content to prepare and then prepare some more.

On December 19, Lyons arrived at Seward's office and summarized Queen Victoria's letter detailing Britain's response to the *Trent* crisis. He wisely withheld the letter itself and explained that the clock would begin ticking once it was officially delivered. If after seven days the captives were not released and an apology offered, then he and the British legation staff would leave and war would ensue. Seward accepted an unofficial copy of the letter. Later that evening, the seemingly ubiquitous *London Times* correspondent Russell saw Seward at a dinner party and asked about the British response. Seward exploded and, as was often typical for the man, he blustered and said far more than was prudent. He shouted to Russell and his other guests: "We will wrap the whole world in flames. No power is so remote that she will not feel the fire of our battle and be burned in the conflagration."[101] Russell reported the conversation. More American troops were soon on their way to the Canadian border.

Seward spent the weekend consulting legal experts and meeting with cabinet colleagues. French minister to Washington Edouard-Henry Mercier told Seward that, although he didn't have official instructions from Paris, the French government supported Britain and knew of British military preparations overseas and in Canada. He added that he believed Lyons would indeed break off diplomatic relations with the United States if demands were not met within the seven-day deadline.[102] On December 23, Lyons was back in Seward's office. The Queen's letter was officially delivered, and the clock began to count the hours to war.

While families across Canada, the United States and Britain woke up on Christmas morning to celebrate the day, the latest British forces began arriving in Halifax, Saint John, St. Andrews and Quebec City from their trying journeys across a frigid north Atlantic. Eleven thousand troops arrived in eighteen ships. They were put up in makeshift quarters in warehouses, schools and church basements. Days later, their equipment arrived. There were fifty thousand new rifles with more than two million rounds of ammunition and sixteen batteries of artillery along with shells and powder. Four companies of engineers disembarked to join the eleven infantry battalions. It was an impressive display but it was doomed from the outset.

For years the Nova Scotia and New Brunswick governments had been arguing with London and themselves about the building of roads and railroads. Coincidentally, a delegation from the two colonies had arrived in London in November just as news of the *Trent*'s fate had reached Westminster. Nova Scotia's Joseph Howe and New Brunswick's Leonard Tilley were there to encourage Russell to supply the money necessary to solve the transportation dilemma that was stymying economic development. In their delegation was Edward Watkin, general manager of the Grand Trunk Railway. The group met with political and business leaders and pressed the case that investment was needed to build an intercolonial railway not just joining Halifax, Fredericton and Saint John but also extending north to Quebec City and Montreal. The railway would bring benefit to Britain and the empire by bolstering New Brunswick's wood and Halifax's shipbuilding industries and linking them to Canada's manufacturers.

Howe and Tilley had prepared their arguments carefully, but were quick to use the *Trent* crisis to their advantage. In meetings with officials and the press they spoke of the possibility of war and how the railway and road work would enable Britain's colonies to better defend themselves against American aggression now and in the future. Howe and Tilley were also unapologetic in discussing their anti-American hopes for a Confederate victory.[103]

The Maritime delegation was correct that the railway was needed, but it was needed that very day. The large contingent of the newly arrived

British soldiers had to get to Canada East and West, and there was simply no good or quick way for them to do so. Some of the hard-pressed British regulars and their equipment were loaded onto three ships. One hit a sandbar, while another found the sea too dangerous and turned back. Only one small ship struggled on through St. Lawrence winds and ice and finally arrived, battered and frozen, at Rivière-du-Loup. The six hundred troops were welcomed by townsfolk, who had been encouraged to do so by French-language newspapers and messages from the pulpit announcing that the young men were coming to save them from the American hordes who were prepared to visit unspeakable horrors upon the land.

Lt. General Williams undertook a number of actions to ready for the American attack that he presumed to be imminent. He believed that the most likely stratagem would be simultaneous attacks on Montreal and Prescott, with advances on Kingston and the Niagara Peninsula.[104] Williams had artillery pieces stationed and reinforced at these positions. He decided that, to protect Montreal, the invaders needed to be kept on the south side of the river, and so he had ten large-calibre, rifled artillery pieces placed on St. Helen's Island. Infantry was positioned near them and on both sides of nearby bridges.[105] This aspect of the plan meant that the eastern townships would be sacrificed. Plans were also made to add artillery and infantry strength to Toronto, Hamilton, London and the Welland Canal. All territory west of London would be allowed to fall to the American invaders. Williams believed that Nova Scotia could and should be defended. He argued that Halifax, with its all-season harbour and access to the coal mines of Pictou and Sydney, should become the centre of maritime warfare, but that Americans would be allowed to take New Brunswick.[106]

Williams argued that the defensive plan suited the types of soldiers that would be fighting the war. Despite the large numbers of British regulars, both the American troops and the Canadian and Maritime militia would consist of untested and undertrained soldiers, and thus the advantage would go to the force with the best-prepared and thoughtfully chosen fields of battle. Williams agreed with Inspector General of Fortifications

Sir John Burgoyne that the long and largely indefensible border would give way to guerrilla warfare, with marauding parties terrorizing civilians and inflicting damage on public, private and military infrastructures. All that would be needed, Burgoyne argued, was two or three successful repulses of such raids to, as he put it, "damp their ardour."[107] Thus, according to the military men planning it, the war would be costly, deadly and ugly—and offer no guarantee of victory.

On December 28, Macdonald finally convinced cabinet colleagues that there was a need for a minister of militia affairs to lead the war preparations. As he had already been acting the part, he appointed himself to the post and continued those efforts. Macdonald asked for more funds to bolster Toronto port defences, but dissuaded Lt. General Williams from dumping boulders into the harbour to trap American ships. He also requested funds to build more and better barracks, and handed over those already prepared to the lieutenant general in command of the recently arrived British troops. Macdonald also shifted the Canadian military leadership with a re-appointment of Lieutenant Colonel Duncan McDougall to be inspecting field officer of the militia. Macdonald had little money and he needed to work through Monck. Nevertheless, he played the few cards he had well.

Meanwhile, thousands of Canada-bound troops remained shivering in Saint John. Arrangements were finally made to gather sleighs and sleds. Soldiers and equipment were loaded, and beneath heavy buffalo robes they headed north behind draught horses lumbering through deep snow in sub-zero temperatures at about three miles per hour. A number of men suffered frostbite. Some deserted when the sorry procession neared the Maine border. After days of horrendous conditions they arrived at Quebec City. They regrouped and began to deploy along the border, with most being stationed at Montreal, Kingston, Toronto, Niagara and Windsor.

The British military staff who were arriving aboard the *Melbourne* had a particularly rough time when their ship encountered treacherous North Atlantic weather and nearly ran out of coal. It finally reached Halifax on January 5. Discouraged by the frozen St. Lawrence and the terrible land travel conditions, the men removed their military insignias, hid their papers, and took a mail ship to Boston, where they purchased Grand Trunk rail tickets for Montreal.

On the same Christmas day that saw the arrival of the British troops in Canada, Lincoln called a cabinet meeting to order. He had been moving toward a decision regarding the *Trent* crisis in the same thoughtful and deliberate manner in which he made all decisions and which his cabinet secretaries were beginning to understand and respect. The five-hour meeting began with Seward reading the Queen's letter and other dispatches that he and Lyons had exchanged, and letters that had arrived from Thurlow Weed in Paris and Adams in London. A consensus was quickly reached that war with England would be disastrous and would favour the Confederacy. Lincoln tipped his hand only in saying that he preferred to fight one war at a time.[108]

As the meeting was breaking up, Lincoln asked Seward to draft an argument supporting the release of Mason and Slidell, while he would write one suggesting that they remain prisoners. On December 26, the cabinet reconvened and Seward slowly read his twenty-six page draft. It was brilliant. He argued that in taking the two men, Captain Wilkes had acted on his own as no specific orders had been given, but that he had acted appropriately. He had erred only in not impounding the *Trent* and taking it to a Prize Court. Therefore, Seward concluded, Mason and Slidell should be released not because Wilkes had broken international law, which was largely unwritten, or that he had insulted British honour, which was irrelevant, but that the release would be consistent with American traditions, principles, and precedents. There would be no apology.

With some minor changes, Seward's report became the official American dispatch to London. He later asked to read Lincoln's argument, but the president admitted that he had struggled with it and in the end found it impossible to finish.[109] He complimented Seward on his handling of the crisis and on the document he had constructed. The man who had for so long seemed to be itching for war ended up providing the graceful instrument through which two great powers could save face and withdraw from the abyss with honour intact and Canada saved.

Seward's offer arrived in London on January 8. Until that point Palmerston had still been sure that war with America was a real possibility and preparations had been continuing.[110] Palmerston took the offer to cabinet and the American terms were accepted. With that, the hollering for war subsided; at least to the level tolerated before the *Trent* had been boarded.

The British warship *Rinaldo* took Mason, Slidell and their secretaries first to Halifax and then to London. With their arrival, the British troops that had remained at their Canadian posts were finally allowed leaves. Men of the voluntary militia who had remained to bolster their units' strength were finally told to return to their jobs, classrooms and farms.

Lincoln, meanwhile, made it clear that the British insults he had heard and the strategic military plans he had entertained were not forgotten. In an interview with newspaperman Horace Peters, the president said: "It was a pretty bitter pill to swallow but I contented myself with believing that England's triumph in the matter would be short-lived, and that after ending our war successfully we would be so powerful that we could call her to account for all the embarrassments she had inflicted upon us."[111] It was an ominous statement, especially when matched with Lincoln's comment about fighting one war at a time and his vague threats to Galt.

While war had been avoided, there was still danger ahead. Southern resentment of Canada had grown with the Underground Railroad. The tepid support for the Union, and then the *Trent* crisis had increased anti-Canadian sentiment in the North. Seward and Sumner still believed that all of North America should be American, and Lincoln's "one war at a time" comment was both a momentary salve and a thinly disguised warning.

The threat of an American invasion of Canada may have ended for the moment, but the Civil War and Canada's role in it had just begun. Having narrowly escaped the ravages of a war for British North America, most Canadians and Maritimers hoped for a return to relative peace. But others had something far different in mind. Thousands joined others who had already left, and headed south to fight both for the Union and for the Confederacy.

3

SARAH EMMA EDMONDS: DONNING THE BLUE AND GREY

N ARMY ON THE MOVE is a magnificent and horrible beast. It eats and drinks and defecates and fornicates. It can manoeuvre with poise and precision or lumber clumsily within a fog of contradictory information, cross purposes and logistical chaos. The beast is both hunter and hunted, existing to kill while offering itself up to be slain.

In July 1861, the beast that was the Union's Army of the Potomac rose from crowded camps around Washington and slowly moved south and west toward the town of Manassas, Virginia. The Civil War's first major battle, called Bull Run in the North and Canada, was nigh. The march was confusing from the start, with stragglers falling behind and others losing their units while searching for food or water. Many suffering from mumps, measles, typhoid fever and dysentery had left their cots to join the march. The troops were joyous about finally going into battle—a battle most, including those who watched as they picnicked on the hillside near the capital, believed would be the first and last big fight of the war. Songs filled the air, and "On to Richmond" was chanted again and again.

Among the untested army's numbers was a young nurse named Franklin Thompson of the 2nd Michigan Volunteer Regiment's F Company. There was more to Thompson's story than met the eye, for he was actually a woman named Sarah Emma Edmonds. She was one of a great number of women who served in the Civil War and one of about 550 who did so disguised as men.[1] Like men, women served for their own reasons but most were moved by a patriotic devotion to the cause, honour, duty, personal ambition, a yearning for adventure, or the chance to make a little money.[2] Women served as cooks, couriers, flag bearers, nurses, spies and soldiers. As many as 60 women were killed in battle and buried as women, but the number who met their death with their male disguises undiscovered is unknown.[3]

Edmonds also concealed the fact that was that she was from New Brunswick. She was born Sarah Emma Edmondson in December 1841, into a large farming family in Magaguadavic, near Fredericton. The youngest of six children, she worked long hours with her four sisters on the farm, and her only brother, an epileptic, did what he could. Like many farm girls of her time, she dressed in what was traditionally men's clothing, grew used to hard labour and was adept with firearms and horses. Her mother, Elizabeth, taught her the secrets of home remedies and she became quite skilled at tending illness and injury. Her father, Isaac, was an angry, embittered man who made life miserable for his children.

When Edmonds was seventeen, her father told her that she was to be married to a man nearly twice her age, whom she had never met. With her mother's help, she fled. She assumed the name Emma Edmonds. Edmonds demonstrated her ability to be independent and self-sustaining, belying her age and the stereotypes attached to women of her time, by securing work first in a hat shop and then in a millinery in a small town ninety miles east of Fredericton.

When her father discovered her whereabouts, she fled again. This time she was assisted by a young man named Linus Seelye, who lent her some of his clothes and helped disguise her as a man to avoid detection and ease her travel. Edmonds settled in Saint John. She purchased more men's clothing, cut her hair, applied dye to her face and hands to darken her complexion, and even had a mole surgically removed from her left cheek. She became Franklin Thompson.

Secure within her new identity, Edmonds found work as an itinerant Bible salesman and moved from town to town and farm to farm. After about a year, in 1860, Edmonds was swindled out of her savings. The brave and desperate nineteen-year-old gathered her last five dollars and moved to the United States to start again. She later claimed to have been motivated to emigrate not just for work but for educational opportunities. Her church pastor had written her a letter of introduction that noted a desire to do missionary work.

Edmonds answered an advertisement for a Boston publisher for "young men willing to hustle." She was hired immediately and found a home in Hartford, Connecticut, where she was soon back to selling Bibles. With a fifty-dollar advance in her pocket and a heavy valise across her back, she was moved to her company's base in Halifax. Her disguise had become so effective that during a short visit home she even briefly fooled her mother and sisters.

In November 1860, she heard of opportunities in the west and took a similar job in Flint, Michigan. In the spring of 1861, as Edmonds was waiting for a train, she heard shouts from a *New York Herald* newsboy announcing that Fort Sumter had fallen and that Lincoln had called for 75,000 troops. She could have easily returned home and avoided the war, but instead decided to enlist.

Edmonds was moved by a desire to fight for the country she had adopted as her home. She later wrote of the war as, "a just cause—the cause of our country that we love; that we shrink from no sacrifice of money, time or life in order to maintain and perpetuate the beautiful Government that our fathers bequeathed to us."[4] She also wrote: "It was not my intention, or desire, to seek my own personal ease and comfort while so much sorrow and distress filled the land. But the great question to be decided was, what can I do? What part am I to act in this great drama?"[5]

She appeared at the 2nd Michigan Volunteers' recruiting station in Detroit as Franklin Thompson. At five foot six, she was about the same height as the average soldier. She easily passed the medical examination, which consisted only of checking her sight and hearing, and making sure she had a trigger finger and at least two good teeth to rip open powder cartridges.[6] On May 25, 1861, after telling the recruiter of her skills with basic medical procedures, she became F Company's Field Nurse.[*]

At the outset of the war, nursing was just being accepted as a profession for women. Only a few years before, in the Crimean War, Florence Nightingale had organized women to work as nurses in British field hospitals. Americans Clara Barton and Dorothea Dix would help to build the profession but, at that point, the dominant opinion in the United States was that women should not be exposed to the blood and gore of battle or be in such close contact with men. This sort of work was considered unbecoming of women and beyond their physical and emotional abilities.[7] Consequently, in the early months of the war, male nurses such as Thompson were seen as preferable to women.

After two months of training, the 1,013-strong Michigan regiment was sent to Washington under the leadership of Colonel Israel B. Richardson. One day Edmonds stood proudly at attention with her compatriots and was inspected by President Lincoln himself. More training followed but it was ad hoc at best, as few knew what to expect or how to really prepare. With the call to march to Manassas, preparations ended.

The Michigan 2nd was ordered to protect a possible retreat route. Edmonds helped ready a field hospital in a small stone church. That night, she and the other nurses listened to young soldiers singing inspirational

---

Much of what we know of Edmonds's story comes from her bestselling memoir, first released in 1864. Some scholars have questioned the book's veracity. In his 1995 Black Confederates and Afro-Yankees in Civil War Virginia, for instance, Ervin L. Jordan noted some errors and exaggerations, but he nonetheless supported her story's fundamental accuracy. In the introduction to its 1999 reprinting, Elizabeth Leonard accepted much of what Edmonds wrote, but again questioned some facts and tales. Cross-referencing her regiment's history, other accounts, and the words of her compatriots written later, leads one to agree with Jordan and Leonard and accept Edmonds account as perhaps fanciful in spots, but largely historically sound.

songs and offering mournful prayers. Many tear-spattered letters were written and left with her and the other nurses.

Through the early morning mists, Union general Irvin McDowell ordered his three divisions forward. Edmonds stood on a hill watching and hoping for the best, with medical supplies in haversacks slung over both shoulders. Within minutes, a Confederate artillery shell tore into a young soldier standing not far away. She ran to him and found a wheezing wound in his chest and his face a bloody pulp. There was nothing to be done but make the dying boy comfortable.

Wounded men quickly began to fill the church. A doctor sent her to the rear for more bandages and brandy, and while she was gone the battle turned in the Confederates' favour. Edmonds returned to find dead and dying strewn everywhere. She and others moved up among the thundering din, whizzing minié balls and black smoke to rescue bloodied and dismembered young men all moaning for water and their mothers.

Then came the unorganized, unauthorized, mad retreat. As men and riderless horses ran by, Edmonds hurried back to the field hospital and found a scene from hell. The pretty little church, once so clean and organized, was piled with wounded. Blood smeared the walls and pooled on the floor. Amputated arms and legs were stacked haphazardly outside along one wall and uncovered dead were laid out along another. Edmonds stitched and bandaged and held men down as doctors sawed mangled limbs. Soldiers were comforted as they breathed their last. Edmonds helped one dying young man cut a lock of his hair and placed it in a packet to be mailed home to his mother.

With the Union army having abandoned the field, and the early evening casting eerie shadows over the day's sad and tragic remains, Edmonds and other medical staff needed to flee or risk capture. They placed water within reach of as many wounded men as possible and ran. Edmonds soon lost her compatriots in the darkness. She stealthily wove her way around Confederate pickets until finally relocating her regiment in Washington. The next day found her in one of the city's many makeshift hospitals tending the sick, wounded, and exhausted.

CANADIAN RECRUITS

Among the thousands who marched with Edmonds on that horrible July day were three brothers from the small town of Wolverton in Canada West. In 1858 Jasper, Alfred and Newton Wolverton had moved to Cleveland to attend school and try to bolster the family lumber business, which had fallen on hard times. In the summer of 1861, they spoke with a recruiting agent from New York who was enlisting teamsters. Lured by the promise of adventure and the opportunity to earn a spectacular combined monthly income of six hundred dollars, Newton and Jasper volunteered with the 50th New York Infantry. They were later joined by their brother. With the blind confidence of youth, the seventeen-year-old Jasper assured his sister back in Canada, "Where we are going we shall in all probability be in no danger at all."[8]

In marching off to war, the Wolvertons joined Sarah Edmonds and thousands of other Canadians and Maritimers who had already been living in the United States when they enlisted. They were among the 102,000 who between 1850 and 1860 had crossed the border to find work.[9] Eighty-eight percent had moved to Northern states, 10 percent to the west, and only 2 percent to what became the South. About half had found jobs in manufacturing, 30 percent in personal service jobs, 18 percent on farms and only about 2 percent in professions.[10]

Charles Riggins was among the Canadian sojourners. He left his family's farm in Fonthill, Canada West, in the spring of 1862, looking for work in Buffalo. He wrote a rather laconic letter home to his brother explaining how his job search ended in military service: "Arrived Buffalo 2 o'clock, got room for 12 a week, went around to see sights, looked for work, found nothing to do so enlisted in the 14th USA."[11] Riggins met a number of Canadians in H Company. Some Canadian recruits made life miserable for others when, tired of training and camp life, they simply deserted. Their actions meant that while Americans in the 14th were given leave, their Canadian compatriots were confined to post lest they dash back across the border and not return. Unlike many others, though, Riggins rather enjoyed his new adventure and spoke glowingly of the bands and the cheers of the crowd when they marched to the trains to depart for Washington.[12]

The vast majority of Canadians and Maritimers living in the United States when the war began were living in the North, and so they, like Edmonds, Riggins and the Wolvertons, enlisted in Northern regiments. Many of those who had found homes and work in the South, not surprisingly, ended up in the Confederates' butternut and grey. An example was Dr. Solomon Secord, the grand-nephew of Laura Secord.* Solomon Secord was born in Stony Creek, near Hamilton, and received his medical degree in Toronto. He practised medicine in Hamilton and then Kincardine. Personal health issues took him to South Carolina to escape the cold winters of Canada West. When the war began a year later, despite the fact that he was an abolitionist, he enlisted as an assistant surgeon in the 20th Georgia Regiment Volunteer Infantry.[13]

Beyond the thousands already in the United States who enthusiastically enlisted, many Canadians and Maritimers left specifically to join in the fight. Among them were the sons of prominent people such as William Lyon Mackenzie Junior, who left home to sign up with a Cincinnati regiment, first for three months and then later for three years.[14] His father was Toronto's first mayor and had led the 1837 Upper Canada rebellion. Another was Fred Howe, son of Joseph Howe, an important Nova Scotia editor and political leader who would spend months visiting Union regiments in a vain attempt to find his son.

Canadians and Maritimers enlisted individually and in groups. Michigan regiments, for instance, were filled when hundreds of enthusiastic volunteers arrived from Canada West's Elgin, Essex and Lambton counties. So many Nova Scotians of Scottish descent enlisted in a Boston regiment that it was named the "Highlanders." Other New England states boasted Highlander regiments bursting with young men from Nova Scotia and New Brunswick. There were Canadians and Maritimers in five hundred Union

---

* *Laura Secord was Canada's Paul Revere, celebrated for braving the night in June 1813 and weaving a nineteen-mile path through dark woods and around American sentries to warn a British garrison that invaders were on their way.*

regiments and in forty-six Confederate regiments.[15] All told, about forty thousand Canadians and Maritimers fought in the American Civil War.[16]

Many of the thousands who crossed the border to enlist were motivated by the siren song of adventure or a cold craving for money, while others, like Edmonds, were inspired by what they saw as a noble cause. Henri Césaire Saint-Pierre, for instance, left his home in Montreal and signed up with the 76th New York Regiment. He later wrote home with an explanation: "We were Christian soldiers fighting for a holy cause and, like the crusaders of old, who wielded their violent swords in their efforts to free their enslaved brethren moaning under the foot of a ruthless conqueror, we devoted all our courage, summed all our energy in the task of breaking to pieces the shackles by which three millions of human beings were kept in bondage."[17]

Enthusiasm for recruitment was such that on April 22, 1861, Joshua Giddings, American consul to British North America, wrote to his secretary of war, Simon Cameron, stating that gentlemen in Montreal, Quebec City and Halifax had each offered themselves as recruiters. All three men were confident that they could quickly raise full regiments and transport them to Washington. Since the war was in its early days and American recruiters were having few problems meeting Lincoln's post-Sumter call for 75,000 men, Cameron assured Giddings that the efforts were unnecessary.[18] Despite Cameron's directive, the *Toronto Leader* a week later reported rumours that American agents were in Canadian cities and towns gathering young men and taking them to a recruiting centre in Chicago.[19] Days later another article noted that Southern agents were in Montreal offering young men a shilling each to come and fight for the Confederates.[20]

In mid-May 1861, with the war only a month old, a growing number of eager Canadian and Maritime volunteers, with or without the help of recruiting agents, were crossing the border to enlist. The situation became so disconcerting that Governor General Head arranged for a statement describing relevant portions of the Foreign Enlistment Act to be published in a number of newspapers and for handbills to be posted in public places throughout the colonies.[21]

Head's reminder that enlisting in foreign armies violated the law did little to stem the tide, and American agents just became more devious. In the summer of 1861, a placard found its way to trees and walls in a number of Toronto's working-class neighbourhoods. It claimed a need for young men for railway work in Pennsylvania. It seemed harmless enough in an era when so many were crossing the border for work. However, all who saw it understood that the poster was really about filling Pennsylvania regiments. Newspapers were filled with similar advertisements offering a range of American jobs. Canadian political leaders deemed them all suspicious.[22]

In August 1861, Arthur Rankin, Canadian legislator and colonel of the 9th Militia District, took it upon himself to travel to Washington, where he later reported to have met with a government official. He returned to Canada and asked the governor general for a leave of absence from his public duties. Rankin then set out to create a 1,600-man cavalry regiment to be composed of Canadian volunteers that he would train and offer for service in Detroit. They were to be called Rankin's Lancers.

One of Rankin's Washington contacts must have leaked something to a reporter, for a September 11 *New York Tribune* article detailed what Rankin was doing and revealed that he had received an American commission to do so. The *Tribune* applauded his efforts.[23] With this evidence of a flagrant violation of the law, Governor General Head initiated an investigation. On October 7, Rankin was arrested for violation of the Foreign Enlistment Act, but only for having accepted the American commission.

Rankin's case drew the issue of Americans recruiting in Canada and the Maritimes out of the shadows. In London, Foreign Secretary Lord John Russell ordered an investigation of Rankin's activities and asked whether his was an isolated case. Lord Lyons, the British minister in Washington, duly met with Secretary of State Seward, who assured him that no government official had offered to work with Rankin, and that no American recruiting agents had been officially dispatched to Canada.[24]

Rankin was in jail, but his operation had gone too far to be stopped. He had brought Michigan's Lieutenant Colonel Tillman and Captain Villiers to his team, and they continued to enlist men for Rankin's Lancers.

They already had phony enlistment papers, ready and waiting in Detroit, stating that all their recruits were from Milwaukee. Tillman had also arranged for about eight hundred posters to be tacked up in Hamilton. Villiers worked with Tillman in the Hamilton campaign and then ran one of his own in Montreal. The Hamilton posters used the old canard of gathering men to work, in this case on Michigan farms, but readers in Montreal were directly invited to join Rankin's Lancers and fight as a Michigan regiment. Tillman and Villiers both signed their Montreal posters with their real names and ranks.

The *Globe* did Tillman and Villiers a great service with the publication of an article about Rankin's Lancers. The story glorified the life of a cavalry soldier: "The [cavalryman] with . . . revolver in his left hand, his sabre in his right, guiding his lance mainly with his leg, and a horse under good training can deal out death upon the front and each flank at the same time."[25]

The governor general was told of the Tillman and Villiers campaigns and he informed Lord Lyons, who asked Seward to investigate.[26] It was found that both men had received legitimate leaves from their Michigan units, although neither had told their superiors what they had in mind for their time away. Seward and Secretary of War Cameron assured Lyons that their government did not condone recruitment efforts in Canada and would stop them if they heard about them.[27]

Rankin's trial ended with his dismissal on a technicality. Governor General Head revoked his Canadian commission. Rankin later justified his actions with a rhetorical question: "Why [should it] be a crime for Canadians to enter the American service? Is not the cause of the United States the cause of civilization and free government?"[28]

The Rankin case had led to American promises being made to stop illegal recruitment, but all the while Canadians and Maritimers continued to leave for the United States to enlist, often with the help of American recruiters. The Rankin case only succeeded in pushing many of those recruiters further underground. They would not stay there long.

DESERTERS HEADING NORTH
AND SOUTH

Joining the many civilians in their rush for the border were increasing numbers of deserting British regulars. Desertion was a concern from the war's outset. In late April 1861, just weeks after the fall of Fort Sumter and in the heat of Seward's threatening words and tone, British commander in Canada Lt. General Sir William Fenwick Williams had written to Governor General Head about a strategy to defend the colonies from an American invasion. He recommended that a detachment of British troops be sent to guard important canals, with specific attention to the Beauharnois on the St. Lawrence. However, he added, there was a risk of desertion whenever troops moved that close to the border. He wrote: "Your Excellency knows as well as I do, that these locations will afford peculiar facility for desertion, and therefore, that it is desirable to send hither only men who are perfectly trustworthy."[29]

Despite Williams's efforts, too many British soldiers were unable to resist the urge to run to an American army that promised the certainty of greater action and rumours of more money and better treatment. American recruiting agents paid special attention to British regulars, for they represented a supply of men already trained for battle and used to army life.[30] Williams ordered extra sentries posted each night, not to keep American invaders out, but to keep his soldiers in.

The problem became worse with the arrival of more British regulars. In late December 1861 — in the troop movements addressing the *Trent* crisis — a number of British soldiers deserted on their way from the Bay of Fundy to Canada when they approached the Maine border. In February 1862, patrols were placed on roads crossing the Maine–New Brunswick border to try to stop desertions. The effort had some effect, but those determined to leave still managed to do so, with British soldiers leaving Saint John and St. Andrews at an alarming rate.[31] The dubious honour of the worst desertion rate was earned by the British 15th Regiment, housed in the old stone barracks in downtown Fredericton. British rear-admiral David Milne ordered all merchant ships to be searched for deserters before they left Halifax.

For regiments stationed in Canada East and West, a favourite crossing was Watertown, New York; men in British uniforms were welcomed
and quickly mustered into Union regiments. On a single evening in July
1862, twenty-seven members of the British 13th Regiment disappeared
from their Toronto barracks. Extra guards were stationed each night and
the doors were locked from the outside. British officers near the Windsor-
Detroit crossing bolstered their guard details and ordered that soldiers be
arrested if found more than a mile from their base.[32] Matters became so
serious at Kingston's Fort Henry that the commander tried to shame his
men by having the daily curfew gun fire an extra shot for each deserter
gone to the United States that day. British officers reminded soldiers of
their patriotic duty to Queen and empire, and threatened them with harsh
punishments if caught on the run. Some were imprisoned. Some had the
letter D tattooed on their chest. But nothing seemed to stem the flow of
British soldiers across the border.

Meanwhile, British soldiers deserting south may well have passed
American soldiers heading north. Throughout the decades before the
Civil War, Canada had become a haven for racial refugees escaping slavery and discrimination. From the war's first days, it had become a sanctuary for those wishing to escape military service. As had been the case with
fugitive slaves, most Canadians felt sympathy for the American deserters.
Folks in border towns and farms across Canada and the Maritimes regularly encountered young men seeking lodging and work, clad in the torn
vestiges of old uniforms.

Canadians came to the support of American deserters in many
ways beyond offers of food, shelter and work. In early October 1861, for
instance, six large and heavily armed Americans headed into the woods
north of Windsor on the trail of Union deserters, with instructions to
return their prey dead or alive. When caught, the deserters claimed to
be Canadians who had been illegally pressed into Union ranks. The
Americans would hear none of it and began hauling the still-protesting
men back to Detroit. The noise alerted a group of Canadians, who
stopped the procession, believed the bound and desperate men, and with

threats and weapons of their own, forced the Americans to free them. A Windsor newspaper article describing the incident referred to the Americans as kidnappers and warned all who might follow them over the river to expect a similarly "warm" welcome.[33]

American soldiers and agents entering Canada to recover deserters became yet another source of tension among Canada, Britain and the United States. Another incident in the Detroit-Windsor area brought the issue to the fore. A Captain Church from Michigan was ordered across the border at Detroit with five unarmed men to find a small group of deserters. They found their erstwhile comrades and, one way or another, persuaded them to return. On their way back, though, they were accidentally discovered by a local magistrate named Billings and a few of his friends. Words were exchanged and the deserters ran—apparently not convinced to return to Michigan after all.

Billings reported the incident to recently appointed Governor General Lord Monck, who, upon investigation, found that the story was not an isolated one. Within days, Lord Lyons was in Seward's office, demanding to know what was going on. Seward asked questions of military officials and then told Lyons that Captain Church had acted on his own and that since he had gone unarmed and allowed the deserting men to flee rather than start an altercation with Billings, he had acted honourably.[34] Seward was quite obviously skirting the larger questions of sovereignty and neutrality, but Lyons allowed the matter to drop. Lyons supported Monck's intention to move more troops to the border near Detroit—not to stop American deserters, but to prevent the incursions of those intent upon retrieving them.[35]

SECOND THOUGHTS

With newspapers filled with stories of deserters running both ways, and then the *Trent* crisis and talk of an imminent American invasion of Canada, many Canadians who had jumped to the lure of joining the Union as a great and glorious crusade had second thoughts. Colonel Rankin, for instance, after working so hard and tossing away his career to raise a regiment of

Rangers, publicly renounced his dedication to the Union cause. He resigned his American commission and declared his loyalty to Canada.

Norman Wade of Granville Ferry, Nova Scotia, felt his loyalty similarly tested. He had left his home in 1859 for a life at sea and found employment on American ships. In September 1861, he had enlisted in the Union navy and was assigned to the 400-ton USS *Young Rover*. In letters home to his parents, Wade explained his reasons for enlisting and touched on the main motivators for nearly all who were doing so: adventure, profit and cause: "When I came back to Boston from Detroit, times were so dull I had a good mind to come home but falling in with an old friend who was going on the *Young Rover* and who got the billet for me, which is not so bad as my pay is twenty-five dollars a month besides the prize money. . . . I am confident our cause is a just one."[36]

Wade served his three-month enlistment largely by playing his part in guarding ports against blockade runners. He then signed up again. When the *Trent* crisis broke, he found his mates suddenly girding up for the new war most thought was coming. He wrote home expressing the fear felt at every level: "If a war should break out between these two Countries there is no telling where it would end, as it is bad enough now."[37] He could not tell his parents whether he would fight or desert.*

The Wolverton brothers similarly felt conflicted fears and spoke with many fellow Canadians who had no desire to be a part of an American army that appeared poised to march north rather than south. While only fifteen years old, the precocious Newton Wolverton was chosen by his peers as their spokesman. Using contacts he had developed through his work in Washington's quartermaster's department, he eventually secured a brief meeting with President Lincoln. He told the president of his concerns and Lincoln said that he understood. The president said: "We are happy to have you Canadians helping the Northern cause and want you to stay. I am not in favour of war with either Britain or Canada. As long as I am president, there will be no such war, you may be sure of that."[38]

---

* *Wade remained in the U.S. Navy until he fell from the mast to his death on September 14, 1862.*

Many Canadian parents felt great trepidation about having their sons so far from home and in constant peril, and wrote to Monck and Lyons asking for help in extricating their children from Union regiments. Most claimed that their boys needed to be saved because they were minors who had run away from home to join the army. In December 1861 alone, at the height of the *Trent* crisis, Lyons and Monck placed ninety-two cases before American authorities.

Lyons continued throughout the war to intercede on behalf of parents, but it was an arduous process of moving through diplomatic channels and contacting regiments in the field. It was all made more difficult by unreliable enlistment records. Most cases bogged down somewhere along the red-taped route or ended when it was reported that the soldier in question could not be found, had deserted, or had died. Lyons was proud on the rare occasions when he was successful in returning a child soldier to his parents.[39]

The problem of so many Canadian and Maritime parents wanting their sons out grew to the point that American Secretary of War Cameron applied to Congress to grant him the power to expedite the process through which he could discharge foreign minors from service.[40] Instead, on February 13, 1862, Congress enacted legislation that ended the practice of petitioning for the release of all underage soldiers. The regulation remained that one needed to be over eighteen to enlist, but the recruit's word was to be taken as proof and once taken it would not be questioned.[*] The new legislation required that Monck inform all distraught parents who suspected their underaged children were in the American army that there was little he could do to help.[41] A growing number of parents nonetheless begged for help, but fewer and fewer releases were secured.

The American legislation hurt many young people whose martial enthusiasm dimmed with the realization that a soldier's life was hard work, with long stretches of boredom punctuated by bursts of terror. Charles

---

[*] *It was a common trick for underaged recruits to put a small piece of paper with the number 18 written on it in their shoe and then swear to enlistment officers that they were "over 18."*

Riggins from Canada West, for instance, who had initially enjoyed military life, became disenchanted when training ended and fighting began. In July 1862, he wrote to his sister, "I am quite shure that if I was home now I would let the south whip the north or vis versa or any other way for all I would care, it is well enough soldiering is very nice in peace & it is all nice enough to fight for ones country but when you are treated as slaves & that too worse than the slaves at the south."[42] Only a month later, Riggins wrote again about how he had made a mistake to enlist and wanted out: "You may write to Lord Lyons & try to get me out if you can—try very hard if you please—I want to get out very bad—tell him that I enlisted under eighteen & that I am only five months over it now. Tell him that I am a British Subject but do not say anything to anyone about it."[43]

THE PENINSULA CAMPAIGN

From the chaos of Bull Run in July 1861 until March 1862, the handsome and egotistical thirty-five-year-old Union general George McClellan built his army. To the frustration of Lincoln and the Northern press, he gathered more and more troops and weapons but, other than small skirmishes, all his massive army did was train.

Riggins and his 14th United States Infantry Division were part of it all. Although they would not meet, Edmonds was there too, still in her guise as Franklin Thompson. Having spent the winter tending the sick and wounded who overwhelmed hospitals, she had developed the thick skin needed for survival when engulfed by so much human misery and sorrow. Her journal records her experience: "Of what an amount of suffering I am called to witness every hour and every moment. There is no cessation, and yet it is strange that the sight of all this suffering and death does not affect me more. I am simply eyes, ears, hands and feet. It does seem as if there is a sort of stoicism granted for such occasions."[44] Edmonds put in long shifts and tried to cheer the sick and dying with card games, letter writing and spirited conversation while tending to their failing bodies.

Finally, on March 14, 1862, McClellan passed the orders that had been anticipated for months, and his enormous army, the largest in American history, began to move. Riggins's and Edmonds's regiments were part of a giant flotilla heading down the Potomac River and south through Chesapeake Bay to Fort Monroe, near the mouth of the James River. The plan had McClellan's army marching northeast up the York Peninsula past Yorktown and Williamsburg all the way to Richmond. Lincoln's concept of McClellan's mission was that it should destroy Lee's army, but his young general saw the war as a mammoth game of capture the flag, with the enemy's capital as his goal. McClellan hoped that the Peninsula Campaign would win him—and the men he encouraged to call him Young Napoleon—the everlasting glory that he so desperately craved.[45]

The campaign began badly as McClellan sabotaged himself by moving slowly and digging in. While helping to construct entrenchments, Edmonds saw the freeing of slaves, and felt the humbling sensation of watching families crying for joy with the dawning realization that they were truly and finally free. She noted her surprise that all were not as she had expected: "Some of them are whiter and prettier than most of our northern ladies. There is a family here, all of whom have blue eyes, light hair, fair skin and rosy cheeks; yet they are contrabands and have been slaves. Yet why should blue eyes and golden hair be the distinction between bond and free?"[46]

As the army began to move, an unyielding rain turned Virginia clay to mud, slowing down the trudging, demoralizing slog to Yorktown. Edmonds suffered with the rest. Damp breezes and malarial mosquitoes wafted from adjacent swamps over the tired, sodden troops—yet they walked on. They walked for five days on two days' rations.

During the Peninsula Campaign, as happened throughout the war and on many fronts, it was common for Canadians and Maritimers to come across countrymen in the field. One day as Edmonds was returning from a scavenging mission, she saw a funeral ending for yet another fallen comrade. She was told that the young man was Lieutenant James Vesey. He was thirty-two years old, had been popular among fellow officers and his men, and was from New Brunswick. Edmonds deeply mourned his loss for they had known each other at home and she had been rekindling feelings for him. On their first chance encounter shortly after embarking on the muddy march, she had avoided eye contact and conversation lest he reveal her disguise. When he did not recognize her, she initiated brief chats. Edmonds was warmed by his stories of home and his affectionate mentions of her, but she managed to maintain her ruse, and then he was gone. She later wrote, "His heart, though brave, was tender as a woman's. He was noble and generous, and had the highest regard for truth and law."[47]

Vesey was not Edmonds's first affair of the heart. In October 1861, Franklin Thompson had developed a close friendship with Jerome John Robbins. Robbins's letters indicated the depth of the friendship, then his growing suspicion about Thompson and his surprise when Edmonds confessed her true identity. When Robbins indicated that he was married, their relationship went no further. Robbins kept Edmonds's secret.[48]

In late April, Edmonds was re-assigned as the regiment's postmaster and then as mail carrier and dispatch rider. Her skills with a horse and determined courage served her well, as her new duties were tough and dangerous and sometimes demanded rides of up to sixty miles. Edmonds was often alone for hours or even days at a time, and she came to know the cold fear of capture and the heat of enemy fire. She became more aware of rumour and camp gossip, and one day heard that a Union spy had been killed in Richmond. She decided that she wished to fill the vacancy. She gave her notice of interest to her direct report, who moved it up the chain of command. After being interviewed and tested, she got the job and declared her oath to the Union for the third time.

Edmonds's first mission was to infiltrate enemy lines and ascertain the strength and preparations around Yorktown. She began with a disguise. She purchased the clothes of a liberated slave, dyed her skin black, shaved her head and donned a wig. She practised the broken English of a field hand and assumed the name Ned. She tested her ruse with friends at the medical station where she had been working and fooled them all—she was ready.

After sunset, she passed through both Union and Confederate pickets. The next morning, she fell in with a group of slaves carrying coffee and provisions to the front lines. It was clear that the men suspected Edmonds, but they played along. The group moved back to Yorktown, where they were ordered to work on reinforcing the breastworks. It was perfect. She was able to estimate height and depth and count artillery pieces. She made special note of the Quaker guns: logs painted black to resemble real artillery pieces, meant to intimidate the enemy. She made rough sketches of the works and hid them in her shoe. After two days she stole away and reported back to McClellan's aides.

Edmonds embarked on nine more missions behind enemy lines. She went disguised as a slave, a peddler and once, ironically, as a woman. Each mission was dangerous and each successful. Explaining her willingness to risk all in such dangerous undertakings, Edmonds later wrote, "I am naturally fond of adventure, a little ambitious and a good deal romantic, and this together with my devotion to the Federal cause and determination to assist to the utmost of my ability in crushing the rebellion, made me forget the unpleasant items, and not only endure but really enjoy, the privations connected with my perilous positions."[49]

With the completion of each mission, Edmonds returned to her regiment and to nursing or riding dispatches and mail. After one assignment that had her in the saddle for three straight days, she was handed a weapon and participated in the battle of Williamsburg. After the bloody battle of May 1862 she recalled, "The dead lay in long rows on this field, their ghastly faces hid from view by handkerchiefs or the caps of their overcoats, while faithful soldiers were digging trenches in which to bury the mangled bodies of the slain."[50] Edmonds searched the wounded for signs of life and helped with the burials.

Although heavily outnumbered, the tough and stubborn Southern defenders stymied McClellan's efforts. With McClellan missing opportunity after opportunity but his army still close and dangerous, Confederate president Jefferson Davis put Robert E. Lee in overall charge of the South's campaign. In late June, showing the audacity for which he would become famous, Lee attacked. His bold gamble became known as the Seven Days Battle. It was an inspired move that took McClellan completely by surprise and left 1,734 Federal troops dead and more than 13,000 wounded or missing.

Edmonds reported men dying from sheer exhaustion.[51] She served
throughout the battle, delivering increasingly desperate messages. At one
point, when an enemy shot panicked her horse, she dismounted and tried
to calm the beast, but it bit her arm and kicked her side. She bound her
bleeding arm in a sling and staggered to a field hospital. Still oozing
blood, she offered assistance to the doctors and helped bind and comfort
the wounded men arriving in alarming numbers from the front.

Still in great pain, Edmonds put herself back in the saddle as aide and
dispatch rider for General Philip Kearny. She was directly involved in five
major battles: Mechanicsville, Gaines' Mill, Savage's Station, Frayser's
Farm and Malvern Hill. Each seemed worse than the last, with fatigue
threatening the morale of all.

The Army of the Potomac had been so close to Richmond that soldiers
had seen its church steeples, but by July 14 the Union's effort was spent.
McClellan blamed Lincoln and a lack of reinforcements for the devastating
loss, but he had simply been out-generalled.[52] Along with the rest of the
devastated and defeated army, Edmonds and Riggins, whose regiment had
played significant roles at the Gaines' Mill and the Seven Days battles, plied
their way through the warm Chesapeake back to Washington.

CONSCRIPTION AND SKEDADDLERS

While the Peninsula Campaign ended well for the Confederacy in July of
1862, in April things had looked dark. The Confederate army was outnumbered and Richmond was under threat. At Shiloh, near the Tennessee-
Mississippi border, Confederate general Beauregard, hero of Fort Sumter
and Manassas, had suffered a stunning loss that cost 107,000 men, a
quarter of those under his command.[53] With only about 5.5 million white
citizens to the North's 22.5 million, the Confederates felt their losses
more deeply. They could not win a war of attrition. To continue the fight,
the Confederacy needed more men than the Southern states' voluntary
enlistment programs could provide.

With McClellan's massive army on his doorstep, Confederate president
Davis had called a council of war. Lee emphasized the significance of recent

Southern casualties, new military needs, and the dwindling numbers of fresh recruits. He argued that those whose patriotic zeal had inspired them to join a year before would soon be seeing their enlistments expire. After a good deal of spirited debate, Davis approved America's first conscription.

Davis signed the law on April 16, 1862. It provided for the draft of all white men between the ages of eighteen and thirty-five. All who had already signed up for one year had their commitment extended to three. The age limit would be raised to forty-five in September, and in February 1865 it changed again to include those from seventeen to fifty. The law eventually excluded railroad and canal workers, telegraph operators, druggists, teachers and those who owned more than twenty slaves.

A number of states declared that the new law violated the concept of states' rights—the very concept that most Southern leaders claimed the war was all about. The governors of Georgia and Alabama publicly stated their refusal to aid in its implementation. However, regardless of opposition in many quarters and the uneven way in which the law's regulations were enforced, the threat of being drafted had its intended effect. Men began enlisting to avoid what would be considered the humiliation of being forced into service.

With the confidence felt in the early spring, Lincoln had approved the closure of Northern recruiting offices. But the combination of McClellan's stalled campaign, western armies bleeding men, and Confederate troops stubbornly holding out within a few dozen miles of Washington, led to their reopening. On July 6, Northern governors were asked to do all they could to encourage recruitment. The response was tepid at best. Two weeks later, governors received a letter from Washington announcing a call for 300,000 men, with each state's quota listed. Again the governors balked. Seward announced the notion of a draft. He sweetened the deal by offering a $100 inducement from the federal government—called a bounty—for every new recruit who enlisted before the draft took place. Union governors were encouraged to top up bounties with state and local cash incentives, and to offer advances upon signing. Those wishing to avoid the draft could pay a substitute a

$300 commutation fee to go in their stead. The Confederate law had a similar clause, whereby a draftee could hire a substitute to take his place.

Lincoln signed the Militia Act on July 17, 1862. It called for each state to raise a nine-month militia, with quotas linked to population numbers. Most states met their quotas, and in those that could not the War Department established a draft. In every state, local tax assessors began making lists of eligible men. Recruitment ads appeared as posters and in newspapers. Most echoed the theme of a Detroit newspaper ad with the large, bold tagline: "Avoid the Draft! $522 Bonus! $10 Advance."[54] There was not a word about duty. Patriotism was being purchased—or at least rented.

As had happened in the South, Northern recruiting offices were overwhelmed with young men wanting to sign up before being drafted. But thousands felt otherwise and fled. While there had been many cases of deserters running to Canada beginning in the fall of 1861, the threat of conscription in the summer of 1862 added draft dodgers to the flood of men pouring over the border. In August, the *Detroit Free Press* reported "an exodus" of men fleeing through the city on their way to Canada.[55] There were similar reports from Chicago, Rochester and Buffalo.

So many young men were making their way over the border that popular crossing points were reinforced with Union soldiers. On August 8, partially to help stem the tide of desertions, Congress passed a law rendering it illegal for those subject to military service to leave the country. When news spread of Lincoln's intention to quickly sign and enforce the law, a new wave of deserters and draft dodgers crossed the border. At Niagara Falls, four hundred men fled in a single day.[56] Some border crossings witnessed screaming matches. Many cases of fights and drawn weapons were reported, and there were riots in Detroit and Buffalo.[57]

Exploitative entrepreneurs quickly appeared to meet the sudden demand for fake discharge papers. Those with genuine documents made good money selling them to forgers, who bleached out names and other personal information and sold copies of blank forms. Many men took a simpler way out, avoided populated border crossings, and quietly slipped across the imaginary line to freedom.

In the Maritimes, soldiers running from their units—and civilians running to avoid becoming part of one—were dubbed skedaddlers. So many young men crossed the Maine border and made their way over a long esker into Carleton County, New Brunswick, that the area became forever known as Skedaddle Ridge. Those on New Brunswick's Montebello Island, within sight of Maine across the waves, renamed an increasingly busy spot Skedaddler's Reach.

By the war's end, about twelve thousand Americans had found their way over the border as either deserters or draft dodgers.[58] As the number of skedaddlers increased over the summer and fall of 1862, Canadian and Maritime opinion of them, which had been positive at the beginning, soured. In provinces where thousands still needed to travel to the United States to find work or liveable salaries, the skedaddling Americans swelled the labour pool and depressed wages. Many farmers who hired cheaper American boys discovered some truth to the skedaddlers' reputation for leaving if work became too hard or before it was done. Skedaddlers saw their reputations further sullied by rumours of un- or underemployed young Americans forming gangs or becoming involved in criminal activity.[59]

WAR'S BRAVERY AND DRUDGERY

After the Peninsula Campaign, Edmonds found herself back in camps around Washington. She was incredibly busy with new outbreaks of camp diseases. Disease would eventually kill more soldiers than battles: of the 360,000 Union troops who lost their lives in the war, 250,000 died from disease.[60] From the camp of his New York regiment, Charles Riggins sent a mournful letter home to his sister in Canada: "Four of our Company are in the hospital—Sick with the measles. Two of them slept in the same tent with me for about a week. I have had a bad headache for about three days. . . . I have broke out all over with a kind of rash & they itch awful bad."[61] Two weeks later things were much worse: "There were three thousand sick men sent away yesterday. There had been five men buried since last night & as I write this they are carrying another one out. They are dying all over the whole army forty & fifty every day."[62]

Typhoid fever took the life of Jasper Wolverton in October 1861, just four months after he had volunteered to serve. In April 1863, his brother Alfred died of smallpox. Peter Anderson, who was to fight with the Wolverton brothers at Antietam, had left Guelph, in Canada West, to enlist with an Ohio regiment and was also in McClellan's camp. He wrote to his sister, "I have been for four months at deaths very door, most of the time delirious with the typhoid fever."[63]

As in every war, Civil War soldiers complained about food, illness, their officers and boredom. Riggins wrote: "We have been here now for six days & the other day we got mouldy crackers with maggots in our bacon— nearly ran away with the same—our coffee is half beans & our sugar is mixed & wet & that is about all we get from day to day."[64] All yearned for home. Jasper Wolverton wrote to his sister: "A great many of those who came with us have got very homesick. Some of them intend returning immediately. We intend to leave when we can't stand it any longer."[65] Riggins seemed to have escaped this heartache. From McClellan's camp in late July 1862, he wrote: "I do not fret like some do that are here about home, home sickness is hurting a good many here, worse than their wounds. . . . I try to be at home where ever I am."[66]

As the soldiers trained and complained, General McClellan rebuilt his army and tried to deflect blame for his disastrous results. Battles continued to rage in the west. New Orleans fell to the Union. In late August, Lee moved 50,000 troops north and met McClellan's Army of the Potomac at the Second Battle of Bull Run. It was another draw and even bloodier than the first, with 25,000 casualties. But a more tragic fight was on its way.

In September 1862, Lee drove into Maryland. His intention was to take the war to the North, and threaten Washington while stirring the considerable Confederate support in that state. He also wanted to lend credence to a Northern peace movement, and add pressure on Britain to recognize the South.[67] On September 15, with only 19,000 troops, Lee formed lines facing the Union's 70,000. They met near a creek called Antietam, and the most deadly battle in the war began.

Edmonds was at Antietam as 2nd Michigan's field nurse. She was moved by the courageous manner in which so many faced their final moments, sincerely believing that a faith in God was the only reason for personal resilience and military victory.[68] Riggins, Anderson and two Wolverton brothers were also among the Canadians at Antietam. Because of strict orders and military censors, they were not able to write home about specifics of the battle, but Riggins managed to sneak a story into a letter to his mother about happening upon a Confederate camp and enjoying the food the fleeing rebels had left behind.[69]

The cost on both sides was unfathomable. In two days, 17,000 men were wounded and 6,000 had died. Lincoln was pleased that Lee had been forced to retreat back to Virginia but could not believe that McClellan had failed to seize the opportunity to pursue and crush him. In early October, Lincoln visited McClellan but could not entice the reluctant general to action. He followed the meeting with a telegram explicitly instructing him to move, but McClellan claimed his horses were too tired. Lincoln responded with rare sarcasm: "Will you pardon me for asking what the horses of your army have done since the battle of Antietam that could fatigue anything?"[70] A few days later, Lincoln fired him.

On her way back toward Washington, Edmonds rode over old battle-grounds—Bull Run, Centreville and more—and encountered disturbing sights. Men and horses lay unburied, swollen and stinking in the sun. She heard of Confederate guerrillas selling Union skulls at ten dollars each.[71]

The fall was a period of relative quiet for Edmonds and her regiment, but in early December she was on the move again. She found herself witness to the Battle of Fredericksburg. Her experience as a dispatch rider had become well known, so she was back in the saddle, serving under the 2nd Michigan's new commander, General Orlando Poe. Edmonds's regiment was now part of an enormous army of about 120,000 troops under the leadership of newly appointed Major General Ambrose Burnside.* On the morning of December 11, the battle began. Edmonds raced along the front, delivering messages.

---

* Burnside's enormous mutton-chop whiskers are said to have given that style of facial hair its name.

Burnside ordered men to attack up a hill on the right flank called Marye's Heights. At the top was Confederate lieutenant General James Longstreet's corps: well dug in, well defended and ready. Union men slowly walked up the hill and into the horror of a merciless killing zone. Tramping over the bodies of hundreds of their falling comrades, most dead and others pitifully writhing in pain and crying for water, wave after appalling wave turned their shoulders against the steel-filled air as if resisting a strong wind. Longstreet's men actually began to cheer each new drive up the hill, each as brave as it was futile.

Among the courageous Union soldiers at Fredericksburg was Canada East's Captain John C. Gilmore. His 16th New York Infantry was advancing but faltering against a withering rain of Confederate lead at Salem Heights. Gilmore grabbed the fallen regimental colours from the blood-soaked mud, waved them high, and then advanced up the hill. Inspired, his men rallied and followed him forward. For his bravery that day, Gilmore was awarded the Congressional Medal of Honor.*

When the Union's rattled General Burnside finally ordered a withdrawal, Edmonds, like everyone else involved, was shaken. She was also sick, having fallen ill during the Peninsula Campaign and never fully recovered. In April 1863, an increasingly ailing Edmonds arrived with her regiment at camp near Lebanon, Kentucky. The combination of illness, fatigue and relentless stress led to a collapse. She later explained:

> All of my soldierly qualities seemed to have fled, and I was again a poor cowardly, nervous, whining woman; and as if to make up for lost time and to give vent to my long pent up feelings, I could do nothing but weep hour after hour, until it would seem that my head was literally a fountain of tears and my heart one great burden of sorrow. All the horrid scenes that I had witnessed during the past two years

---

* *Gilmore remained in the United States after the war, enjoyed a career of dedicated service and retired a brigadier general. He is buried at Arlington National Cemetery.*

seemed now before me with vivid distinctness, and I could think of nothing else.[72]

Suffering from emotional trauma and malaria, she coughed, shivered and endured nightmarish hallucinations. Despite her emotional and physical incapacitation, Edmonds remained lucid enough to realize that if she entered one of the many hospital tents for treatment, her identity would be discovered. She came up with only one option—she left.

On April 19, 1863, she limped from camp and purchased a ticket for the first train out, disembarking in Cairo, Illinois, where she checked into a hotel to rest and recover. When she finally emerged, wan and weak, Edmonds discovered her name on a list of deserters. After another few days spent regaining strength, she left Cairo, her men's clothes, and Franklin Thompson behind.

While Edmonds was again reinventing herself, the momentum of the war shifted. On July 4, 1863, the Confederate commanders at Vicksburg, Tennessee, surrendered what many had believed to be an impregnable fortress of a city to Union General Ulysses S. Grant. With Vicksburg's fall, the Mississippi belonged to the Union, and the Confederacy was split in two. On the same day, Robert E. Lee began his retreat after being beaten at Gettysburg, Pennsylvania. While Vicksburg was important, Gettysburg became engulfed in a romantic aura. The setting was beautiful, the sacrifice both horrible and heroic; the magnificent, seemingly unbeatable Lee was beaten; and in commemorating the fallen four months later, Lincoln's eloquence would reach its zenith.

Many Canadians and Maritimers were at Gettysburg. Charles Riggins was there. His 14th U.S. Infantry arrived on July 2, the battle's second day, and took up a position at Little Round Top. His regiment engaged Confederates charging up the wooded section of the hill on the Union's far left. Under heavy fire and taking casualties, they held the line and then moved back up the hill where they helped to hold it.

The 20th Maine included about twenty New Brunswickers. On July 2, playing their part in the desperate attempt to hold Little Round Top, but with ammunition nearly spent, Colonel Joshua Chamberlain ordered a bayonet charge down the hill. George Leach from Fredericton and Alex Lester from Saint John were among the men who ran down Little Round Top that afternoon, and among the forty who died saving the day for the Union—helping seal the Confederacy's fate.

Canadian Francis Wafer was there too. In the spring of 1863, while completing medical training at Queen's Medical College in Kingston, he had been approached by Union recruiters. Seeing an opportunity to gain some first-hand medical training, he enlisted with New York's 108th Regiment as its assistant surgeon. Wafer gained some field experience before arriving at Gettysburg on the battle's second day. He performed surgery in a small stone house on Taneytown Road, with artillery thundering and shells crashing nearby. Through fear and fatigue, Wafer sawed and sewed and marvelled at the stoicism of the blood-soaked, wounded men.[73]

PRISONERS

Also at Gettysburg, but on the Confederate side, was Canada West's Dr. Solomon Secord. He had been promoted to surgeon in early 1863 and reassigned to General James Longstreet's Corps. He was in the woods on the third day of the battle when General George Pickett's Virginians left the cover of the trees to take their fateful walk up a gentle rise to meet devastatingly relentless Union fire. When the rains came the next day and Lee's defeated army began to withdraw, Secord volunteered to stay behind and continue tending the ten to twelve thousand wounded left on the field. He was taken prisoner but, according to common practice, allowed to continue to treat the suffering men of both sides.

Two weeks later, Secord was sent to Virginia's Fort Monroe, then to another prison at Fort Norfolk, and finally to Maryland's Fort McHenry. He was among seven thousand Confederates captured at Gettysburg. Secord carefully noted the schedules of the McHenry guards and which were most alert. On October 10, he escaped. He slowly made his way south and eventually located his old regiment. He returned to service as the Georgia 20th's surgeon. He was later promoted and served in the office of the Inspector of Hospitals in Richmond.

Secord was one of many Canadians and Maritimers who spent time as prisoners of war. Shortly after being granted a transfer from support to active combat duty, Alonzo Wolverton had been captured, though he quickly escaped. He rose to the rank of lieutenant and led men in many battles including the decisive struggle at Chattanooga in November 1863. Later that year he was captured again and imprisoned in Villanow, Georgia. Conditions were so horrible that many contemplated suicide. Wolverton was one of those released after signing a pledge to never again bear arms against the Confederacy.[74] He ignored his pledge, and by October was part of General Sherman's ruthless drive across Georgia to the sea.

E.L. Stevens left Sackville, New Brunswick, in February 1863 to enlist with Maine's 1st Infantry Volunteers. On May 5, 1864, he was wounded and captured at the sprawling Battle of the Wilderness. For three weeks he was transferred through several camps until being placed in the notorious and barbaric Andersonville prison. He was exchanged for a Confederate soldier in December.

Saint John's Robert Hayborn left home in 1852 to find work in the United States and his brother soon joined him. With the outbreak of war, they enlisted in the 1st Louisiana Cavalry. The brothers fought at Shiloh, Chancellorsville, Williamsburg, Corinth and Murfreesboro. At Gettysburg, a minié ball pierced his right arm and, suffering a loss of blood, he fell and was captured. He was taken to Camp Chase in Ohio and then to Fort Delaware. He was exchanged on March 7, 1865.[75]

Some prisons allowed men to write home, and military officials sometimes wrote to families with the news of a loved one's capture. Mary Elizabeth Gray, for example, received a letter at her home in Kingston from John Collins of the 11th U.S. Infantry Recruiting Office, Watertown, New York. He gently informed Ms. Gray that her brother Edward had been captured by Confederates in a battle outside Petersburg. He did not know where Edward had been taken but supposed it was to one of the many camps around Richmond. He tried to console her by explaining that he too had a brother captured and had not heard from him since March. He ended with a hope that peace might soon return to the land.[76]

Governor General Monck and British minister Lyons tried to intercede on behalf of Canadian and Maritime prisoners, but were hampered by their excessive workloads and inadequate staff, and the need to deal with sketchy information and an American government often unwilling or unable to help. Another complication was that any British subject who enlisted with the Confederate or Union forces had broken the law. This point was made in a circular from Lyons to all British consuls in the United States on May 3, 1862.[77] Further, British foreign secretary Russell (in 1861 he was raised to a peerage and was no longer Lord but Earl Russell) was of the opinion that the United States had the legal right to consider those captured in uniform as prisoners of war and therefore to treat them as they would captured Americans. How could Britain claim to be maintaining its neutrality when so many of their citizens were being captured in uniform? Lyons was thus given a direct order: "You should abstain from making any formal official demand for the liberation of such Prisoners and . . . you should not call upon the U.S. authorities to lay down any general rule or make any formal declaration as to the course they will take regarding them."[78] Lyons and Monck backed off a little, acting only when there was undeniable proof that a particular person had been unwillingly pressed into service and his regiment was known. It was clear that little could or would be done.

CRIMPING

As the war progressed and the need for recruits increased, the issue of Canadians and Maritimers being forced into service became a more serious problem. For instance, in January 1863, Ebenezer Tyler was asleep in his house on Wolfe Island, not far from Kingston, when a group of armed American soldiers led by Captain Haddock arrived by boat, pulled Tyler from his bed, and ferried him to New York.[79] Haddock claimed Tyler was an American deserter. Tyler insisted he was a native Canadian who had never left his homeland. He was nonetheless pressed into uniform and shipped away.

Tyler managed to contact a British consul and Lord Lyons was soon in Seward's office. Monck and Lyons were at that moment dealing with a number of cases of Canadians being either mistaken for American deserters or flagrantly kidnapped and forced into military service. The Tyler case seemed cut and dried, and Lyons demanded action.

Seward reluctantly agreed. He issued a statement that referred to the Tyler case as a "violation of the sovereignty of a friendly state."[80] He understood the enthusiasm that had led to the soldiers doing what they did, but chastised them for having done it. Seward took the matter to Lincoln, who personally promised that Haddock would be dishonourably discharged and Tyler would be allowed to leave his regiment and return home to Canada.[81] Tyler was soon home with his family.

The Tyler case was unique only for its happy ending for, like him, many Canadians and Maritimers came to know the process of crimping. Crimping is not immoral or illegal, as it refers simply to encouraging and helping someone to enter military service. The word assumes a menacing and pejorative turn, however, when implying that men are unwillingly enlisted through trickery, force, or the threat or actual use of violence. That form of crimping became common practice.

Lincoln's 1862 Militia Act had fuelled crimping in Canada and the Maritimes, but his Enrollment Act in March 1863 made it increasingly common, open and aggressive. The law established new quotas for Northern congressional districts and provided greater cash incentives for enlistment. The federal government offered $100 for each and every man between the ages of twenty and forty-five. When local and state governments chipped in, the total bounty often became $300, and in some places as high as $500. The sums were quite generous, as they equalled most men's annual income. The new law continued the allowance of a $300 commutation or substitution fee for those whose means outpaced their patriotism. With the news of battlefield carnage and Matthew Brady's stunning photographs making it all so real for those at home, the market for young men willing to serve as substitutes rose—and with it the ruthlessness of unscrupulous crimpers filling their pockets by filling demand.

Initial attempts to implement the draft had met with protests, and riots broke out in Indiana, Illinois, Ohio and Wisconsin. The worst riots tore up New York City streets for five days and nights. Poor New Yorkers attacked the homes and businesses of the rich who could afford commutation fees. African-Americans were beaten up and some lynched. The city's large Irish community acted against other ethnic minorities and African-Americans who were seen as economic competitors. The violence subsided only with the arrival of five regiments of soldiers rushed in from Gettysburg.

Despite the riots and simmering opposition, by the fall of 1863 enlistments began to trend up. Meanwhile, many young men recognized a chance to turn a profit and began to shop around and offer themselves to provost marshals offering the highest reward.[82] Others began bounty jumping; that is, they enlisted in one community, collected the bounty, deserted, enlisted in another, and then started all over again.

Many entrepreneurially minded men offered themselves as brokers. For a cut of the bounty, brokers would help connect recruits with recruiters. Many bounty brokers were honest, but plenty of others duped young men into believing that they could not enlist without a broker and that the exorbitant percentages demanded for brokerage services were common practice. By the fall of 1863, bounty brokers had grown so numerous and powerful that it became difficult for anyone to enlist without one.[83]

As the wealth and influence of brokers increased, many began openly advertising their services in newspapers and on posters hung in bars, post offices and other public places. They offered competitive rates to recruits and not only good value but a list of available substitutes for those with the means and desire to avoid service. Many opened offices near recruiting stations. By the end of 1863, most provost marshals had stopped advertising for recruits and simply sub-contracted the job out to brokers. Men approaching marshals on their own were often referred to brokers, and when enlistment was complete, the provost marshal paid the appropriate broker, who then paid the recruit, minus the brokering fee. A provost marshal in Utica, New York, signed a $750,000 contract with broker Aaron Richardson to fill the town's quota.[84]

Some bounty brokers became quite wealthy by intimidating or buying out competitors. In order to meet their obligations to the provost marshals, increasingly rapacious brokers hired staff to do administrative work and to be runners, venturing out in search of more recruits. Like the brokers themselves, runners worked on commission.

Government pressure on provost marshals to meet quotas was passed on to brokers, who pressed their runners for more men. This hierarchy of demands led many runners to employ ruthless and illegal means to meet their personal quotas. In New York and Boston, for instance, many immigrants walking down ships' gangplanks were directed to runners' stations where, without explanation, they were signed up, suited up and marched onto a troop train before they understood what had happened. Many brokers and runners made deals with captains which allowed them to enter immigrant ships before any had disembarked and offer men more money than they had seen in their lives to enlist or, alternatively, to con them into believing that enlisting was simply a part of entering the country.[85]

When the pool of young men began drying up, in many states, runners began employing even more vicious tactics. Runners went to bars and made young men drunk, or drugged them, and then shipped them off. The new "recruits" awoke hung-over and in uniform. Many runners simply snatched victims from the streets. Young men down on their luck or those afflicted with mental disabilities were especially easy prey.

Authorities were aware that the brokers were engaging in such practices, and legal action was taken in the most egregious cases. As Commander of Military District of the East, responsible for the Canadian border, Major General John Dix hated brokers. While conceding that they were providing a valuable service to the Union, he sought to end their illegal and immoral actions.[86] As the need for men continued to increase, however, even Dix relented and, except for a few cases where brokers were fined or jailed, he and most other authorities turned a blind eye.

In April 1864, a runner named Holley brought two Canadian boys to a broker named A.B. Pratt, who had two principals in need of substitutes. One of the two boys was rejected by the provost marshal at Albany's 14th

District, but Joshua Long was accepted. After having seen so many young men cheated, the provost marshal suddenly felt a rush of guilt, and asked Long how much he was being paid. When Long replied that he was promised $150, he was told he could be getting the entire $300. Long said nothing. At that point a clerk named Eliakim Chase pounced on the broker and knocked him down several stairs. Chase was convicted of assault. Pratt went back to his broker business and Long entered the army.

The incident was widely reported, but the lesson learned seemed to be that a deal struck between a broker and a potential recruit was fair game. It was up to the recruit if he wished to offer himself up for service and be swindled while doing it. No one seemed concerned that Long was a Canadian, or that British neutrality was being compromised by the recruitment of a British subject.[87] The *New York Times* called the entire situation "a necessary evil."[88]

With crimping happening so openly in the United States, American authorities showed little interest in stopping similar activities in Canada. The necessary evil of American runners filling their demand by sourcing the Canadian and Maritime supply had, in fact, been going on for some time. The number of American crimpers in Canada grew with the demand for fresh troops and the potential for profit. In December 1863, the British consul in Boston reported two cases of American men coming to his office asking for advice regarding Canadian crimping laws. Both men were open about their plans to advertise jobs in the United States—one on a farm and the other in a quarry—with the notion of forcing everyone they hired into the military and then claiming their bounties.[89]

American crimpers scoured Canadian and Maritime streets, bars and schools, attempting to meet their quotas by tricking, conning, or drugging and kidnapping young men and boys just as others were doing in America. Prostitutes were hired to seduce men into signing bogus contracts. As warnings of their tricks were publicized, the crimpers just thought up new ruses.

Monck was told of crimpers posing as Canadian police officers. The most well-known case involved William Fisher and Thomas Miller. In

July 1864, they were arrested by Canadian police in Windsor and then spirited across the river to Detroit. They appeared before a magistrate, who offered to drop all charges if the two joined a Michigan regiment. Fisher and Miller were pressed into military service. Their case was brought to Seward, whose inquires revealed that the police officers and magistrate were all frauds.[90] Months later, Miller was found and offered a discharge. Fisher had already deserted.

In January 1863, an order was given to all British regulars to beware of being tricked into desertion by American agents. In October, a $50 reward was offered to anyone offering information about men involved in crimping British soldiers. Despite the warnings, a group of British merchant sailors had been hoodwinked. They wrote to Boston's British consul in September 1864, and reported their story. They spoke of drinking in a bar in Quebec City and then waking up in the United States. After being sold in Lebanon, New York, they were transported further south. Each man was given $200 and their kidnapper was paid $1,000. The kidnappers had bragged of the lucrative deals they had done in stealing British and Canadian sailors.[91]

Many of the British soldiers stationed along the American border had come from Ireland, and crimpers encouraged desertion by exploiting anti-British, Irish nationalism. Sergeant James Campbell was stationed in Montreal. He told of being harassed by well-known American crimper Edward Kelly while walking along Notre-Dame Street. Kelly tried to convince the unwavering sergeant that there were over a quarter of a million loyal Irish fighting in Union ranks, and once the war was over they would be organized and turned against Canada, where they would hang every British soldier they could find.[92]

Crimpers paid special attention to the many Black communities in Canada and the Maritimes. In August 1862, Secretary of War Stanton authorized the raising of what were then called coloured regiments. The decision was a clarion call for the thousands of racial refugees who had made their homes in Canada and the Maritimes, and many left to enlist. The 1st Michigan Coloured Regiment was augmented by many from

Canada West's Elgin county, and a number of Black men from Nova Scotia and New Brunswick left to join the famed Massachusetts 54th. The number of African-Canadians who crossed the border to join the 200,000 African-Americans who served in Union ranks cannot be reliably estimated, but it is certain that crimpers found their job easy when dealing with young men eager to fight for a cause so close to their hearts. One such recruit was Henry Jackson, who left Guelph to join the 17th Michigan. He wrote, "I wish to impress upon your mind that the war is a trial between freedom and slavery not only here but all over the world."[93] Jackson was killed in November 1863 at the Battle of Campbell's Station, in Tennessee.

Some young people sealed their fates by trying to out-trick the tricksters. Canadian Peter Daly, for instance, had the temerity to write to Monck complaining that he had voluntarily enlisted in the Confederate army but then, after having completed his enlistment, moved north on news of larger bounties. He had enlisted as a substitute. He wrote: "I took a Drafted mans Place and He gave me 25 Dollars and said He would send me more when I was in the army but my Lord He Has Not Done as he said He would, and I have been in the service of the United States nine months."[94] Daly seemed oblivious to the law he had broken in enlisting in two foreign armies. There is no evidence of Monck offering him assistance.

Many parents falsely claimed that their sons had been coerced. The father of James Cunningham, for example, wrote to the governor general with a detailed description of how his son had been drugged and torn from his home in Toronto to serve in the Union army. Monck discovered that not only had young James negotiated a bounty with a runner but then once in the United States and enlisted, he had mailed part of his earnings home. Monck refused to intervene and Cunningham remained in the army.[95]

Monck and Lyons also refused to help bounty jumpers. In April 1865, the *Nova Scotian* reported that two men from Saint John were found to have been bounty jumping. They were taking enlistment money and then deserting and re-enlisting again and again. Both were caught and executed.

Lord Lyons asked Seward to investigate 235 cases of young people being coerced into service against their will.[96] Monck grew increasingly frustrated with his inability to stop the crimping. In January 1864, he reported to the British Colonial Office that, despite his best efforts, crimping was a growing problem, and he asked for help.[97] He wrote several more times; by May his letters were taking a tone of utter despondency. The financial reward of the increasingly lucrative bounties overwhelmed the risk of being caught.[98] Monck told Lyons that as long as the Americans offered so much money in bounties, it would be impossible to end crimping.[99] Monck was told by both Lyons and Russell that continuing to negotiate with Seward and the Americans was a waste of time.[100]

In 1862 and 1863 Canada, Nova Scotia and New Brunswick all enacted legislation making it easier to arrest and convict crimpers, and they raised fines and jail terms. The Canadian government also announced that crimpers would be charged under the Foreign Enlistment Act, and subject to a possible six months of imprisonment and fine of $450. Further, in January 1864, it declared that willing deserters would be charged under the Mutiny Act, which carried a maximum penalty of six months' hard labour.

The Canadian Committee of the Executive Council tabled a report in the legislature on May 10, 1864, praising the use of members of the British military for apprehending crimpers. It said that in Brockville the previous January, members of the 4th Regiment had apprehended two Americans who had drugged a young Canadian and were carrying him off to be enlisted in the United States army. Two others were found engaged in the same activity and were also arrested. Two of the group were convicted, and one sentenced to four, and the other to five, years in prison.[101] In support of the Committee's recommendations, the paltry $10 reward offered for soldiers or civilians offering information leading to conviction was raised to a more enticing $200. Kingston and Montreal offered an additional $50. Special constables were hired and placed in cities known to be favourites for crimping activities. Additional border guards were hired.

In August, 1864, Monck approved the death sentence for two deserters, but the decision was commuted and they instead spent six months in prison. In the spring of 1865, the Canadian legislature passed a new law making it easier to convict crimpers by allowing police magistrates to hear cases and allowing convictions to stand even on the testimony of a single witness. Despite all the concern and all the efforts to put a stop to it, crimping continued. In 1864 and 1865, only ninety-one people were convicted of crimping in Canada.

The saddest cases involved crimpers visiting schools and enticing boys with offers of money, drink and girls. Michael Boyle, for instance, wrote to the governor general in early July 1864 of an American agent who had visited his son at his Toronto school and absconded with him. Alfred Broissoit, was only fifteen when snatched from his Montreal school.[102] Neither boy was heard from again.

When Sarah Emma Edmonds regained her health, she rejoined the army as a nurse; this time as herself. She served in Virginia hospitals far from front-line action. At Harper's Ferry, quite by chance, she was reunited with Linus Seelye—the young New Brunswick man who had helped her to escape her father so many years before. He had come to the United States and found work as a carpenter. They renewed their friendship and it soon turned to romance.

Not all who fought by choice or by force were so lucky. Until the guns fell silent, Canadians and Maritimers continued to fight, to volunteer to fight, or to dodge crimpers to keep from fighting. Deserters and skedaddlers crossed the border in both directions. All the while, Canadian and Maritime political leaders struggled within their malfunctioning political systems to exert what control they could. Confederate president, Jefferson Davis, was in precisely the same situation. A perfect storm of military, political, economic and diplomatic disappointments was turning desperate measures into viable options. Davis decided to save the South by looking north—and he had just the man he needed to make it happen. Davis decided that Canada would help turn the tide toward victory and redemption.

4

———◆———

JACOB THOMPSON AND THE
CONFEDERATES IN THE ATTIC

I T WAS THREE O'CLOCK on that fateful July morning. Robert E. Lee stepped from his cramped quarters into the cool morning mist. From beyond the eastern horizon came streaks of ghostly grey that smudged the stars and offered Cemetery Ridge in silhouette. It was a mile away, up a long gentle rise and topped with a low rock wall. On and behind the ridge were 75,000 men of the Army of the Potomac. Encamped to the north and west of the fish-hook-shaped Union line were 60,000 men of Lee's Army of North Virginia, as potent a fighting force as the continent had ever seen. They were outnumbered, on inferior ground, far from home, and yet still believed themselves to be invincible.

Lee's latest northern advance, which had brought them all to this place and this moment, had begun on June 10, 1863. Lee had ordered a march up the west side of the Blue Ridge Mountains. The Union's newly appointed General Joseph Hooker did just as Lee had predicted and turned north as well, trying to keep his forces between the Confederates and Washington. Lee's slow advance was a terrific combination of skill, bluff and luck, with the Union missing many chances to stop it. Lee's last communication with President Davis had repeated their belief that the effort would be strategically successful if it encouraged negotiations to end the war.[1]

There were skirmishes and significant battles as Lee slowly moved north. On June 27, he had stood studying a map of Pennsylvania and pointed at a small town at the hub of an intersection of roads. "Thereabout," he said to the gathered officers, "we shall probably meet the army and fight a great battle, and if God gives us the victory, the war will be over and we will achieve the recognition of our independence."[2] The next day he learned that Hooker had been replaced by General George Meade, who was at that moment rushing north to catch up with the men had been appointed to lead. Three days later, Lee's army approached Gettysburg, Pennsylvania.

On the afternoon of July 1, Union and Confederate skirmishers met outside and then pushed each other through the small town. Lee was not able to take the Union's right later that day, and the next day, despite enormous effort and losses, failed to take its left at Little Round Top. Today he would attack its centre.

It was now July 3, 1863. Lee mounted Traveller, the imperturbable grey stallion that had served him so well and for so long, and set out to find General Longstreet. Minutes later the booming of artillery pierced the gathering dawn. It was Lt. General George Ewell, on the Confederate left. Lee had told him to wait for Longstreet's men, but now guessed that the Union's cautious but clever Meade had forced his hand. There was nothing he could do but trust Ewell, and so he nudged Traveller forward.

Lee and Longstreet mumbled a respectful good morning, but then Old Pete, as his men called the heavily bearded general, repeated the point he had made the night before—that with the Union entrenched on the high ground, an attack would be foolhardy. He argued that they should disengage and swing south toward Washington, allowing them to fight when and where they chose. Lee disagreed, saying the enemy was there and there he must be confronted.[3]

After frustrating delays, an artillery barrage began at 1:07 in the afternoon. It shook the earth and belched enough smoke to eclipse the scorching summer sun. Confederate artillery fired in salvos along their curving two-mile line. Union cannon answered, and for nearly two hours the deadly exchange thundered.

Then there was silence. Confederate major general George Pickett had been busy all morning organizing his Virginians for the attack he had been afforded the honour to lead. The barrage was over but there was still no order to advance and so he rode off to find Longstreet. He found Old Pete sitting on a fence, looking morose and unable to bring himself to issue the order to advance. He finally looked up at Pickett and nodded.

As a warm breeze urged the black smoke away, Union men along the ridge and from the hills on either side witnessed a glorious display. Beneath nineteen fluttering blue flags, Pickett's 12,500 men stepped smartly into the field's open expanse. The perfectly formed line was a mile wide. And they walked. They were resplendent in the sunshine and spectacular in their discipline. Then hell was visited upon them.

The full fury of one hundred field artillery pieces opened up. Enfilade fire rained down from Cemetery Hill on their left and Little Round Top on their right. Hot metal tore into flesh and bone, and mutilated men screamed over the cacophonous din. Blinding smoke rolled and rose. And yet the Virginians walked on.

Musket fire announced their coming within range of the rock wall, and more men fell. There was a startled cheer from the Union line when, at about a hundred yards out, the Virginians stopped and reoriented their line with a textbook-perfect left oblique. Further down, with Confederates falling in greater numbers and yet somehow continuing their advance, Union boys were chanting vengefully "Fredericksburg—Fredericksburg."

A scattered few made it to the wall, to be met by the Union bayonets. There was no serious breach. There was no order to fall back. The battered and bloodied men, with most of their officers wounded, dead or lost, simply sensed it was time and turned around.

Out of range and back in the relative protection of the trees, wide-eyed and bloodied survivors staggered past Lee, who sat tall upon the stoic Traveller. To a few torn-up men who met his eye, he said that it was all his fault. Pickett, covered in soot and dirt and blood, stood gazing up at Lee in shock and exhaustion. Lee ordered him to prepare his division for a possible counter-attack. Pickett shook his head and muttered, "General Lee, I have no division now."[4]

The next day, a pounding torrential rain masked the sound of Lee's army leaving, with only a skeleton force left behind to cover its retreat. A wagon train heaving with wounded and dying stretched for eleven miles as the once indomitable army began its long, slow and sad slog home.

On that same day, the fourth of July, hundreds of miles west, the Union's General Ulysses S. Grant received a message. For several months, he had been concentrating his efforts on capturing Vicksburg. The city rested on a hairpin turn on the Mississippi River, halfway between Memphis and New Orleans. It was a formidable fortress, glaring down at the river from high bluffs and protected by miles of impenetrable bayous, malarial bottom land, and crisscrossing rivers and streams. To win the city was to gain control of the Mississippi and cut the Confederacy in half; so, since November, Grant had been trying one thing after another to take it. His determination, daring and unorthodox ideas brought failure after failure, but Lincoln stood by him, despite mounting calls for his dismissal. Confederate forces eventually withdrew to the city, initiating a long and tortuous siege. By the summer of 1863, Vicksburg's defenders had dug themselves into defensive trenches and its citizens retreated into caves to survive the near constant artillery bombardment. Finally, with food running out and options gone, the Confederate commander surrendered the city and his thirty thousand troops.

The silence at Vicksburg and Gettysburg announced a turning point in the war. The Confederacy was severed and there would be no more major invasions of the North. Talk of recognition from Britain that had been revived with Southern victories in early 1862 had already faded, and Gettysburg and Vicksburg ended any further serious consideration. From that point forward, despite the fortitude of the Southern people, the courage of its soldiers and the brilliance of many of its generals, the end of the Confederacy had begun.

Jefferson Davis had spent much of the summer of 1863 seriously ill. On July 5, he was conducting official business from his bed, amid swirling rumours that he was dying.[5] While waiting for word from Pennsylvania, he was told that Vicksburg had fallen. On July 9, reports from Gettysburg finally arrived. Lee offered his resignation. It was refused.

Davis somehow rallied himself and set about managing the arguments over who was to blame for the two major defeats and, soon afterwards, for the loss of Arkansas and his home state of Mississippi. Davis suffered the indignity of his home being taken and ransacked by a marauding Northern regiment. With the Union forces doing little to capitalize on their victory in the east but still pushing hard in the west, Davis stuck with generals who were being viciously criticized. He reorganized the Army of Tennessee and moved troops and respected commanders to shore up that threatened sector. A tour of western cities and camps helped calm complaints and boost morale; but it would not last.

Southern cities continued to fall. By December, Tennessee was gone. Lincoln issued a Proclamation of Amnesty and Reconstruction that offered pardons to Southerners who would swear allegiance to the United States. Although only a few stepped up, the proclamation was yet another signal that the war was entering a new phase. Dwindling numbers of Southern recruits were unable to fill the gaps left by death, injury, illness, imprisonment and desertion. Soldiers were going hungry, as were the growing number of refugees. The army's uniforms and shoes were falling apart, and too many ammunition cases were empty. The value of Confederate dollars was continuing to plummet in the face of falling bond sales and rising inflation. Rampant counterfeiting made the situation worse. Despite England's neutrality proclamation that prohibited such activities, ships for some time had been built in England and smuggled out for the Confederate navy, but it looked as if future construction would be delayed and more ships might never be delivered.

Davis's cabinet was squabbling. The Confederate Congress reconvened in early January 1864, with speakers competing to see who could be most critical of the administration's handling of the war. Good news had become a stranger in Richmond. As options were weighed and desperate actions taken, two events and one man suggested that part of what might save the South would perhaps be to look north.[6]

THE EVENTS: JOHNSON'S ISLAND AND
THE *CHESAPEAKE* AFFAIR

Davis's new idea would be based on something Canadians already knew —
there were Confederates fighting their war from Canada. In early
November 1863, Canadian governor general Monck was told by an official at the British consul in Baltimore that Confederates in Montreal were
attempting to purchase two ships and use them to attack the Union prison
on Johnson's Island and liberate Confederate comrades. Johnson's Island
lay in Lake Erie, less than half a mile from Sandusky, Ohio, and housed
about two thousand prisoners. It was poorly designed, with bad drainage
and barracks that were fiery hot in summer and icy cold in winter.
Prisoners often ate rats to survive.[7] The island prison was protected only
by a few soldiers, Erie's waters and the fourteen-gun, iron-clad steamer
Michigan. The *Michigan* had plied the Great Lakes since 1822, serving as
a recruiting vessel and a training ship for naval artillery personnel. In
1855, 1857 and again in 1861, British authorities had complained that it
violated the letter and spirit of the 1817 Rush-Bagot Agreement, which
limited the number and size of ships on the lakes and the power of the
armaments they could carry. The protests were ignored.[8]

Monck investigated the jail break rumours and found that there was
a legitimate cause for concern. On November 11, he so informed British
minister in Washington, Lord Lyons, who told Secretary of State Seward.
Warnings went to the prison and Northern governors, and the Johnson's
Island guard was enhanced. The *Michigan* was moved closer. Canadian
militia and British regulars were moved to protect the Welland Canal and
major ports on the Canadian side of Lake Erie. Canadian premier John
Sandfield Macdonald (no relation to Liberal-Conservative party leader
John A. Macdonald), who had taken office in May 1862, went to Buffalo
to consult with its mayor and Department of the East commander General
John Dix about what other precautions could be taken.

When the Johnson's Island attack failed to happen, newspapers and
officials on both sides of the border speculated as to whether the preparations had unnerved the Confederate conspirators, or whether Monck had

made the whole thing up to curry favour with the Lincoln administration.[9] Seward sent a commissioner to Quebec to speak with Monck. The governor general insisted that the information upon which he acted was from a reliable source—but he refused to reveal that source.

Though questioned by many, Monck had already earned grudging respect from Confederate leaders. Confederate secretary of the navy Stephen Mallory had told Davis of Monck's diligence, noting that back in July 1861 he had sent sixty-seven men to Canada to organize an expedition from Canada into the North, but that Monck had proved himself a man of strength and principle when he intervened to stop it.[10] Canadians seemed proud that Monck had prevented the Johnson's Island raid; even the pro-South *Toronto Leader* praised his swift action.[11] Much of the Northern press was similarly pleased, with the *New York Times* echoing most others in lauding Monck for what it called a "thoroughly friendly act."[12] Other papers offered no quarter and criticized Canadians and Maritimers for being too soft in allowing Confederates to operate so freely in their cities in the first place.[13]

In the days that followed, a number of newspapers fed a new and growing frenzy arising from reports of Confederates sweeping over the border and invading Northern cities.[14] A large group of armed people gathered in Buffalo to protest against the authorities who they claimed had been negligent in defending them. General Dix recommended to Seward that more troops be placed along the border and that fortifications be augmented and new ones constructed. Seward decided to wait.[15] Northern governors called up militias and demanded that Lincoln send troops to protect their ports.

Concerns about dangers from Canada were amplified by the *Chesapeake* affair. The Union steamer *Chesapeake* left New York on December 5, 1863. Two days later, off the coast of Cape Cod, her captain and crew were swarmed by seventeen young passengers who took the ship. The chief engineer was killed and the captain wounded. After brief landings at Mount Desert and Grand Manan islands, the pirates took the *Chesapeake* to Saint John, New Brunswick, for coal. Some of passengers were allowed to row to shore and the chief engineer's body was weighted and thrown into the bay.

News of the *Chesapeake*'s capture spread quickly. Newspapers on both sides of the border demanded action.[16] American consuls in New Brunswick, Nova Scotia and Canada were alerted that Union ships had been sent orders to pursue and capture the *Chesapeake*. It was established that the pirates were led by twenty-three-year-old John Braine, who had spent time in a Union prison for activities perpetrated in the name of a secret society called the Knights of the Golden Circle. Upon his release, he had moved to New Brunswick, where he met Canadian Vernon Locke, who had a letter of marque signed by Confederate Secretary of State Judah Benjamin. The letter had been written for a third man and for a ship called the *Retribution*, but it had been enough for Locke and Braine to concoct a plan. They would take the *Chesapeake*, rename it the *Retribution*, and then steam it to Bermuda, where it would be offered to the Confederate navy operating there.

With more and more publicity and less and less coal, the *Chesapeake*'s crew grew desperate. Braine jumped ship near Petite Rivière, Nova Scotia, and, with the help of sympathetic locals, he escaped arrest and made his way to Halifax. With a shrinking crew, the *Chesapeake* carried on, hugging the coast, to LaHave, still searching for coal. Two Union warships, the *Ella and Anna* and the *Dacotah*, were in hot pursuit. In Sambro Harbour, the *Dacotah* captured the *Chesapeake* and a Canadian ship called the *Investigator*, which had arrived to refuel her. The crew, including Nova Scotians Alexander and William Henry and John Wade, were put in irons and the *Chesapeake* was towed into Halifax's inner harbour.

With the ships bobbing just off shore, American secretary of the navy Gideon Welles sent a telegram ordering that the *Chesapeake* be turned over to the Canadians, but he said nothing of the prisoners. Nova Scotia's provincial secretary Charles Tupper and lieutenant-governor Doyle demanded that the ship and prisoners be immediately released, as the American captain had flagrantly violated international law and Canadian and British neutrality. Tupper advised Doyle that if the demands were not met, the Halifax batteries should fire upon the *Dacotah*.[17] Meanwhile, a crowd of about one hundred and fifty gathered on Queen's Wharf became irate when word spread that the Henry brothers and Wade were being held in irons.

American vice-consul at Halifax, Nathaniel Gunnison, had obtained a warrant for John Wade's arrest and stood on the pier with a Halifax police officer ready to serve it. They watched with trepidation, surrounded by roiling Haligonians, as Wade was rowed to shore. As the little boat neared, the crowd surged forward. Guns were drawn. In the melée that ensued, the officer and diplomat were surrounded and threatened, and Wade was helped to escape in another boat. In the confusion, the Henrys escaped as well.

The *New York Herald* reported on the "Halifax Riot" and called the city's people and officials "Blue Noses—men with the cold blood and feeble circulation of reptiles."[18] Gunnison sent a telegram to Seward explaining that Nova Scotia officials had done little to stop the people of Halifax from helping Wade and the Henry brothers to escape, and that Braine was being hailed as a hero in the city's pubs, with nothing being done to arrest him.

Seward sought to defuse the affair by reporting that the *Dacotah*'s captain had acted without orders. He claimed Lincoln had promised that the captain would be reprimanded for entering foreign waters and for his treatment of the prisoners.[19] The incident soon faded from the headlines.

The trials of those involved dragged on for over a year. It was discovered that Alexander Keith[*] of Halifax, who had played a lead role in helping Wade to escape, had been acting for some time as a Confederate agent. Papers were produced which proved he had been involved in purchasing twelve thousand muskets to be shipped to the South. It would be three months before the *Chesapeake* was returned to Portland.

The Johnson's Island and *Chesapeake* incidents demonstrated both the degree to which Canadian, Maritime, British and American officials understood how quickly a small incident could explode into a new *Trent* crisis, with potentially catastrophic consequences, and how adroit they had become at the diplomacy needed to address them. Suspicion, distrust

---

* *Keith's uncle, also Alexander, was a former mayor of Halifax and also a successful brewer.*

and rancour remained nonetheless. American consul James Howard, in a dispatch to Seward, described Canadians as "stupidly bad," "rotten rubbish" and "the dregs of society." And worse: "Any notorious offender may murder the Governor . . . of Massachusetts, may take the steamer to this province, and walk the streets of St. John . . . with impunity, there being no power to arrest him for an offense within the Extradition Treaty."[20]

In London, American minister Adams met with Foreign Secretary Russell to express disappointment with the British and Canadian governments for allowing Confederate activity in Canadian cities. Russell explained that with the British proclamation of neutrality, its colonies were open to both Americans and Confederates.[21] Adams reported the conversation to Seward, adding—perhaps unnecessarily—that he saw Confederate activity in Canada as a Southern tactic meant to disrupt relations between the North and Britain in the hope of dragging Britain into the war.[22]

THE MAN: CLEMENT VALLANDIGHAM

Ohio congressman Clement Vallandigham was a Copperhead. The loosely organized group's name was taken from the venomous snake, known for striking without warning. Copperheads believed that neither the hope of reuniting the Union nor the freeing of slaves was worth the Civil War's expenditure of blood and treasure, and so negotiations with the Confederacy should be undertaken to end it. Many Copperheads were also motivated by a desire to rebuild the shattered Democratic Party and nominate a candidate who could defeat Lincoln in November 1864. The movement also attracted those in the Midwest who believed national economic policies were geared to eastern needs and felt themselves beyond the pale of Richmond's passions and Washington's power. If peace could not be quickly negotiated, or their outlier ideas respectfully considered, the Copperheads would seek the establishment of a new, independent republic made up of Ohio, Indiana and Illinois. Lincoln said he feared the Copperhead movement, the "fire in the rear," as he called it, more than military failure.[23]

Vallandigham became one of the most effective leaders of the Copperhead movement. He had entered Congress in 1858 opposed to the march to war. When war began, he delivered fiery anti-war speeches at home and from the House floor. By 1862, he had been defeated when his district was gerrymandered away, but he continued to speak his mind at well-attended peace rallies throughout the North. His speeches became increasingly popular and radical—and, to some, treasonous.

On May 1, 1863, after an especially passionate speech at Mount Vernon, Ohio, Vallandigham returned to his home in Dayton. That night, with orders from Union general Ambrose Burnside, soldiers pounded on his front door. He jumped from his bed to a window and fired two pistol shots over the soldiers' heads. Men burst through a side door and, amid his wife's screams, he was dragged out and to jail. Vallandigham was charged with treason and there was talk of execution. Lincoln became involved and decided that the political costs and constitutional questions involved in proceeding were not worth the noose, so he arranged to have Vallandigham escorted under a flag of truce to Murfreesboro, where he was released to Confederate general Braxton Bragg. Lincoln quipped that Vallandigham's head could go where his heart already was.[24]

Not really needing this new problem, Bragg arranged papers and transport for Vallandigham, who made his way to Wilmington, North Carolina, boarded a blockade runner to Bermuda, and then took a transport to Nova Scotia. Word had leaked of his arrival, and a crowd welcomed him to the Halifax docks with three cheers to Jefferson Davis and another round to the Confederacy.[25]

Vallandigham received an equally kind reception at Quebec City. At a dinner in his honour at the prestigious Stadacona Club, he was introduced to Canada's political and business elite, including John A. Macdonald. On July 15, Vallandigham arrived in Niagara Falls and checked into a two-room suite at Clifton House, just blocks from the town's natural wonder. The hotel had become the centre of Confederate activity in the lively border town. The next day he met with several Americans, including Joseph Warren of the *Buffalo Courier*, well-known Illinois Copperhead Richard Merrick and Indiana congressman Daniel Voorhees.[26] Vallandigham gave them copies of a speech in which he accepted his nomination as the

Democratic Party's candidate for the governor of Ohio. He would run his campaign from Canada and use it to promote the Copperhead agenda.

Over the next few weeks, hundreds of American politicians and Copperhead leaders, as well as American and Canadian newspaper reporters, sat with America's most notorious candidate. His presence in Canada and his incendiary views split public opinion. The *Toronto Leader* spoke highly of Vallandigham and his Copperhead goals, calling him "intelligent, amiable and a martyr to his cause."[27] George Brown, on the other hand, set out in his *Globe* to insult and vilify Vallandigham for a project designed to hurt the United States. Brown argued that his presence and actions in Canada threatened to bring American troops across the border. Vallandigham wrote harsh letters in response, and the ensuing duel of words lasted for weeks.[28]

Among the Canadians who visited Vallandigham was influential Montreal member of the legislature Thomas D'Arcy McGee. The short, stocky, hard-drinking and charismatic McGee, who had a brother serving in the Union army, was on a speaking tour of the Maritimes and Canada, promoting the idea of unifying Britain's colonies into a single union in order to build railways and offer greater protection from aggressive American expansionism.[29] At McGee's invitation, Vallandigham travelled to Drummondville, Canada East, where on August 16 he addressed a crowd of about two thousand. A few days later, McGee introduced him from the floor of the Canadian legislature. The next day, Vallandigham took a chair to the speaker's left, an honour rarely bestowed, to hear passionate speeches relating to Canada's position on America and the Civil War. Most notably, he heard McGee warn about United States's preparations to send one hundred thousand troops to invade Canada, with the goal of splitting Canada East and West as the first step to annexation.[30]

Back in Niagara Falls, Vallandigham continued his gubernatorial campaign by employing the well-established Confederate communication network. Routes from Wilmington to Bermuda to Halifax, and overland routes through Canada East and West had been used from the outset of the war by Confederate officials to communicate with Europe and each other. Codes had been created. In a number of cities, drop spots had been established for the exchange of documents and messages. Couriers such as Robert E. Lee's uncle, Cassius Lee, for example, lived in Hamilton and moved freely throughout Canada and the Maritimes, helping to provide the lifeblood of communications to the Confederacy.

Vallandigham soon discovered that the owner of Clifton House had become annoyed by the number of men tramping through his establishment and tired of the negative attention that his famous guest was bringing to his business. The Copperhead leader was asked to leave. On August 24, Vallandigham and his family moved to a two-room suite at Hirons House in Windsor. On the day of their arrival, the Detroit River teemed with politicians, newspapermen and admirers plying its waters to meet with the famous candidate-in-exile.

Secretary of State Seward's spies reported on Vallandigham's words and actions, and Lincoln and the Republican political establishment did all they could to frustrate his electoral bid. Money was forwarded to Ohio and other states with credible Copperhead candidates. Anti-Copperhead, pro-Republican rallies were organized, with the largest taking place at Madison Square Garden. Lincoln approved fifteen-day furloughs for soldiers wanting to return home to vote.

Lincoln spent much of October 13, 1863 pacing the floor, awaiting word on the mid-term election results. Finally, news arrived that Republican John Brough had defeated Vallandigham in Ohio by more than one hundred thousand votes. Lincoln was ecstatic and rushed off a telegram exclaiming, "Glory to God in the highest. Ohio has saved the Nation."[31] Copperhead candidates lost in every state but New Jersey. Vallandigham and the Copperheads were defeated but not beaten—they would be back. Meanwhile, Jefferson Davis had a Canadian trick up his sleeve.

JACOB THOMPSON AND THE CANADA PLAN

For Jefferson Davis, the Johnson's Island and *Chesapeake* incidents, along with Vallandigham and his Copperhead movement, offered sparks of opportunity amid the dark desperation of the spring of 1864. They led him to wonder if the Confederate presence in Canada and Canadian sympathies for the South could be used to establish a "second front" that could operate from Canadian cities and hurt the North—irritate it, distract it, and cost it time, energy and money.[32] Perhaps agents could continue attempts that had already been made to gather Confederate soldiers who had escaped Northern prisons and were living in Canadian and Maritime cities, and bring them back to active duty. Confederate agents in Canada could encourage support from secret societies and Copperheads to make Lincoln a one-term president. They could help coordinate efforts to create a separate northwest republic that could negotiate an end to the war, with the Confederacy and slavery intact. They might even instigate a Union invasion of Canada, which could lead to an American-British war with all the benefits that happy event would accrue to the South.

Davis consulted broadly and earned cabinet and congressional support for the secret second front. The Confederate Congress approved five million dollars. If the Canada Plan were to work, a special man would need to lead it. Davis and Secretary of War James Sedden and Secretary of State Judah Benjamin agreed that Jacob Thompson fit the bill perfectly.[33]

Jacob Thompson was born in Leaside, North Carolina, on May 15, 1810. He was a smart, witty, ambitious and ruggedly handsome man who had graduated from the University of North Carolina, taught at the university for two years, and then earned a law degree. His brother was a doctor who moved west to exploit the excitement and opportunities of the opening frontier. Thompson joined his brother in Mississippi and established a thriving law practice. At twenty-eight, he married sixteen-year-old Catherine Jones, whose father was a wealthy plantation owner. With his savings and Catherine's huge dowry, they built a large estate near Oxford, about seventy miles south of Memphis. It soon grew to three estates that together earned them a substantial annual income.

Thompson was always interested in politics and was elected to the House of Representatives in 1835 and then re-elected four times. In 1856 Thompson volunteered to put his ambitions for the Senate aside to allow fellow Mississippian Jefferson Davis to run. The two became friends as he helped Davis win his seat. In 1857, Thompson was plucked from private life to serve as President James Buchanan's secretary of the interior. While working in Washington, he came to know Lincoln, Stanton, Seward and many of the others with whom he would later struggle. With Lincoln's election in November 1860, Thompson became increasingly outspoken in his support of Southern causes, and two months later he resigned.

In 1863, Thompson was elected to the Mississippi legislature. He also served as a colonel in the Confederate Army, fought at Shiloh as one of General Beauregard's dispatch riders and then served as inspector general for General Pemberton. In the summer of 1863, a Union regiment at Vicksburg was working just above the mouth of the Yazoo River when it was interrupted by a boatload of Confederates that floated into them beneath a white flag. Thompson was recognized and taken to a Union ship, and General Grant was summoned. Grant briefly interviewed Thompson, quite correctly concluded that he was a spy, but also that nothing of value had been learned. Grant ordered him and the others released.[34]

Thompson had maintained a regular and warm correspondence with Jefferson Davis, offering unsolicited advice on a number of matters. In late March 1864, Davis asked Thompson to meet him in Richmond. With Secretary of State Benjamin in attendance, Davis outlined the mission and its overall goals, but made it clear that specific tactics would be up to Thompson himself. Davis told him that University of Virginia law professor James Holcombe had been sent to Halifax in February to test the viability of the Canada Plan and to see if arrangements could be made to help Confederates wishing to return south. Upon his arrival, Holcombe had informed Monck of what he was up to, and affirmed that he would be careful to observe British neutrality.[35] He got word to Confederates in the Maritimes, Toronto and Montreal, and arranged for several to get home before he returned to Richmond with the advice that Davis's idea for the establishment of a larger Confederate presence in Canada was a good one.

Davis arranged for Thompson to have one million dollars in cash to use at his discretion. In an intentionally vague letter dated April 27, Davis wrote to him: "Confiding special trust in your zeal, discretion and patriotism, I hereby direct you to proceed at once to Canada; there to carry out the instruction you have received from me verbally, in such manner as shall seem most likely to conduce the furtherance of the interests of the Confederate States of America which have been entrusted to you."[36]

With the understanding that Thompson would lead the mission, Davis appointed Holcombe and former Alabama senator Clement Clay as co-commissioners. Holcombe left first; Thompson and Clay departed on May 3. The two ran the Union blockade from Wilmington to Bermuda and then boarded a British ship for Halifax. Thompson and Clay stopped at the city's Saverly House, where Southern sympathizers congregated with Confederate soldiers who had either deserted or escaped from Northern prisons. There were similarly well-known spots around the Maritimes, including Hesslein's in Saint John and Fredericton's Barker House. Young Southern patriots mixed openly with adventurers, opportunists, prostitutes and spies.

Spies had been a part of the conflict between the North and South from the day Fort Sumter's cannon had announced the war's arrival. Many were efficient and provided information that altered polices and battles, while others were bumblers who were easily fooled, offered information that could be gleaned from newspapers, or simply got in the way. Many were women. All were amateurs, for no professional intelligence agencies existed in North America. As the war progressed, more spies openly walked the streets of Richmond and Washington and, as demonstrated by the exploits of Sarah Emma Edmonds, passed through enemy lines with relative ease. Spies also plied their trade with varying degrees of success in London, Paris and Canadian cities and towns.

As early as June 1861, Lyons and the Duke of Newcastle had been firm with Governor General Head and Seward in stating that the use of "secret agents" in Canada was intolerable. Newcastle told Head that he should never meet with such people and that he should do all he could to find them and get rid of them.[37] As the George Ashmun case revealed, Seward ignored the warning. That American spying continued was made evident on November 14, 1861, when Lyons wrote to recently appointed governor general Monck, warning that "a perfectly reliable source" had informed him that three parties were in Canada making drawings of fortifications and naval defences. The spies had visited Toronto, Montreal and Quebec City, and Monck was to find and deport them and all other spies he could find.[38] However, Monck was as flummoxed as Head in his attempts to shut down the clandestine American activities.

Part of the spy operation involved a rapid increase in the number of American consuls in Canada and the Maritimes and their expanding mandates. Until the war, consuls had primarily handled trade issues and assisted American citizens while promoting emigration to America. In January 1862, Seward responded to a letter from Congress admitting that consuls had been ordered also to ferret out Confederate activities and report on sympathy for and assistance to the South.[39]

Seward's forthright admission of his government's secret operations drew a predictable reaction. Monck had just approved new consular openings at Kingston and St. Catharines and held a list of requests for more at small border towns.[40] Seward continued to request the establishment of even more consuls, arguing through Lyons that they were needed to stop smuggling. Lyons reported to London and Monck that he knew that Seward was not being truthful.[41] New consuls were nonetheless opened.

It was in the midst of this intrigue, on May 30, 1864, that Thompson and his co-commissioner, Clay, arrived in Montreal. Thompson established headquarters at the St. Lawrence Hall—a large, ornate and well-appointed hotel that offered great service, tremendous meals and a discreet staff. It was so openly pro-Confederate that it bragged of having the only bar in the city that served mint juleps. Montreal's Donegana Hotel was home to hundreds of other Confederates. Many nearby boarding houses also became acquainted with the warmth of Southern charm. Thompson opened a bank account at Montreal's Bank of Ontario and left Clay there with $93,000 to organize operations. Clay had fallen ill on the trip north. His health and a sad yearning to be home with his wife was already limiting his effectiveness, so Holcombe remained in Montreal to help him while Thompson moved on to Toronto.

Thompson took a suite of rooms at Toronto's Queen's Hotel. The Queen's was the city's most luxurious hotel, boasting an elevator, a large dining room offering fine wines and cuisine, running water in all of its well-appointed rooms, and from its Front Street location a stunning view of the harbourfront.* By the spring of 1864, the Queen's had become infamous as the centre of Confederate activity in Canada West. Thompson was welcomed by the hundred or so Confederates who had rooms at or near the grand hotel. He quickly learned to spot local officials and Union detectives and newly arrived Confederates, conspicuous with their leathery tans, worn clothes and distinctive accents.

Toronto's George Denison was among the many Canadians whom Thompson came to know and rely upon. Denison came from a wealthy and influential family. He was well educated, a lawyer, a one-time city alderman, and founder of both the Canadian Rifle Association and the Queen's Plate horse race. Denison was also a militia lieutenant colonel and commandant who used his inherited wealth and political power to advocate for increased support for the militia, with special attention on cavalry. His 1st Toronto Independent Troop of Cavalry became the governor general's body guard.

Denison regularly visited Thompson at the Queen's and often welcomed him and his compatriots to his large estate for dinners and quiet afternoons.[42] Denison later wrote: "I was a strong friend of the Southern refugees who were exiled in our country, and I treated them with the hospitality due to unfortunate strangers driven from their homes."[43] Denison was concerned that Thompson and his people were beset by Union agents who hindered their efforts, and he did all he could to help. He was to help a great deal, and paid a handsome price for doing so.

---

* The Queen's was torn down in 1928 to make room for the even more stately Royal York Hotel.

THE NIAGARA PEACE INITIATIVE

Throughout his time in Canada, Thompson juggled a number of people, plans and plots. One of his first initiatives began with meetings in Montreal and Toronto about an idea to distract the North with the intention of influencing the upcoming presidential election. Thompson met with Clay, who in turn met with Copperheads William "Colorado" Jewett and George Sanders. Jewett was an influential Copperhead leader who had been travelling throughout the Midwest for over a year, stirring up support for the movement. He had come to Canada in the fall of 1863, delivering speeches in which he urged listeners to exert pressure on Britain to help negotiate an end to the war. He conducted a number of interviews with Canadian newspaper editors, to whom he regularly submitted open letters.[44] Following the tour, he offered his services to Thompson.

George Sanders was the former editor of New York's *Democratic Review*. He was a navy purchasing agent before the war and had been arranging arms purchases for the Confederacy since the first battle at Bull Run. Davis recalled him and then sent him to Toronto to help Thompson, with specific instructions to create support for the Copperhead peace movement. He had arrived on June 1, 1864. Sanders was witty, eccentric, and alternatively an infuriating and charming man, who became an instant hit on the Montreal cocktail circuit.[45]

With Thompson's encouragement, Holcombe, Clay, Jewett and Sanders devised a plan whereby a meeting would be held and a framework for a peace settlement established. For it to succeed, they needed a Northerner with gravitas. When their first choices did not work out, they involved newspaper publisher Horace Greeley. Jewett and Sanders told Greeley that they were fully empowered by Jefferson Davis to negotiate a peace arrangement with Lincoln, and only needed a well-positioned Northern intermediary such as him to begin the process. Greeley bought the ruse and within days welcomed Jewett to his New York office.[46] The con was on.

Greeley was an influential Republican Party leader and friend of William Seward, who had founded the *New Yorker* and then the unashamedly partisan *New York Tribune*. His opinions were read and considered in the United States, Canada, the Maritimes and around the world. Most famously, on August 20, 1862, Greeley had filled the *Tribune*'s front page with an open letter to Lincoln entitled "The Prayer of Twenty Millions." The letter criticized Lincoln for his conduct of the war and most blisteringly for his having missed the opportunity it offered to free all the slaves in Union-held territory. Lincoln had responded two days later with an open letter of his own in which he stated his goal for the war more clearly than he had ever done, arguing that his first and only objective was the preservation of the Union with the eradication of slavery simply a possible tactic to attain that end.

On July 7, 1864, Greeley wrote to Lincoln about his having been contacted by rebels in Niagara Falls, Canada. He detailed all that they promised and wanted. Greeley had obviously given thought to Jewett's conversation, however, for he told Lincoln, "Of course I do not endorse Jewett's position averment that his friends at the Falls have 'full power' from J.D., though I do not doubt that he thinks they have."[47] Greeley argued that a meeting should nonetheless take place. Pressuring Lincoln to agree, Greeley wrote: "I therefore venture to remind you that our bleeding, bankrupt, almost dying country, also longs for peace—shudders at the prospect of fresh conscriptions, of further wholesale devastations, and of new rivers of human blood; and a wide-spread conviction that the Government and its prominent supporters are not anxious for peace." Greeley listed what he thought would be six conditions for peace. The first two were: "The Union is restored and declared perpetual. . . . Slavery is utterly and forever abolished throughout the same."[48]

Lincoln shared Greeley's doubts about the Confederates in Canada but could not afford to be seen as lacking interest in ending the war, and so he responded that he would meet anyone sent from Davis to discuss peace. He echoed Greeley's note, however, and wrote that any discussions would be based on the restoration of the Union and the abolition of slavery.[49] Excited by this even tepid support, Greeley abandoned his reserve and wrote to Lincoln that he had become convinced that Clay, Sanders and Thompson were fully empowered by Davis to carry on negotiations. Lincoln displayed impatience with a rather sharp response stating that he did not want another letter but to meet the men. Lincoln offered safe conduct for Thompson, Clay, Holcombe and Sanders to come to Washington.[50]

The president sent his personal secretary, Major John Hay, to Greeley's New York office on July 16 to move the process along. Through Hay, Lincoln urged Greeley to proceed and reiterated his offer of safe passage to Washington for the Confederates. With this support, Greeley took a train to the American side of the falls.

Greeley settled into a suite of rooms, surrounded by reporters from his own and other papers. Over the next three days, he sent cables and then crossed the suspension bridge to meet with Holcombe and Sanders at Clifton House on the Canadian side. Thompson remained in Toronto. Greeley told them of Lincoln's offer of safe passage and tried to persuade them to return with him to Washington. The Confederates balked. With each meeting, Greeley felt his hopes fade. Sanders finally admitted that they were, in fact, not accredited by Davis and only wanted to hear what Lincoln had to say on the matter of peace.

That evening, Hay arrived at Greeley's hotel with a handwritten letter from the president dated July 18. Addressed "To Whom It May Concern," the brief letter said:

> Any proposition which embraces the restoration of peace, the integrity of the whole Union and the abandonment of slavery, and which comes by and with an authority that can control the armies now at war against the United States, will be received and considered by the Executive Government of the United States, and will be met by liberal terms on other substantial and collateral points, and the bearer thereof shall have safe conduct both ways.[51]

Greeley worried not only that he had been duped by Thompson's Confederates but that he had erred in not being clear with them from the outset regarding these preconditions. He and Hay argued over the next step and finally agreed to take Lincoln's letter to Clifton House the next day.

Sanders and Holcombe were aghast, or at least feigned being so. They told Hay and Greeley that Lincoln's pre-conditions were unacceptable and interpreted them to mean that the president was not serious about wanting peace. The talks ended in acrimony and accusations. Greeley left for New York. Hay stayed another day and met Sanders and Holcombe again, but then he left too with the realization that the entire episode had been a ploy.

Over the next several weeks, newspapers in the North, South and Canada carried articles about what were widely interpreted as botched peace negotiations. Clay sent an open letter to the Associated Press that was printed in a number of newspapers. He spoke of how Holcombe and Sanders had arrived ready and able to negotiate peace but that they had been hoodwinked by a double-crossing president who wanted only war. Clay also wrote accusingly of the process: "a rude withdrawal of a courteous overture for negotiation at a moment it was likely to be accepted. . . . If there be any citizen of the Confederate States who has clung to the hope that peace is possible, Lincoln's terms will strip from their eyes the last film of such delusions."[52] Lincoln's letter had handed Thompson's men an outstanding propaganda opportunity.

Greeley obtained Lincoln's permission to publish many of the letters that had passed between him, the president, and Thompson's men. It did not help. The story of what happened changed with each new telling, but a consensus developed that Lincoln had begun to bargain in good faith and then, having suddenly changed his mind, presented preconditions that he knew the South could never accept.[53] The newspaper coverage smeared both Greeley and Lincoln, with the editor appearing to be a naive and amateur fiddler and the president a cold warmonger, uninterested in peace.

Even loyal Republican and Lincoln supporters criticized the president's handling of Thompson's Niagara Falls initiative because the "To Whom It May Concern" letter clearly stated that the war was being fought not just for the restoration of the Union but also for the emancipation of slaves.[54] Critics were, of course, ignoring Lincoln's Gettysburg Address and Emancipation Proclamation. Henry Raymond, editor of the *New York Times* and chairman of the Republican Party's National Committee, nonetheless told Lincoln that after the Canadian meetings, the electoral tide had turned against him and the party. If elections were held soon, he told the president on August 22, he would be defeated and the party would lose in Congress and in states across the North.[55]

Thompson's Niagara Falls initiative also led members of Lincoln's cabinet to begin conspiring against him and testing the waters for a run at the Republican presidential nomination. On August 19, Thompson met in Toronto with Judge Jeremiah Black, who had been sent by Lincoln's secretary of war, Edwin Stanton, to ask his opinion about the strength of the Copperhead movement and whether a new Republican contender in 1864 could be nominated if he advocated a negotiated peace with slavery left untouched.[56]

Lincoln told New York secretary of state Chauncey Depew that he had suspected from the outset that Davis had not accredited Thompson's men in Canada and that the negotiations would end in failure. With the political fallout mounting, and then Greeley making a public display of having pushed him to act, Lincoln was pressured to make a statement. He confided to Depew, "The attention of the whole country and of the army centred on those negotiations at Niagara Falls, and to stop the harm they were doing I recalled Mr. Greeley and issued my proclamation 'To Whom It May Concern.'. . . Their mission was subterfuge. But they made Greeley believe in them, and the result is that he is still attacking me for needlessly prolonging the war for purposes of my own."[57] Lincoln decided to say nothing.

Thompson had won, for Lincoln had been embarrassed, Northern political fissures widened and the Copperhead movement boosted. Lincoln asked his cabinet: "Does anyone doubt that the only thing the Confederate agents were authorised to do was to assist in selecting and arranging a candidate and a platform for the Chicago convention?"[58] He was partly right. The Niagara Falls fiasco would indeed reverberate at the Democratic Party convention in Chicago, but a great deal would happen first.

THE *PHILO PARSONS* ON LAKE ERIE

Confederate Captain Charles Cole had a chequered military career. He had served with General Nathan Bedford Forrest, been captured and imprisoned. He then escaped and, although he never mentioned it, was also expelled from the army on account of theft and dishonesty.[59] In the summer of 1864 he was in Sandusky, Ohio, on his way to hide among other Confederates in Canada, when he heard of Thompson's operations. He wrote to Thompson in July, offering a new twist on an old idea. Cole's plan was to steal the Union steamer *Michigan*, which protected the Johnson's Island prison, and then use it to spring the two thousand or so imprisoned Confederates, who could then be organized to launch raids from Canada that would wreak havoc on the North.

Thompson warmed to Cole's idea and asked him travel Lake Erie to become acquainted with the schedules and security arrangements of various harbours. He was also to ingratiate himself with the *Michigan*'s captain and crew. Thompson sent Cole four thousand dollars, which he quickly spent on a luxury hotel suite and new clothes for himself and his girlfriend in order to assume the guise of a wealthy oil man.[60]

Confederate navy captain John Beall had worked under the direction of Confederate navy secretary Stephen Mallory to help build a volunteer navy of eighteen ships that acted like a secret coast guard. He had lived in Toronto for a few months in 1862 and in the spring of 1864 had returned. Thompson contacted him about Cole's plan and he was soon recruiting twenty Canadian-based Confederates to execute it. Their mission would be to take over the American steamer *Philo Parsons* at Detroit, release her crew, and then go on to Sandusky, where they would pull alongside the *Michigan*, on which Cole would be waiting. Beall and Cole would then coordinate efforts to capture the *Michigan* and move her quickly to the suddenly vulnerable prison. It all made sense. Thompson gave $25,000 to a courier named Bennett Young, who took it to Beall at Buffalo's Genesee House. Beall met with Cole at Sandusky, and then stole back across to the border to Windsor to finalize his plans.

One of Beall's recruits was ammunitions agent Bennett Burley.

Burley, or Burleigh as he was known in Canada, had come from his native Scotland to try to sell a new underwater mine to the Confederacy, but the mine did not work. He had then become a member of Beall's privateers and, for the last number of months, had been living in Canada, where he orchestrated the purchase and delivery of ammunition being manufactured for the Confederacy in a small foundry in Guelph.[61]

Cole connived for several weeks, befriending the *Michigan*'s crew. He was often on the ship and several times hosted generous dinners for the captain and officers at his hotel or on a rented ship. He also visited a number of Johnson's Island prisoners and told those he trusted of the date of the *Michigan* highjacking and jailbreak.

On September 18, Beall boarded the *Philo Parsons* in Detroit. He somehow talked the captain into making an unscheduled stop to pick up a group of young men and then sixteen more men came on board at Amherstburg, carrying a large box and some rope. At 4:00 p.m., after stopping again at Kelley's Island, the box was opened, the men armed themselves, and Beall informed the captain that he was commandeering the ship. Many heavy objects were thrown overboard to make it faster. Beall ordered it to steam at top speed for Middle Bass Island, about ten miles from Johnson's Island, to gather wood for fuel. Passengers and crew were put ashore.

A small steamer called the *Island Queen* then unexpectedly approached, and a half-hour skirmish ensued. Shots were fired and the ship's engineer hit in the face before Beall's crew prevailed. Beal declared the *Island Queen* taken in the name of the Confederacy. Its crew and passengers, including twenty-six unarmed Union soldiers from the 13th Ohio Regiment who had put up a gallant struggle, were put ashore. A couple of men were held back as potential hostages. A passenger was found to have eighty thousand dollars on him, but Beall allowed him to keep it. The *Island Queen*, too small to be of much military use, was scuttled and sunk. By then, it was 9:00 p.m., the appointed hour, and from a safe distance, Beall and his men watched the *Michigan* and awaited its signal. And they waited.

Cole had been betrayed. On the day it was all to happen, he had invited the *Michigan*'s officers to dinner but, with the meal and drugged wine ready to be served, a group of soldiers burst in and arrested him. Cole was charged with being a spy and locked up on Johnson's Island.

Not knowing Cole's fate, Beall ordered the *Philo Parsons* closer to Sandusky where, under the light of the full moon, he was startled to see the *Michigan*'s lights ablaze and crew standing ready on deck. Seventeen of Beall's twenty crewmen promptly mutinied. A deal was made and the ship turned back into the lake. Most of the crew and the hostages were let off at Fighting Island in the Detroit River. The ship then steamed to Windsor. The remaining crew stole everything of value, including a piano, and then scuttled the ship.

Burley fled back to the foundry in Guelph. Beall took a train to Toronto and reported to Thompson at the Queen's Hotel. Thompson told him that the *Michigan–Philo Parsons* escapade was front-page news in Canada and Northern states. On Thompson's advice, Beall decided that it was time for a hunting trip and promptly left for the Muskokas, north of the city.

When informed of Cole's fate, Thompson wrote a letter of protest to Colonel Hill, Johnson Island's commandant of post. He argued that Cole had done nothing wrong and that it was illegal to hold him solely for being suspected of contemplating an illegal act. Further, Thompson argued, "If you can justly condemn Captain Cole as a spy, every soldier and officer of the United States coming within the armies or limits of the Confederate States could be tried and condemned as such. We admit your right to return him to prison as a recaptured prisoner, but any other punishment, in our judgment, would be against justice and the law."[62] Cole remained behind bars.

Not satisfied to stay in hiding, Beall sent an article to the *Toronto Leader* that sought to explain and justify his actions by directly addressing Canadians: "The United States is carrying on war on Lake Erie against the Confederate States (either by virtue of right or sufferance from you), by transportation of men and supplies on its waters; by confining Confederate prisoners on its islands, and lastly, by the presence of a 14-gun steamer patrolling its waters. The Confederates clearly have a right to retaliate, providing they can do so without infringing on your laws."[63]

Many American newspapers used the *Philo Parsons* episode to renew their anti-Canadian rhetoric. The *Detroit Tribune*, for instance, reported in an editorial that was reprinted in the *Globe*, "These pirates have grossly violated the rights of asylum to Canada, and if our neighbours were animated by one spark of generous humour they would feel insult that has been perpetrated as keenly as ourselves, but the bitter and senseless prejudice which has warped their feelings has also blunted every sense of honour and propriety."[64]

The bogus Niagara Falls peace initiative and then the *Philo Parsons* escapade led Union general John Dix to maintain an even closer eye on Thompson and his men. Shortly after the botched *Philo Parsons* incident, Dix wrote to Stanton, "That it is one of the chief purposes of the insurgents to advance their own cause by bringing about a rupture between the two countries through their agents and officers in Canada there can be no doubt."[65]

Lyons was in Quebec City visiting Governor General Monck when informed of the latest border troubles and was shaken by the thought that Thompson's actions might unravel years of his best efforts to maintain peace. He collapsed in bed for twenty-four hours.[66] Lyons was justifiably perturbed, for the *Philo Parsons* incident had ramifications far wider than merely military. American generals and Lincoln's cabinet questioned Canada's sincerity and its ability to patrol its border. British acting-minister to Washington Joseph Burnley, stepping up during Lyons's absence and subsequent illness, assured Seward and Russell that Monck was doing all he could to arrest the men responsible and to avoid future incidents.[67] The Americans were unconvinced. Seward called the *Philo Parsons* episode "hostile and piratical" and promised consequences.[68]

In September 1864, the number of American ships on the Great Lakes was increased. From Sandusky, Major General Hiscock wrote to Stanton, praising the fleet's growing numbers as well as the improved quality and armaments of individual ships. He noted the purpose of the action and who was to blame: "to prevent the rebels who find security in Canada from seizing steamers engaged in commerce and converting them into war vessels, with a few of which they may, if not prevented, do us incalculable mischief. . . . Ex-Secretary Thompson is employed in Canada in setting on foot expeditions of the most dangerous character."[69]

By early October, General Hooker had ordered another regiment to move north to guard Buffalo and Detroit. Dix ordered guns installed on five tug boats and sent them to guard critical ports, while extra funds were sent to expedite the construction of an armed revenue cutter fleet.* The additional ships were in plain violation of the 1817 Rush-Bagot Agreement. Burnley reminded Seward of the agreement and the importance to British-Canadian-American relations of abiding by it, but Seward was unmoved. He dryly replied to one of Burnley's letters of protest: "Any excess . . . which may thus be occasioned in the armament of United States vessels in that quarter over the limits fixed by the Arrangement of April 1817, will be temporary only, and as it has been made necessary by an emergency probably not then foreseen, may not be regarded as contrary to the spirit of the stipulations of that instrument."[70]

Thompson must have smiled as he read of each Union soldier, gun, ship and dollar deployed north rather than south. His individual operations may have been failing, but he was successfully distracting the enemy. His undertakings on the lakes were not finished, nor were a number of other initiatives that would soon come to fruition.

CHICAGO

The American peace movement, spearheaded by the anti-Lincoln machinations of Thompson and the Copperheads, had sputtered as the Union made successful military advances in 1863, but it was revived in the late spring of 1864, not by Union defeats but by the enormous prices paid for its victories. Lincoln had appointed Ulysses S. Grant his general-in-chief. Grant summoned the same determination that had earned his reputation in the west, and in May and early June fought important battles in his Overland Campaign: The Battle of the Wilderness, and battles at Spotsylvania and Cold Harbor. They were unprecedented in their

---

* *"Revenue cutter" was a term used to describe ships of a special fleet, later to become the Coast Guard.*

ferocity and cost the Union 55,000 casualties. With increasing numbers of Northerners questioning the price of victory and the profits of peace, hope for the Confederacy rose.

The Copperhead movement crept back into the headlines and brought Vallandigham, still in Canada, back to public attention. In February 1864, peace movement agitators Dr. Thomas Massey from Ohio and Harrison Dodd from Indiana had visited him in Windsor and brought news of the growing strength of secret organizations that were dedicated to ending the war. Secret societies had long been part of American life. The Order of American Knights had grown in the Midwest and recently changed its name to the Sons of Liberty, to claim a spiritual connection with the courageous activities of the American Revolution. Massey and Dodd told Vallandigham that the Sons of Liberty had three hundred thousand passionate members in Illinois, Indiana and Ohio. They were organizing themselves into county-based military units, each swearing their lives to defeating Lincoln in November in order to end the war. Vallandigham was further told that he had been elected to lead the Sons of Liberty as its Supreme Grand Commander, from his exile in Canada. He accepted, and there were soon rumours of his beginning a campaign for the Democratic presidential nomination.[71]

A few weeks later, Kentucky captain Thomas Hines met with Jefferson Davis. Hines was well respected for his cavalry exploits with Brigadier General John Hunt Morgan's brave and free-ranging regiment. Hines was a rather small, effeminate man but he showed great strength in the saddle, fortitude when captured and determined grit in working with Morgan and five other officers who tunnelled their way out of the Ohio Penitentiary. Hines had an idea. He told Davis he would work with Thompson and Vallandigham to coordinate Sons of Liberty regiments and Canadian-based Confederates to perpetrate prison breaks at Chicago's Camp Douglas and Johnson's Island. The new army would initiate a popular revolution to realize the Copperhead dream of ending the war and establishing a Midwest republic, with Chicago as its capital.

Davis approved the idea and Hines left for Toronto. Secretary of War James Sedden's written orders to Hines stated that he was "to proceed to

Canada through the U.S. . . . collecting any members of Morgan's command . . . in Canada and to employ them in any hostile operation against the United States consistent with neutral obligations in the British Provinces."[72] Hines was given access to two hundred bales of cotton, which he sold to finance his activities.

Hines met Thompson at the Queen's Hotel and they developed his idea into a plan. On June 9, Thompson sent Hines to Windsor to meet with Vallandigham, and two days later he joined them. Vallandigham bragged about his growing popularity among the people in Ohio and throughout the Northern states, and invited Thompson to join the Sons of Liberty.[73] Thompson accepted. Now that he was a member, Vallandigham was able to tell him of the 300,000 fellow members who were waiting for a signal to rise up and overthrow state governments in Missouri, Kentucky, Ohio, Indiana and Illinois, and replace them with provisional governments dedicated to peace. Thompson came onside and forwarded $500,000 from his Canadian account to bankroll the endeavour.[74]

Vallandigham left Windsor for Ohio to deliver a number of inflammatory speeches meant to build interest in the Copperhead cause and the Sons of Liberty plots. He also hoped to earn publicity by being arrested again. General Ambrose Burnside, head of the military's Ohio Department, had arrested him the first time and now refused to offer him the compliment of attention. Vallandigham was soon back in Canada.

Thompson reported to Davis on July 1 that the uprising would begin as scheduled in mid-July. He wrote: "Though intending this as a Western confederacy and demanding peace, if peace be not granted, then it shall be war. There are some choice spirits enlisted in this enterprise, and all that is needed for success is unflinching nerve. . . . In short, nothing but violence can terminate the war."[75] Hines reported to Davis that he expected success in simultaneous prison breaks at Chicago, Rock Island, Columbus, Indianapolis and Johnson's Island, and in the attack on Chicago that he would personally lead. Hines expected that he and Thompson would soon command fifty thousand men.[76]

Thompson began coordinating the purchase of rifles and ammunition through James Holcombe. Holcombe arranged for weapons to be secured in New York and sent to him in Montreal. On July 27, Holcombe assured Thompson that things were going well but that that he needed more money to close arms deals. His letter indicated the growing Confederate links between Canada and the North: "Our friends are here and urge the promptest measures, as the time is very brief. They have contracted for five thousand; these will cost thirty thousand in gold. No payment until they are received. Bill Canada Bank of England, payable to their order, can be cased, and should be sent in small denominations at once to New York."[77]

On July 22, Thompson met with Confederate captain John Castleman and colonel Hines in St. Catharines. They sat with a number of men who had arranged to become delegates at the Democratic Party's national convention in Chicago, which had been scheduled for July 1 but had been postponed when news of possible rebel trouble from Canada had leaked. Thompson was asked to forward more money and more guns.

They met in St. Catharines again on August 7. Excuses were made and more money requested. Thompson sent a coded message to Davis asking him to organize a military diversion in Kentucky for mid-August to draw Union troops south. Thompson issued a warning and prediction: "The rank and file are weary of the war, but the violent abolitionists, preachers, contractors, and political press are clamorous for its continuance. If Lee can hold his own in front of Richmond, and Johnston defeat Sherman in Georgia prior to the election, it seems probable that Lincoln will be defeated."[78]

Thompson seemed unaware of the fact that anything he said or did was soon reported to Seward. And the efficiency of Seward's spies meant that Lincoln was kept fully aware of the ideas and activities swirling in the interconnected worlds of the Copperheads, secret societies and what was becoming known as the Confederates' Canadian Cabinet. Lincoln and his advisors were divided as to the legitimacy of the threats posed, but Lincoln took them seriously and so actions were taken to address them.[79]* Shortly after the St. Catharines meeting, more soldiers were sent to Chicago to increase security at the convention and more troops were sent to the state houses in Indiana, Illinois and Ohio.

With delays and additional troops sapping the enthusiasm of their followers, Sons of Liberty leaders continued to try to rally their people. Sixty Canadian-based Confederates met at the Queen's, and Hines gave them instructions, a hundred dollars each and train tickets for Chicago. They arrived on August 28, the day before the convention was scheduled to begin at the Amphitheatre. They waited for the thousands of armed and determined men that Illinois Sons of Liberty leader Amos Green had promised. None arrived. Green and the twelve thousand dollars that Thompson had sent him were gone. Many of Thompson's men exercised the better part of valour and quietly slipped away.

From Toronto, Thompson hastily concocted a revised plan. He ordered Castleman and Hines to gather as many men as they could and to commandeer a train, cut telegraph lines and liberate Confederates at the Rock Island and Springfield prisons. The rebel force was then to burn bridges and cut remaining telegraph wires except for one, through which messages could be sent to Washington and elsewhere explaining what had happened. The plan was set but, as in Chicago, it fizzled. They were betrayed and Castleman was arrested. The others fled back to Canada.

The failed disruption at Chicago and the prison break fiascos, coupled with the *Philo Parsons* episode, drew even more attention to Thompson's Canadian operations. Stanton and Seward began to receive more regular and alarming reports. On September 30, for instance, General Dix telegraphed Stanton that Thompson had been seen in Sandwich, Canada West, with known Confederate colonel William Steele and that they were planning some kind of "piratical expedition" on the lakes. The next day, Detroit's

---

* *Historians have argued the same question. Wood Gray (1942) and Frank Klement (1984) contended that the threat was somewhat exaggerated at the time by Republicans seeking to exploit fears for their party's political gain. In 2006, however, Jennifer Weber, in* The Rise and Fall of Lincoln's Opponents in the North, *wrote that Lincoln was justified in fearing the "fire in the rear" because the threat was real and could well have affected the outcome of the war.*

provost marshal reported, "As the case now stands, the rebel agent in Canada residing in Sandwich, Col. Jacob Thompson, has organized an expedition in Canada to seize American trains."[80]

Nothing seemed to be working for Thompson as planned, but with the actions he was taking and the reports and rumours piling up on Washington desks, he continued to exact a price in Union men, money and attention. His quiet activities were often the most effective. For example, Thompson worked in Toronto with Confederate agent Beverley Tucker, who arranged for cotton to be shipped to Canada and traded for bacon on a pound-for-pound basis, then secreted back to the hungry South. Other work was done to try to disrupt and devalue the American currency. Meanwhile, Clement Clay, from his Montreal office, and without Thompson's knowledge, approved a scheme that was far from quiet. It promised to lead to the invasion and the war that Thompson had been sent to Canada to precipitate.

THE ST. ALBANS RAID

By October 1864, Lord Lyons, whose health had been questionable for some time, had been diagnosed with neuralgia and was feeling the effects of three years of intense stress. He had spent a couple of enjoyable weeks with Governor General Monck and his family at Monck's official residence, the idyllic Spencer Wood. He developed a cloying friendship with Monck's effervescent adult daughter Feo and, uncharacteristically, enjoyed himself. With Monck and his family, Lyons visited parts of Canada, seeing Shawinigan Falls, Montreal, and Toronto. He toured the American side of Niagara Falls to avoid contact with the Clifton Hill Confederates.

Duty soon had Lyons back in the United States, and on October 20 he was in tails at a New York City dinner party attended by several dignitaries, including General Dix. During cocktails, Lyons saw Dix receive a telegram and rush from the room. A half an hour later he was back and, before the startled guests, began berating Lyons: Confederates had swarmed across the Canadian border and taken St. Albans, Vermont.

The raid had been led by Thompson's experienced Confederate agent and courier Bennett Young. Young was a handsome twenty-one-year-old from Jessamine County, Kentucky. He had ridden with General Morgan in Ohio and been captured and imprisoned, but escaped to Montreal in early 1864. He met Clement Clay, who encouraged him to return to Richmond via Halifax and Bermuda. With a letter and instructions from Clay, Young met with Secretary of War James Sedden, who commissioned him as a first lieutenant and ordered him back to Canada.

Thompson had involved Young in a number of missions, including the peace negotiations with Horace Greeley and the attempted disruption of the Democratic Party's National Convention in Chicago. From his hotel in St. Catharines, Young had helped plan a prison uprising in Columbus, Ohio's Camp Chase. He made it to Ohio with about thirty men but nearly all lost their nerve at the last minute, so Young was soon back in St. Catharines, and still seeking his first success.

Young met with Clay in Montreal and the two hatched the plan for the St. Albans raid. Clay gave Young two thousand dollars to cover expenses. Working through Clay's contacts at St. Lawrence Hall, Young carefully gathered twenty fit, experienced young Southern men who shared his passion and willingness to die for the cause.

They left Montreal on different trains and arrived in St. Albans over several days. Claiming to be members of a Canadian hunting and fishing club, they booked into different hotels and Young and another man scouted the town. On October 19, at three o'clock in the afternoon, they gathered at the town's main intersection. With a silent signal they threw their greatcoats to the ground, revealing Confederate uniforms with intimidating twin navy sixes strapped across their chests. Young bellowed from his hotel's front porch that the town was theirs in the name of the Confederacy. With much shouting and brandishing of weapons, the townsfolk were shepherded into the public square. When a couple of men put up a fight, shots were fired and one resister was hit in the leg.

Amid the crying and quaking, several of Young's raiders entered and robbed the town's three banks of about two hundred thousand dollars.

From satchels came fifty four-ounce bottles of Greek fire that exploded buildings into flames.* For forty-five minutes the rampage continued; and then it got worse.

The raiders hadn't noticed that a Union captain named George Conger, who happened to be there on leave, had slipped out of the crowd. He quickly assembled men to retake the town. As the raiders were gathering horses to make their escape, shots rang from second-storey windows. Men in the crowd pulled weapons from beneath jackets and joined the fray. The raiders threw their remaining bottles of Greek fire against the houses from which the shots were coming, and returned fire from horseback as they fled. Three raiders were hit and a civillian was killed.

Eight miles outside town, with Conger's posse giving chase, Young and few breathless men reined their sweating horses near a bridge. They took control of a farmer's load of hay and waited. When the posse galloped into sight, the raiders set the bridge and hay alight and opened fire. By nine o'clock, all twenty raiders were back in Canada. They changed into civilian clothes, got rid of the horses and split up. Young finally had his success.

He set off on foot to report to Clay in Montreal, but stopped at a farmhouse to ask for food and drink. A woman allowed him in and he settled before the fire to rest. Within minutes, about twenty-five members of the posse burst into the small room, threw him to the floor and beat him. Bloodied and stunned, Young was tossed into the back of a wagon with men on either side holding weapons to his head. He shouted that his captors had violated British neutrality. The men yelled back and hit him again. Young suddenly rose, knocked both men out of the wagon, grabbed the reins and shouted to the horses. The two men recovered quickly though and pounced on Young, one beating him with the flat side of a sword. From out of nowhere appeared a British officer, who stopped the beating and demanded to know what was going on.

---

* Greek fire was a liquid incendiary mixture of phosphorus and bisulfide of carbon, placed in glass jars and used to start fires, much like a Molotov cocktail.

The red-coated soldier heard the shouted story from both sides. Thinking quickly, he assured the vigilantes that many of Young's compatriots were already under arrest and talked them into releasing him. In exchange, he promised he would take charge of Young and that he and the other Confederates would be returned to St. Albans to face trial. The promise worked and Young was taken to jail.

While Lord Lyons was being publicly dressed down by General Dix in New York, Governor General Monck was reading a telegram from frenzied Vermont governor, J. Gregory Smith.[81] Smith had surmised that the raid was part of a larger invasion and so he called out all the reserves he could to protect other towns and important railway junctions. Unaware that their capture was already in progress, Monck ordered the raiders arrested. Meanwhile, Dix telegraphed an order to Vermont that American troops should find and arrest the raiders even if it meant crossing the Canadian border. Lyons protested, and Dix admitted that he was issuing the order without authorization from Washington.[82]

The raid from Canada, along with Conger's posse and the Dix order, meant trouble. Secretary of State Seward was quickly involved and sent a message to acting British minister Joseph Burnley, still in charge pending Lyons's official return to duty, insisting on the immediate extradition of the St. Albans raiders.[83] A couple of days later, with the men still in the Canadian jail, he repeated his demand.[84]

Even before the St. Albans raid, Seward had sent a message to Foreign Secretary Russell in London stating that recent incidents demonstrated that Britain's pledge of neutrality could not be trusted and, therefore, that Canada and Britain should prepare themselves for the abrogation of the Rush-Bagot Agreement and the re-arming of the Great Lakes.[85] The raid made the bad situation worse and had even moved Robert E. Lee to write to Jefferson Davis arguing that adventures such as occurred at St. Albans were illegal and ill-advised. Men sent to carry out such activities, he argued, would be better put to use in battle or protecting Southern cities.[86]

The press on both sides of the border exploded with recriminating articles. American papers were nearly unanimous in their condemnation of Canada's involvement in the raid; meanwhile, Canadian papers decried the raid itself while expressing outrage at Conger's cross-border incursion.[87] The *Montreal Gazette*, for example, echoed even the normally pro-Southern papers in editorializing: "It is the first duty of the Government of Canada and the people of Canada to see that the right of asylum which their soil affords is not thus betrayed and violated. The Government must spare no pains to prevent it. [But] to surprise a peaceful town and shoot people down in the streets, at the same time committing robbery, is not civilized war; it is that of savages."[88]

Thompson's people did themselves no favours by entering the newspaper fracas. From his cell, Young penned a letter to Montreal's pro-South *Evening Telegram* explaining his actions. He wrote that he had intended to burn a number of Vermont towns in retaliation for the Union's burning of Southern cities and towns. With impressive temerity, Young continued that he had been captured in Canada by American citizens and that each should be charged with violating Canadian neutrality.[89] An editorial in the *Toronto Leader*, while not condoning the raid, allowed that it supported Young's point. If, it argued, the Union army can act with impunity in destroying property in the South, then why could Confederate forces not use every means at their disposal to do the same thing in the North?[90]

Young's letter was followed by another from Thompson's agent George Sanders arguing that Young was a prisoner of war and must be treated as such, for he had been hired by the Richmond government with the express purpose of organizing the St. Albans expedition. It was not a raid or a bank robbery, Sanders contended, but a legitimate act of war.[91]

With newspapers keeping the raid hot, Burnley, Russell, Monck and the Canadian government did all they could to cool matters by reassuring everyone that they opposed the attack, and held no regard for those who carried it out or for the Confederates in Canada who had organized and financed it. Burnley wrote to Monck saying that Lincoln was pleased by the actions taken so far in the St. Albans and *Philo Parsons* cases. He said that Lincoln believed that the raid and acts of piracy on the Great Lakes were attempts by the Confederates in Canada to embroil the United States and Britain in war and that his government would not fall into the trap.[92]

At the same time, rumours of more plots along the border were brought to Seward's attention and he alerted Monck and Burnley. There were stories of planned piracy on the Great Lakes, of more border raids and of plotters in Montreal eager to put a number of Northern towns to the torch. Unlike Lincoln, Seward publicly criticized Canadian efforts to stop it all as being tepid at best: "It is not the Government or the people of the United States that are delinquent in the fulfillment of fraternal national obligations."[93]

With the rumour mill churning, Vermont's Governor Smith called out militia units and asked Secretary of War Stanton to send him cavalry supplies, including five hundred carbines, pistols, sabres and other equipment. Demonstrating the attention being paid to the northern border, Stanton replied that very day and sent the governor everything he requested.[94] The next day, Stanton wrote to General Grant outlining aspects of the affairs in New York State, including the levels of security of forts, canals, ports and cities "from rebels imported from Canada." Grant acknowledged the threat and suggested that new recruits that were currently being organized in the state for his army should be diverted to defend the northern border.[95] About two thousand recruits were kept from Grant and assigned instead to Dix.

The St. Albans raiders were brought before Magistrate Charles-Joseph Coursol at St. Johns, a short distance southeast of Montreal, on October 25.* The courtroom was packed with American, Canadian and Maritime reporters and a large crowd that included many who had arrived by train from Montreal, decked out in Confederate uniforms. Young and the others were defended by lawyers paid for through Clay's funds and hired by George Sanders. Their chief counsel was John C. Abbott, who was McGill University's dean of law and in 1891 would become Canada's prime minister. There were six charges, all extraditable: robbery, attempted

---

* St. Johns is now called Saint-Jean-sur-Richelieu.

arson, horse-stealing, assault, intent to murder and murder. After three days it was decided that tensions in the small town were simply too high and so the proceedings were moved to more secure facilities in Montreal. Young and his compatriots lived at the home of their jailer, where Sanders arranged fine food, good wine and expensive prostitutes. They also welcomed a number of visitors, including Clay and Thompson.

The hearing began again on November 3. It dragged on through days of arcane legal arguments and delays. Attempts were made to procure documents from Richmond meant to prove that the defendants were commissioned by Davis, but first Monck and then Lincoln refused to allow messengers safe passage. The decision to deal with each charge separately slowed the proceedings even more.

As the preliminary hearing ground along at a glacial pace, Thompson carried on with exploits that he had been planning for weeks. His actions turned the already complex and volatile situation volcanic.

BURNING CHICAGO AND NEW YORK

By October 1864, General Grant's relentless assault on the South was visiting unprecedented horror upon cities, soldiers and civilians. Petersburg saw combatants dug into the mud of zigzag-shaped trenches, where they lived and fought—and many died. Cities and crops were burned. Homeless refugees wandered wide-eyed and hungry. It was total war.

The *Richmond Whig* saw the war for what it had become and called for revenge upon the civilians and cities of the North. Its October 15 editorial, printed just days before the St. Albans raid, urged:

> Burn one of the chief cities of the enemy, say Boston, Philadelphia, or Cincinnati. If we are asked how a thing can be done, we answer, nothing would be easier. A million of dollars would lay the proudest city of the enemy to ashes. The men to execute the work are already there. There would be no difficulty in finding there, or here, or in Canada, suitable persons to take charge of the enterprise and arrange its details.[96]

Thompson had been planning for just such an attack. In his Toronto hotel suite, he met with three selected conspirators: Captain Thomas Hines, Colonel Robert Martin and Captain John Headley, to discuss how it could happen. They agreed that spectacular events in major Northern cities could galvanize support for the Sons of Liberty and their drive to end the war to the Confederacy's advantage. They decided that the day of the presidential election, November 8, would be perfect to demonstrate the secret society's power and resolve. Thompson arranged for Hines and men named Walsh and Morris to organize an attack on Chicago. The city was a natural choice, as there were already many Canadian-Confederate connections there and it was designated as the capital of the Copperheads' new republic. They developed a plan whereby Confederates would be sprung from Camp Douglas and other Illinois prisons. Fires would be set and bombs exploded in various predetermined locations, and Chicago's military officials would be captured or killed. With an army of 25,000 recently sprung Confederate prisoners, the state would be taken.[97]

Thompson believed that New York City was also ripe for attack. The city's mayor, after all, had made a number of rabid and popular anti-war, anti-Lincoln speeches, and then the draft riots had shown popular support for those sentiments. Thompson appointed John Headley and men named McMaster, Horton and Wood to lead the assault on New York. They were convinced that twenty thousand Confederates, its Sons of Liberty members and vast numbers of others would celebrate their liberation from Lincoln and the war, and support the attack while welcoming the Canadian-based Confederates as heroes.[98]

When news of Thompson's plans leaked out, the Chicago operation fizzled. On November 2, Seward telegraphed military commanders and told them of the Confederate raiders coming from Canada.[99] On November 9, Chicago's Colonel Benjamin Sweet and Brigadier General John Cook, commanding the District of Illinois, organized a dragnet that scooped up all of Thompson's conspirators and other assorted ne'er-do-wells. The ever-resourceful Hines escaped by hiding inside a box-spring mattress upon which lay a woman friend, feigning illness.[100]

On October 30, eight Confederates from Toronto arrived in New York. They travelled in pairs to avoid detection and checked into a number of lower Manhattan hotels. With letters of introduction from Thompson, they met several times with New York Copperheads. Through the force of his personality and power of his contacts, James McMaster, who was the owner and editor of the *New York Freeman's Appeal*, became the group's chief spokesman. McMaster claimed to have met with New York's Governor Seymour, who supported what was about to happen and promised not to send troops to stop it.[101] After New York was taken, McMaster insisted, Seymour would help bring the governors of New Jersey and other New England states together, secede from the United States, and form another republic akin to the Northwest republic. Emboldened by such support and grand ideas, the group made its final preparations.

As with the Chicago plot, the plans were leaked. On November 7, Major General Benjamin Butler, who had taken effective but brutal control of New Orleans after its capture by Union forces, moved five thousand troops into New York. The *New York Times*, reporting on Confederate activities in the city, applauded Butler's arrival: "The wisdom of the Government in selecting the man who had scattered the howling rabble of New Orleans like chaff, and reduced that city to order most serene, approved itself to the conscience of every patriot and made Copperheads squirm and writhe in torture."[102]

Obviously betrayed, the conspirators postponed their attack. Lincoln's re-election on November 8 further deflated their élan. Contact was made with Thompson in Toronto, who encouraged the group to ignore the collapse of the greater plan and carry on.[103] They hid and waited.

With the quiet that followed the election, Butler's troops were withdrawn. Their departure excited the patient conspirators. Their numbers had been dwindling, but those who remained were the most passionate about their cause. They devised a new reason for the old plan. They would set fire to the city just to scare the people of the North and to let Lincoln know that there would be repercussions for burning Southern property.[104] Headley purchased bottles of Greek fire from a chemist next to Washington Square. On November 25, the group set out with ten bottles each. They checked into various hotels and waited. At 8:00 p.m., they emptied some of the bottles, lit their matches, and then moved to other pre-arranged hotels and theatres to set more fires.

Bells echoed down Broadway as nineteen hotels and several theatres simultaneously burst into flames. There were panicked screams as people dashed from burning buildings. Many jumped from first- and second-storey windows, while others scrambled down ladders. Thompson's Confederates joined the crowds and enjoyed the chaos. The Winter Gardens was among the theatres evacuated. The audience had gathered at the opulent theatre to raise funds for the erection of a statue of Shakespeare in Central Park and to attend a performance of *Julius Caesar* featuring three of America's most talented and respected actors: Junius Booth, his son Edwin, and the star of the family, John Wilkes Booth.

It quickly became apparent that much of the Greek fire was ineffective and many of the fires had been improperly set. Many snuffed themselves out, while others were quickly handled by alert fire brigades. Within hours, all of the hotel and theatre fires were extinguished. Despite the alarm and terror, no one was seriously hurt.

The conspirators ate a leisurely breakfast the next morning at a Broadway and 12th restaurant and read about their exploits in the morning papers. Some enjoyed an afternoon in Central Park, but when they returned downtown it was discovered that some of their co-conspirators had been arrested. The afternoon edition of the *New York Times* reported that a couple of weeks earlier, a man from Canada had told authorities in Washington about the plots to burn American cities and asked for one hundred thousand dollars in return for information regarding the perpetrators. He had named names.[105] Headley and his group took a train north that evening and the next day reported to Thompson in Toronto.

It was discovered that Godfrey Hyams of Arkansas was the man who had betrayed the New York mission. He was also implicated in the selling out of other operations. Hyams had been living at the Queen's Hotel for some time and Hines had warned Thompson about him, but

Thompson liked and trusted him. Hyams left the hotel that day, but stayed in Toronto.

A few days later, Thompson met a woman called Katie McDonald. She had travelled from New York to ask him for money to support the trials of men arrested for having abetted those who tried to burn the city, among whom was her brother, the editor of New York's *Day Book*. Thompson agreed to consider her request, but was then told that New York detectives had arrived in Toronto, apparently having followed McDonald. Thompson advised the men who had been to New York to go into hiding.

Meanwhile, Lord Lyons had again fallen ill. He had fainted in his office on November 6, and the next day had temporarily passed his duties on to his secretary and sometime acting minister, Joseph Burnley. Five months later, Lyons was replaced by Sir Frederick Bruce, the younger brother of former Canadian governor general Lord Elgin. Bruce had served as lieutenant-governor of Newfoundland as well as in South America, Egypt and China.

Lyons's last official meeting before returning to England was with Seward. The two had worked together for three years and both had grown to be nuanced and effective diplomats. In his final message to Seward, Lyons assured him that Monck was doing a good job in dealing with Thompson and that he needed to be patient with the Canadian efforts. Despite this assurance, Lyons had just written to Russell stating that more needed to be done to stop Thompson and his men, because the pressures being put on the American government to respond were becoming impossible to resist.[106] After a month spent trying to recover in his darkened room, Lyons finally rallied sufficient strength to travel and on December 12 he left America for the last time. He would be missed.

THE *GEORGIAN*

Thompson was still not done. In late October 1864, he had persuaded his Canadian friend Lt. Col. George Denison to front the purchase of the steamer *Georgian* from Kentucky's Dr. James Bates for eighteen thousand dollars. Captain John Beall, who had commandeered the *Philo Parsons*, returned from hiding to organize its crew. The ship was to be taken to Port Colborne on Lake Erie's north shore, only twenty miles from Buffalo. It would be armed and outfitted, and then used to free the Johnson's Island prisoners, some of whom would provide crew for more ships. The *Georgian* would form the core of a ghost navy working from Canadian ports and prowling the Great Lakes. It would bomb American cities and bring terror to the North.[107] Final plans were made in Toronto and then the conspirators left for Port Colborne to await Beall and the *Georgian*.

As happened with so many of Thompson's plots, an informer surrendered the plan. With telegrams already flying regarding the fallout of the St. Albans raid and the New York attacks, Monck, Seward and Burnley learned of this latest threat.[108] Seward telegraphed General Dix, who wrote to Secretary of War Stanton for help. Stanton and Seward consulted with Lincoln, and General Grant was asked to take troops from his forces to augment border defences. Grant noted in a wry telegraph to Dix that all the troops he believed were needed had been sent. He added, "It seems to me that you and General Butler ought to be able to take care of Jake Thompson and his gang."[109] Dix did what he could with what he had, and alerted governors and military leaders. Buffalo's harbour was reinforced, and guns were affixed to more tugboats. The next Sunday, news flooded Detroit that Confederates were on their way across the river from Canada on the *Georgian*. Church bells sprang people from their pews and men to the docks to defend their city—but the rumour of attack had no substance.

Monck had the *Georgian* examined but no weapons or anything untoward were found. Bates claimed he was working for a lumber company and refitting the ship to haul wood. Days later, the *Georgian* left port, moving northward past Detroit and into Lake Huron, tracked carefully throughout its journey by American ships. It eventually moored at Collingwood, far from the American border on the south shore of Lake Huron's Georgian Bay. Seward sent Monck a message asking him to continue to pay special attention to the *Georgian*, as a number of American mayors along the lakes, especially at Buffalo, remained concerned that their cities would soon be bombarded.[110]

Thompson's plan, meanwhile, proceeded. The *Georgian* was to be out-fitted with armaments from Guelph. He did not know that local authorities in the town had been growing suspicious of activity in the foundry of Adam Robertson and Son, which for some time had been casting solid shells and grape shot. They had their suspicions too about a man named Bennett Burley, or Burleigh (earlier a participant in the *Michigan* plot), who was living with the Robertsons and was often seen leaving town with wagon-loads of foundry products. Their concerns landed on Monck's desk at the same time as the governor general learned about the *Georgian*. Monck investigated and discovered that the Guelph factory had been selling arma-ments to the South for some time and that it was preparing to supply the *Georgian* with a cannon and ammunition.[111] Monck had the *Georgian* put under twenty-four-hour surveillance and John A. Macdonald began an investigation into the Guelph foundry and Lt. Colonel Denison.[112]

Meanwhile, a cannon that had been boxed in a Robertson and Son crate and sent to a man named Duncan Smitten was seized in Sarnia. With it were two heavy barrels, improbably marked "Potatoes." On November 19, more ammunition in transit from the Roberston foundry was seized at Spanish River. A keen-eyed officer recognized Burley and arrested him. The ammunition runner was charged with murder for the part he had played in the seizure of the *Island Queen* in the *Michigan* incident the previ-ous September.[113] Attorney General John A. Macdonald approved the arrest and ordered the interception of all other Robertson shipments.

On November 21, Monck ordered the Guelph factory's warehouse seized until the owners signed a bond pledging that nothing in it and noth-ing that would be manufactured in the future would be sold to Confederates or those who would transport it to Confederates. The bond was signed.

The next day, Macdonald supported Monck with a proclamation ban-ning all exports of armaments to the United States. On November 30, more boxes of ammunition from the Guelph plant were discovered in Sarnia in the possession of men believed to be Confederate agents. Meanwhile, despite the many eyes upon the *Georgian*, its captain managed to disappear.

SETTLING THE SCORE

While the Chicago and New York missions and the *Georgian* intrigue
were being played out, Bennett Young and his St. Albans co-conspirators
remained in Montreal. Proceedings began again on December 13. This
time, chief counsel John Abbott questioned the legality of Magistrate
Charles-Joseph Coursol's hearing the case. He went back to the legal
arguments of the John Anderson case and in a complex argument he drew
the Webster-Ashburton Treaty and Canadian law together to contend
that Coursol had no jurisdiction in the matter before him.

Coursol considered the argument over lunch and then shocked the
court by agreeing with Abbott and ordering the St. Albans raiders released.
Crown lawyers scrambled to stay the implementation of the decision, but
Montreal police chief Guillaume Lamothe did not wait. He had been put
in charge of a receipt for $84,000 of the money stolen from St. Albans
banks. Minutes after Coursol's announcement, he surrendered it to an
agent working for Thompson, who rushed to the Bank of Ontario's back
door, after closing time. He was met by a bank official who arranged for
the transfer. The money went from Thompson's contact in the bank to
his agent on the street, to Chief Lamothe and then to Young and the
others. They took it and ran.[114] Through Thompson's intervention, they
had stolen the money again.

The release of the St. Albans conspirators and the pilfering of the
money sparked outrage in the North. The *New York Times* reported, "It
may be said that this will lead to a war with England. But if it must come,
let it come."[115] The *New York Herald* called for war and blamed an inef-
fectual Canadian government and legal system for all that had been happening throughout the Civil War. "The next raid," it threatened, "is likely
to be avenged upon the nearest Canadian village which gives refuge to the
marauders."[116]

General Dix ordered his troops to find Young and his cohorts and
bring them to justice in the United States, no matter where they were or
who claimed jurisdiction in the matter. This was the second time Dix had
ordered his troops to ignore the border and British neutrality. The *London*

Times called Dix's order a declaration of war against Canada.[117] The *Times* may have been overstating things a little, but not much.

At that moment, as was his wont and his mission, Thompson made a tense situation worse. He ordered another already planned raid on America to immediately proceed. On December 16, John Beall led a number of men over the border to intercept a train transferring several Confederate generals from Johnson's Island to New York's Fort Lafayette. The train was not intercepted and the generals were not freed, but Beall, who had so many times narrowly escaped capture, was arrested. The raid was a fiasco of bad planning and misunderstandings, but it offered one more example to those screaming about Confederates who seemed to have carte blanche to wreak havoc from across the border.

There were long debates around Lincoln's cabinet table regarding the many overlapping incendiary issues tied to the suddenly ramped-up problems on the border, and specifically about Dix's latest directive to ignore it. On December 17, Lincoln overturned the order with a new one stating that any American troops needing to cross into Canada had to first clear their plans with Washington. Lincoln's order ended the practice established following the 1837 Upper and Lower Canadian rebellions, when it had been agreed that troops in "hot pursuit" could cross the line to apprehend their prey. Lincoln was wisely taking away the power to initiate international incidents from zealous generals such as Dix and Joseph Hooker, who had also publicly stated that he would have no compunction about ordering his troops into Canada.[118]

Despite Lincoln's order, American patience with Canada had ended. Throughout the Civil War, the floors of the Senate and House of Representatives had heard fiery anti-Canadian speeches with every outrage from across the border. In October 1864, the House had been debating the 1854 Reciprocity Treaty, which had created a free-trade zone between Canada and the United States and brought great benefits to the Canadian economy. On the day that Coursol freed the St. Albans raiders, the House was scheduled to vote on whether to abrogate the treaty. Congressmen voted 87 to 57 to end it. And on January 12, the Senate voted 38 to 8 in support of killing the treaty. Iowa senator James Grimes spoke for many when he argued in a long speech that the decision to end the treaty involved a number of long-debated economic and political issues but that many senators were now voting in direct response to Canada's decidedly mixed support for the Union, its harbouring of Confederates, and the numerous cross-border incursions it had allowed. Grimes said he was one of those who hoped that the treaty's abrogation would result in no more need for Northern defences, for it would lead to Canada's annexation.[119]

A second agreement between Canada and America also hung in the balance. Days after the St. Albans Raid, Seward had warned Britain's foreign secretary, Russell, that border tensions could lead to the abrogation of the Rush-Bagot Agreement.[120] Congress had been shouting for its abrogation for years, with Charles Sumner, the powerful chair of the Senate Foreign Relations Committee, among the loudest. On November 23, Canada and Britain were informed that that the agreement would be repealed in six months.[121] The Great Lakes would be remilitarized.

On December 17, tensions worsened when Lincoln signed a law stating that no one could enter the United States without a passport. The Canadian and New Brunswick borders were long and largely undefended, so the law was meant less to stop traffic than to express displeasure. The *Toronto Leader* saw it for what it was: "a vindictive expedient."[122] The law nonetheless threatened workers, by making travel for employment in the United States more difficult. The thickened border would also punish Canadian businesses by complicating bilateral trade. Macdonald met with the presidents of the Great Western and Grand Trunk railways, who predicted that the passport regulations would cost their companies eighty thousand dollars a month.[123]

Not since the *Trent* crisis of 1861 had Britain and the United States been so close to war. Once again, Canada was paying the price in insults meant to intimidate, actions designed to injure and threats too real to ignore. The situation in December 1864 was as treacherous as it was complex. But other events at the time complicated the situation even more and made the stakes higher still.

Canadian and Maritime political leaders were trying to stave off invasion and annexation from within a rickety political system that no longer reflected the colonies' demographic realities or evolving independence. In particular, they lacked the structural and fiscal capacity to defend the people for whom they were responsible. The Civil War was making clear to all that tinkering with old ways would not do. Canada and the Maritimes had to reinvent themselves to save themselves, and they needed to act quickly or there might be nothing left to save. A leader was needed who would be willing to risk his career by telling the hard truths and getting essential changes made. In May 1864, a man few Canadians believed had the capacity or desire to be that kind of leader stepped forward.

5

———◆———

GEORGE BROWN AND THE IMPROBABLE NATION

B Y MAY 1864, THE Confederacy was dying and Canada was struggling to be born. In the white brick legislative building in Quebec City that was home to Canada's government, seventeen men entered a non-descript committee room with casual chatter, light jokes and an air of nonchalance. But the tension was palpable. Many of the men did not trust each other. Many did not like each other. Some hated each other.

George Brown was there. The owner-editor of Toronto's influential *Globe*, former leader of the Reform party and now member of the legislature for South Oxford, rose as the others took their seats. He walked to the door and, with a dramatic flourish, locked it and pocketed the key. "Now gentleman," he said, glaring at the startled, silenced and somewhat bemused group, "you must talk about this matter, as you cannot leave this room without coming to me."[1]

The matter at hand was an idea that had been tossed around for years as a way to end the political and economic instability that had challenged

British North America and stunted its development for over two decades. With the Civil War, this challenge was threatening its very existence. The word "Confederation" had come to represent the notion of ending the current political structure and creating a new and efficient federated one, its two levels of government better able to address divisive and paralyzing regional, ethnic, religious and linguistic cleavages. Some dared to dream of extending Confederation to include the Maritime colonies of Nova Scotia, New Brunswick and maybe even Prince Edward Island and Newfoundland. Others hoped to include the vast northwestern territories that began at Lake Huron and touched towering Rockies and Arctic ice. But dreams are not plans, and progress had been stifled by a general lack of incentive and political courage.

Brown was not the first to call for Confederation. That distinction fell to Alexander Galt. Galt was born in Scotland and came to Canada in 1828 with his businessman father. By the 1840s, he had become a visionary entrepreneur, with interests in real estate, manufacturing and railways. Galt entered politics in 1849, toyed with the idea of annexation to the United States, lost his seat, and then was re-elected in 1853.

In July 1858, John A. Macdonald's Conservative government fell over arguments about the establishment of a permanent capital. Governor General Head offered Galt the premiership, but he declined and instead suggested that George Cartier of Canada East form a new government with Macdonald. Ignoring Galt's advice, Head offered the government to George Brown. When Brown's cabinet resigned in order to run for re-election, according to the parliamentary practice of the day, Macdonald's Conservatives voted to defeat the temporarily reduced government. After only two days, Macdonald was back in power. He then moved his old cabinet out of their jobs for one day and back the next, thus avoiding their having to quit and run again. It was a dirty but legal trick called the "double shuffle." Brown was humiliated.

Attempting to shore up his numbers, Macdonald moved to pry Galt from the Reform party with the offer of a cabinet seat. Galt agreed on condition that the Cartier-Macdonald administration adopt Confederation as a goal of the new government. An agreement was struck and Galt became finance minister. He was confident that the idea of Confederation would find traction in Canada and the Maritimes, where local politicians and business people would see the economic advantage of a broader union.[2] In 1857, Nova Scotia's legislature had passed a resolution to investigate such a union. Further, Galt knew that the notion of a more independent British North America was growing popular in London among those in politics and civil society known as Little Englanders, or the Manchester School, who were of the opinion that the cost of governing and defending colonies no longer matched the benefit.[3] While not a Little Englander himself, the Duke of Newcastle, British secretary of state for the colonies, saw the writing on the wall and at least twice in the late 1850s had urged his Canadian governor general to see what could be done to support talk of constitutional change among colonial politicians and his Maritime lieutenant-governors.[4]

Both Cartier and Macdonald were lukewarm to the Confederation idea, but good to their word, and so they allowed Galt to introduce a proposal to broach the subject with Britain. The resolution was so vaguely worded as to appear harmless and so it passed. Shortly afterward, just before the House was about to end its session, Governor General Head surprised many by announcing: "I propose in the course of the recess to communicate with Her Majesty's Government, and with the Governments of the sister Colonies, on another matter of very great importance. I am desirous of inviting them to discuss with us the principles on which a bond of a federal character, uniting the Provinces of British North America, may perhaps hereafter be practicable."[5] Head's brief statement was like a clanging bell announcing the need for a fundamental change in the political makeup of British North America, and seemed to offer Galt's proposal the support of the Crown.

Two months later, Galt, Cartier and John Ross, president of the Executive Council, packed their high hopes and left for London. The cool autumn air was as chilly as their welcome. Henry Labouchère was Palmerston's secretary of state and, like the Duke of Newcastle, had encouraged Head to support Canadian efforts at uniting the North

American colonies.[6] However, within weeks of Head's statement, the Palmerston government had fallen. There was confusion in the Colonial Office as new colonial secretary, Sir Edward Bulwer-Lytton, no friend of the Little Englanders, was either unaware of, or perhaps unwilling to acknowledge, previous colonial directives.[7] A minor scandal erupted over whether Head had been directed to make his pro-Confederation remarks. Lytton seemed to misunderstand the complexity of the Canadian situation and the storm gathering in the United States. He was worried that Confederation was a half-baked scheme meant mostly to extricate the current Canadian government from a political mess and, further, that if Confederation talks moved forward too quickly, his office would lose control of the process and outcome. He expressed these concerns to Galt and the others in a circular dispatch written in November, and then in another to Head in December.[8] Lytton ordered that moves toward a wider federation should be delayed to allow time to build a consensus in Canada and the other colonies.[9]

With the Galt initiative effectively shelved, George Brown entered the fray. Brown, another Scot, had been a force in Canadian politics and civil society since shortly after arriving in Toronto from New York intent upon using his knowledge of the newspaper business to start a new paper in Canada West. Founded in 1844, the *Globe* was by the late 1850s a powerhouse. It boasted British North America's largest subscription list, the newest and most efficient printing technology and distribution system, and correspondents connected by telegraph who presented the latest daily news and opinion to a broad urban and rural readership. Brown poured profits back into the paper while investing in real estate and land development. In 1851, he won a seat in Kent County, in the remote southwest of Canada West, as a member of the Reform party.

Canadian political parties in the 1850s were shifting coalitions of independently minded men that were slowly coalescing into two major groups. The Tories or Liberal-Conservatives (or simply Conservatives) were led by Cartier and Macdonald, who did their best to hold together what they called "loose fish." The Reformers were precursors to the

Liberal Party, who increasingly recognized Brown as their leading voice. Brown spoke for those who opposed the current constitutional system, which gave Canada East and West equal votes in the legislature, resulting in the need for a double majority for anything to happen: that is, party support and French/English support. He advocated a new system of representation by population to reflect the fact that the population of predominantly English-Protestant Canada West had outdistanced that of French-Catholic Canada East, and yet the Constitution still guaranteed each an equal number of seats. Brown's calls for "Rep by Pop" were interpreted by opponents as either a bigoted attack on French Catholics or a desperate attempt to change the rules of a game his Reform party seemed unable to win. Brown did little to help himself or his cause, by his too frequent mentions of his disdain for "Popism" or a desire to end the power of the Catholic church, and his personal attacks on opponents, which betrayed anger and impatience.

In January 1858, Brown had written a long letter to a political ally, saying that he believed the future lay in forging a federal union between Canada and the Maritime colonies. It would, he reasoned, solve the political and economic problems plaguing them all, and end the ethnic and religious bickering that had no place in the public sphere. And it would allow a strong base for expansion to the west. "No honest man," he wrote, "can desire that we should remain as we are. . . . A federal union, it appears to me, cannot be entertained for Canada alone but when agitated must include all British America."[10] Shortly afterward, following the embarrassment of his two-day ministry, he stood apart from many in his party and spoke in favour of Galt's Confederation motion. When Galt's mission to London ended in a disappointing failure, Brown dropped the idea—but only for a while. Six months later, beginning on May 10, 1859, the *Globe* ran a three-month series of articles outlining the problems with the current political structure and reviving arguments for a new federal union.

Brown worked assiduously to convince Reform members of the need for a convention to adopt Confederation as party policy. On November 9, in Toronto's cavernous but ornate St. Lawrence Hall, 570 skeptical and scrappy party members were gavelled to order. For two days motions came to the floor advocating a number of ideas, including inviting the Maritimes to join a British North American government, altering only the present Canadian political structure, and even dissolving Canada to create separate French and English governments. A compromise was finally approved whereby the party would support the creation of a new general government under what they called "some joint authority," with details to be worked out later.

Everyone waited for Brown's response. And he let them wait. Finally, with sunlight fading from the large windows, and gaslights creating golden shadows on the carved gods and gargoyles that glared down from massive crown mouldings, Brown rose to speak. The hot, crowded room fell silent.

He began slowly with innocuous remarks, and then, as his volume and pace increased, there were cheers as he announced support for the convention's Confederation motion. He then played the note that resonated with so many Reformers and Canadians in general—anti-Americanism. He held up Confederation as a way to create a new Canadian system of government that would be loyal to Britain while avoiding what he called the fundamental errors at the heart of the American system. Those mistakes, he argued, had been played out over the past decade in the increasingly rancorous debates that were splitting the United States apart and had been seen particularly in Kansas, where Americans were killing each other over an inability to compromise. He said Canadians wanted a strong and British-style government and no part of the failing republic. "I have no fear," he said, "that the people of Upper Canada would ever desire to become the fag end of the neighbour republic."[11] He concluded with a grand vision: "I do look forward with high hopes to the day when these northern countries shall stand out among the nations of the world as one great confederation!"[12] The thunderous applause marked Reform Party unity and a hard-won triumph for Brown.

The Cartier-Macdonald administration had allowed the idea of Confederation to wither, but Brown had resuscitated it. Two months later, Conservative finance minister Alexander Galt returned to London to repeat his request for Britain's support to begin Confederation negotiations. Lytton again said no. However, after discussions with his cabinet colleagues, Lytton told Galt that the official position of the British government had moved slightly, in that it would not promote Confederation but would no longer oppose it if there was an overwhelming desire on the part of Canadians to bring it about.[13]

In February 1860, George Brown took the train to Quebec City, ready to kick-start the Confederation debate. Governor General Head read a rather flaccid speech from the throne that ignored the issue altogether. The Conservative government had little to offer as it struggled to hold the confidence of the House in the face of a belligerent opposition and divisive forces within its own caucus.[14]

As the first opposition speaker responding to the speech from the throne, Brown announced his intention to move two resolutions based on the Reform party's November convention agreements. His short speech was met by partisan laughter and hoots of derision from government benches, which included Premier Cartier, Galt and Macdonald.

On April 30, in a four-hour speech, Brown was finally able to present his resolutions to the House. The debate lasted several days. On May 7, 1860, a motion expressing the legislature's desire to end the Canada East–Canada West union was defeated 66 to 27. A second motion, promoting the idea of a new federation, lost 74 to 32. With many of its members supporting the government on both resolutions, Brown's party crumbled around him.

Confederation had lost again. The previous two years had seen Brown humiliated by what Macdonald repeatedly called his two-day "ephemeral government," and then by the scuttling of Confederation and the splintering of his party. His personal life mirrored his political difficulties for, while the *Globe* remained strong, he had seen his many other business ventures suffer in the devastating 1857–59 recession. On top of everything, his health began to falter.

Brown was bedridden over the winter of 1860 and missed the entire 1861 session. In the June 1861 election, he lost his seat and with it the

Reform party leadership. He turned his focus to the *Globe* and other business interests, with special attention to his growing Lambton County land-
holdings near Sarnia. Like the government and his party, Brown abandoned
Confederation as an impossible ideal. He offered his still-influential public
voice in opposition to Macdonald and his Conservatives and the power
of railway interests. He also upheld Northern views in the arguments that
were leading to war in America. His health continued to suffer as his days
of public service seemed behind him. Brown did not realize in the fall of
1861 that events south of the border were already beginning to do for
Confederation what he and Galt could not.

A CHANGED MAN, AN OLD IDEA AND NEW THREATS

The Civil War began in April 1861. By December's *Trent* crisis, even
sceptical Canadians and Maritimers realized that the war involved and
threatened them. Their political leaders, however, recognized their inability to act quickly or decisively in the face of those threats. Palmerston
had become Britain's prime minister again in 1859, and this time with
Little Englanders such as William Gladstone at his cabinet table.

In May 1862, in reaction to American threats and British encouragement, the Cartier-Macdonald government introduced the Militia
Bill. It was intended to raise fifty thousand men and augment Canadian
defence capability with fortifications and arms. The Reform opposition
had attacked its enormous expense. The bill, after all, represented about
10 percent of the government's annual budget. The government could
not say if the shocking cost would necessitate increased taxation. In fact,
it could not even be specific about how the money would be spent. Many
who represented French ridings shouted the bill down for its plan to
conscript recruits if there were insufficient volunteers. The government's
faltering efforts to pass the bill were not helped by the fact that Macdonald
chose the middle of the debate to fall into a week-long drinking binge.

The Militia Bill was defeated with a vote of 61 to 54. Fifteen
Conservative members had defected, and with them gone, the

Cartier-Macdonald coalition had dissolved. The party that had held power since 1854 by managing shifting loyalties and clever political manoeuvring was forced to resign. Sandfield Macdonald, who had assumed the leadership of the Reform party after Brown's defeat in 1861, formed a government with his Canada East lieutenant, Louis-Victor Sicotte. Sandfield Macdonald was opposed to Confederation. Far from a visionary leader, he was a manager and technocrat of average skill who filled his cabinet with equally uninspired and uninspiring men. Governor General Monck recognized the limitations of the new administration and in a dispatch to London called it "a wretched lot . . . incapable of rising above the level of a parish politician."[15]

The British and American press heaped scorn on the Canadian government for the defeat of the Militia Bill, arguing that Canadians simply did not have the strength or stomach to defend themselves.[16] Little Englanders such as Gladstone, John Bright and Richard Cobden had a field day, as the troublesome, expensive and unreliable colony looked as if it might yet drag Britain into a war with the United States. They called for British North America to be set adrift.[17] Even those who supported Canada found it difficult to remain sanguine. The Duke of Newcastle, for instance, wrote a long letter to Monck expressing tremendous frustration and foreboding: "Everybody in the States will look upon it as little less than an invitation to come and annex it. The event will create as much joy in New York as it has caused concern in London."[18]

The Sandfield Macdonald–Sicotte government was shamed into action and tripled the defence budget so that some work could be done, but it was not nearly enough. There were still far too few troops, forts and weapons. A Maritime intercolonial railway, which could move men and equipment quickly in a time of crisis, remained a dream.

George Brown missed it all. His tenuous health led to the first extended holiday of his life. In July 1862, he arrived in Britain, where he enjoyed a leisurely time in London and Edinburgh. While there, Brown met Anne Nelson, the attractive, charming and highly intelligent daughter of a wealthy Scottish publisher. He was smitten. Thirty-three-year-old

Anne was well educated, well read and articluate. She had lived in Germany and France, and enjoyed debating political matters from a decidedly liberal point of view. The two were married at a lavish ceremony, and set out for Canada in December. Even the mammoth swells of the frigid North Atlantic could not diminish the happiness they found with each other.

The forty-three-year-old Brown came home a changed man. He returned to the *Globe* and to his growing Bothwell estate and related businesses with a temper less quick and a disposition more tolerant. He found in Anne a confidante who persuaded him to put aside personal affronts and quick, cheap victories in favour of steady long-term progress. In March 1863, he was back in the legislature after easily winning a by-election in South Oxford. Brown bided his time on the government's back benches. He did not ask for a cabinet post; nor was one offered.

Three months later, Union victories at Vicksburg and Gettysburg altered the trajectory of the Civil War. Lincoln still faced tremendous and competing challenges, but Jefferson Davis was juggling even more problems. So many Southern troops were deserting that on August 1 Davis issued an order offering amnesty to any soldiers who returned to duty. Slaves were taken from plantations to do construction work and other jobs that soldiers had previously done. Across the South, food shortages were being felt and in Mobile, Alabama, troops had to quell a food riot. The Confederate currency was devaluing rapidly and Confederate bonds were becoming harder to sell. North Carolina farmers were having their property confiscated in an attempt to collect desperately needed tax revenue.

By the fall of 1863, the war's outcome was still far from certain, but the South's declining morale and rising financial, human and physical costs revealed a discernible trend. The increasing likelihood of a Northern victory caused great consternation in Canada and the Maritimes, for it was becoming clear that the United States would emerge from the war stronger than it had ever been. The Northern economy would be richer and more technologically advanced thanks to the impressive manner in which it met its need for war *matériel*. More rail had been laid and telegraph lines strung; harbours had been enlarged. The agricultural capacity of the North would also be greatly increased by Lincoln's 1862 Homestead Act, which was opening vast swaths of fertile land in the west to the plows of thousands of immigrants. And the United States would emerge from war with the largest, most advanced, best-trained, and most battle-hardened military the world had ever seen. Canadians and Maritimers were justifiably concerned that an angry behemoth of a country would have the ability to easily right past wrongs and pursue its old dreams of Manifest Destiny.

Brown was among those who realized that in order for the United States to wreak havoc on Canada, an American military invasion might not even be necessary. The American-Canadian Reciprocity Treaty was soon due to expire. At the outset of the war, Lord Lyons had worried about the treaty becoming one of its victims. Lyons and Monck exchanged a number of letters about the treaty's importance and agreed that the best way to keep it in place was to remain quiet about it.[19] In February 1862, Congress had created a three-man commission to examine the treaty question, and by June Lyons was warning Monck that Canada should be prepared to see it abrogated.[20]

The economic effects of the treaty's repeal would damage Canada's nascent industrial development. But there were other concerns. British investors controlling Hudson's Bay Company stock still claimed ownership of the vast swathe of territory called Rupert's Land. Brown knew that the land was ripe for development and that if Canadian interests did not quickly exploit its potential then Americans certainly would. He editorialized in the *Globe*, "Cooped up as Canada is between lake, river and the frozen North, should all the rest of the continent fall into the possession of the Americans, she will become of the smallest importance . . . nothing more or less than the handing over of the vast North West Territory, not only commercially but politically, to the United States."[21] He believed that American annexationists were biding their time and would pounce when the war ended.

By early 1864, the only Canadians who were not afraid were not paying attention. While Confederation had been a good idea before, the war had rendered it an imperative. Canada's constitutional questions needed to be solved once and for all; further delay would be suicidal. It was in this charged atmosphere that the Canadian Parliament convened in February.

Jammed in the gridlock that had paralyzed the Sandfield Macdonald administration throughout the previous session, the government proposed little and did less. Brown was silent and spent most of his time at his desk writing to Anne, who had just given birth to a healthy girl. Finally, on March 14, he interrupted one of the House's endless arcane debates by suddenly rising to propose a startling resolution. He proposed that a committee made up of members from both parties be formed to investigate the possibility of constitutional change: "I simply ask the House to say that a great evil exists, that a remedy must be found, and to appoint a committee to consider what that remedy should be."[22]

A spontaneous and shouting debate erupted, in which Galt, John A. Macdonald and Cartier all derided not what Brown had actually said but things he had said in the past. They accused him of having the wrong idea, an anti-French idea or a self-serving idea regarding federation. The debate raged on, with Brown making his final point two weeks later. Referring to military, economic and territorial threats from the United States, he thundered that Canadians needed to "stand shoulder to shoulder to fight their own battle for progress and prosperity, and if need be, to meet and do their best unitedly to repel a common foe."[23]

The debate reached a climax, but then events suddenly caused it to fizzle. In late March, an unrelated shift of political support in Canada East led the Reform government to resign. John A. Macdonald quickly hammered together a Conservative coalition and then the House rose so that cabinet ministers could seek re-election. The whole messy affair was proving Brown's point about Canada's dysfunctional political system.

While the Canadians dithered, the Civil War continued on toward its inexorable end. In March 1864, Ulysses S. Grant had been placed in supreme command of the Union forces. Lincoln finally had a general who agreed with him that the strategic objective of the Army of the Potomac should not be the capture of Richmond but the destruction of the Southern armies. Grant began reorganizing his army. He announced an end to prisoner exchanges, dealing a blow to the South, which already could not refill its diminishing ranks. The order also inadvertently led to the inhumane treatment of prisoners on both sides, with men suffering from disease and deprivation, and at places such as Georgia's hellish Andersonville, starvation.

When Grant put his plans into action, the battered and shrinking Army of Northern Virginia was forced to manoeuvre with the wile and fury of a cornered beast. In May, it drew Grant into one of the bloodiest battles of the war: The Wilderness. Two days of chaotic fighting in dense woods saw some men burned alive in forest fires that the battle had ignited. It ended in a draw, with more than 17,000 Union and nearly 8,000 Confederate casualties. Grant did not recoil or regroup as his predecessors would have done, but kept coming. Before the Union attack at Cold Harbor, many of Grant's men pinned notes on their backs stating, "Here lies the body of. . . ." The carnage on both sides reached proportions that were horrifying even to war-weary Americans numbed by over three years of staggeringly large casualty lists.

While Grant moved in America, Otto von Bismarck moved in Europe. The ambitious and charismatic Prussian had become minister-president in 1862 and immediately began preparing military, diplomatic and economic means to unify Germany. In the spring of 1864, the first of Bismarck's territorial conquests began with a Prussian-Austrian attack on Denmark. Palmerston recognized the danger that a strong and unified Germany would pose to Britain, but made the tactical error of announcing that his government would stand by Denmark. It did not. Bismarck's belligerence led to a reassessment of British military preparedness and the realization that the 14,500 troops spread thinly along the American border protecting colonies that seemed unwilling to defend themselves might soon be needed elsewhere. Little Englanders such as Robert Lowe insisted that all British troops be immediately withdrawn from Canada and the Maritimes to prepare for deployment in Europe.[24] Palmerston refused to consider such a drastic action, but the undeniable strength and potential of Grant's and Bismarck's forces was altering the way in which Britain saw the world and, in consequence, its view of Canada.

The only ray of hope for Britain was that Louis Napoleon had been successful in his Mexican adventure. French troops had taken Mexico City in June 1863. The bold—or perhaps reckless—move was an affront to America's Monroe Doctrine, as it re-introduced a European power into the western hemisphere. It was, however, welcomed by Palmerston, who saw it as helping Britain by drawing French troops, money and attention away from Europe, while poking at America's pride.[25]

It was from within this cauldron of events, threats and opportunities that Brown rose in the House once again in May 1864 to renew his call for a select committee to investigate constitutional change. The intervening months had chastened Canadian members and this time the resolution quickly passed. Within days, Brown stood in that Quebec City committee room and slid the key into his pocket. Both Macdonalds, Cartier, McGee, Mowat and others were there, and Galt would soon join them. Brown forced them to talk, and talk they did. Eight meetings took place and all the old hatreds, suspicions and hard feelings were put aside. The Civil War and its impending conclusion meant that the colonial leaders could no longer afford to play their old partisan games.

On June 14, the committee reported back to the House. It recommended the creation of a new federal system applied either to a reconfigured Canada East and West or to all British North American provinces. Committee members did not unanimously endorse the recommendation. Of the three who opposed it, the most important was John A. Macdonald, who insisted on a recommendation for a legislative union: one central government with no sub-national provinces.

The committee had done a tremendous service in bringing bipartisan support to the most divisive of issues, but its report was immediately swamped by the very inanities it was designed to address. Later that same day, the government fell—again.

Brown was infuriated, but like Grant, he refused to yield and instead pushed forward. He arranged a meeting with his old rival John A. Macdonald. The two had been political opponents for years, and their professional rivalry had grown to become a personal, visceral hatred. But Brown put those feelings aside and invited Galt and Macdonald for a chat in his room at the St. Louis Hotel.

The next day, Macdonald rose in the House. Everyone expected an announcement of dissolution and yet another election, the fourth in two years. Instead, he elicited gasps from both sides when he stated that a coalition had been formed and that Brown would be joining his government with the goal of bringing about constitutional change from the midst of crisis. Joseph Dufresne, a member from Canada East who had all but given up on Canada, rushed across the floor and hugged Brown around the neck, hanging there ludicrously before dropping to the floor and then jumping up to vigorously pump his hand.

Brown had taken the biggest political gamble of his life for the good of his country. Even the *Toronto Leader,* which seldom missed an opportunity to slam Brown, reported, "Events which occurred today may be pregnant with results of vastly greater importance than perhaps ever befell Canada."[26] The paper was right.

FORGING AN UN-AMERICAN VISION

The American Revolution and the country it created were the world's first and most successful expressions of the broad sweep of eighteenth-century Enlightenment thought. Thomas Jefferson and James Madison played essential roles in translating those thoughts to the events, needs and documents of their time, thereby providing America's ideological foundation. The civic humanist and republican ideas of the Enlightenment were sound, and the political structure constructed to reflect them was brilliant.

In November 1863, Abraham Lincoln referred to those ideas in the brief address in which he dedicated the Gettysburg cemetery to the thousands of young men who had given their lives in the epic battle four months earlier. Among those who travelled with the president from Washington to Pennsylvania was Canadian Reform party member of the legislature William McDougall. McDougall listened as Lincoln's two-minute address broadened the war's goal from preserving the union to reinventing America, as a signal to the world that a people could indeed organize themselves according to the core Enlightenment concepts of freedom and equality. As Lincoln memorably declared, "Four score and seven years ago, our fathers brought forth, upon this continent, a new nation, conceived in liberty, and dedicated to the proposition that all men are created equal. Now we are engaged in a great civil war, testing whether that nation, or any nation so conceived, and so dedicated, can long endure."[27]

McDougall understood Lincoln's point but, like his compatriots who would join him in Charlottetown and Quebec seven months later to create their own nation, he did not agree. While freedom and equality are noble concepts and certainly worthy of forming a society's foundation, the Civil War was proving to Canadian leaders that the United States was far from an inspirational beacon to the world. The fact that the country dedicated to freedom and equality had for three hundred years enslaved millions of its people, and was at that moment arming its citizens to butcher each other over the promise of its creed and its concept of federal power-sharing, was sufficient evidence that the American experiment had failed. Even the promise of the Emancipation Proclamation was belied by blood, Northern desertions and the race riots that followed its announcement. While McDougall and other Canadians disagreed about many things, on one fundamental point there was no dispute—America at war with itself offered only a negative example of political concepts that Canada must reject, and structural mistakes that it must avoid.[28]

Brown, Macdonald, Galt, Mowat, McGee, Cartier, McDougall and the others charged with the awesome responsibility of creating that country were practical men not poets, and practising politicians not angels. They were also working in the shadow of a clock and a crisis. Consequently, rather than seeking to persuasively express the philosophical basis for their actions, as the American colonists had done when they entrusted

Jefferson and others to draft a declaration of independence, they acted according to their experience and the already fully formed utilitarian ideas that they brought to the table. Those ideas were complex and reflected their late nineteenth-century mindset rather than the eighteenth-century ideological values of their American counterparts.

Most important among the concepts that informed their deliberations were those of Edmund Burke, an Irish nationalist and British member of parliament. In 1790, he had written the influential *Reflections on the Revolution in France*, an uncompromising critique of the revolution, its leaders and its ideas. He argued that governments should not be based upon abstract theory that might be temporarily popular with mobs on the street, but rather upon long-tested and respected tradition. He warned about the dangers inherent in political leaders' becoming "entangled in the mazes of metaphysic sophistry." [29] Circumstances, rather than a blind adherence to some set of ideological principles, should dictate practical solutions. Brown, Macdonald and the others, quite appropriately, did not mention Burke's anti-ideology ideology, but it was present throughout their deliberations and it informed their decisions.[30] When later explaining the political structure they had designed, for instance, Macdonald conjured Burkean ideas to defend it: "I am satisfied to confine myself to practical things—to the securing of such practical measures as the country really wants. I am satisfied not to have a reputation for indulging in imaginary schemes and harbour ideas that may end sometimes in an annexation movement, sometimes in Federalism, and sometimes in a legislative union, but always utopian and never practical."[31]

Important among the practical measures to which Macdonald referred was the anti-Enlightenment and un-American notion that power must not be split among government branches or rest with the executive; it must rest, rather, with Parliament: "A great evil in the United States is that the President is a despot for four years. . . . Under the British Constitution, with the people having always the power in their own hands and with the responsibility of a Ministry to Parliament, we are free from such despotism."[32]

Linked to the Canadian founders' belief in the primacy of Parliament was their agreement that members of parliament needed to be more than simply delegates sent to echo the views of constituents. They should be educated, thoughtful leaders, unencumbered by whims of the un- or ill-informed electorate.[33] This common understanding again reflected Burke, who, in a speech to the people of his Bristol constituency, had bluntly stated that he would all but ignore them, as he believed that members of parliament needed to act not according to the desires of their constituents but according to their considered opinion.[34]

Ancillary to the rejection of a presidential system in favour of a parliamentary system rich with independent members was an abhorrence of the American brand of democracy. Canadian and British leaders alike saw American democracy as akin to mob rule, to be avoided at all costs. The Canadians preferred constitutional liberty. Cartier spoke in favour of the notion with an argument for restraint in democracy: the United States "founded [its] federation for the purpose of carrying out democracy on this continent but we felt . . . convinced that purely democratic institutions could not be conducive to the peace and prosperity of nations."[35] Cartier and the others were not damning democracy itself but rather the unbridled and often undisciplined, ill-informed power of the majority— the mobs that had wreaked havoc on the streets of Boston and Paris and to whom, it was believed, too many American politicians bowed far too easily, until they had tilted so far forward as to fall into civil war.

Also important were ideas regarding minority rights. At the outset of talks among Canadian political leaders in that summer of 1864, Macdonald's was the voice most strongly advocating a legislative union in which one parliament would rule without the divided powers of sub-national governments. He was quickly swayed, however, by the realization that the project was doomed from the start unless the rights of the French Catholic minority were protected, and that the best guarantor of those rights was a two-tier federal system. Cartier was essential in making this point. He wanted to ensure that Canada East would have its unique language, religion, education and system of law protected in a new federal structure. He convinced Macdonald and the others that only through the establishment of legitimate sub-national governments, with sufficient power to protect those rights, would French Canadians support the creation of a new country—the state must protect the nation. However, he said that if the structure was sound, and through it French rights secure, then French Canadians would be among the new country's most loyal citizens.[36]

Despite their agreement on the need for provincial governments, Brown and the others were unanimous in their desire to locate overwhelming constitutional power in the parliament of a central government. The United States had been built on the assumption that the states existed first as independent entities, and that they created the central government by surrendering only tiny slivers of their sovereignty. Brown, Macdonald and the others on their committee saw the concept of states' rights as the fundamental flaw in the American system which had caused the Civil War. As Macdonald argued, "The various States of the adjoining Republic had always acted as separate sovereignties. . . . The primary error at the formation of their constitution was that each state reserved to itself all sovereign rights, save the small portion delegated. We must reverse this process by strengthening the General Government and conferring on the Provincial bodies only such powers as may be required for local purposes. All sectional prejudices and interests can be legislated for by the local legislatures."[37] In response to James Chandler, a member of Nova Scotia's legislature who worried about locating too much power at the centre, Macdonald said: "We should concentrate the power in the Federal Government, and not adopt the decentralization of the United States. Mr. Chandler would give sovereign power to the Local Legislatures, just where the United States failed. . . . Mr. [Alexander] Stephens, the present [Confederate]Vice President, was a strong Union man, yet when the time came, he went to his state."[38]

The essence of the committee's thinking was that a new Canadian parliament would be afforded all the power it needed to tend to the interests of the country as a whole, while checking the power of the provincial governments by listing important national concerns as federal powers. Second, a reserve clause would note that any power not specifically allocated to the provincial governments would be held by the central parliament. If this were not enough, the central parliament would also have the power to disallow any laws passed by a provincial government that were deemed to contradict the welfare of the country. The federal government alone would speak for Canada.

Brown and his colleagues emphasized that the creation of this new federal state would not sever links with Britain. To the contrary, there was unanimity in the desire to maintain the trans-Atlantic ties that the Americans had so violently cut in the Revolutionary War. After all, beyond economic and military necessity, there existed a spiritual link to Britain. Macdonald later exclaimed as a campaign slogan, "A British subject I was born, a British subject I will die." His phrase was effective because it reflected the collective consensus. Even George Cartier took pride in being a British citizen, wore clothes tailored in London and named one of his daughters Reine-Victoria. He saw the maintenance of British ties as essential to ensuring the survival of French Canada, for its cultural uniqueness would certainly decline if it was allowed to be placed in the American melting pot. Cartier said of his proud French, and Catholic, nation, "If they had their institutions, their language, and their religion intact today, it was precisely because of their adherence to the British Crown."[39] Indeed, Canadians and Maritimers were sentimental enough to love all things British, while practical enough to know that if the British ties were cut, their days of independence from the United States would be numbered.

CONFEDERATION CONFERENCES

The stately *Queen Victoria* steamed into Charlottetown's beautiful harbour on September 1, 1864. The picturesque Prince Edward Island town was home to seven thousand people and the well-kept Georgian homes of its capital city stretched along streets rising from the tranquil bay. As Brown wrote to Anne, "It is as pretty a country as you ever put your eye upon."[40] Eight Canadian delegates, including Brown, McDougall, Cartier,

Galt, McGee and Macdonald, changed into fine clothes in preparation for the expected grand welcome. It did not come. Few had noticed their arrival, as most of Charlottetown was preoccupied by the Slaymaker and Nichols Olympic Circus. The Canadians watched, bemused, as the province's provincial secretary, W.H. Pope, rowed himself to the ship in a little dory and did his best to greet them warmly.

The Island's lieutenant-governor, George Dundas, hosted a reception at Government House that evening. It was the first of the many social gatherings during which the delegates from various provinces grew to know, like and trust each other. While Brown had been essential in getting them all to Charlottetown, in that first reception John A. Macdonald proved himself Confederation's indispensable man.

Macdonald had been late in warming to the idea of Confederation. He had always seemed fixated on immediate, practical, partisan and political matters. In Charlottetown, however, his inestimable skill with people and his ability to forge unlikely coalitions became the movement's single most important asset, a fact not lost on him when, beside his signature in a Charlottetown guest book, he listed his occupation as "cabinet maker." He charmed the Maritime delegates; he charmed their wives. He talked more, smiled more, drank more and persuaded more about more than anyone there.

The Canadians had arrived well prepared. Cartier, Macdonald and Galt began with three days of presentations outlining the legal, political and military reasons for Confederation, their dreams for a country that would someday stretch to the Arctic and Pacific oceans, and then intricacies of the financial details. Brown spoke the next day for over four hours about the proposed constitutional structure. Having heard the Canadians, the Maritime delegates met and dropped their pretense of a narrow Maritime union—they were in. The conference moved to Saint John and eventually, with more meetings, to Halifax. Promises were made to resume the talks in Quebec City in October.

At the final dinner before the recess, hosted by Nova Scotia's Charles Tupper at the Halifax Hotel, Macdonald rose to present a toast. He thanked

his hosts, and spoke admiringly of all that had been accomplished. He
spoke of the delegates proudly drawing upon Britain's long tradition of
parliamentary democracy. Macdonald praised the American Constitution
for its bold uniqueness but also noted the flaws in the American system that
the Civil War had laid bare. "It is for us," he said, "to take advantage by
experience, and endeavour to see if we cannot arrive by careful study at
such a plan as will avoid the mistakes of our neighbours. . . . If we can only
attain that object—a vigorous general government—we shall not be New
Brunswickers, nor Nova Scotians, nor Canadians, but British Americans,
under the sway of the British sovereign."[41] He went on to argue that a
larger, stronger union could better defend itself against aggressive American
intentions, and he equated the proposed new Canada to the Confederacy:
"The gallant defence that is being made by the Southern Republic—at this
moment they have not much more than four millions of men—not much
exceeding our own numbers—yet what a brave fight they have made."[42]

The conference resumed on October 10 in Quebec City. Once again,
each delegation demonstrated its commitment to parliamentary democracy by including government and opposition among their members.
This time even Newfoundland sent two delegates. They met in a grey
stone building with tall arched windows through which delegates could
marvel at the beauty of the St. Lawrence River, churning far below the
towering bluff. Quebec's old stone buildings and the cobbled streets of
lower town charmed, but skies that had been so clear in the Maritimes
offered only dark days and endless rain. There would be fewer walks and
buggy rides, but just as many grand balls and multi-course dinners. The
champagne flowed as freely as the rain. Canadian premier Sir Etienne-
Paschal Taché was the chair, but Macdonald again ran the show.

The conference moved quickly to determine details of the structure
of the proposed government and the division of powers between the central parliament and provincial governments. Progress slowed when talk
turned to the Senate. It was finally decided that the best way to ensure that
ultimate political authority lay with the House of Commons would be to
establish an appointed Senate. As appointees, senators would be expected

to provide only what Macdonald called "sober second thought" in their consideration of bills, while the elected members of the House exercised genuine power.

On October 20, the day after the long debate on the Senate had ended, news arrived of the raid on St. Albans, Vermont. For the next stressful week, Canadian leaders balanced communications with Monck relating to the capture of the raiders, and threats from General Dix and Seward, with efforts to keep the Quebec conference on track. Distracting as these events were, they clearly demonstrated that danger from the United States was more than just another debating point.

New Brunswick's Leonard Tilley and Nova Scotia's Charles Tupper led their delegations with aplomb. They and the two island delegations were secure in the knowledge that, while it had been agreed that Canada would get two votes on all conference matters since the proposed deal would divide them into Ontario and Quebec, the four Maritime delegations could still outvote them if they wished. The arithmetic ensured that Maritime matters would not be taken for granted. Support for the inter-colonial railway was guaranteed, and less-industrialized New Brunswick negotiated a financial subsidy to be paid by the new federal government.

As discussions moved forward, however, Prince Edward Island and Newfoundland delegates found themselves first frustrated and then angered. Neither bordered the United States, and so neither shared the visceral fear of the Americans felt by the others. Both resented the small number of members of parliament that would be afforded by their tiny populations and saw no benefit in the intercolonial railway that so excited the delegates from Nova Scotia and New Brunswick. Nor were they moved by Brown's talk of expanding to the west. They were drifting away, and even Macdonald's charm could not hold them.

The conference ended on October 27. All thirty-three delegates, even those from Prince Edward Island and Newfoundland, voted to support the seventy-two resolutions and agreed to take them to their respective legisla-tures for ratification. But first there would be a tour for the Maritimers who had not seen the Canadian province with which they had just voted to partner. They began the next day in Montreal. Then, in Ottawa, they marvelled at the Parliament Buildings that would house the new government. The Gothic buildings, although still under construction, inspired awe with their size and grandeur, and with the magnificence of their commanding presence on a cliff overlooking the mile-wide Ottawa River.

Macdonald then withdrew to his home in Kingston, surrendering to exhaustion and the bottle. Brown stepped up and hosted the group in Toronto. At a grand luncheon at the city's Music Hall, he delivered the keynote address, explaining to the large audience what the Confederation delegates had done and why they had done it. It was November 3, the day that Magistrate Charles-Joseph Coursol had the St. Alban's raiders before him in court. Brown knew those gathered to hear him were nervous. The papers had been filled for weeks with stories of the raid and its consequences. Brown began by explaining constitutional principles that would render the government more efficient, and emphasized the economic advantages and the opportunity for western expansion that Confederation would offer. He concluded with what his anxious audience may well have believed to be his strongest argument: "The delegates have unanimously resolved that the United Provinces of British North American shall be placed at the earliest moment in a thorough state of defence. . . . I cannot doubt they [Americans] have plenty of work already on their hands—and I confess that notwithstanding the fierce ebullitions of the American press, I have faith in the good feelings of our neighbours . . . but any fight would show, in the hour of trial, that the spirit which was manifested in 1812 has not died in 1864."[43]

DEFENDING AN INDEFENSIBLE LINE

Brown's bold words were meant to soothe and inspire, but they rang hollow when measured against reality. Earlier in the year, the Colonial Office had asked British army engineer Lieutenant Colonel W.F.D. Jervois to tour Canada and the Maritimes and assess what would be needed to mount a viable defence should the Americans invade. Months later, the various irritants that had been stirring Canadian-American distrust and increasing the possibility of American aggression had led the Colonial Office to dispatch Jervois again to complete a new assessment. His second *Report on the Defence of Canada* was released just days after Brown's luncheon speech, on November 9. Jervois's new conclusions were jarring. Constructing and augmenting border fortifications, building a credible Great Lakes fleet, and training and properly arming a sufficient number of men would cost a staggering £1.75 million. Even if all that were accomplished quickly and properly, Jervois argued, an American invasion would lead to a surrender of the southwestern part of Canada West, with effective defensive positions possible only in St. Catharines and Toronto. Even those cities would likely have to be surrendered. With all the preparations done, and all that territory given up by retreating British soldiers and Canadian militia, Jervois still believed that victory against the United States would be possible, but only if the British navy attacked American coastal cities from bases in Halifax and Bermuda, and then negotiated to have Canada returned.[44]

The Canadian cabinet soberly digested the report and responded with a proposal to appropriate $50,000 as the first installment of the $2 million needed to fortify Montreal, and an additional million dollars to train and arm more militia.[45] The proposal was predicated on the condition that Britain would contribute even more money and troops, while backing a loan so that Canada could pay its share. Brown was dispatched to London to determine whether the British would support the new defence plans and appropriations as well as the Quebec Conference's seventy-two resolutions.

Before setting sail, Brown learned that Abraham Lincoln had been re-elected to a second term as president. The outcome had by no means been certain. In fact, Lincoln had been so sure that he would lose that in August he had written a note insisting that each of his cabinet secretaries promise to commit themselves to saving the Union in the months between the November election and March inauguration of a new president. He folded the copies so that none could read them before signing.

In the Chicago convention that Jacob Thompson had tried but failed to sabotage, the Democrats had nominated disgraced Union general George McClellan. He was as weak a presidential candidate as he had been a general, and stood on the shaky Copperhead platform of peace through negotiation and the creation of two separate American states. The party's platform had been primarily written by Clement Vallandigham—in his Canadian hotel room.

McClellan's candidacy had been doomed when, on September 3, 1864, Union general William Tecumseh Sherman took Atlanta. Lincoln's steely determination to preserve the Union through victory was vindicated. Voting day was on November 8 and by midnight the decision of the people was unmistakable. Lincoln defeated McClellan by more than a million votes; and 116,887 soldiers had voted for the president, while only 37,748 had voted for their former general. Lincoln was instantly stronger than he had been, with a Union victory more certain and the North more united. For Canadians, all of this meant more foreboding than ever before.

On November 16, Brown left New York harbour aboard the *Persia*. Coincidentally, among his travelling companions was Lt. Colonel Jervois. Immediately upon his arrival in London on December 3, Brown was taken to meet the new colonial secretary, Edward Cardwell.

Cardwell was the Oxford-educated son of a Liverpool businessman and had been a member of parliament since 1841. In cabinet posts in both the Aberdeen and Palmerston administrations, his intelligence won him great respect; his ambition and drive led him to seek positive change in every matter he tackled. Cardwell's correspondence with Governor General Monck revealed a man with a keen understanding of, and interest in, British North America. While Palmerston, Gladstone and cabinet colleagues had slightly shifted in their opinions of Canadian Confederation, Cardwell brought a sense of firm purpose and direction. He was unwilling to simply to wait for the Canadian colonies to come to a consensus on reorganizing themselves and their relationship with Britain. The war and the growing certainty of Northern victory had robbed Britain of the luxury of patience. Cardwell wanted Monck and the Maritime lieutenant-governors to actively push for change, and had penned a number of letters to that effect.[46]

In January 1864, there had been about 11,000 British troops in Canada and another 3,500 in the Maritimes. In July, Cardwell argued in cabinet that there were too few troops to mount a credible defence but enough to provoke an attack. Cardwell had read a report from British captain James Goodenough, who had been sent by the Duke of Newcastle to spy on American military preparations of the Great Lakes. Goodenough's May 1864 report stated that the number of American ships and fortifications under construction, and the improvements being made to harbours and connecting roads, allowed no other conclusion: the Union was preparing for war in Canada.[47] It was Cardwell who had sent Lt. Colonel Jervois to write a second report.

Monck had been keeping Cardwell up to date on the Confederation conferences and had sent a copy of the seventy-two resolutions that had been hammered out in Quebec.[48] The day before Brown arrived in London, Cardwell had sent a message to Monck praising the resolutions and offering his full support for their implementation.[49]

It was in this light that the colonial secretary welcomed Brown with open arms. They discussed the resolutions and the issues related to them for several hours. Cardwell told Brown what he had assured Monck. He agreed fully that the economic and military dangers facing the British North American colonies were real and that reorganization according to the model of the Quebec resolutions was not only intelligent but essential.[50]

Over the next few days, Brown met with Britain's political elite, and all echoed Cardwell's points. Chancellor of the Exchequer William Gladstone, Colonial Office Undersecretary Sir Frederick Rogers and Foreign Secretary Earl John Russell all offered support and sought Brown's views on the defence question in light of the St. Albans raid and other mischief that Thompson had instigated.

Brown sent a report to Macdonald that summed up the effusive British reaction to the Confederation proposals and what he believed were the main reasons for it: "There is a manifest desire in almost every quarter that ere long, the British colonies should shift for themselves, and in some quarters evident regret that we did not declare at once for independence. I am very sorry to observe this, but it arises I hope, from the fear of invasion of Canada by the United States, and will soon pass away with the cause that excites it."[51]

Brown was able to enjoy Christmas with Anne's family. While he had followed news of the St. Albans raid and its international ramifications in the pages of the *London Times*, upon his arrival back in Toronto on January 13, he was surprised by the level of tension that greeted him.

FRUSTRATION, ELATION AND DESPAIR— JANUARY TO APRIL 1865

George Brown returned to Quebec City to chair cabinet preparations for the parliamentary session that was to begin on January 19, a month ahead of schedule. It had been hoped that the only important order of business would be the debate and vote to ratify the seventy-two Confederation resolutions agreed to in the fall. However, the American reaction to Jacob Thompson's irritating Confederate incursions, made worse by Coursol's release of the St. Albans raiders, had been swift and the consequences portentous. Confederation would have to wait.

Lincoln had approved new regulations regarding American troops pursuing criminals over the border as well as a new passport law to control access to the United States. Seward had announced the end of the Rush-Bagot Agreement, clearing the way for a remilitarization of the Great Lakes, and Congress had voted for the abrogation of the 1854 Reciprocity Treaty. The American media supported all these measures as fervently as it had expressed outrage in the previous three years at what was generally perceived as Canada's pro-South proclivities and activities. A *New York Times* editorial praising the Reciprocity decision stated: "The first object of reciprocity was the cultivation of a strong and intimate friendship with Canada but the war had proved the futility of this."[52] Many papers pressed for stronger retributions toward Canada. The *Chicago Tribune*, for instance, urged General Dix to sweep over the border and "take Canada as a St. Bernard would throttle a poodle pup."[53]

Attorney General Macdonald and Governor General Monck had discussed Coursol's decision to release the St. Albans raiders and agreed that it had been an abomination. They had correctly predicted the swift and negative American reaction.[54] Macdonald, as always, remained calm in the face of crisis: "We must perform our duty, however, irrespective of the smiles or frowns of any foreign body and will never be hurried into extra exertions by proclamations like those of General Dix, or prevented by any feeling of indignation from carrying our laws into full force.[55]

On December 20, days after Coursol had made his fateful decision, Macdonald had approved a two-hundred-dollar reward for information leading to the recapture of Young and his men. Young was arrested later that day. Others were picked up in Maine where they had, surprisingly, tried to disappear by enlisting in the Union army. More were arrested in Newfoundland, having found work on a whaling ship. They were all brought back to Montreal to await a second hearing.

Meanwhile, Macdonald ordered an investigation of Coursol and Montreal police chief, Guillaume Lamothe, who had helped return the stolen St. Alban's money to the thieves. Coursol was found to have made a decision far above his pay scale. Lamothe, meanwhile, had been motivated by politics: he was a Reform Party supporter determined to embarrass the Conservative government. The Canadian government announced that it would pay fifty thousand dollars to the St. Albans banks to cover the better part of the money that Lamothe had returned to the raiders.

With these short-term responses complete, Monck and Macdonald moved to implement changes that would address longer-term issues. The Western Frontier Constabulary Force was created to mirror work already being done in Canada East under the leadership of William Ermatinger, former police officer and field inspector of the volunteer Active Militia. Led by Gilbert McMicken, the new force would coordinate border patrols and improve surveillance on Union and Confederate activities. Macdonald spoke admiringly of McMicken: "He is a shrewd, cool and determined man who won't easily lose his head, and who will fearlessly perform his duty."[56] McMicken was a Conservative member of the legislature for Welland and mayor of the small border town of Clifton. McMicken had also worked with Confederate agent James Holcombe to gather Confederate soldiers in Canada and return them to the South, though there is no evidence that Macdonald knew about this.[57]

Macdonald drafted a new law granting the Canadian government the power it needed to better defend the border against American incursions and to arrest and deport Confederates attacking the North from Canada. Monck had communicated with Seward, Lyons and Cardwell about how the law should be structured.[58] The Alien Act allowed for any foreign national even suspected of engaging in acts interpreted as hostile to a nation friendly to Canada to be fined up to three thousand dollars, have his property seized and be deported. It was overwhelmingly passed on February 6, 1865.

Canadian leaders were not the only ones worried about the ratcheting up of border tensions. In a report from London, American minister Adams reminded Seward that the British Parliament still contained many friends of the Confederacy and enemies of the North. He reported that Southern agents in Britain and Europe were taking full advantage of the propaganda gift the American actions of the past few weeks had handed them. He wrote to Seward on February 9: "The insurgent emissaries and their friends are busy fanning the notion that this is a prelude to war the moment our domestic difficulties are over."[59] He asked Seward to do all he could to defuse the situation.

Foreign Secretary Russell composed a remarkable letter addressed to European Confederate agents, including Mason and Slidell, with copies to Monck and Lincoln. The letter stated, in part, that the "so-called" Confederate States had been undertaking a number of violent acts, including raids onto American soil from Canada, with the intention of inciting an Anglo-American war. He cited recent actions taken by Canada to stop them and continued, "I trust you will feel yourself authorised to promise that such practices will cease, and shall be entirely abandoned for the future."[60] Lincoln was so pleased with the letter that he had General Grant send a copy under a white flag of truce to General Lee. Lee refused to accept the letter, however, and sent it back to Grant with his compliments.

Unknown to all those trying again to avoid a broader war was that two months earlier, on December 3, Jacob Thompson had sat down in his Toronto hotel room and composed a long and detailed report to Confederate Secretary of State Benjamin. He acknowledged his failures but tried to sound hopeful: "I have relaxed no effort to carry out the objects the Government had in sending me here. I had hoped at different times to have accomplished more, but I still do not think my mission has been altogether fruitless."[61] He admitted, "A large sum of money has been expended in fostering and furthering these operations and it now seems to have been too little profit. But in reviewing the past I do not see how it could have been avoided, nor has it been spent altogether in vain. The apprehensions of the enemy have caused him to bring back and keep from the field in front at least 60,000 to watch and browbeat the people at home."[62]

Thompson wasn't finished, but he realized that his mission needed to wind down. With Beall's botched December train-highjacking attempt outside of Buffalo, Thompson had been forced to listen to yet another report rife with excuses and failure. He told those who wished to leave to pack up and return to the South, and paid the travel expenses of any who asked. The next week, Brigadier General Edwin Gray Lee, Robert E. Lee's cousin, arrived at Toronto's Queen's Hotel with a message. Thompson was to be relieved. Benjamin's letter praised the work Thompson had done, but said, "From reports which reach us from trustworthy sources, we are satisfied that so close espionage is kept upon you that your services have been deprived of value which is attached to your further residence in Canada. The President thinks, therefore, that as soon as the gentleman arrives who bears this letter . . . that you transfer to him as *quietly* as possible all of the information that you have obtained and the release of funds in your hands and then return to the Confederacy."[63]

The news surprised and angered Thompson, who argued that he had a great deal of work left to do. He shared the information he had with Lee but made no preparations to leave.[64] With Lee establishing himself first in Montreal, Thompson remained active in Toronto. Many of his compatriots were in jail in Toronto, New York and Chicago, and he was determined to do all he could to help them. He forwarded money to help defray the legal costs of Bennett Young and his co-perpetrators of the St. Albans raid. Thompson also wrote letters to Jefferson Davis asking for copies of the men's commissions so that they could be tried as prisoners of war rather than spies or common criminals. He did the same for Beall, who was on trial in New York. Confederate secretary of the navy Stephen Mallory sent copies of Beall's commission with a note stating that Jefferson Davis had authorized everything that Thompson and his men had done.[65]

On January 4, Confederate courier Lieutenant S.B. Davis arrived in Toronto. The presence of Macdonald's newly hired and empowered detectives, along with Seward's ever-present spies, meant that that the Queen's Hotel was no longer safe, so Davis was spirited to George Denison's home. Thompson gave the messages he needed Davis to deliver to Richmond to Denison's wife, who had been helping Confederate couriers sneak information across Union lines for some time. Secret pockets were sewn into the linings of clothing and boots, and photographs miniaturized and hidden in the back of buttons. Messages were sometimes written in pencil on silk ribbons and then sewn into clothing. In Davis's case, Mrs. Dension sewed Thompson's letters into the civilian clothing they had procured for him. Davis dyed his light hair black and then Lt. Colonel Denison hid him in a carriage and drove him to the Mimico train station.[66] Despite the precautions, on January 15, Lieutenant Davis was arrested in Newark, Ohio, found guilty of treason, and sent to Andersonville prison to await his hanging.

Thompson wrote directly to his old acquaintance Abraham Lincoln. He noted that Lieutenant Davis was a Confederate officer who had been acting on his behalf to gather documentation for an upcoming extradition trial. His letter concluded, "You have a right to retain him as a prisoner of war, but I declare on my honor he is not a spy."[67] Lincoln intervened and Davis was paroled.

Davis had been carrying messages regarding Acting Master Bennett Burley, the ammunitions dealer who had been doing business from the foundry in Guelph, Canada West. He was on trial in Toronto for his part in the *Philo Parsons* adventure. Burley had been found guilty of unlawful warfare and ordered extradited to the United States, but the verdict was under appeal. While waiting for Burley's day in court, Thompson had written to James Mason, the Confederate minister in London. He sent copies of court transcripts with an appeal: "I think you will agree with me that in this case not only is a great outrage about to be perpetrated on a citizen, but a great wrong is to be done and an insult offered to the Confederate States."[68] He asked Mason to put pressure on the British government to demand that Governor General Monck intervene and stop the extradition of Burley to the United States. Thompson was obviously unaware of the fact that Mason's power had shrunk to a size as pitiable as his ability to manoeuvre.

Thompson also wrote to Jefferson Davis, who sent a letter directly to the court on Burley's behalf. It is important for what it revealed about Davis's view on all that had been transpiring in Canada.

Now, therefore, I, Jefferson Davis, President of the Confederate States of America, do hereby declare and make known to all whom it may concern, that the expedition aforesaid undertaken in the month of September last, for the capture of the armed steamer *Michigan*, a vessel of the war of the United States, and for the release of the prisoners of war, citizens of the Confederate States of America, held captive by the United States of American at Johnson's Island, was a belligerent expedition ordered and undertaken under the authority of the Confederate States of America and that the Government of the Confederate States of America assumes the responsibility for answering for the acts and conduct of any of its officers engaged in said expedition, and especially of the said Bennett G. Burley, an Acting Master of the Confederate States Navy.[69]

Davis went on to write that all those involved had been ordered to "abstain from violating any of the laws and regulations of the Canadian and British authorities in relation to neutrality."[70] Burley was released.

Confederate Captain John Beall was not so lucky. Beall was on trial in New York City for his involvement in a number of Thompson's activities. The court found that he was an officer of the Confederate government acting on orders, but that no soldier is immune from prosecution for illegal actions based on that excuse. Judge Advocate-General John Bolles submitted: "If, then, such unlawful command be given and obeyed, its only effect is to prove that both he who gave and he who obeyed the command are criminals, and deserve to be gibbeted together."[71] Beall was found guilty and on February 24 was hanged.

DEBATING IN A HURRICANE

Having made efforts to avert war and ease cross-border strains and mistrust, the Canadian legislature re-initiated its delayed deliberations on Confederation. The debates began on February 6, 1865, with a long and detailed oration by John A. Macdonald. He was followed the next day by Cartier and the next by Brown. All the old arguments were restated in long but articulate and persuasive speeches. The need for increased defence capability took a more central place than had been the case even the previous September and October. Nearly every member spoke, and sixty made direct mention of Confederation as being necessary to create a state that was larger, more stable and better able to protect itself against American aggression. McGee was perhaps most inflammatory in his speech:

> They coveted Florida, and seized it; they coveted Louisiana, and purchased it; they coveted Texas, and stole it; and then they picked a quarrel with Mexico which ended by their getting California. They sometimes pretend to despise these colonies as prizes beneath their ambition; but had we not had the strong arm of England over us we should not now have a separate existence. The acquisition of Canada was the first ambition of the American Confederacy, and never ceased

to be so, when her troops were a handful and her navy scarce a squadron. Is it likely to be stopped now, when she counts her guns afloat by the thousands and her troops by hundreds of thousands?. . . only vigorous and timely preparation would protect British North America from the horrors of a war such as the world has never seen.[72]

While less flamboyant, George Brown made the point most effectively:

A revolution has occurred in Great Britain on the subject of colonial relations to the parent state—the government of the United States has become a great warlike power—our commercial relations with the republic are seriously threatened—and every man in British North America has now placed before him for solution the practical question: What shall be done in view of the changed relations on which we are about to enter? Shall we continue to struggle along as isolated communities—or shall we unite cordially together to extend our commerce, develop the resources of our country, and to defend our soil?[73]

Opponents of Confederation also presented their arguments, but it appeared that the well-organized government, confident in its argument and parliamentary majority, would win the day. Then disturbing news came from New Brunswick. Premier Leonard Tilley had been a strong advocate of Confederation throughout the two conferences and had returned to Fredericton determined to see the resolutions ratified. A quiet, cautious, churchgoing, teetotalling widower and father of seven, Tilley faced an unexpected storm of opposition to Confederation with the stoicism for which he was known. Then he made a mistake. The electoral timetable was against him, as he was scheduled to go to the people in March. Nova Scotia's premier, Charles Tupper, and Macdonald both wrote a number of letters to Tilley urging him to present the resolutions to his House before dissolution.[74] With his majority and opposition leaders behind him, ratification could have been easy. More than that,

Macdonald argued, the debate would educate the people and thereby ease his re-election by developing support for the cause.[75]

New Brunswick was a fragmented colony. Its most evident division was between the north, which saw itself more closely linked to Montreal and the rest of Canada, and the south, which had firmer cultural and business ties with the United States. Confident that he could carry the north and persuade the south, Tilley called the election. All other issues were either forgotten or folded into what became a Confederation referendum. He lost. He even lost his own seat. There were celebrations in some quarters and charges of corruption in others. A *Morning News* editorial claimed that American money had been spent freely and influenced the outcome of the election: "The alternative of Confederation or Annexation is more than ever confirmed when we see how completely American influence can control elections of the Province."[76]

News of the defeat arrived in Quebec City on March 6, just as the Canadian Confederation debates were wrapping up. Newfoundland was delaying in dealing with the question. Prince Edward Island, as expected, had declared that the scheme held nothing for its people. Its premier resigned, the government fell into disarray, and finally the legislature voted no. In Nova Scotia, Joseph Howe had roused himself from the semi-retirement of a boring patronage post to lead the charge against Confederation. He tapped into the pride that Nova Scotians based on their prosperity, linked to lumber, coal and shipbuilding, and their worldliness, afforded them by their busy Halifax port. Howe exploited that pride by inviting Nova Scotians to ask themselves if Confederation would serve only Canada and therefore be unnecessary for Nova Scotia's future.[77] The Conservative Tupper disagreed with Howe and continued to fight. He was supported by Liberal leaders Adams George Archibald and Jonathan McCully, but victory was by no means secure.

It appeared that Confederation would fail, but Brown and Macdonald took the Maritime body blows and continued the fight for ratification. Finally, at two thirty in the morning on March 10, 1865, with a spring blizzard raging outside, the Canadian House voted 91 to 33 in favour of the resolutions. Despite the disappointing news from the Maritimes, plans were made to leave to seek British parliamentary approval in London. Macdonald was worn out, his personal finances were in disarray and he did not want to go. Brown, too, was tired and felt guilty for having spent so much time away from Anne and their growing children. But the two former enemies nonetheless prepared to leave.

THE END

As Macdonald and Brown were arranging their departure, word arrived that the Canadian and British efforts to assure the Americans of their goodwill following the St. Albans raid were having their desired effect. On the same day that the legislature ratified Confederation, Seward wrote to Monck that the passport law as it applied to Canadians was being rescinded, though Maritimers would still need to show passports to cross the border. Shortly afterward, Seward announced that the Rush-Bagot Agreement would not be abrogated after all.

News from the battlefield was soon even more significant. Thousands of men and boys had spent the last months shivering outside Petersburg, Virginia. Through the winter of 1864–1865, Lee's options had continued to shrink, along with his army. He had established a line of fortified trenches from Petersburg, Virginia, all the way north to Richmond, thirty-five miles away. The spring brought no relief. Grant's mammoth army continued its long siege of the embattled Petersburg. Meanwhile, Union general Sherman was continuing his march across South Carolina to the sea, leaving a fifty-mile swath of destruction in his wake. Cities were burned, telegraph poles were torn down and railway track was ripped up. Southern leaders knew what he was going to do and where he was going, but they could not stop him.

On March 4, 1865, Lincoln had delivered his second inaugural address. Just as he stood to speak, two days of steady rain suddenly stopped, the dark clouds parted and the sun shone down upon him. Thousands had gathered to listen. All knew the war was nearing its end and much of what he said pointed to the rebuilding that would soon need to be done. But he also promised that fighting would continue until the bitter end. Few noted that, just thirty-five feet away, the famous actor John Wilkes Booth watched the speech with teeth clenched in rage.

Shortly afterward, Lincoln accepted Grant's invitation to join him at City Point, Virginia. He arrived on March 25. Five days later, Grant's troops were finally able to breach Lee's flank, leading to an end of the stalemate and a Union victory on April 1 at Five Forks. The next day, Grant ordered an attack along the entire Confederate line. Lee had no alternative but to withdraw what remained of his bedraggled and starving army. Lee sent a telegram to Richmond, and within hours Jefferson Davis was on the run with his government in a valise. His officials set fire to cotton and to documents that could not be carried, and the flames quickly got away from them. The fires consumed much of the city, along with Confederate dreams of statehood.

On April 4, with a guard of only twelve blue-coated sailors, President Lincoln arrived aboard a small boat at Richmond's Rocketts Landing. The city was largely abandoned, with smoke still rising from smouldering buildings. Resplendent and instantly recognizable in his black suit and tall stovepipe hat, Lincoln walked hand-in-hand with his son, down charred streets. Faces peered through broken windows and African-Americans, who just days before had been enslaved, filled the streets and formed a buoyant parade behind him. Cheers greeted Lincoln when he arrived at Richmond's Capitol Square. He nodded at a guard and then entered the Confederate White House. He sat for a moment at Davis's desk. He said nothing. He took nothing.

Lee led what was left of his army west, but it was clear that they were done fighting. He sent a message to Grant, and on April 9, 1865, the two met at a house in the little crossroads village of Appomattox Court House. Lee arrived in a freshly brushed full dress uniform. Grant stepped into the small parlour to meet him in a mud-spattered private's uniform. Lee offered his sword and Grant refused it. Grant accepted Lee's offer of unconditional surrender and then allowed Lee's men to keep their horses and return to their homes.

The modest home in which Lee surrendered was owned by Wilmer McLean, who had moved there after his farm near Manassas had been the site of the war's first battle. MacLean could legitimately claim that the Civil War had begun in his front yard and ended in his parlour. As Lee and Grant emerged from the house and descended the steps, a Union honour guard snapped to attention. Among those standing ramrod straight was Canadian John McEachern, there with his Maine regiment.

Lincoln arrived back in Washington on April 9 and went immediately to the home of his friend and cabinet ally William Seward. Seward had been in a carriage accident and suffered a number of lacerations as well as a fractured arm and broken jaw. On April 10, the city erupted in celebration. When a band appeared outside the White House, Lincoln asked them to play "Dixie."

Four days later, on April 14, Good Friday, Lincoln presided over a cabinet meeting in which Grant spoke of the surrender that he expected soon from Confederate general Johnston, who was leading the last Confederate army left in the field. Later that afternoon, Assistant Secretary of War Charles Dana brought a message to Lincoln that Confederate agent Jacob Thompson had left Canada and was attempting to flee to Europe. He had been spotted in Portland, Maine. Secretary of War Stanton wanted Lincoln's permission to have Thompson arrested. Lincoln refused and offered an aphorism as explanation: "When you have an elephant by the hind leg, and he's trying to run away, it's best to let him run."[78] Thompson made it to his ship and believed himself through with the United States. But the United States was not through with him.

With the sun down and most of his staff gone for the day, Lincoln wrote a final note. It was to George Ashmun, who had been Seward's agent in Canada and the man who had sat with the president and Galt years before. He would see Ashmun the next morning.

It had only been five days since Lee's surrender had brought peace to America. The war was over, but Lincoln understood the immensity of the challenges still ahead. For the next couple of hours, though, he would take his mind off such serious matters and enjoy a good comedy. He took the arm of his wife, Mary, and set out for Ford's Theatre.

———————•◆•———————

JOHN A. MACDONALD: THE INDISPENSABLE MAN

A DEVILISHLY HANDSOME, roguishly charming and gifted actor, John Wilkes Booth had, by 1862, surpassed the fame even of his father and older brother, who were respected thespians in their own right. He led a nomadic lifestyle and hotels had become his only home. When in Washington, he spent a good deal of time at Ford's Theatre, on 10th Street, just blocks from the White House. He had appeared thirteen times on the Ford stage, most recently in *The Apostate*, on March 18, 1865.

A few weeks later, on the Good Friday morning of April 14, the twenty-six-year-old visited the theatre to pick up his mail. While there, he learned that the president, his wife, and General and Mrs. Grant would be attending that evening's performance of *Our American Cousin*. He went upstairs to check preparations on what would be the president's private box, then hurried away.

Around 9:30 that evening, Booth dismounted his horse in the alley behind the theatre and asked a stagehand named Edman Spangler to hold the reins. He entered, and then left through a side exit to purchase a whiskey at Taltavull's Star Saloon next door. When Booth returned to the theatre, he entered through the front door, stirring no suspicion from the doorman. He made his way upstairs to the back of the unguarded presidential box, where he waited patiently for the point in the play he knew quite well, when only one actor would be on stage.

Booth held a dagger in one hand and a single-shot derringer pistol in the other. Through a small hole in the door that he had drilled that afternoon, he could see President Lincoln and his wife and, because Grant could not attend, Major Henry Rathbone and his fiancée, Clara Harris, enjoying the play. When the moment was right, Booth quietly slid open the door, pointed the derringer at the back of the unsuspecting president's head, and fired. Rathbone jumped to his feet and Booth slashed him with the dagger. Booth then yelled "*Sic semper tyrannis*" and leapt twelve feet to the stage below, breaking his fibula bone inches above his right ankle. To a stunned audience, he shouted, "The South shall be free," and then hurried out the back door to his waiting horse.*

Pandemonium gripped the theatre. Two doctors joined the throng crowding around the unconscious president, and they agreed that the wound was mortal. Lincoln was carried through a chaotic crowd to the Peterson boarding house across 10th Street, where he was laid diagonally across a small bed.

Six blocks away, in his three-storey home overlooking Lafayette Square, Secretary of State William Seward was resting in bed, still recovering from the injuries he had sustained in the carriage accident. He wore a steel brace, painfully securing his broken jaw, and his fractured arm was hanging over the bedside. At about the time that Booth had left the saloon, a co-conspirator, the intimidatingly large and well-dressed Lewis Powell, knocked on Seward's front door, claiming to be delivering medicine. He pushed past a servant and rushed to Seward's third-floor room.

---

* *Eye witness accounts and Booth's diary entries tell different versions of the event, including what was yelled and whether Booth broke his leg when hitting the stage or in a fall from a horse while fleeing. The version related here is the most commonly held view.*

Seward's son Frederick stopped him at the bedroom door, and Seward's daughter Fanny and army nurse George Robinson stepped out to see who was there. Fanny and Robinson left Frederick alone to deal with the visitor, at which point Powell suddenly pulled a revolver from beneath his overcoat and, when it misfired, smashed it against Frederick's head. The horrible noise brought Fanny and Robinson back. Powell then attacked Robinson with a long Bowie knife, ran into Seward's room, leapt onto the bed, and with Fanny screaming, began slashing at Seward. One blow nearly sliced off Seward's cheek. Several more strikes sent blood spattering onto the bed and walls. The commotion roused another of Seward's sons, Augustus, and he and the bleeding Robinson pulled Powell from the bed. But they could not hold him. Yelling "I am mad! I am mad!" Powell ran back outside to his partner, David Herold, who had been holding their horses. They dug in their spurs and vanished into the night. Seward lay crumpled on the floor, entangled in torn and blood-soaked nightclothes and sheets, gasping for air and barely conscious.

Minutes later, there was a knock on Edwin Stanton's door. Two clerks who had been walking along 10th Street heard the shouts announcing Lincoln's shooting and had run to tell the secretary of war. The gruff, magnificently bearded Stanton rose from his bed, got dressed, and came downstairs to the alarming news. He reacted stoically when the clerks added that, while rushing over they had also heard that Seward had been assaulted and possibly killed. It appeared that the government was under attack. But Stanton had earned his reputation as a tough, cool and decisive man, and those qualities would serve him and his country well in the minutes and hours to come.

Stanton called for guards to be placed at the homes of all cabinet secretaries and at the vice president's rooms at the Kirkwood House Hotel, only two blocks from Ford's Theatre. He then rushed to Seward's house, where the gruesome scene left him staggered. It appeared, however, that the steel jaw brace had saved Seward's life by deflecting what could have been fatal thrusts. General Montgomery Meigs, the army's quartermaster general, Secretary of the Navy Gideon Welles and the

District of Columbia's Supreme Court Justice David Carter had also been told of the attack and soon joined Stanton at Seward's home.

Leaving Seward in the care of his doctor, the stalwart group risked the night and hurried to the Peterson house. Stanton pushed his way through the growing crowd standing silently in a cool rain and strode into the tiny bedroom where the president lay dying. When told that recovery was impossible, he slumped into a chair and, uncharacteristically, cried. In a moment, he stood, wiped his face, gathered himself and left for a back parlour where, for all intents and purposes, he stationed the government of the United States.

Stanton ordered telegraph communications to be set up from the Peterson house. Dispatches were written, more guards posted and General Grant recalled to Washington. All bridges leading from the city were to be closed and all ships on the Potomac and trains moving in and out of the capital stopped. While the Mexican border and eastern seaboard ports could remain open, Stanton had the Canadian border sealed. As interviews with witnesses began, it was quickly established that John Wilkes Booth had shot the president. No one could identify Seward's assailant; nor could anyone guess if the night's violence was over.

Washington's police headquarters was just a few doors away, and detectives soon joined the cabinet secretaries, army officers and doctors crowding into the narrow, three-storey Peterson house. When told of the tragic events, Vice President Andrew Johnson pulled a dark hat low over his head and walked the two blocks from his hotel to the Peterson house, with only Provost Marshal Major James O'Beirne as protection against assassins who, for all they knew, lurked in every shadow. Johnson left a short while later for his more easily secured Kirkwood House suite. Stanton remained in charge and continued to sift clues, direct the investigation and manhunt, and issue government statements. Among the many leads that he received was word that a man named John Surratt had often been seen with Booth and lived a few blocks away at his mother's H Street boarding house. Stanton ordered him arrested.

A group of detectives were soon at the Surratt house, where a boarder named Louis Weichmann told them that Surratt was not home. They nonetheless pushed their way in and searched the house. John's mother, Mary, confessed to having recently seen Booth, but said her son had been away for some time in Montreal. With that admission, only hours after Booth's fateful shot, Canada entered the picture.

Back at the Peterson house, Stanton was reminded that just hours before, Confederate agent Jacob Thompson had been spotted on his way out of the country, and Lincoln had refused to have him stopped. Stanton ordered Thompson's arrest. With that order, Canada moved toward the picture's foreground.

Abraham Lincoln died at 7:22 a.m. on Saturday, April 15. The news spread quickly around the world. John A. Macdonald issued no public statement. George Brown was devastated and sat alone in his study, where he composed a long and heartfelt eulogy for the *Globe*—the first issue to be published with a black border. His kind words were echoed in nearly every newspaper in Canada and the Maritimes. Special church services were held, and flags on public buildings and ships in harbour were pulled to half-staff. Later, when Lincoln's funeral train made its way from Washington to Illinois, hundreds of Canadians crossed the border to pay their respects at Buffalo and then again at Detroit.

As in the United States, however, not everyone in Canada mourned the president's death. From Montreal, United States consul general John Potter reported to the State Department that news of Lincoln's shooting had sparked celebrations among the city's many Confederate agents and sympathizers. He told of a special dinner having been held at St. Lawrence Hall to hail Lincoln's death, with toasts drunk to his passing. More ominously, the consul general stated that he had just been informed that before the assassination, Confederates were heard bragging that Lincoln would not live another week. Potter also informed the State Department that the previous October, Montreal's St. Lawrence Hall had welcomed John Wilkes Booth, who stayed in the city for two weeks and spoke with many well-known Canadian-based Confederates.[1] Stanton's Department of War agent,

Colonel Lafayette Baker, dispatched a number of Washington detectives to Montreal to investigate.[2] In a subsequent letter to Seward, Potter provided more detail about those he called the Confederate's Canadian Cabinet: "There are many facts which tend to prove that these persons were not only cognizant of the conspiracy but the conspiracy was planned in this city."[3]

Three hours after Lincoln died, Andrew Johnson was sworn in as America's seventeenth president in his Kirkwood House sitting room. Johnson was born in North Carolina to illiterate and poverty-stricken parents. He made a little money as a tailor and, after his wife taught him to read, served five terms as a Democratic congressman. He was elected to the Senate in 1857. Johnson remained loyal to the Union when Sumter's guns forced a choice, and when Grant's armies took the state in 1862, Lincoln appointed him Tennessee's military governor. In 1864, Lincoln ran for re-election as the leader of the National Union Party, a coalition of Republicans and like-minded Democrats. In an attempt to demonstrate reconciliation with the South, the party convention in Baltimore chose Johnson as Lincoln's running mate. Many doubted Johnson because he was from the South and others disliked his gruff manner. Anger and bitterness seemed to motivate his decisions. He saw opponents as enemies and compromise as weakness. Johnson did himself no favours when he appeared drunk at the inauguration and delivered a slurring, ramble of a speech while some laughed and Lincoln hung his head. One thing that few people worried about was whether the stocky, barrel-chested Johnson would be tough with the South or those responsible for the terrible Good Friday crimes. He told those who came to wish him well, "When you ask me what I would do, my reply is, I would arrest them; I would try them; I would convict them; and I would hang them."[4]

It happened just like that. Only days after the murder, detectives arrested Mary Surratt. Lewis Powell had the bad luck of showing up at the boarding house at the moment of her arrest and was taken too. Edman Spangler, to whom Booth had handed his horse, and Samuel Arnold, who was implicated by a note addressed to him and found in Booth's belongings, were also arrested. Three days later, detectives arrested George

Atzerodt, who had taken a room directly above Johnson's in the Kirkwood House in order to carry out his part of Booth's plan to assassinate the vice president. Atzerodt had lost his nerve and spent the night drinking and wandering the streets. Dr. Samuel Mudd had been in contact with Booth and the others before the assassination, and mended Booth's leg afterward. Detectives took him to jail too.

John Surratt could not be found. It was later established that for some time he had been a courier and spy as one of Thompson's Canadian-based Confederate agents. In Montreal and Washington, he had become involved with Booth and others in a plot to kidnap Lincoln and take him to Richmond. The president was to be swapped for a return of Confederate prisoners and a declaration allowing the South and slavery to stand. On March 17, they had gathered on the road often taken by Lincoln to the Soldiers' Home, where he liked to get away from the constant flow of White House callers. Lincoln did not show up.

After the failed kidnap attempt, Booth kept contact with the others, but Surratt left to resume his work out of Canada. He signed into Montreal's St. Lawrence Hall on April 6. Shortly afterward he was asked to investigate the viability of springing the twelve thousand Confederates from the deplorable conditions of New York's Elmira Prison. Surratt was there when he heard news of the assassination, and fled immediately back to Montreal. He was hidden by a Catholic priest named Father Charles Boucher in the village of St. Libone, forty-five miles north of the city. Surratt spent three months there, but when suspicions arose that he had been spotted, he was moved to Murray Bay, an even more remote community on the St. Lawrence, and later back to Montreal, where he stayed with another priest. In September, Surratt was helped to disguise himself and escape on the *Peruvian*, bound for Liverpool.[5]

While Surratt was hurrying back to his Canadian friends, the days after the assassination saw a massive manhunt for Lincoln's killer. Jottings that Booth made in an appointment book while on the run reveal him as a man who, after a week, had grown hungry, dirty, tired and dispirited.[6] On April 24, with a scrap of rumour that Booth was in Virginia, the 16th

New York Regiment's first lieutenant Edward P. Doherty was ordered to assemble his best men to pursue and capture him. Doherty was born in Canada East and had moved to New York in 1860, where days after Lincoln's first call for troops he had joined the 71st Volunteers. He had seen action in a number of battles and in the autumn of 1863 had been assigned to defend Washington.

Doherty and twenty-six men, accompanied by detectives Everton Conger and Luther Baker, took a steamship to Belle Plain, Virginia, and questioned everyone they encountered. They followed a trail of clues to Jack Garrett's farm, where Booth and David Herold were found hiding in a barn. Doherty ordered it surrounded and sent a reluctant Garrett inside to convince them to surrender. When Booth refused to give himself up, sticks and pine twigs were thrown against the walls with the threat to fire the barn. Garrett and Herold emerged with their hands in the air. With Booth still inside, Doherty's men set the barn ablaze. Sgt. Boston Corbett had crept to the back and could see Booth through gaps in the barn board. Without Doherty's order, and with flames consuming the barn and Booth walking menacingly toward the door with a rifle in hand, Corbett aimed his .44 Colt revolver and shot him.*

Lincoln's assassin was dragged from the burning barn and for two hours he lingered in agony on a bed pulled onto Garrett's front porch. Seconds before drawing his last breath, he whispered, "Useless. Useless."[7] Booth's body was returned to Washington where, for a time, it was buried beneath the floor of the Washington Arsenal. Doherty, meanwhile, would be cheated out of the largest portion of the reward money by the more ambitious detectives.

While Booth was being hunted, the intense questioning of his compatriots suggested that authorities believed the assassination had been an elaborate conspiracy involving not only Canadian-based Confederates but possibly Jefferson Davis himself. Kentucky lawyer and former secretary of

---

* *Boston Corbett was an interesting man; after having been tempted by a prostitute, he cut his testicles off with a pair of scissors to avoid again offending God with such impure thoughts.*

state Judge Advocate General Joseph Holt led the investigation. Holt was a brigadier general and had been a friend and political ally of Stanton since they served together in President Buchanan's cabinet. He was also respected and feared as a smart and ruthless lawyer. Holt and Stanton had a hand in the composition and release of President Johnson's first public proclamation regarding the assassination of Lincoln and attempt on Seward's life, which was released on May 2. It reflected their conviction that Canada was at the bottom of the tragedy and stirred up the already virulent anti-Canadian sentiment across America.[8] Reprinted in newspapers across Canada, the Maritimes and the United States, the proclamation said in part:

> Whereas it appears, from evidence in the bureau of military justice that the atrocious murder of the late President Abraham Lincoln and the attempted assassination of the Honourable William H. Seward, Secretary of State, were incited, concerted, and procured by and between Jefferson Davis, late of Richmond, Virginia; Jacob Thompson, Clement C. Clay, Beverly [sic] Tucker, George Saunders [sic], William C. Cleary, and other rebels and traitors against the government of the United States, harbored in Canada.[9]

The new president offered a $100,000 reward for Davis, $10,000 for Cleary and $25,000 for the others. Johnson's proclamation made evident to all that Canada's involvement in the Civil War had not ended with the Appomattox handshake. Two Montreal newspapers carried identical editorials in response to the proclamation, criticizing Johnson for trying to drag Canada into the assassination and for claiming, with no evidence, that American criminals were being hidden in Canada. It also suggested that the only man to have benefitted from Lincoln's murder was President Johnson himself, and that a note Booth had sent to Johnson's hotel on the day of the murder was proof that perhaps he should be the one under investigation.[10]*

---

* *Booth's handwritten note to Johnson said, "Don't wish to disturb you; are you at home?" Booth and Johnson had never met.*

Jacob Thompson wrote a letter from Europe that was published in the *Globe*, the *New York Tribune* and elsewhere denying any involvement in the assassination: "I aver upon honor that I have never known, or conversed, or held communication, either directly or indirectly with Booth . . . or with any of his associates, so far as I have seen them named. I knew nothing of their plans. . . . I know there is not half the ground to suspect me than there is to suspect President Johnson himself."[11] Tucker and Clay wrote similar letters and, like Thompson, challenged Johnson to produce evidence to prove that Booth had planned the assassination with them in Montreal.[12] But American investigators were gathering evidence that seemed to prove just that: Lincoln's murder had indeed been planned in Montreal.

MACDONALD GOES TO LONDON

On the day that President Johnson officially implicated Canada in Lincoln's assassination, John A. Macdonald was in London, England. Governor General Monck had been looking forward to being a part of the Canadian delegation and to visiting his Irish home and family. However, with Lincoln's murder, the uncertainty that followed, and Macdonald's absence abroad, Colonial Secretary Cardwell had ordered Monck to stay in Canada to deal with whatever might come.[13] Four days after the killing, Macdonald and Brown left Monck behind and sailed out of New York harbour aboard the *China*.

The ice had thawed between the two former rivals, but they would never be friends. They would never really understand each other. In fact, although Macdonald was Canada's most well-known and powerful political leader, few really understood him at all. Born in Scotland, Macdonald had moved to Canada when he was five. The family settled near Kingston, where his alcoholic father continued his habit of failing in every business venture to which he turned his hand. When only fifteen, Macdonald began articling at a law office, and five years later he was running his own firm. An intelligent, hard-working, ambitious young man, he was soon a successful corporate lawyer and businessman who would enjoy directorships in a number of financial institutions and gather investments in land, banks, railways, and road and shipping companies. In the 1850s, a business partner's bad decisions and untimely death cut Macdonald's success short. That calamity was followed by the long and deep international recession. Business problems coupled with an insufficient and unreliable income would plague him for the rest of his life.

The tall, gangly young man with the wild and wiry black hair, prominent nose and dancing, bright eyes, married the cheerful and lively Isabella Clark, his first cousin, in 1843. Within two years she was beset with a mysterious illness from which she never recovered. She became addicted to the opium prescribed for her undiagnosed condition. Macdonald took her to a number of Canadian and American doctors, and on one occasion they endured a horrendous journey to supposedly medicinal hot springs in Savannah, Georgia. Nothing helped. The home of the jovial and fun-loving Macdonald was, ironically, nearly always dark and silent. After an exceptionally difficult birth, they mourned the death of a son. A second, named Hugh, survived, but would be brought up mainly by relatives.

An unhappy domestic life was not the only reason that Macdonald found the bottle. It was, after all, a time when heavy drinking was the norm and, as notoriously hard-drinking Ulysses S. Grant and Andrew Johnson proved, drunkenness by public figures was excused. Macdonald's drinking became even worse when Isabella died, after twelve pain-filled years, in December 1857. One of his favourite drinking buddies was D'Arcy McGee, who was found one morning curled up under the editor's desk at the *Ottawa Citizen*. Macdonald admonished his colleague and friend saying, "Look here McGee, this Cabinet can't afford two drunkards, and I'm not quitting."[14]

The blinding light of Macdonald's strengths, seen at their best during the Confederation conferences, more than made up for the shadows of his dark side. The momentous spring of 1865 called on his strengths again: the Civil War had ended, the president was slain, Britain was impatient, the Maritimes were losing faith and the border was again in peril. Macdonald reluctantly packed his bags to pull Canada through it all.

The British government's support and recognition of Confederation was already assured. In January, Prime Minister Palmerston had written a letter advising Queen Victoria that: "whenever the Civil War in America shall be ended, the Northern states will make demands upon England which cannot be complied with, and will either make war against England or make inroads into your majesty's North American possessions which would lead to war; and it is felt by the majority of the Cabinet that the best security against a conflict with the United States will be found in an adequate defensive force."[15] Her majesty recorded in her journal that her prime minister had spoken with her about the danger of war with the United States "and of the impossibility of our being able to hold Canada, but," she added, "we must struggle for it."[16]

Cardwell had already written several directives in which his government's position could not have been made clearer. In April, he had penned his sternest letter yet to New Brunswick's recalcitrant lieutenant-governor, Arthur Gordon, who never seemed to like or even fully understand his job and did not support Confederation. Cardwell bluntly required him to convince members of the New Brunswick government to see the connection between Confederation and the province's survival as a British entity. He added a not-so-veiled threat: "New Brunswick, as a separate Province, appears to be able to make no adequate provision for its own defence, and to rest in a very great degree upon the defence which may be provided for that by this Country. It will, consequently, be likely to appear to your Advisors reasonable and wise that, in examining the question of the proposed Union they should attach great weight to the views and wishes of this Country, and to the reasons on which those views and wishes have been based."[17] When Nova Scotia's lieutenant-governor, Sir Richard MacDonnell, publicly expressed doubts about Confederation, Cardwell had him transferred to Hong Kong and replaced by loyal military man Sir William Fenwick Williams.

Even if assured, Britain's support had been expressed almost exclusively in private. Macdonald was in London to encourage a more public demonstration of British policy. That weapon could be wielded to caution

Americans still keen on annexation and to turn opinion among Maritimers and reluctant Canadians: if they did not want to become American, then they would have to become Canadian.

Brown and Macdonald joined George Cartier and Alexander Galt at London's luxurious Westminster Palace Hotel on April 30. They were taken on rounds to meet political and business leaders, all of whom gave private guarantees of support for Confederation but, in matters of defence, only promises of further discussions. On May 18 they met Queen Victoria. All were dressed for the occasion, with a delighted and nervous Galt terrified that his ill-fitting breeches would split with a deep bow.[18] Her majesty was courteous but limited herself to small talk, and impressed Cartier with her fluent French. It was not the conversation but the effect that mattered. When she left the room, they could boast of what amounted to royal support for the Quebec resolutions. Cardwell followed this substantial if symbolic victory with a letter to Monck and his lieutenant-governors, ordering them to do all they could to see that Confederation came about according to the Quebec plan.[19]

This was all good news, but the issue of defence persisted. In meetings with British cabinet members, the Canadians spoke of their displeasure with the current preparations and with plans that would see the surrender of nearly all of Canada West and New Brunswick, should an American invasion occur. They reported on the Canadian legislature's promise of an annual million-dollar expenditure to equip and train militia and bolster fortifications in Montreal and improve canals if the British government would pledge to back Canadian loans and supply Great Lakes naval defences. Palmerston's government was stymied, however, by its shaky majority in the House, Bismarck's power in Europe, fear of provoking the United States, and the growing strength of Little Englanders— especially Gladstone, Richard Cobden and John Bright. Palmerston and Cardwell could still make only private assurances.

Galt expressed the frustration of the Canadian delegates in a letter to his wife:

I am more than ever disappointed at the tone of feeling here as to the Colonies. I cannot shut my eyes to the fact that they want to get rid of us. They have a servile fear of the Unites States and would rather give us up than defend us, or incur the risk of war with that country. . . . I doubt much whether Confederation will save us from Annexation. Even Macdonald is rapidly feeling as I do . . . meantime a war might arise between England & the U.S. in which our country would grievously suffer.[20]

Upon their return, Macdonald, Cartier, Brown and Galt prepared a nine-page report to Monck that detailed their negotiations in London and analysed how the issues that were raised related directly to their simultaneous fear of and need for the United States. They had asked for British help in saving the Reciprocity Treaty with the United States and, at the same time, in negotiating with the Hudson's Bay Company to keep the vast northwest territory out of American hands. They told Monck of their arguments regarding defence and their vision of Confederation as an essential step in bolstering military strength. The report made clear that the Civil War and its outcome brought the defence issues that had been debated for years to a critical point.[21]

Events would soon bolster their argument, for as they were striving to save a country as yet unborn, a rebellious group of angry Civil War veterans was about to inadvertently change the game by delivering a genuine threat to British North America, a threat that could finally push the already tense situation to its breaking point.

CANADA AND THE LINCOLN CONSPIRACY TRIAL

Gas lamps hissed in the newly built courtroom on the third floor of Washington's Old Arsenal Penitentiary. The dazed defendants entered in chains, their heads covered with thick canvas hoods; only Mary Surratt, in deference to her gender, was spared the indignity. The men's haggard appearance bespoke the foul conditions in which they had been held; in solitary confinement, hooded, manacled, and with steel bars immobilizing their hands. Around a large table sat a military commission made up of eight generals and a colonel, and led by Judge Advocate General Joseph Holt. In a glaring but ignored conflict of interest, Holt acted as both chief prosecutor and the commission's legal advisor—in effect, the judge. There had been a debate over the establishment of a commission rather than the use of a civilian court for the trial, but Stanton had insisted, the attorney general had vouched for its legality and President Johnson had approved.

The prosecution set out not just to prove the guilt of those in the docket but also to demonstrate the complicity of Jefferson Davis and his Confederate secret service in Canada. Charged with an "illegal and traitorous conspiracy" to murder Lincoln, Seward, Johnson and Grant in aid of the rebellion against the Union, were John Wilkes Booth, John Surratt, Jefferson Davis and "Canadian Cabinet" members Jacob Thompson, Clement Clay, George Sanders, Beverly Tucker and William Cleary.[22]

The prosecution's first witness, called on May 12, was a War Department spy named Richard Montgomery, who had infiltrated the inner circle of the Canadian-based Confederates. The first words heard in evidence at the Lincoln conspiracy trial were his: "I visited Canada in the summer of 1864, and excepting the time I have been going backward and forward have remained there for two years."[23] He detailed many meetings with Thompson, Clay and others in Montreal, Toronto, Niagara Falls and St. Catharines. Montgomery claimed that Thompson told him in the fall of 1864 that Lincoln could be "put out of the way" at any time. He was told at a Montreal meeting in January 1865 that a plan to "take care of Lincoln" was in place and only needed Richmond's approval to be implemented. Montgomery spoke of Thompson having met with Booth in Montreal. After the assassination, Montgomery claimed, Thompson expressed disappointment that Seward and Johnson had not also been killed as planned, as the decapitation of the government had been left incomplete.[24]

Montgomery was recalled on June 12 to add to the testimony since heard from others regarding Thompson's clandestine activities. He testified to Thompson's either directing or having knowledge of all

Canadian-based Confederate terrorist activities, including the attempted burning of New York and the St. Albans Raid. He told of Thompson's supporting a Dr. Blackburn, who gathered clothing from yellow fever victims in Bermuda and had them sent through Halifax into the United States with the hope of spreading the disease among northerners. He told of plans hatched in Montreal to poison New York drinking water. Montgomery also testified that Canadians were in support of these and other Confederate activities. With direct reference to the St. Albans Raid, he claimed, "The sympathies of nine-tenths of the Canadians are with Young and his men; and the majority of all the newspapers justify or excuse his act as merely retaliatory, and they desire only the authority of the Confederate States Government for it to refuse their extradition."[25]

Tales of Canada's role in the conspiracy were heard over and over again from the 370 witnesses called. Sanford Conover, for instance, testified on May 20 that he was a Union spy and *New York Tribune* journalist who infiltrated the Confederacy's secret Canadian operation. He claimed to have moved to Montreal in October 1864, under the assumed name of James Watson Wallace and to have worked with Thompson, Clay, Sanders and others. He testified to having met John Surratt several times in Canada and to have seen Booth once, in late October, at St. Lawrence Hall. He swore that Thompson told him of a dispatch that Surratt had delivered from Jefferson Davis authorizing the assassination of Lincoln and other top officials, and that Thompson had invited him to join in the enterprise. Conover testified that he had submitted an article to the *Tribune* warning of the plot against Lincoln being hatched in Canada, but that publisher Horace Greeley had neither printed it nor warned the government, as Conover had hoped he would.[26]

Conover went on to testify that, after the assassination, he had been sent back to Montreal to investigate the Canadian-Confederate connection and that he had encountered John Surratt again. He also said that on May 22, after the commission had begun its work, he met with Tucker, Cleary and Sanders, who showed no remorse for the president's death. Cleary, he testified, had been especially upset that Lincoln had not pardoned John

Beall for his involvement in the *Georgian* incident and had "considered the killing of the President as an act of retributive justice."[27]

Another important witness was Louis Weichmann. He had been a regular at the Surratt house and a friend of John Surratt, Lewis Powell and Booth. He corroborated the testimony of others that the plot against Lincoln had begun with a meeting between John Surratt and Jefferson Davis in Richmond. According to Weichmann, Davis supported the plan to kidnap Lincoln, and he had Surratt take a dispatch with his authorization to Thompson in Montreal. Thompson then withdrew $184,000 from his Canadian bank account to finance the operation. This is where, according to Weichmann and a number of other witnesses, Booth had entered the picture.

Their testimony established that by late 1864, John Wilkes Booth was spending more time and energy on political matters than on the stage. Born in Baltimore, an ardent racist and a strong supporter of states' rights and the Confederate cause, he had come to hate Lincoln and everything for which he stood. Through David Herold and John Surratt, Booth had ingratiated himself among Confederate spies with charm, boasts, manipulation and lies.

While many conflicting stories were told at the trial, investigators later established that in the second week of October Booth had indeed arrived in Montreal and taken a room at St. Lawrence Hall. He spoke with a number of Confederates, including notorious blockade runner Patrick C. Martin. On October 27, Booth and Martin visited the Bank of Ontario and exchanged $300 in gold coins for £60 gold sterling. After ten days in Montreal, dealing with spies, money and a mysterious trunk he claimed contained theatrical costumes but needed to be moved through Canada, Booth returned to the United States.

While these facts were noted at the trial, they were lost in the fog of witnesses embellishing or confusing them. Most conflated the plot to kidnap the president in March with plans to execute multiple assassinations in April. Some witnesses simply lied. Richard Montgomery and Sanford Conover, for instance, both claimed to have spoken with Thompson in Montreal after he had already left the city. On June 8, two weeks after

Conover's testimony, the *Montreal Evening Telegraph* published an affidavit that was read into the trial record. A gentleman from Montreal argued that the man calling himself Sanford Conover was impersonating him.[28] The accusation was true: the false Conover's real name was established as Charles Durham. But his testimony was allowed to stand.

After the trial, it was proven that Judge Holt had arranged for Durham—as Conover—and other witnesses to tell the stories that he and Stanton wanted told. Money was paid to ensure that they stuck to the tales they had agreed to tell.[29] A year later, Montgomery would appear before the House Judiciary Committee investigating the trial and the commission and admit that he had perjured himself.[30] The committee also found that Durham/Conover had not only lied on the stand but had also instructed others to do the same, and paid them for their efforts. In November 1866, he would be arrested for committing perjury before the House committee, found guilty and sentenced to ten years in prison.[31]

Never mentioned throughout the trial was that Confederate president Jefferson Davis had been captured on May 10, and that "Canadian Cabinet" member Clement Clay had surrendered the next day. Throughout the trial, both languished in horrid conditions at Virginia's Fort Monroe, and Stanton and Holt elected to leave them—and the truth—behind bars.

At the time, of course, the trial's findings were all that mattered, and its conclusions were unequivocal. Special judge advocate John Bingham said it best in his summation: "Surely no word further need be spoken to show that John Wilkes Booth was in this conspiracy; that John Surratt was in this conspiracy; and that Jefferson Davis and his several agents named, in Canada, were in this conspiracy."[32]

On June 29, the long trail of witnesses finally came to an end. The commission had decided beforehand that only a majority was needed to convict and only two-thirds to sentence death. Mary Surratt, Lewis Powell, George Atzerodt and David Herold were to be hanged. Sam Arnold and Mike O'Laughlen, childhood friends of Booth's, and Dr. Samuel Mudd were sentenced to hard labour for life, and Edman Spangler for six years. President Johnson signed off and then stopped an attempt to appeal Surratt's sentence. On an overcast July 7 afternoon, a large crowd gathered in the courtyard outside the makeshift courtroom to witness the multiple hanging, and America's first hanging of a woman. The spectators fell silent as the four prisoners were led past rough-hewn coffins that lay beside the red brick wall, and then up the stairs of the newly constructed gallows. At 1:26, soldiers pushed supports away and a trap door opened. With gasps from the crowd, the convicted conspirators dropped six feet to their deaths.

Few mourned their fate or questioned the commission's conclusions. An article in July's *Atlantic Magazine* summarized the consensus opinion:

> We have the authority of a high Government official for the statement that "the President's murder was organized in Canada and approved at Richmond"; but the evidence in support of this extraordinary announcement is, doubtless for the best of reasons, withheld at the time we write. There is nothing improbable in the supposition that the assassination plot was formed in Canada, as some of the vilest miscreants of the Secession side have been allowed to live in that country. . . . But it is not probable that British subjects had anything to do with any conspiracy of this kind. The Canadian error was in allowing the scum of the Secession to abuse the "right of hospitality" through the pursuit of hostile action against us from the territory of a neutral.[33]

The quick arrests, trial, executions and incarcerations could have allowed President Johnson to move the United States a step away from the horrors and costs of war and assassination. Rather than healing Southern, British and Canadian wounds, however, the controversial process and wild accusations poured salt onto them. Meanwhile, Jefferson Davis and Clement Clay waited in Fort Monroe, and Johnson faced the problem Lincoln had wanted to avoid—what to do with them. At the same time, a great number of Confederate officers were fleeing north to Canada, becoming Attorney General Macdonald's problem. But diplomacy would soon be the least of his worries: thousands of Civil War veterans were preparing to right an injustice and promote a cause by using their newly acquired military skills to attack Canada.

NEW THREATS OF INVASION AND ANNEXATION

On the day that the Lincoln conspirators fell to their deaths, Macdonald arrived home from London. He was welcomed by darkening economic, political and military storms. Confederation was key to responding to all three and yet, despite the gathering consensus that change was essential, the project enjoyed no momentum. Newfoundland and Prince Edward Island had gone cold on the idea and Nova Scotia was rife with anti-Confederation talk led by the revitalized Joseph Howe. An anti-Confederation government held power in New Brunswick.

Then Sir Étienne-Paschal Taché died. With the death of Canada's premier and titular leader in July 1865, Monck called on Cartier, Brown and Macdonald in turn and all three considered the top job. All had done it before and all wanted it again, but they knew if one of them became the premier, then the great coalition would be shattered. With their consent, Sir Narcisse Belleau, a non-entity from the Legislative Council, was appointed. The coalition was saved and Macdonald continued as Canada West's attorney general, returning to his portfolio as minister of the militia while acting, and still openly recognized, as the government's real leader.

Macdonald had controlled his drinking while in London, but upon his return home he fell off the wagon. Parliament resumed, but Macdonald was seldom in attendance. Despite reports of his being ill, Macdonald's peers and the public knew what was meant when it was whispered that John A. was "off again." But this time he was not off for long. Threats from America soon had him back on his feet and at his post. The new threats were galvanized by a group of angry Irish-Americans called the Fenians.

The origins of the Fenian movement date back to 1541, when Henry VIII went to Dublin to declare himself "King of Ireland, Annexed and Under the Realm of England." Generations that followed saw England's attempts to render Henry's proclamation a fact matched by the struggles of Irish nationalists to make it history. By the 1840s, Ireland was a land of tears. A blight destroyed potato crops, visiting famine on an already impoverished people. Political anger and economic desperation were wed in the Young Ireland Movement, leading to the 1848 Rebellion. It was ruthlessly crushed by British soldiers and an even harsher British rule. Hungry for freedom or simply hungry, over a million people fled the troubled isle, most for the United States and Canada.

By the outset of the Civil War, close to 1.6 million Irish had moved to the United States. About a million had come to Canada and the Maritimes, many to Halifax, but most to Toronto, Montreal and the eastern townships south of the city. Their sheer numbers were the source of significant economic and political power, and their contributions to the building of both societies was inestimable. As many Canadian and American Irish climbed ladders of success and influence, however, negative ethnic and religious stereotypes were reflected in nativist distrust and blatant discrimination. Irish newspapers, clubs and organizations teemed with resentment and a romantic yearning for a home that many had never even seen. One of those organizations was the Fenian Brotherhood.

The Fenians' goal was simple—the end of British rule in Ireland. It was formed as a wing of the Irish Revolutionary Brotherhood in 1858 by Irish-American New Yorker and veteran of the '48 Rebellion John O'Mahoney. He had adopted the name from an ancient and brave Irish militia—the Fenia. He sought to raise awareness, money and armed men.

Three years later, thousands of Irish-Americans and -Canadians enlisted in the Union army and fought bravely in the Civil War, many in specifically Irish units. In November 1863, Irish soldiers were given leave to attend a national Fenian Convention in Chicago.[34] They held a second convention in Cincinnati in January 1864. Governance, fundraising and recruitment were formalized, and local groups called "circles" sprang up in every city and town with a significant Irish population.

The Canadian branch of the Fenians, called the Hibernians, was established in Montreal by Michael Murphy and W.B. Linehan.

Membership in Canadian circles grew with every anti-Irish taunt and bout of violence that accompanied annual St. Patrick's Day parades. Hibernians were motivated by the growing power of their American compatriots. Their publication, the *Irish Canadian*, echoed many of the American groups' goals. Young men were encouraged to take up arms to defend themselves against Irish-Catholic–hating Orangemen and to prepare for the ultimate struggle to liberate Ireland.

Hibernian leaders saw the movement toward Confederation as dangerous, for it would weld forever what they considered the undesirable link between Canada and Britain. They spoke against it and encouraged Irish throughout Canada and the Maritimes to vote for candidates pledged to oppose it.[35] In November 1864, it became Hibernian policy and the editorial stance of the *Irish Canadian*, that Canada should be annexed to the United States.[36] The growing militancy alarmed a number of Canadians. The *Globe* noted, "It is certain we have in our midst an armed secret organization . . . there can be no moral doubt these Hibernians identify with the Fenians in the neighbouring United States."[37] Many Hibernians, in fact, began referring to themselves as Fenians.

Thomas D'Arcy McGee was a pugnacious man who, at the beginning of the Civil War, was a member of the legislature for one of Montreal's predominantly Irish ridings and a cabinet minister. While serving as a legislator, he also found time to lecture across British North America, publish poetry, write a book detailing the history of Ireland and earn a law degree. He had been part of the 1848 Rebellion, but while working at newspapers in New York and Boston he had rejected the ideas of his youth. McGee's active and influential life, and his impassioned political stance, resulted in his becoming loved by many Irish-Canadians, who were proud of one of their own doing so well. He was also hated by many others, and certainly by the Hibernians, who saw him as a traitor to their cause. McGee faced many threats to his life and he seldom spoke in public without worrying that each appearance might be his last.[38]

McGee and Macdonald were good friends who saw eye to eye on Irish nationalism and the danger posed by Fenians in the United States and Hibernians in Canada. In the fall of 1864, McGee warned of increased Fenian activities on both sides of the border, and cabinet approved the hiring of more spies to infiltrate Canadian and American circles.[39] The new spies reported to Gilbert McMicken, head of the Western Frontier Constabulary Force. While Canadian spies were already tied into Hibernian networks, the new spies were soon in attendance at American Fenian meetings and informal gatherings.

The career of Henri Le Caron demonstrated the degree to which Canadian spies had successfully infiltrated Fenian ranks in America. Born Thomas Beach in England, he became so enthralled by the romanticism of the Civil War that at the age of nineteen he changed his name and sailed to New York, where he enlisted in the 8th Pennsylvania Reserves. He fought at Antietam, Fredericksburg and Chickamauga. He ended the war as a first lieutenant and settled in Nashville. He had fought in units with a number of young Irish men and knew of the Fenians and their goals. He was shocked when, after the war, he was told by a friend he had met in the service, the prominent Fenian leader John O'Neill, of plans to attack Canada.[40] Le Caron's English patriotism stirred and he wrote to his father, who wrote to Lord Cardwell—and he soon became one of Macdonald's spies.

Le Caron attended Fenian meetings and infiltrated the organization to the point that he became one of its chief spokespersons and organizers. Meanwhile, he was writing to McMicken and eventually reporting personally to Macdonald and, under three aliases, to the British home office. The effectiveness of the Canadian infiltration of the American Fenians resulted in Macdonald's being well informed and justifiably nervous. In December 1864, he learned of armed Hibernians openly drilling in a number of Canadian communities, with the expressed purpose of helping their American comrades to overthrow him and his government.[41]

Monck was hearing similar warnings from London. The growth in wealth and numbers of the radical Irish nationalists in the United States, Canada and Britain, along with their increasing militarization and reports of their intention to attack British ships in American harbours, led the British ministry in Washington to take them seriously.[42] In December

1864, Foreign Secretary Russell ordered Monck and British consuls in the United States to heighten their diligence and report any word of Fenian activity immediately and directly to him.[43]

William Seward had meanwhile quickly recovered from the wounds suffered in the carriage accident and assassination attempt, but he was never the same. Old friends and colleagues were shocked upon seeing him, as he was as changed in physical appearance as he was in the uncharacteristic sense of calm surrounding him. His two sons had recuperated slowly from the tragic night, but his wife, who had for some time suffered poor health, never did. She had died in June. Despite his pain and heartbreak, Seward was back at his desk, dealing with a new president he supported but with whom he often disagreed, and with a host of new problems involving Britain and Canada.

Russell wrote to Seward complaining that the Johnson administration had been allowing the Fenian Brotherhood to actively and openly plot against Canada. Seward responded with a reminder that the group had done nothing illegal. In America, he sneered, the Constitution protected free speech and assembly.[44] Johnson spoke privately with British minister Frederick Bruce and assured him that his government was doing all it could to discourage the Fenians, but Macdonald's spies in America were reporting that Johnson and Seward had met with the Fenian Brotherhood's treasurer, Bernard Killian, at the White House. The president had given Killian his assurance that if Canada was invaded and its government overthrown, the United States would acknowledge the legitimacy of a transitional Fenian government.[45]

As the Fenian movement grew in the United States, O'Mahoney, its founder, was criticized for his lavish spending and for his contention that the movement should focus only on the ultimate goal of fighting for Irish independence in Ireland. At an August 1865 Fenian convention in Philadelphia, one-armed retired brigadier general Thomas Sweeny became the brotherhood's secretary of war. William Roberts was elected president. In their opposition to O'Mahoney's tactics and strategy, a Fenian schism was revealed. Sweeny and Roberts proposed an exploitation of the opportunity presented by the numbers of unemployed, experienced and trained Irish-American soldiers in their ranks, to restructure and formalize the movement's military wing, recruiting even more veterans and purchasing more weapons. Sweeny and Roberts openly advocated using the powerful force they could create to attack Canada, establish a provisional government and then trade Canada for Ireland's freedom.[46]

This was not the first time Irish-Americans had threatened Canada. In 1848, the colony had been struggling through a decade of violent unrest and rebellion, during which the Parliament Buildings had been burned in a riot started largely by conservative businessmen, and powerful political and economic leaders had actively sought annexation. Governor General Lord Elgin had been in the midst of it all and in April had written to London of another threat: "A secret combination of Irish in Montreal is found and bound together by oaths, having designs imical to the Government; that the number enrolled is at least 17,000 and that they look to the acquisition of arms and powder stored on St. Helen's Island."[47] The significant difference between 1848 and the post–Civil War situation was not just that the war had ramped up anti-Canadianism and that there were thousands of battle-ready soldiers available, but that talk of Confederation now gave Irish-Canadian nationalists greater reason to attack Canada sooner rather than later, because a confederated Canada would be stronger and more difficult to conquer. And there was more.

The perfect storm had also been abetted by American consul general to British North America John Potter, a diligent but arrogant former Wisconsin congressmen who had arrived in Montreal in July 1864. After speaking with just a few Montreal businessmen, Potter reported to Seward early the following year that Canadians yearned to be annexed to the United States and that the desire to become American was growing stronger every day.[48] He ignored all evidence to the contrary, including the opinions of the popular press, the building of fortifications, the training of militia and the Confederation initiatives.

Potter's views dominated a convention hosted by the Detroit Board of Trade on July 12–14, 1865. The convention's purpose was to discuss the future of the Reciprocity Treaty and so delegates from American and Canadian Boards of Trade were invited. Potter wrote to Seward proposing that he and others use the convention to promote the end of the treaty as a way to damage the Canadian economy, thereby advancing the day when Canadians would beg to become Americans. Seward, who had long advocated—and still fervently believed—that Canada should become part of the Union and improve the American economy through the expansion of territory and influence, supported Potter's stand.[49]

Potter arranged for others to carry his message to the convention floor, but he spoke at a large meeting hosted by the New York delegation. Potter's remarks were interrupted by a group of Canadian hecklers in the audience, but he was undeterred. A *Globe* article reported on his speech, noting that American talk of making economic policy decisions, such as the killing of the Reciprocity Treaty, to promote annexation had become the convention's dominant theme.[50] Other newspapers, including the *Montreal Gazette* and the *Halifax Morning Chronicle*, picked up the story, with similar attacks on Potter and his ideas.[51] A group of Montreal merchants collected signatures demanding Potter's recall and sent it to Macdonald and Monck.[52]

While Potter and the convention made headlines, his ideas were not particularly new. In 1863, the same argument had been made by America's consul to British North America Joshua Giddings. He had flooded Seward with reports urging that the treaty be immediately scrapped, with the intention of causing such economic pain in the British colonies that they would beg to be subsumed by America.[53] At the 1864 National Union Party convention in Baltimore where Lincoln was nominated as presidential candidate, *New York* founder and *Times* editor Henry Raymond had earned great cheers from the floor when he argued that at the war's conclusion Canada should be attacked and made American, and that getting rid of the Reciprocity Treaty should be the first step.[54]

The Civil War's conclusion, which freed thousands of armed veterans to march on Canada, made these old ideas more viable and so, to Canadians, more alarming than ever. Seward did nothing to calm growing Canadian fears and left Potter at his post. Civil War hero and soon-to-be Johnson administration cabinet secretary, Ulysses S. Grant, visited Montreal the next month and was asked about the American desire to swallow Canada. He diplomatically ducked the question of annexation and invasion, but left the door open by telling reporters that the United States would consider invading Canada if Britain supported France in Mexico.[55]

McMicken had Canadian spies in Philadelphia and Detroit, so Macdonald received first hand reports of both meetings. Canadian spies had also infiltrated a number of major American Fenian circles and were attending their meetings in New York, Cincinnati and Chicago. They were paid $1.50 per diem with a bonus for the submission of useful information. McMicken told Macdonald that the plans to invade Canada were real and that preparations were underway.[56]

After the Philadelphia meetings, the Fenian leadership kept Seward's support a secret, but no longer concealed their designs on Canada. They needed the publicity for their recruitment and fundraising efforts. Fenian goals and plans filled American newspapers. The *New York Herald*'s front page of October 24, for instance, reported on the growing power of Sweeny and Roberts, and noted that the Fenian Brotherhood boasted over half a million members, with representation in every Northern state and many Southern ones. As before and during the war, the paper seemed to relish anti-Canadian, anti-British rhetoric: "Their first step will be to seize Canada with an army of one hundred thousand fighting men. . . . The Fenians will establish a provisional government, and operate for the deliverance of Ireland. The United States will play the neutral game, precisely like Great Britain in our contest with the rebels. . . . England will find before many years, that the neutrality game is one that two nations can play at."[57]

CAMPOBELLO ISLAND

While Fenians prepared, New Brunswick pondered. Pressure, politics, fear and hope had been slowly changing minds about joining Canada. Despite having been formed by the slimmest of margins, New Brunswick's Smith-Wilmot government had assumed its mandate to be the death of

Confederation, but when it sent delegates to London to argue against all that Macdonald was proposing, Cardwell had informed them that the British government fully supported the adoption of the Quebec resolutions. They were offered neither lavish dinners nor an audience with the Queen.

A by-election scheduled for November 6 in New Brunswick's York riding was seen as a test of Confederation's popularity. Former premier and determined Confederation advocate Leonard Tilley wrote to Macdonald arguing that his man Charles Fisher could win if eight to ten thousand dollars was poured into the campaign.[58] Macdonald made arrangements with many of his political allies as well as Grand Trunk Railway executive Charles Brydges, and Fisher soon received all the money he needed. Even George Brown, who had resigned from cabinet over a patronage spat and was now focusing on his businesses and newspaper, contributed $500.

With the money to buy drinks, favours and votes, Fisher crisscrossed the riding, reminding everyone of his attendance at the Quebec conference and of the political, economic and military value of Confederation. He painted his opponent as pro-American, anti-British and a tool of the Fenians.[59] To parry this thrust, anti-Confederation speakers were shipped in from Fredericton and Halifax, to warn of the untrustworthy and distant Canadians and tout the advantages of stronger ties to the nearby Americans. Many unscrupulous folks refused to stay bought and bargained for the price of their votes.[60] In the end, Fisher won decisively and the Smith-Wilmot government and the anti-Confederation movement faltered.

While the York by-election offered a victory to celebrate, new Fenian activity needed to be addressed. In the week after the York contest, forewarnings of an impending attack surfaced in Canada West. Macdonald called for militia units to be mustered in the southwestern portion of the province, and banks in the small town of London took the precaution of removing money from their vaults and hiding it.[61] Macdonald notified Grand Trunk's president that he had approved plans to slow the Fenian advance by tearing up rail lines.[62] The rumours proved unfounded, however, and the militiamen went home.

In February 1866, the Fenian's Sweeny-Roberts faction met in Pittsburgh and outlined not just an intention but a plan for the invasion of Canada. It would involve a number of simultaneous cross-border attacks led by regiments of Civil War veterans. Specific Canadian fortifications, canals and railway centres were targeted. Fifteen hundred dollars was approved to establish a secret service corps in Canada that would organize Hibernians to cut telegraph wires and burn bridges to frustrate Canadian militia and British regulars attempting to meet the advancing Fenians.[63] Brigadier General Sweeny boasted that by May, all of Canada and the Maritimes would be under the Irish flag and their authority would be recognized by President Johnson.[64] American and Canadian reporters had been invited to the conference, so Sweeny's plans and promises became quickly and widely known.[65]

The growing public awareness of Fenian invasion plans brought the question of the American government's stance on those plans, and the Fenian Brotherhood in general, to President Johnson's February 9 cabinet meeting. After the president was told of the military preparations on the Canadian border, a long debate ensued on the advisability of denouncing the Fenian talk of invasion. It was finally decided to remain publicly quiet but to send word to local law enforcement officials to be extra vigilant.

Asking police to do their jobs was the very least the president could do, but at that moment it was about the most he could muster. Johnson was in the middle of a titanic struggle with Congress about reconstruction policies that would see him veto, among other things, the First, Second and Third Military Reconstruction Acts, the Freedman's Bureau Act, the Civil Rights Act and the Tenure of Office Act, which gave Congress control over whom he could fire from his cabinet.[*] Johnson would veto twenty-nine bills, doubling the previous record held by Andrew Jackson. Congress overrode fifteen of those vetoes. Political gridlock ground the gears of progress, and the broken country suffered as the branches of government fought a lot and fixed little.

---

[*] *The fight over the Tenure of Office Act led to the House passing articles of impeachment, although the Senate did not concur. The act was later found to be unconstitutional. Johnson was thus the first president to assume office as a result of an assassination and the first to be impeached.*

In this unprecedented political turmoil, Johnson needed to hold on to the friends he had and make no new enemies. The power of the politically active Irish communities in so many northern cities had therefore to be considered when determining his response to Fenian threats on Canada. Johnson was honest in making this point with a *London Times* reporter: "The Government, surrounded by difficulties in its internal policy, and anxious to obtain support from any quarter against the violent party in the North were desirous of avoiding, if possible, any collision with the popular sentiments of the Irish masses."[66]

The British government inadvertently made things worse by sending soldiers to Dublin to raid a number of houses suspected of harbouring Irish nationalists. Two hundred Fenians were arrested, many of whom were naturalized American citizens. Parliament then suspended the right of *habeas corpus*. Reaction to these moves was explosive, and the Fenian Brotherhood organized a mass rally in New York to protest. On March 4, an even larger rally was held, at which one hundred thousand people gathered to hear speeches denouncing Britain and all things British. Sweeny was among the speakers and at one point he shouted, "There are enough Irishmen in the City of New York to drive the British rule off the continent of America. Every redcoat sent out [to Canada] makes the power of England in Ireland become less. We want her to send all her soldiers to Canada. Let them come. We will be able to kill them all."[67]

American minister to Britain, Charles Adams, was in regular contact with Seward throughout the spring on the topic of the growing Fenian troubles and the administration's silence.[68] Adams was also working to secure the release of the American Fenians in British prisons. Meanwhile, Seward had several discussions with British minister to Washington Bruce about the jailed Americans and the blatant threats the Fenians were making toward Canada. Seward agreed to offer no direct support to Sweeny or his men because, from his point of view, he told Bruce, the worst thing that could happen at that point would be for Fenians to launch an attack on Canada with the new threats of a British-American war that would follow.[69] Someone was lying.

Meanwhile, McMicken's spies told of the ongoing military preparations on the border.[70] They believed that nearly five thousand Fenians were amassing at a number of locations and that the coordination with Hibernians was continuing apace for an invasion that would come on March 17—St. Patrick's Day.[71] On March 7, days after the huge New York rallies, and with McMicken's reports on his desk, Macdonald mobilized ten thousand volunteer militiamen. Monck ordered two regiments of British regulars, who were about to leave Halifax, to stay in the city and on duty. Major rail stations were ordered to remain open and engineers told to keep their engines warm. Crews were to sleep on the trains to enable them to move troops and equipment at a moment's notice.[72] Macdonald received more reports from his spies saying that plans existed to capture all members of cabinet and that McGee would be specifically targeted for assassination.[73]

St. Patrick's Day came and went without an invasion. But Canadian and American border towns had been shaken. Many frightened Canadians had suffered a sleepless night, with candles burning and weapons loaded. The Fenians had not come, but the fears stirred and preparations instigated were nonetheless significant. George Brown interpreted the situation to Canada's advantage in the pages of the *Globe*:

> The Fenians have. . . . given our Republican neighbours an opportunity of seeing how earnest and unanimous is the love of the people of British North America for British alliance, and how utterly groundless has been the impression so diligently propagated, that the desire for annexation to the United States was general in Canada.[74]

Just as Canadian militia men were returning to their families, Fenians threatened New Brunswick. In an attempt to regain influence, John O'Mahoney had organized a gathering of about five hundred Fenians in Eastport and Calais, Maine.[75] The plan was to take New Brunswick's Campobello Island and use it as a base from which they could harass

British ships and, with any luck, provoke a British-American war. O'Mahoney was convinced that Seward knew of the plan and was sympathetic to it.[76]

From Eastport, Maine, came a Fenian proclamation to the people of New Brunswick stating, in part, "Republican institutions have become a necessity to the peace and prosperity of your Province. English policy, represented by the obnoxious project of Confederation, is making its last efforts to bind you in effete forms of Monarchism. Annexation to the United States is not necessarily the only means of escape. Independence for the present is the best one."[77] The bold and provocative proclamation appeared in public places in several New Brunswick towns and found its way to American, Maritime and Canadian newspapers.

New Brunswick militia were mobilized and two British regiments moved in from Halifax. British ships of war *Pylades* and *Rosario* began cruising the American shoreline and more ships set out from Halifax to boost their presence. British major-general Hastings Doyle took command. Defensive positions were thrown up at likely invasion spots, the largest at St. Andrews.

With tension mounting, a group of Fenians, emboldened by nationalist fervour and ale, took boats to New Brunswick's tiny Indian Island. They burned down a Customs House and stole a flag before rowing quickly back over the border. The escapade was more of a prank than an attack, but it raised the temperature and many New Brunswickers began evacuating their families from vulnerable border towns such as St. Stephen.

The Americans finally reacted. Seward sent marshals, and Navy Secretary Gideon Wells approved the taking of the Fenian ship *Ocean Spray*, which had arrived at Eastport loaded with 129 cases of rifles, ammunition and other supplies. The next day, April 18, the hero of Gettysburg, General George Meade, arrived at Eastport with an artillery unit and took control of the situation. Meade crossed the border, visited St. Andrews and then met with Major-General Doyle. Meade let it be known that he would arrest any Americans attempting to cross the border with the intent of breaking neutrality laws.

Like the St. Patrick's Day invasion that never came, the comic fiasco
of the aborted attack on Campobello Island proved an important point.
British regulars and local militia would and could quickly and effectively
mount a credible defence. They also demonstrated that, despite its public
silence and perceived support of Fenian designs on Canada and the
Maritimes, the Johnson administration would enforce neutrality laws and
stop Fenian incursions over the border. The long and legitimate menace
of invasion also significantly helped New Brunswick's pro-Confederation
advocates, as fear altered perceptions and opinions.

New Brunswick's York by-election the previous November had
been followed by the slow crumbling of the anti-Confederation administration when Robert Wilmot resigned from the coalition and began
speaking in favour of joining Canada. Further, after years of insubordinate
intransigence, Lieutenant-Governor Arthur Gordon finally did what
Cardwell and Monck had asked, and put pressure on New Brunswick's
political leaders to support the future offered by the Quebec resolutions.
Premier Smith still opposed Confederation but offered no alternative.

As New Brunswick's spring parliamentary session dragged on, dealing
with minor matters but not the major issue facing it, more pressure arrived
from Nova Scotia. While the irascible red-headed firebrand Joseph Howe
continued to lead a strong anti-Confederation crusade in the province, he
was winning rhetorical battles but losing the war. Gordon was told—and
he told the premier—that Nova Scotia's Parliament was about to bring
Confederation to a vote and that everyone predicted a win.[78]

It was the first week of April 1866, nearly two years after Macdonald
and the Canadians had steamed into Charlottetown offering their
Maritime cousins a broader, safer, British, un-American union. News of
the Fenians gathering in Eastport had broken, the militia had been called
out and families were making plans to escape the murderous American
rampage. Political and civil society leaders who had been arguing against
the need for Confederation suddenly found their tongues stilled or audi-
ences gone. Nova Scotia's Catholic Church leaders, for instance, had
opposed Confederation, but in the heat of Fenian fears a pastoral letter

was read in pulpits and printed in newspapers across the province. It stated, in part, "Current events and all reliable sources of information within our reach point to one conclusion, that, namely, British aid and protection in the hour of danger and emergency can be secured on one condition only—and that condition is the UNION OF AMERICAN BRITISH PROVINCES."[79] While there were some, most notably Howe, who would carry on, the Fenian threat and the scrambled military response all but washed away resistance to Confederation like a Fundy tide.

On the day that troops were assembling on the Halifax pier to move to quell the Fenian invasion, the Nova Scotia legislature heard passionate speeches proclaiming the absolute and immediate necessity of Confederation. The point made over and over was distilled by one member: "The whole police [policy] of the United States has been acquisition of territory. Their ambition is insatiable. . . . If we remain disunited . . . the time may come when we shall have the British flag lowered beneath the stars and stripes, and the last gun fired from the Citadel as a British fort."[80] On April 18, the day General Meade arrived in Maine, the Nova Scotia legislature voted 31 to 19 for Confederation.

With the Fenians gone, but with reignited fear of America still in the air, New Brunswick's government fell into a mess of shameful partisan manoeuvring that ended with its resignation. Leonard Tilley returned to the premier's chair and called an election. One of his first campaign moves was to contact Macdonald and ask for money. He estimated a need for $40,000 to $50,000 to carry the campaign.[81] Macdonald raised it from party stalwarts and he again wrote to Grand Trunk's president Charles Brydges, who came through as he had in the York by-election. Galt personally delivered envelopes of cash.

The campaign was hard fought, with many of those opposing Confederation claiming that Macdonald had actually stage-managed the Fenian scare to manipulate public opinion.[82] On June 21, 1866, the last of the votes were counted and Tilley and Confederation were found to have won the day. Three weeks later, with a 31 to 8 vote, the New Brunswick legislature passed a resolution supporting Confederation.

FENIANS ATTACK CANADA

The O'Mahoney faction of the American Fenians was devastated by the Campobello failure and in a May 5 editorial the *New York Times* announced the death of the entire movement.[83] At the Roberts-Sweeny headquarters on Broadway, however, the more militant and determined faction was stronger than ever. Plans to take Canada remained paramount. Fenians were soon on the move north from Cincinnati, Tennessee and even New Orleans. Retired Civil War officers were in charge: Brigadier-General C.C. Trevis would lead the attack from Chicago and Milwaukee; Brigadier-General W.F. Lynch would cross Lake Erie and the Niagara River from Cleveland and Buffalo; and Brigadier-General S.P. Spear would attack from New York and Vermont.[84] Sweeny's plan involved ten thousand armed invaders supported by artillery.

Macdonald had been reading reports of renewed Fenian activity, but with the false alarms of two months before and then the Campobello fiasco, he had dismissed them. By late May, however, the reports were becoming more frequent and convincing. The Fenians *were* coming. On the last day of May, he ordered fourteen thousand militiamen to pre-determined border locations.

In cities, towns and villages, men left their families, farms and jobs to hoist a rifle and risk their lives. An audience enjoying an opera at the Toronto Music Hall gasped when a uniformed officer of the Queen's Own Rifles interrupted the performance to announce from the stage that the United States was about to attack Canada and that all militia volunteers must assemble by six the next morning. After a loud cheer, the orchestra played "God Save the Queen."

Many of those gathering their weapons to stand against Civil War veterans were veterans themselves. James Wesley Miller, for instance, had left his home in Peterborough, Canada West, in October 1861 to join the New York 6th Cavalry. He had seen action in a number of important battles, including Gettysburg. Miller was back home in Peterborough when he heard the call. He joined his militia unit and others from surrounding villages such as Lakefield and Ashburnham, on a train for

Cobourg on Lake Ontario's northeast shore.[85] Another Civil War veteran who responded to the call was Newton Wolverton, the youngest of the four brothers from Wolverton, Canada West, to join the war.* While Miller and Wolverton would see no action, like thousands of others they were prepared to do battle against their former brothers in arms.

On June 1, the invaders crossed the line. Beneath a cloudless, starry midnight sky, retired Union colonel John O'Neill gave the order. Leaving reinforcements behind, about fifteen hundred men, dressed mostly in old uniforms from Tennessee, Kentucky, Ohio, New York and Indiana regiments, slipped across the Niagara River in small boats. At 3:30 in the morning, they assembled at a wharf just outside Fort Erie.

With news of the landing, British lieutenant-colonel George Peacocke led three companies of infantry, an artillery battery and Canadian militia to the Niagara Peninsula. O'Neill divided his force of invaders, intending to forage for horses and food, and then have one unit move west toward Port Colborne and the Welland Canal, while the other advanced toward St. Catharines. At six o'clock in the morning on June 2, Peacocke's Lieutenant-Colonel Alfred Booker arrived at the village of Ridgeway with about nine hundred Canadians of the Queen's Own militia unit, many of whom were students from Toronto's Trinity College. The Fenians had taken the high ground and built earthworks. Both sides deployed skirmishers and then, with bayonets fixed, the opposing lines advanced.

Private A.G. Gilbert of Peterborough was on the ridge as a member of the Queen's Own Company 7. He later wrote of the battle:

> One look at one another, then a shot from No. 5, and soon a continuous roar of musketry greeted us, and bullets in showers whizzed past our ears. The battle was now opened in earnest, and nothing but the whistle of bullets and the roar of the rifles could be heard. . . . But we could not open fire yet; and there we stood,

---

* *Newton had left the Civil War in 1864, while Alonzo had remained in the service until the end, leaving as a second lieutenant with the 9th U.S. Coloured Artillery.*

about the most exposed and dangerous position in the field, receiving the Fenian fire, but dare not return it. And it was at this time that we had the sensation fully and keenly experienced, of facing death in its most terrible form—in full health, young, active, very fond of life.[86]

The Fenians reinforced their right and their left, and the cry went up for a cavalry charge. The Queen's Own girded themselves in textbook fashion by forming a square to repulse the horses, but the Fenians reacted by quickly moving to their flanks and filling the air with enfilade fire. The Canadians were forced to withdraw, leaving the Fenians with the field.

Generals Meade and Grant both hurried to Buffalo. Grant ordered Meade to stop further border incursions. American law enforcement authorities and militia were alerted. The American steamer *Michigan* arrived at the scene, and her crew confiscated a cache of hidden weapons. Meade then took a train to St. Albans, Vermont, to address reports of five hundred Fenians moving north. O'Neill heard this news along with a startling report that about five thousand Canadian militiamen and British regulars were heading toward him from Chippawa, just a few miles away, and decided to withdraw. The ragtag, retreating Fenians made it half-way across the Niagara River, and then were captured by an armed American tugboat and put in the *Michigan*'s brig.

The Fenian raid and Ridgeway battle moved President Johnson to finally break his silence. On June 6 he issued a proclamation stating that the Fenians had violated neutrality laws and warning Americans against helping them or anyone else with designs upon Canada. The next day, thirteen hundred Fenians, ignoring the presidential proclamation, marched north from St. Albans and crossed into Canada, where they established picket lines and waited for reinforcements. Meade, meanwhile, had ordered those reinforcements stopped. Sweeny was arrested. The Fenian invaders quietly retreated back across the border and went home.[87]

FENIAN PRISONERS

Eighty-one Fenian raiders were in Canadian custody, hundreds in American jails, and no one knew what to do with them. Their fates rested on the delicate complexity of the Canadian-American-British relationship. Seward initially suggested that those held in the United States should be allowed to escape, but the decision was finally made to release them all on bail. The young Civil War veterans were then offered free transport home on their promise never to participate in another attack on Canada.[88] None were ever prosecuted.

The American prisoners languishing in Canadian jails were not so lucky. On a clear and warm afternoon on June 5, Toronto businesses closed for a public funeral to honour the five members of the Queen's Own militia who had lost their lives at Ridgeway. The *Globe* captured the mood of the day: "We have buried our dead but the lesson which they have taught us will live long after all those who were present at the ceremonies have followed them to the tomb . . . there lurks a desire to force this country into a connection with their neighbour by means of border troubles. . . . The autonomy of British America, its independence of all control save that to which its people willingly submit, is cemented by the bloodshed in the battle on the 2nd of June."[89]

The Canadian legislature reconvened three days later in the recently finished and grand Parliament Buildings overlooking the Ottawa River. Macdonald introduced a motion stating that American requests for the extradition of the Fenian prisoners would be ignored. He suspended *habeas corpus* and stated that the prisoners would be tried by Militia General Courts Martial.

American reaction was explosive. In Washington, Seward led the charge by fuming to British minister Bruce that the Canadian decision was unacceptable and that Britain would be held responsible.[90] Bruce wrote to Monck: "The future relations of Canada [with the United States] and its deliverance from any chance of becoming a battlefield of Fenianism will depend in a great measure on the tact and temper with which this question of the prisoners is managed."[91] This time it was Monck's turn to rage a little. He let London know that he was sadly disappointed with Bruce's handling of the entire matter, believing him to be pandering to the Americans. He also argued that Britain could not at the same time support Confederation and Canada's growing independence and then interfere in a case of jurisprudence that was so obviously a Canadian matter. In his demand, Monck was channelling the growing Canadian nationalism that the Confederation debates and Fenian excitements had bolstered: "The course of justice cannot be interfered with at the dictation of a foreign power."[92]

The British government, of course, was simply doing as it had done throughout the war in seeking to avoid confrontation with the United States. Monck understood, and he pledged to use his influence with Macdonald to try to postpone the Fenian trials until emotions in Canada and the United States had subsided. As he put it in a dispatch to the Colonial Office: "I think you may safely dismiss from your mind all fears of any difficulties arising from the treatment of the Fenian prisoners. I am resting on my oars with regard to these prisoners until Congress shall have adjourned, which will probably be in a few days and we shall then try them in statutable felony before the ordinary courts."[93]

As Monck suggested, the imprisonment of American veterans had become a part of the ruthless struggle between Congress and the president and a factor in the upcoming 1866 mid-term elections. Congress passed a resolution demanding that Johnson act to have the prisoners immediately released from Canada. Trying partly to court the same Irish vote that Johnson was seeking, Massachusetts congressman and chair of the House Foreign Affairs Committee Nathaniel Banks condemned the president for interfering with the Fenian raids, arguing that if he had just let events play themselves out, then Canada would have fallen. On July 2, Banks introduced a bill that contained changes to the neutrality laws that would encourage Fenians or others to undertake Canadian invasions in the future. The bill also suggested provisions for Canada and the Maritimes to join the United States as four new states and two territories. Fenian leader William Roberts praised the bill for its demonstration that radical Republicans were supportive of the Fenian cause, while Charles Sumner and others in the Senate expressed their intention to kill it through either filibuster or death in committee.[94] The bill sank into Banks's House Committee, however, and never emerged.

While the bill vanished, its promotion had been widely reported in Canadian and Maritime papers and, coming so soon after the Fenian raids, it boosted the pro-Confederation forces by serving as yet another catalyst for gelling the burgeoning sense of nationhood. As noted by the *Toronto Daily Telegraph* a few days after the Banks bill made headlines, and with the Fenian raids still on peoples' minds, "the covenant of our nationality had been sealed with blood."[95] D'Arcy McGee made a similar observation to Monck, calling his old Fenian enemies "wretches" and a "scourge." But he concluded, "Our population are up and united as one man; we are three millions; we are on our own soil." [96] A *Globe* editorial almost thanked the Fenians for their role in uniting Canadians: "The events of the last fortnight have not only shown unmistakably that the true British spirit beats universally throughout our country—that the people of Canada are ready, as one man, to defend their homes and fire-sides. . . . The Fenians have unwittingly done an essential service to the Canadian people, by inspiring them with a degree of confidence in their defensive strength which they did not before possess."[97]

In August, perhaps encouraged by the House bill or perhaps trying to regain the momentum lost by the failed Canadian incursions, Roberts organized a Fenian picnic in Buffalo. Macdonald ordered ships to full alert in lakes Erie and Ontario and three thousand militiamen to Fort Erie. On August 15, at another Fenian picnic, in Chicago, Illinois's Governor Oglesby, Senator Logan and two congressmen spoke of brave Fenians, treacherous Englishmen and a criminal president who prevented the raiders from taking Canada.[98] Macdonald and Monck met to discuss the increasingly anti-Canadian rhetoric in Congress and on the part of state officials—and President Johnson's silence. If Fenians launched another attack, they concluded, the Americans might not this time help in stopping it. Monck asked for more British troops for the Canadian border and for forty thousand state-of-the-art Snider-Enfield breech-loading rifles.[99]

Monck's requests for more military assistance initiated a fresh round of discussions at the British cabinet table on the subject of Canadian defence. The arguments brought forward ignored the quick defence that Canadian and Maritime militia had recently launched and the pledges of money and men that had been made. Powerful Tory and Little Englander Benjamin Disraeli argued, "It can never be our pretence or our policy to defend the Canadian frontier against the United States. If the colonists can't, as a general rule, defend themselves against the Fenians, they can do nothing . . . what is the use of these colonial dead weights which we do not govern."[100] Despite these reservations, British domestic politics, as always, needed to be considered. The government could not be seen to be allowing Fenians to succeed anywhere if it hoped to keep on successfully battling them at home. The British Parliament grumbled but voted another fifty thousand pounds for Canadian defence, and more troops were sent in September. Fortunately, by the time Britain's 61st Regiment arrived, the new danger had gone cold and so the men were sent on to the West Indies. Their arrival nonetheless reassured Canadians and Maritimers who still feared American intentions after years of Civil War threats and insults followed by Fenian scares.

As the American fall mid-term elections approached, Johnson's policies on Canada and the Fenians became hot-button issues in Irish districts. A *New York Tribune* article, for instance, attacked the president for having supported the raids by meeting with Fenian leaders and then saying nothing while public plans were made, but then double-crossing them when those plans were executed. It concluded: "A weak policy is always wrong at both ends and bad in the middle; and thus the President has failed to satisfy Irishmen, Americans and Canadians."[101] A similar point was made by many Fenian leaders, including a general whom Meade had known in the Civil War, who told him, "We have been lured on by the Cabinet, and used for the purpose of Mr. Seward. They encouraged us on this thing. We bought our rifles from your arsenals, and were given to understand that you would not interfere."[102]

President Johnson was sorely disappointed when the voters of Maine, Vermont, Pennsylvania, Indiana and Ohio elected his political opponents. The elections in the more heavily Irish New England states were still to come. The president announced that no Fenians would be prosecuted and that all captured arms would be returned to their owners. He fired Attorney General William Dart, who had publicly advocated stopping the Fenian raids, and ordered Seward to work harder to free the Fenians still in Canada.

The Fenian trials had been postponed to allow time to heal wounds, but they could be delayed no further. Amid new rumours of Fenians on the border and American belligerence fanning the increasingly hot embers of Canadian nationalism and anti-Americanism, the trials began on October 8. The Americans were charged with having entered Canada to wage war on Her Majesty. They were brought before the court one at a time and defended by Toronto lawyers who were paid by the American consul. It all moved quickly. Robert Lynch and Catholic priest Father John McMahon were the first to be found guilty and sentenced to be hanged.

Seward jumped to intervene. He asked for trial transcripts and wrote to Bruce asking that Britain review the cases and act to prevent the sentences from being carried out. The Colonial Office had written to Monck with the same request.[103] As he had with the case of former slave John Anderson years before, Macdonald respected the legal process while being too smart to hurl himself into whirlpools of political peril, and so said nothing. Canadian newspapers were not so circumspect. Most united in supporting the courts with a nationalist fervour that lashed out at American and British attempts at intervention. Maritime papers joined the chorus. The *St. John Morning Telegraph* reflected the thoughts of many in its November 6 editorial: "It is to be hoped that Canadian Courts will deal with the convicts without reference either to England or the States. . . . We hope the sentence of the Courts will be firmly carried out, notwithstanding the rage of the American Fenians and the diplomacy of Mr. Seward."[104]

The trials continued, with more guilty pleas and death sentences. With Fenians on Canada's death row and Johnson's government unable to save them, and with an increasingly fierce struggle between parties and branches of government, voters in New England went to the polls. Nearly every Johnson candidate in predominantly Irish districts was defeated. With the elections lost, his cabinet divided, and so many of his vetoes overturned, President Johnson's political influence had evaporated. He carried on with his constitutional authority but was bereft of political capital. In his State of the Union address, delivered a few weeks later, he expressed regret that there had not been more progress in resolving the differences between the United States and Britain that remained as a result of actions taken during the war. He noted that he had issued a proclamation condemning attacks on Canada from the United States, although he failed to mention his tacit support for the raids or that his proclamation had been issued only after they had taken place. He also spoke of his government's attempts to intervene in the Canadian trials and expressed hope that the prisoners would be treated with "clemency and a judicious amnesty."[105]

MACDONALD CLOSES THE DEAL

With the Fenians and the new threats from America on his mind, Macdonald had spent the fall of 1866 focusing on at last bringing Confederation to fruition. Once he had the approval of the Canadian, New Brunswick and Nova Scotia legislatures in hand, the last necessary step was to shape the Quebec Resolutions into a bill and request that the British Parliament pass it. Delegates from Nova Scotia and New Brunswick were so anxious to move the process along that they ignored the advice of Monck and Macdonald and had hurried off to London in July, without their Canadian counterparts. They were met graciously but there was little they could do without the Canadians.

Macdonald delayed his departure both to deal with the Fenian issue and to push through long-awaited legislation for the public funding of separate Catholic schools. He was also reluctant to leave because of the instability of the British government. Lord Palmerston, his earlier ally, had died on October 18, 1865, and Earl John Russell had again become prime minister. In the general election that soon followed, Russell was defeated and a Tory government brought to power. Lord Derby, the next prime minister, had appointed Benjamin Disraeli chancellor of the exchequer. Fortunately for Macdonald, Lord Carnarvon had replaced Cardwell as colonial secretary, and he was as anxious as his predecessor to see Confederation come into being. Carnarvon had written to Derby in October: "[Confederation had] become a necessity to us and it was a question of confederation amongst themselves, or of absorption by the U. S."[106] Derby agreed.[107] But still Macdonald demurred.

Monck became as frustrated as the Maritime delegates cooling their heels and wetting their whistles in London. He wrote a scathing letter to Macdonald, demanding that he move to exploit the momentum that Confederation had gathered. Macdonald replied with a coolness that must have brought the preternaturally calm governor general to a boil: "With respect to the best mode of guiding the measure through the House," Macdonald replied, "I think I must ask your Excellency to leave somewhat to my Canadian parliamentary experience."[108] Macdonald ended with kind compliments, but his point was clear and the power play won.

Macdonald was also drinking again.[109] In August, for ten days in a row, he failed to show his face in the House. The length and depth of this bender was remarkable even for him. Monck's daughter Elizabeth was appalled when, at a formal Spencer Wood dinner party, Macdonald drank so heavily that he threw up on the family's new drawing room chairs.[110] Galt wrote to his wife of the problems the government was facing and complained, "Add to all this that Macdonald has been in a constant state of partial intoxication and you may judge whether we have had a pleasant week. . . . Macdonald is in such a weak maudlin state, that he is wholly unfit for the emergency."[111] At one point Monck dispatched an aide to Macdonald, ordering him back to his duties. A dishevelled Macdonald told the young man that if he was there at the behest of the governor general then his Excellency should go to hell, but if he was there of his own accord then he could take the trip himself.[112]

Macdonald eventually shook his demons. The timing of his delay was actually quite clever: for he understood the British Parliament's schedule and wanted to arrive in London with little time for the Maritimers or the

British government to significantly alter the Quebec resolutions. The apparent procrastination that infuriated and exasperated so many was really just another illustration of a masterful political strategist at work, and a man perhaps quite adept at timing his binges.[113]

With the Fenian trials in progress, on November 7, 1866, Macdonald, Galt, Cartier, up-and-coming Conservative Hector-Louis Langevin and two Reform cabinet ministers finally set sail from New York for London. They showed courage in moving through the United States. Fenians had already put a bounty on McGee's head. A week after the delegation's departure, Monck prepared to leave for England to spend Christmas with his family and to be in London for the conference. The British consul in New York City warned him that a number of Fenian informants feared for the governor general's life and urged extreme caution.[114]

The Canadian delegation checked into the Westminster Palace Hotel that they had come to know so well. On December 4, they joined the Maritimers in a grand and high-ceilinged meeting room to begin work on the seventy-two Quebec resolutions. Macdonald was again the indispensable man. He manoeuvred, charmed and cajoled. He personally redrafted the words that he had played such a large part in writing two years before. Carnarvon's senior advisor, assigned to oversee the work, described Macdonald as the conference's "ruling genius."[115]

On December 11, after a day off enjoying Carnarvon's hospitality in the English countryside, Macdonald awoke to flames engulfing his curtains, bed and bedclothes. He leapt up, tore off his burning nightshirt, frantically pulled the flaming sheets and curtains onto the floor and doused the lot with water. He ran for Cartier and Galt, who breathlessly rushed in with more water to put out the rest of the fire. An errant candle had been the culprit. Another minute or two and the Fathers of Confederation could have been fatalities.

The next day, Macdonald was back at work with scorched hands, a burned shoulder blade and singed hair, but still ready to lead the discussions. Some minor changes were made regarding the apportioning of powers between the federal government and the provinces. But the essence of what had been decided in Charlottetown and Quebec remained unaltered: a highly centralized, federal state, loyal to the monarchy. The new nation and Constitution would be founded not on Thomas Jefferson's ringing declaration of "life, liberty and the pursuit of happiness" but rather on a more staid promise of "peace, order and good government." The phrase was both process and goal. In its modesty, and with an eye to the blood just spilled south of the border and more recently at Ridgeway, the phrase was as brave as it was so very Canadian.

The final draft was rewritten as a bill and introduced by Carnarvon in the House of Lords on February 12, 1867. He tried to put it all in context: "This Confederation of the British North American Provinces . . . in population, in revenue, in trade, in shipping, it is superior to the Thirteen Colonies when, not a century ago, in the Declaration of Independence, they became the United States. We are laying the foundation of a great State—perhaps one that at a future day may even overshadow this country."[116] It passed without amendment and with little comment. On March 8, following not a single word of debate, the House of Commons passed the bill. Queen Victoria signed it a couple of weeks later. The Civil War had thus seen the destruction of one country and the renewal of another; and with that signature, the immeasurable role it had played in the creation of one more was nearly complete.

Macdonald had been in the galleries of the British Parliament for both historic moments which marked the birth of a nation and the crowning achievement of a career already long and distinguished. With the passage of the British North America Act, Macdonald had forged a nation and frustrated America's dream of Manifest Destiny. But Seward and other dreamers were not yet ready to surrender. Despite the guns having fallen silent, the Civil War was not really over and Macdonald could not yet rest.

— • —

DANGER IN THE WAR'S SHADOW

T HE CLOCK'S FIRST GONG announced midnight. Few heard the second, as 101 guns roared in succession, announcing the start of the glorious day. An enormous bonfire was set ablaze. Every church bell in Ottawa chimed, and spontaneous cheers erupted from the crowd on Parliament Hill. It was July 1, 1867, and Canada had been born.

There were twenty-one gun salutes in Saint John, Kingston and Hamilton, and fireworks in Montreal and Toronto. In many towns, shops closed for the day as people enjoyed parades, dances and concerts. But the black bunting on a number of Nova Scotia shops and the black border on some of its newspapers spoke for those who still believed they had been hoodwinked into a bad deal. The *Halifax Morning Chronicle*'s headline read, "Died! Last night at twelve o'clock, the free and enlightened Province of Nova Scotia."[1]

John A. Macdonald had been appointed the new country's first prime minister. He and several of his colleagues had been rewarded with knighthoods. He was enormously popular even among those who opposed him and his policies. To his countrymen, he was simply Sir John or John A. He was a rascal, but he was their rascal.

Macdonald had come back from the final London conference happy and married. After a decade as a widower, he wed Susan Agnes Bernard, who offered love and the stability that had been too long absent in his life. He kept his promise to reduce his drinking—not end it, mind you. The now lively Macdonald household hosted dinner parties as one would expect of a head of government and, according to current practice, all expenses came out of his pocket.

The Civil War had been over for two years, but neither the United States nor Canada had yet to emerge from its shadow. Lingering judicial questions and humanitarian concerns needed to be addressed. Of greater importance was the link drawn between Canada and America's competing urge for territorial expansion and the settlement of claims against Britain for having allowed Confederate ships to be built in its harbours. As he listened to the church bells and gunfire echo down the Ottawa River late into the warm July night, Macdonald understood that Canada was still more an idea than a fact. He knew that there were men in Washington determined to erase that idea before it could take hold. Until crucial issues were settled and those men confronted, the Civil War was not really over and Confederation not yet complete.

QUESTIONS OF JUSTICE

The trials of Fenian raiders captured on Canadian soil had caused international consternation in the winter of 1866. When their sentences were announced in January, there had been outrage. Twenty-five Fenians had been found guilty and sixteen sentenced to death. Macdonald was as politically astute and generous in dealing with such matters as Lincoln had been. He quietly commuted the sentences to life imprisonment and the sixteen joined their comrades in Kingston's penitentiary. Over the next four years, he arranged for all to be released and many received full pardons. In so doing, Macdonald respected Canadian law and American diplomatic appeals. He allowed punishment without creating martyrs.

Among the other judicial questions demonstrating the war's continued effects on Canada's civil society was the matter of Lt. Col. George Denison. The colonel had spent the war playing an interesting game; he had served as an officer in the Canadian militia while maintaining his very public support for the Confederacy. He was the only member of the Toronto City Council who voted against sending a letter of condolence following Lincoln's assassination. He later wrote a history of the Fenian Raids that, while exaggerating his role, burst with nationalistic pride at the way Canada had defended itself against invasion.

Denison insisted on being compensated for losses suffered as a result of his association with Jacob Thompson's Canadian-based Confederates. In late October, 1864, as part of what would become the *Philo Parsons* incident on Lake Erie, Thompson had arranged for Denison to purchase the steamer *Georgian* from Kentucky's Dr. James Bates for eighteen thousand dollars. Through another arrangement with Thompson, Denison had then purchased a second ship called the *Georgiana*. It was also moored at Collingwood, on Lake Huron's charming Georgian Bay. In February 1865, Denison hired William MacDonald to perform a number of upgrades on the *Georgiana*. MacDonald had been one of Thompson's men and was a fugitive for having been involved in the burning of New York. In April, under the power of the Alien Act, John A. Macdonald, as attorney general, had the *Georgiana* seized. Denison was on board when Toronto's Collector of Customs arrived to do the deed.

Denison protested through political channels, and then the courts, with the unconvincing claim that the ship had not been purchased for Thompson and that the modifications had nothing to do with preparations for armaments. Long after Appomattox, Godfrey Hyams, the agent who had infiltrated Thompson's inner circle and warned Canadian and American authorities of many Confederate activities, was called to testify at a hearing intended to settle Denison's monetary claims. He explained that the ship was indeed being outfitted for use as a Confederate privateer. He told of grenades, guns, Greek fire, and other weapons being gathered for the ship at the time it was seized. He also identified the

Toronto arms manufacturer that Thompson had regularly used. Hyams took police to the Agnes Street house that had served as Thompson's arms factory. He showed them the secret rooms and doorways, the twenty-six shells still on shelves awaiting delivery, and the secret compartments on wagons still parked outside.[2]

The case dragged on through a number of frustrating appeals. It was finally resolved in November 1867. As part of the settlement, Denison was required to pay Thompson thirteen thousand dollars for it had been established that, despite his claims to the contrary, it was his promissory note that had allowed the ship to be purchased in the first place.[3] The case ended up proving in court what many suspected and others knew: Canada had supplied arms to the South.

HUMANITARIAN ISSUES: CONFEDERATE REFUGEES IN CANADA

When Robert E. Lee and then other Southern generals offered their swords in the spring of 1865, they were faced with the conundrum of remaining in the shattered South or fleeing the land that would be ruled by their enemies. Many fled, and a number came to Canada. Their arrival bolstered the already substantial Confederate communities in the towns where they settled. The stories of three prominent refugees tell the tale.

Jubal Early was a celebrated general, having led troops in several major battles, and offered punsters the chance to quip that Gettysburg was lost because Early arrived late. He was later accused of allowing a mass hanging of deserters and he was relieved of duty in late March 1865 for his failure in the Valley Campaign. At the war's end, Early fled to Mexico but, finding conditions there inhospitable, he moved on to Cuba and then, in the spring of 1866, to Toronto. He happened to arrive on the same day that Union general William Tecumseh Sherman was being welcomed with great pomp and afforded the honour of conducting an inspection of the city's militia. Early was miffed at being ignored, but accepted the hospitality offered at George Denison's grand home.[4]

When Early was in Mexico, Lee had written explaining that he was preparing a history of the war but needed documents relating to its final years. Early promised to help.[5] Instead, he gathered papers and began a book of his own, writing the bulk of it in Toronto. It was released by Toronto publisher Lovell and Gibson and became a sensation in Canada and the United States. The book was like Early himself—unrepentant, stubborn and proud. Along with Southern journalist Edward Pollard's work, Early's book established the idea of the "Lost Cause" as the lens through which generations of Southerners interpreted the war.

Early enjoyed life in Toronto, lived for a time in Niagara Falls and then in Drummondville, in Quebec's idyllic eastern townships. When President Johnson declared a general amnesty for all former Confederates on Christmas Day 1868, Early packed up and went home to Virginia.

General George Pickett revealed himself the master of the understatement when, asked why his famous Gettysburg charge had failed, he laconically responded, "The Yankees had something to do with it."[6] Pickett and his wife, Lasalle, moved to Montreal in early 1866. They stayed at a fine house owned by a gentleman on an extended stay in England, and then at the comfortable St. Laurent Hotel. He cut off his famous ringlets and settled into civilian life, accepting salutes every day from the city's many Southerners and Southern sympathizers. Pickett soon found, however, that one cannot eat notoriety. Lasalle was eventually forced to sell her jewelry and they moved to Sherbrooke, where they lived quite modestly, while she gave French, Latin and piano lessons. They, too, left Canada with the news of the Johnson amnesty.

The most important Confederate refugee in Canada was Jefferson Davis. He was a devoted family man with a sincere and boundless love for his wife, Varina, and their seven children. Davis was a skilled military tactician and dedicated public servant who worked tirelessly for the advancement of the public good, as he saw it, through a long career untainted by even a whisper of scandal. Davis had received word from Lee that Petersburg had fallen on April 2, 1865, and hours later he left Richmond. On May 10, he was recognized and arrested by a passing group of Union soldiers near Irwinville, in south Georgia. Twelve days later, the worn and bedraggled ex-president was taken to a cold, damp cell in Fort Monroe, where he was shackled and humiliated.

Varina had sent their children north to Montreal, where they lived with her mother and sister, who had been there for some time. They attended school and settled into a quiet life in their new home. Varina worked tirelessly to secure the release of her husband, and was eventually allowed to live nearby to visit him. In June 1867, President Johnson approved Davis's parole. Varina gathered the haggard and ill ex-president and left the next day to join their children in Montreal.

They arrived to a hero's welcome. Former Confederate consul to Havana Colonel C.J. Helen and Confederate minister to Britain James Mason, who had been living for over two years in Niagara Falls, had organized the welcome. A large and boisterous crowd cheered, clapped and sang.

After a brief time with their children, the two set off on a tour of Canada. At the harbour in Kingston, a cheering crowd greeted them on arrival and mobbed them as they stretched their legs on shore. Denison helped organize their reception in Toronto and it was magnificent. Six to seven thousand people applauded as the steamer docked. A *New York Times* reporter was there and noted that at a luncheon in Davis's honour, "all the Confederates in the City, besides large numbers of Canadians, paid their respects."[7] Davis smiled and shook hands, but was obviously not well. Denison observed, "I was so astonished at the emaciation and weakness of Mr. Davis who looked like a dying man, that I said to a friend near me, 'They have killed him.'"[8]

It was then on to Niagara Falls and another large crowd. A band welcomed them with "Dixie" and "Bonnie Blue Flag," followed by a rousing three cheers for Davis and another three for Mason. Not sure of Davis's plans in Canada, the *New York Times* article concluded, "If he remains in Canada he may spend it at this little town of Niagara where a pleasant Confederate society is springing up."[9]

Davis returned to Montreal, where Varina's entire family soon joined them. Toronto publisher John Lovell arranged for them all to move from their rather run-down boarding house to a Mountain Street mansion, paid for by Canadian supporters. It was there that Davis concerned himself with personal finances, which were abysmal, and with efforts to regain his health, which was awful.

Just before the fall of Richmond, boxes of official Confederate government documents had been gathered and shipped through Halifax to Montreal, where they were stored at the Bank of Montreal. Varina arranged for some of the boxes to be brought to them so that Davis could begin work on a history of the Confederacy that he had said he wanted to write. After only a short time, however, it proved too much for him: one afternoon, Davis stood and walked away saying, "Let us put them by for awhile, I cannot speak of the dead so soon."[10]

When September came, the family moved to Lennoxville to be near Jeff junior, who was enrolled in Bishop's College. He was welcomed at the school by a number of other children of Confederate refugees.[11] The family stayed at the modest Clark's Hotel and continued to welcome a steady stream of visitors. Finance Minister Alexander Galt was among those who called on Davis and fussed over gifts for the children.[12] Autumn among the riotous colours of Quebec's hardwoods promised tranquil beauty for recuperation, but Davis could not really rest, as his trial for treason was set for late November. On November 19, the Davis family left Montreal to face his accusers in an America still struggling to reconcile the horror it had inflicted upon itself.*

ISSUES OF SURVIVAL: THE *ALABAMA* AND ANNEXATION

From the outset of the Civil War, Canadians had worried about what would happen when it ended. Two days after Lee's surrender, Macdonald had written to George Brown, predicting that the Union, "flushed with success," would turn its armies and fleets northward to take Canada. He spoke of Seward's goal of seeing the United States "overspread the continent."[13]

---

* *Davis was never tried. A motion to restore his American citizenship was approved by Congress in 1976 and signed into law by a president born in Georgia. Davis may have enjoyed the irony.*

By late 1868, however, the mighty American military had been largely demobilized. There were only about fifty thousand men left in uniform, and most were deployed in the south and west. The threat of armed intervention in Canada was consequently greatly reduced. Nonetheless, the expansionist goals of many American policy makers remained. If Canada could not be won through invasion, perhaps it could be bought or traded for. Both potential tactics stemmed from the unresolved wartime issue of the *Alabama* claims.

The claims arose from one of Lincoln's first aggressive acts—the blockade of Southern ports. Lincoln had hoped to suffocate the South by stopping shipments of armaments and supplies in and cotton out. Davis had already issued letters of marque in an attempt to create a privateer navy and sent agents to Britain to have ships bought or built.[14] Thirteen ships were eventually obtained—among them was the *Enrica*. Working from offices in Liverpool, Confederate agent James Dunwoody Bulloch arranged financing and then placed the order for the *Enrica* with Birkenhead's Laird Brothers in October 1861.[15]* Code-named "290," the 900-ton, iron-clad steamer was, according to the paper work, a freighter to be sold to a Spanish company. Its design, however, clearly indicated that it was to be a battleship. The *Enrica* was launched in May 1862.

American minister to Britain, Charles Adams knew of the secret Confederate shipbuilding operations and specifically about the *Enrica*. He asked Foreign Secretary Earl Russell to have it inspected and seized as tangible proof that Britain had violated its declaration of neutrality. While a bureaucratic shuffle ensued, the wives and children of the crew and some of the shipbuilders boarded the *Enrica* for what was to be a short test run on the Mersey out of Liverpool. It all looked innocent enough. Around the first bend, though, the passengers were put ashore and the *Enrica* put to sea. She steamed to the Azores, where armaments were installed and ammunition loaded. On August 25, the *Enrica* was re-commissioned as the CSS *Alabama* and joined the growing British-made Confederate navy.

---

* *Bulloch's nephew would later be president: Theodore Roosevelt.*

The *Alabama* became a predator, sinking sixty-four American commercial vessels and an American warship. Secretary of the Navy Gideon Wells ordered the USS *Kearsarge* to find and sink the *Alabama*, and a global hunt began.

With the *Alabama* and others wreaking havoc on American trade, and Nova Scotia and New Brunswick helping to make a mockery of Lincoln's blockade, Seward and Adams became increasingly agitated with the British government's willful blind eye toward its role in Confederate naval operations, a blindness they claimed was making the war longer and harsher. Adams's protests increased in intensity and frequency. After the turning of the tide with Gettysburg and Vicksburg, the Palmerston government finally put a stop to the building of Confederate ships. In September 1863, Palmerston ordered that two large iron-clads, known as the Laird Rams, be seized and purchased for the Royal Navy. Meanwhile, Confederate ships already made possible through the winks and nods of British law makers continued to do their work.

A few weeks later, Adams petitioned the British government to consider an arbitration process to determine the amount of compensation owed the United States in respect of Britain's illegal support of the building of the Confederate navy. The suit involving all British-made and procured ships, but was named after the most notorious and so became known as the *Alabama* claims. Palmerston refused to acknowledge the suit.

In July 1864, after months of prowling the world's seas, the *Kearsarge* waited near Cherbourg, France, where its prey was being repaired. A challenge was issued. The two slowly emerged from the harbour and engaged in a spectacular and fiery battle. The *Alabama* whirled and brawled, but was outgunned and sunk.

With the war's end, neither country had forgotten the *Alabama* claims suit, but neither brought it to the top of their agendas. Britain was dealing with increasingly troublesome events in Europe and its government was changing at an unprecedented rate. The United States needed to mourn a president and heal a nation under the chaotic rule of a federal government battling itself. Into this vacuum stepped William Seward.

Seward was not the man he had been before or during the war. The assassination attempt had rendered one arm useless and sapped his vigour. His wife's premature passing had broken his heart. He had lost political capital because of his support for the embattled President Johnson. As before the war, though, he was passionate about American expansionism, and winning Canada remained a key goal.[16] Seward saw the settlement of the *Alabama* claims as a tactic in that pursuit.

In early 1867, Seward first spoke with Britain's minister in Washington, Sir Frederick Bruce, and offered to trade the money owed the United States in an *Alabama* settlement for Britain's Bahamian Islands. He then wrote to Adams in London to see if Britain would cede British Columbia in exchange for the money owed.[17] Seward believed that taking the British colony, composed mostly of the small towns of Victoria and Vancouver, would help American progress by ridding the west coast of a European power. At the same time, it would provide more ports to spur Asian-American trade and, by taking the continent's west coast, put pressure on the rest of Canada to eventually become American.[18] Seward's ideas leaked and by May 1867 were being openly discussed and became the subject of editorial newspaper debate in Britain, Canada and the United States.[19]

Russian minister to Washington Edouard de Stoeckl made things even more interesting by asking Seward if America was interested in purchasing Alaska. Russia and America were close allies at the time and both saw Britain as a strong and dangerous competitor. Consequently, Czar Alexander II was quite receptive to the argument that if America owned Alaska, then there would be increased pressure on Britain to sell or cede British Columbia and perhaps even all of its North American territory to the United States. Russia would win either way because Britain would no longer have a North American Pacific presence.[20]

The offer thrilled Seward, who agreed with the czar's geopolitical analysis.[21] He also realized that the purchase would bring prestige for him and his state department, while meeting his long-held goal of expanding America. Seward negotiated well and quickly, and bought Alaska for only

$7.2 million. President Johnson signed the treaty ceding Alaska to the United States on the same day—March 29, 1867—that Queen Victoria signed the British North America Act that created Canada.

The purchase instigated a storm of protest in the United States against what many called "Seward's Folly." There were some, however, who recognized and supported his Manifest Destiny strategy. The *New York Tribune*, for instance, praised the purchase as part of a move to eventually swallow Canada and argued, "When the experiment of the 'dominion' shall have failed, as fail it must, a process of peaceful absorption will give Canada her proper place in the great North American Republic."[22] Chair of the Foreign Relations Committee Charles Sumner was a vehement believer in Manifest Destiny and saw the annexation of Canada as a part of that vision. In the Senate debate approving the Alaska purchase, Sumner sold the idea to his colleagues as a significant step toward American occupation of all of North America.[23] Upon the Senate's ratification of the treaty, Seward wrote to Adams that the *Alabama* claims should now be brought back to the fore because, "now they could be settled in one way, by such acquisition from England as would enable us to round off our North-Western territory."[24]

The British Columbia legislature had passed a motion in March 1867 expressing its desire to join Canada. The Alaskan purchase, however, drove a wedge between those in the colony's civil society who wanted to maintain ties with Britain and its American ex-patriots, many of whom began to fly the stars and stripes from their homes and shops. British Columbia's Governor Frederick Seymour wrote to the British Colonial office, fretting that the power of the annexationists was growing, and was supported by money flowing in from San Francisco.[25] In September, those concerned with growing American influence watched with dismay as six American warships dropped anchor in Victoria's harbour.

If Canada was to survive, British Columbia needed to become Canadian, and Macdonald needed to move quickly to shore up support for Confederation and win the western colony. He demonstrated the political genius for which he was so highly respected by first negotiating new financial arrangements between his government and Nova Scotia and then moving Joseph Howe, still the province's chief anti-Confederation spokesperson, into his cabinet. Demands to leave Canada slowly faded from Nova Scotia's political discourse.

In late 1868, Macdonald sent George-Étienne Cartier and William McDougall to London to negotiate the purchase of Rupert's Land, the great swath of territory north and west of Canada that was owned by the Hudson's Bay Company. Seward wanted the land for America and had sent feelers to Britain about arranging an American purchase. The negotiations were protracted—the American elephant was always present in the room—but an agreement was finally made whereby Britain would loan Canada three hundred thousand pounds to make the purchase. Minnesota railway men and Washington annexationists ground their teeth as Canada suddenly took ownership of land from the Great Lakes to the Rockies and north to the Arctic, and did so for a pittance.

Macdonald then turned his attention to British Columbia, where arguments continued to rage between those who wished to join the United States, centred mostly in Vancouver, and those who preferred to join Canada, predominantly those in Victoria. In October 1869, at Macdonald's behest, Britain's Lord Granville, who had become secretary of state for the colonies the previous December, had sent a note to British Columbia's political leaders stating that Britain preferred the colony to join Canada. Of more significance was that Macdonald promised that Canada would assume the colony's debt and build a railway connecting it to Canada within ten years. Canada had proven that it wanted British Columbia, the Americans would not risk war to take it and Britain would not risk losing North America by surrendering it. British Columbia officially joined Canada in July 1871.

In late 1868, with Macdonald negotiating the Hudson's Bay Company land and British Columbia out from under him, Seward had moved to settle the *Alabama* claims. Union general and Northern hero Ulysses S. Grant had been elected to the presidency in November; Seward's time in office was ending and he had to move fast. He initiated new talks that led to the signing of the Johnson-Clarendon Convention in January 1869. The agreement lumped the *Alabama* claims with a number of other grievances that Britain and America had left unresolved since 1853.

President-elect Grant let it be known that he did not like the terms of the agreement.[26] Senator Charles Sumner, at that point Seward's ally, thought Johnson-Clarendon was an abomination because it did not demand a British apology or establish the amounts that would be paid. Further, it left Canada Canadian. He delivered a long speech slamming its terms and concluding that America remained interested in taking Canada as settlement for the *Alabama* claims.[27] To make the swap more tempting to Britain, Sumner said that the United States demanded $15 million for the loss of property and an astronomical $110 million for indirect costs, including increased marine insurance premiums, and lost trade and economic expansion opportunities. Michigan senator Zachariah Chandler made a motion that Britain should immediately cede Canada to the United States as a down payment on all *Alabama* claims. He said that he could rally sixty thousand volunteers from his state who would gladly cross the border, take Canada and hold it hostage until Britain agreed.[28] The lame-duck Senate voted 54 to 1 against the Johnson-Clarendon Convention.

Sumner and Chandler could bluster and Seward could steam, but the next steps would be Grant's. After years of Johnson's harsh and troubled leadership, the country was ready for a strong and skilled chief executive. Unfortunately, it did not get one. While scandal and misdeed never touched Grant personally, almost from the outset his administration was soiled by corruption and bureaucratic blunder. Grant was an intelligent and able man but a poor administrator. The skills that had put him in the White House were not those he needed to succeed once in office.

As he had hinted during his brief visit to Canada after the war, Grant was an expansionist. He considered Chandler's boast silly and had said many times that he would never sanction military action in order to win more land. However, in the same breath he had told aides that the settlement of the *Alabama* claims would end with the United States owning Canada.[29] He was among those who believed that the Civil War had been prolonged by Britain's declaration of neutrality and actions it took that helped the South, most significantly the building of ships for the Confederate navy. He had also made many public and private remarks about his disdain for Canada on account of its Southern sympathies and its harbouring of Confederates who acted against the United States. In one of his early cabinet meetings, he spoke of his hatred of Britain and Canada: "If not for our debt, I wish Congress would declare war on Great Britain, then we could take Canada and wipe out her Commerce as she has done ours, and then we would start fair."[30]

In February 1869, days before Grant took office, British minister to the United States Sir Edward Thornton and Macdonald exchanged a series of letters concerning rumours of another Fenian invasion. Macdonald argued that he would prepare for it but would not ask the Americans to help stop it. Thornton agreed, noting that he had told the Americans about the rumours and that it was up to them to take action.[31] Grant's secretary of state, Hamilton Fish, had taken word of Fenian plans to one of the administration's first cabinet meetings. He recommended that the raids be stopped and that arms being assembled near the Canadian border be seized. President Grant silenced the room by snapping, "The British did not seize or stop the *Alabama*."[32]

The decision was eventually made to alert American ships on the Great Lakes with orders to stop the Fenians, and local law enforcement agents were told to capture the arms. The Fenians lost their nerve and nothing of consequence occurred. Grant's cabinet debated using detectives to investigate future Canadian raids, but Grant said no, adding, "The British did not employ detectives to prevent raids from Canada during our war."[33]

In July 1869, Macdonald dispatched Finance Minister John Rose to Washington to meet with Fish. The secretary of state was a graduate of the Columbia Law School and had been a New York congressman, governor and senator. His slow-talking nature and long, sad face fringed with scraggly chin-whiskers disarmed those who met him, but he was as intelligent as he was shrewd. Fish was also as determined an annexationist as his president and his predecessor. Fish explained to Rose that Sumner's harsh words in the Senate expressed the thoughts of most Americans. He felt, nonetheless, that Canada and the United States needed to rationally address matters of concern but that a resolution of the *Alabama* claims needed to occur first. They talked about a joint commission to settle the claims.

Rose left for Britain shortly afterward to try to initiate discussions. Fish did the same with Grant, but hit a wall. The president stated in a cabinet meeting that he believed the *Alabama* discussion should be postponed for perhaps a year. He predicted that time would lead to Britain's becoming desperate to settle and thus willing to withdraw from Canada, allowing all claims to be settled through a money-for-land swap.[34]

Grant publicly revealed his harsh feelings for Canada and Britain in his State of the Union address:

The Imperial Government is understood to have delegated the whole or a share of its control or jurisdiction of the inshore fishing grounds to the colonial authority known as the dominion of Canada, and this semi-independent but irresponsible agent has exercised its delegated power in an unfriendly way. . . . It is hoped that the government of Great Britain will see the justice of abandoning the narrow and inconsistent claim to which her Canada provinces have urged her adherence.[35]

In November 1869, Fish invited British minister Thornton to his home. As they settled into large wingback chairs and puffed cigars, Fish said that he and Grant both wanted to see the United States ultimately take control all of North America. He said that Canadian-American fishing disputes and the *Alabama* claims needed to be settled, and that Grant would give up his pressure to take Canada only if Britain offered amenable terms in respect to both issues. Thornton felt the offer was reasonable and forwarded it to London.[36]

Fish reported to cabinet with the argument that Canada should not immediately be taken, but that Britain might yet surrender it to the United States to settle the *Alabama* dispute.[37] Grant agreed to be patient. When told of the Fish-Thornton agreement, Senator Sumner was furious. He wrote a long memo to Fish arguing that the United States must exploit the *Alabama* claims in order to force Britain to surrender Canada immediately. He concluded, "Therefore, the withdrawal of the British flag cannot be abandoned as a condition or preliminary of such a settlement as is now proposed. To make the settlement complete, the withdrawal should be from this hemisphere, including the provinces and the islands."[38] Sumner and Grant had earlier parted ways over an issue involving the purchase of Santo Domingo (later the Dominican Republic), and over a number of impolitic personal attacks that Sumner had made on the president. His power was somewhat reduced from its previous strength, but because the Senate would eventually need to ratify whatever was decided, his views remained significant.

Fish met with Thornton several more times over the coming months and at one point bluntly enquired whether Britain would mind if the United States simply annexed Canada. Thornton replied that Britain would not stop the United States from doing so if Canada expressed an interest but, he added, Canadians seemed somewhat bitter about thoughts of annexation.[39] Macdonald heard of the exchange and launched protests to Westminster and directly to Thornton. Thornton softened his stand only a little, telling Fish the next time they met that Macdonald was unhappy about British policy. The policy, however, did not change—nor did American goals. In an April 1870 cabinet meeting, Grant stated that if Canada would simply agree to join the United States, the *Alabama* claims could be "settled in five minutes."[40]

Fish told Thornton of Grant's desire to settle the claims by trading for Canada, and noted that every cabinet secretary supported the president.[41] Despite overwhelming evidence to the contrary, Fish said that he believed the majority of the Canadians wanted annexation. Thornton finally balked and questioned the veracity of the American interpretation of Canadian public opinion.[42] The talks were going nowhere. Canada refused to concede; Britain refused to push it. The three-nation joint commission that Fish and John Rose had discussed two years before seemed to be the only way forward. Besides, the 1872 presidential election was coming up and Grant needed a foreign policy victory.

On February 2, 1871, Macdonald received an invitation to join a five-person British delegation as part of a Joint High Commission to meet in Washington to settle all claims outstanding from the Civil War. Macdonald pondered his participation, but decided he needed to be there to represent Canadian interests—compensation for the Fenian raids, protection of fishing rights and, above all, to ensure that Canada was not traded in whole or part for the *Alabama* claims.

Despite the simmering postwar tension with the United States, Macdonald had enjoyed a series of political triumphs since July 1867—but he had also suffered more personal tragedy. On April 7, 1868, his trusted friend and political ally Thomas D'Arcy McGee, having completed a late-night speech in the House, was enjoying a cigar as he walked a few blocks home to his Sparks Street boarding house. As he took out his key to unlock the door, he was felled by a gunshot. Word screamed through the city and Macdonald rushed to the scene in time to kneel on the cobblestones and hold his friend's head in his hands. McGee was dead—Canada's first political assassination.* Hibernian Patrick Whelan was found guilty of the murder and hanged after uttering his final words: "God save Ireland and God save my soul."[43] Investigations were undertaken to determine if American Fenians had ordered the assassination, but no connections were found.

In February 1869, Macdonald and his wife, Agnes, had welcomed a beautiful baby girl they named Mary. By June, doctors diagnosed hydrocephalus, a brain ailment that led to the enlargement of her head, crippled limbs, and a sad lack of intellectual development. Macdonald was unerringly gentle and loving. Every day he read Mary stories and rubbed her legs to ease her pain; or perhaps his.

Despite years of drinking too much, eating too little and never taking exercise, Macdonald had always enjoyed robust health. But on November

---

* *McGee is the only Canadian political leader to have been assassinated. There has never been an attempt on the life of a Canadian prime minister.*

6, 1870, while in his office, he suffered a piercing pain and collapsed. He had passed a gallstone of such ghastly proportions that his life was in danger. For weeks, first his office and then the rooms normally reserved for the Speaker of the House, were his hospital. Newspapers prepared obituaries.[44] But by July, he was well enough to be moved to Charlottetown for a recuperative holiday. For months he handled nothing but the most urgent matters. When he returned to work in the fall, Macdonald was stronger but not fully recovered.

Sadness and tragedy were not strangers to Macdonald. Somehow he was able to compartmentalize office pressures, personal heartache and physical discomfort, and he departed for Washington. He brought Agnes and the deputy ministers of fisheries and justice, but left his bottles behind. Throughout the negotiations he did not touch a drop. The little group of Canadians settled into the Arlington Hotel and prepared to save Canada from the Civil War's last battle.

THE WASHINGTON CONFERENCE

The conference began on February 27, 1871, with the five American and four British delages, and one from Canada, meeting at the State Department library. Fish led the American delegation, and the British group was led by a short, heavily bearded man with the long name, Lord De Grey and Ripon. First on the agenda was the fisheries question. Macdonald refused to compromise on every proposal the Americans made at the table and those that British delegates brought him in private. He insisted that the fisheries would neither be sold nor traded, regardless of the effect on the *Alabama* claims issue. Macdonald's obduracy exasperated the British delegates, who had arrived believing that the Canadian prime minister would comport himself as British, or least an obedient colonial.[45]

It was estimated that, from 1854 to 1864, Americans had taken six million dollars' worth of fish a year from Canadian waters.[46] When the Reciprocity Treaty ended in 1866, a system of licencing American fishermen had been established, but it was all but ignored. In January 1870, Macdonald's government had built six military cruisers, at a cost of a million dollars, to keep Americans out of Canadian inland fisheries and to enforce the three-mile off-shore limit.[47] A number of American ships were stopped and their catches and nets seized. These facts led Macdonald to emphasize that the fisheries were economically important, and symbols of Canadian sovereignty that he simply could not deal away.[48]

On March 21, Macdonald was able to write home with the good news that De Grey and Ripon had conceded that any agreement made in Washington would need to be ratified by the Canadian Parliament. Fish was perturbed: he suddenly and unexpectedly had to deal with Canada as an equal. In a letter to Charles Tupper, Macdonald crowed about the concession that had just been won. Also, he could now offer a great incentive to Newfoundland and Prince Edward Island, because if they wanted to enjoy the benefits of whatever fisheries agreement was made with the United States, they would need to join Canada.[49]

Day after frustrating day, the British delegates showed a united front. Night after infuriating night, those delegates badgered Macdonald to give ground. They grew desperate. In an act of astonishing diplomatic effrontery, Macdonald's frequent letters home to his cabinet and to Governor General Lisgar were re-routed back from Lisgar to the British delegates.[50] They thus knew the game Macdonald was playing, for they knew his fallback positions and that he had full authority to make independent decisions—but still they could not best him. The British delegates were reduced to threatening that if Macdonald did not act according to their interests, Britain might not offer military support in the future and Canada would be doomed to fall to America. They also tried to bribe him with an appointment to Her Majesty's Privy Council, a powerful group of advisors to the Queen that, they expected, any British subject would be humbled and honoured to join.[51]

Meanwhile, America's interest in Canada persisted. Days before the meetings had begun, Michigan senator Jacob Howard had introduced a motion stating that the United States should annex Canada, from Sault Ste. Marie to the Pacific. On March 15, Fish told the British delegation of Seward's old idea to take British Columbia in compensation for the *Alabama* claims. Later, Fish met privately with De Grey and Ripon to see about reducing *Alabama* payments for whatever part of Canada he was willing to give away.[52] Howard's motion did not come to a vote and neither of Fish's proposals was seriously entertained—but the pressure remained.

Finally, after thirty-seven meetings held over nine weeks, the Washington Conference was over. On May 5, 1871, the delegates met to sign the Treaty of Washington. It had been agreed that two international tribunals would be established. One would rule on the *Alabama* claims made by the American government and the other on claims made by individuals. Britain agreed to express regret for having involved itself in arming the Confederacy but would not suffer the diplomatic humiliation of an apology. Canada was not asked for an apology and did not offer one. Canada would receive $5.5 million for ten years of access to its inland fisheries and enjoy the elimination of duties on many Canadian products entering the United States, including wood, fish oil, bait, salt and coal. Most important, Canada remained Canadian with no mention made of land swaps or annexation.

Macdonald had reason to be proud of what he had won and of having averted the catastrophe. He knew he had pushed the British as far as they could go and the Americans further than they wished. He wrote to Tupper, "The expectations by the American people of a settlement of these matters have been strung to a very high pitch, and the disappointment, in case the negotiations end in nothing, will be very great. If this attempt to settle the *Alabama* question should fail, no peaceable solution of it is possible, and the war cloud will hang over England and Canada."[53]

When Maritime political leaders and fishermen expressed happiness that the agreement had finally set new rules that, with any luck, would be obeyed, Macdonald was even more upbeat. Upon his return to Ottawa, he spoke of the Washington Treaty as a Canadian victory. In a speech to the House of Commons on May 3, 1872, which lasted four and a quarter hours, Macdonald detailed what had been at stake, what could have been lost, and what had been won. He began by noting the significance to Canada's nationhood; it was now firmly established, in that the agreement needed to be ratified by three bodies: the American Congress, the British Parliament and the Canadian Parliament. He returned to that point several times.[54]

He explained that the negotiations had led to an agreement between Canada and Britain that they would not press the Americans to apologize for the Fenian raids and compensate Canada. Instead, there had been a deal whereby Britain would pay Canada's Fenian losses of four million pounds and the funds would be used for railway construction. As part of the agreement, he continued, Britain promised to come to Canada's aid in the event of another invasion from America.

Macdonald spoke of the American duties that would be removed on a number of Canadian products, representing a re-introduction of the Reciprocity Treaty by degrees. He also talked of the Washington Treaty's bonding agreement, which would allow freer transport of American and Canadian goods to each other's markets, and overseas.

Finally, Macdonald reiterated that the Washington Treaty had finally ended Civil War irritants, established Canada as a fact, and rendered its border safer:

> But I say that this Treaty which has gone through so many difficulties and dangers, if it is carried into effect, removes almost all possibility of war. If there was ever an irritating cause of war, it was from the occurrences arising out of the escape of those vessels, and when we see the United States people and Government forget this irritation, forget those occurrences, and submit such a question to arbitration, to the arbitration of a disinterested tribunal, they have established a principle which can never be forgotten in this world.[55]

The international *Alabama* claims tribunal met the next year in Geneva, with the United States represented by Charles Francis Adams, Jr., called out of retirement to serve. In September 1872, it was agreed that Britain would pay the United States $15.5 million plus interest for the damage caused by the British-made Confederate ships. As per the

Washington Treaty agreement, there was no talk of trading all, or even part, of Canada.

The *Alabama* claims tribunal and the Treaty of Washington ended the American Civil War. Britain's long decline from its period of global dominance was underway and the growth of the German military machine would, in a few decades, invite the final phase of that process. The United States emerged from the Civil War scarred and broken, but its industrial might, supported by the strength of its fleet and fuelled by the wealth of its resources and the ingenuity of its people, could be felt around the world, even throughout its long and painful period of reconstruction and redemption. Its era of global domination had begun.

The war that had threatened to crush Canada and the postwar machinations that could have kidnapped it from the road upon which it was embarked were finally over. There were still harsh words, accusations that demanded apology, and hatred and suspicion that needed reconciliation. But there was hope. The Canadian experiment, with its unique centralized parliamentary democracy governing a bilingual, multicultural, tolerant country with too much geography and too few people, was underway. Canada emerged from the war unified in its un-American political and social values, led by a determined and visionary leader, secure in its heritage and bristling with the power of its potential.

POSTSCRIPT

And what of our guides, those six people whose lives led us on our journey of understanding? After disappearing into Africa, John Anderson never reappeared. The inauguration of President Grant put William Seward into retirement. He enjoyed a trip around the world and then settled into his Auburn, New York, mansion. Seward died in October 1872, a month after the announcement of the *Alabama* claims tribunal.

Jacob Thompson eventually returned to Mississippi to find that his three estates had been destroyed by Union marauders. He moved to Memphis, where his personal fortune, or perhaps his wife's dowry, or maybe money he had taken from his Canadian adventure, allowed him to live in ostentatious comfort. The Grant administration filed a two-million-dollar law suit against him, but it was quietly dropped after the 1876 election. Thompson died with his papers burned and secrets secured in March 1885.

George Brown never returned to politics. He focused on his impressive land holdings and other investments, while his *Globe* remained the most widely read newspaper in Canada. In March 1880, Brown was shot by a disgruntled *Globe* employee and died of his wounds two months later.

Except for a brief stint in opposition, Sir John A. Macdonald remained the prime minister of Canada until his death in office in 1891. Without his skills, determination and vision, it is quite likely that Canada would not have been created or survived. Macdonald's legacy is Canada itself.

A month after the war ended, Sarah Emma Edmonds left the service and returned home with fellow New Brunswicker Linus Seelye. They were married two years later and had three children and adopted two more. Edmonds wrote a book entitled *Nurse and Spy in the Union Army: Comprising the Adventures and Experiences of a Woman in Hospitals Camps and Battlefields*. It was a smashing success, selling 175,000 copies. In 1884, Edmonds attended the reunion of the 2nd Michigan Volunteers. Her comrades in arms convinced her to ask that the charge of desertion be dropped and that she apply for a veteran's pension. Many wrote letters detailing her contributions and supporting her claim. It took a House bill, signed by President Arthur, to make it happen. Edmonds was granted an honourable discharge and a pension of twelve dollars a month.

In obtaining her pension, Edmonds joined many other Canadians who had earned theirs. It is impossible to quantify how many Canadians were also drawing pensions, Canadians who, like Edmonds, had joined one army or the other when they were already in the United States and then remained there after the war's end. However, by 1883 the American government was mailing 615 monthly pension cheques over the border to veterans who had returned to their Canadian homes.[56]

In 1893, Edmonds and her husband moved to the home of their adopted son George in LaPorte, Texas. Edmonds died on September 5,

1898, and was buried with full military honours in a Grand Army of the Republic portion of a Houston cemetery beneath a headstone that reads, with deceptive simplicity, "Emma E. Seelye, Army Nurse." How modest. How Canadian.

30   William Teatero, *John Anderson Fugitive Slave*, p. 64.

31   Macdonald to Freeman, December 27, 1860. LAC. *Macdonald Papers*. Vol. 673.

32   Richard Gwyn, *John A*, p. 151.

33   Macdonald to Matthews, August 3, 1859. LAC. *Macdonald Papers*. Vol. 673.

34   *New York Times*, December 21, 1860

35   Ibid., January 4, 1861.

36   Teatero, *John Anderson Fugitive Slave*, p. 74.

37   Freeman to Macdonald, October 6, 1860. LAC. *Macdonald Papers*. Vol. 540.

38   Macdonald to Freeman, October 18, 1860. LAC. *Macdonald Papers*. Vol. 540.

39   *Province of Canada Sessional Papers*. Vol. 19, no. 4.

40   Ibid.

41   *Toronto Leader*, November 24, 1860.

42   *Globe*, November 28, 1860 and *Hamilton Daily Spectator*, November 29, 1860.

43   Ibid., November 14, 1861.

44   Ibid., November 30, 1860.

45   Patrick Brodie, *The Odyssey of John Anderson*, p. 49.

46   Ibid., p. 50.

47   *Detroit Daily Advertiser*, December 5, 1860. Cited in Brodie, *The Odyssey of John Anderson*, p. 52.

48   Ibid., p. 53.

49   *Baltimore American*, December 3, 1860. Cited in Brodie, *The Odyssey of John Anderson*, p. 53.

50   Queen's Bench Reports. *Province of Canada Sessional Papers*. Vol. 20, no. 4.

51   Ibid.

52   William Renwick Riddell, "The Fugitive Slave in Upper Canada," p. 356.

53   Macdonald to Freeman, December 20, 1860. LAC. *Macdonald Papers*. Vol. 673.

54   *Quebec Mercury*. Reprinted in the *Globe*, December 25, 1860.

55   *Globe*, December 25, 1860.

56   Ibid.

57   Ibid.

58   Ibid.

59   *Globe*, December 22, 1860.

60   Macdonald to Freeman, December 27, 1860. LAC. *Macdonald Papers*. Vol. 673.

61   Henning to Chamerovzow, December 17, 1860. Cited in Reinders, "The John Anderson Case," p. 399.

62 Ibid., p. 400.

63 *London Post*. Cited in the *Globe*, January 22, 1861.

64 *London Times*, January 12, 1861.

65 Reinders, "The John Anderson Case," p. 394.

66 H. Sweet (ed.), *The Jurist*, p. 13.

67 Ibid., 81.

68 Newcastle to Williams, January 1861. *Province of Canada Sessional Papers*. Vol. 19, no. 4.

69 Crook, *Diplomacy During the American Civil War*, p. 3.

70 Jasper Ridley, *Lord Palmerston*, p. 552.

71 Reinders, "The John Anderson Case," p. 401.

72 *London Times*, January 16, 1861.

73 *Liverpool Post*. Reprinted in the *Globe*, February 2, 1861.

74 Brodie, *The Odyssey of John Anderson*, p. 80.

75 *Globe*, February 2, 1861.

76 *Toronto Leader*, January 21, 1861.

77 Brodie, *The Odyssey of John Anderson*, p. 81.

78 Macdonald to Head, March 16, 1861. *Province of Canada Sessional Papers*. Vol. 19, no. 4.

79 Brodie, *The Odyssey of John Anderson*, p. 83.

80 *New York Times*, January 30, 1861.

81 *New York Herald*, January 30, 1861.

82 *New York Times*, January 30, 1861.

83 *Peterborough Examiner*, January 3, 1861.

84 Ronald White, *A. Lincoln*, p. 349.

85 *Toronto Leader*, February 18, 1861.

86 Ibid.

87 *Peterborough Examiner*, February 21, 1861.

CHAPTER TWO: WILLIAM SEWARD AND THE POWER OF DIVIDED LOYALTIES

1 Ernest Paolino, *The Foundations of the American Empire*, p. 2.

2 Glyndon G. Van Deusen, *William Henry Seward*, p. 535.

3 Ibid., p. 209.

4 Paolino, *The Foundations of the American Empire*, p. 8.

5 Amanda Foreman, *A World on Fire*. p. 122.

6   Newcastle to Head, October 28, 1860. LAC. *Head Papers*. Reel M-194.

7   Foreman, *A World on Fire*, p. 161.

8   Van Deusen, *William Henry Seward*, p. 271.

9   Dean B. Mahin, *One War at a Time*, p. 40.

10 Norman Ferris, *Desperate Diplomacy*, p. 8.

11 Ibid., p. 9.

12 Ibid., p. 15.

13 Ibid., p. 24.

14 Crook, *Diplomacy During the American Civil War*, p. 3.

15 Ferris, *Desperate Diplomacy*, p. 17.

16 Kenneth Bourne, "British Preparations for War with the North," p. 604.

17 Ibid., p. 603.

18 White, *A. Lincoln*, p. 392.

19 Walter Stahr, *Seward*, p. 223.

20 Ibid., p. 269.

21 Carl Sandburg, *Abraham Lincoln*, p. 145.

22 Douglas Southall Freeman, *Lee*, p. 113.

23 Sandburg, *Abraham Lincoln*, p. 250.

24 Jefferson Davis, Message to Confederate Congress, April 29, 1861. Brooks Simpson et al. (eds.), *The Civil War*, p. 332.

25 Crook, *Diplomacy During the American Civil War*, p. 9.

26 David George Surdam, *Northern Naval Superiority and the Economics of the American Civil War*, p. 155.

27 Winks, *The Civil War Years*, p. 47.

28 *New York Herald*, April 17, 1861.

29 Lyons to Russell, April 22, 1861. Copy to Head. LAC. *Head Papers*. Reel M-194.

30 Winks, *The Civil War Years*, p. 48.

31 Ferris, *Desperate Diplomacy*, p. 26.

32 Ibid., p. 27.

33 Bourne, "British Preparations for War with the North," p. 602.

34 Ibid., p. 631.

35 Wilkins to Head, April 21, 1861. LAC. *Head Papers*. Reel M-194.

36 Head to Wilkins, April 22, 1861 and Head to Morgan, April 22, 1861. LAC. *Head Papers*. Reel M-194.

37 Seward to Lyons, May 3, 1861. Copy to Head. LAC. *Head Papers*. Reel M-194.

38   Stahr, *Seward*, p. 293.

39   E.L. Pierce, *Memoir and Letters of Charles Sumner*. Vol. 4, p. 37.

40   Van Deusen, *William Henry Seward*, p. 298.

41   Ferris, *Desperate Diplomacy*, p. 25.

42   Ibid., p. 31.

43   Ibid.

44   Head to Newcastle, April 29, 1861. LAC. *Head Papers*. Reel M-194.

45   Lyons to Head, May 2, 1861. LAC. *Head Papers*. Reel M-194.

46   Ferris, *Desperate Diplomacy*, p. 66.

47   Winks, *The Civil War Years*, p. 47.

48   Henry Adams to Charles Francis Adams, Jr., June 10, 1861. Cited in Simpson et al. (eds.), *The Civil War*, p. 411.

49   Lyons to Newcastle, June 25, 1861. Copy to Head. LAC. *Head Papers*. Reel M-194.

50   White, *A. Lincoln*, p. 371.

51   *New York Times*, July 26, 1861.

52   *London Times*, July 30, 1861.

53   Mahin, *One War at a Time*, p. 57.

54   *Globe*, July 29, 1861.

55   Donald Creighton, *John A. Macdonald*. Vol. 1, p. 310.

56   William Wilgus, *The Railway Interrelations of the United States and Canada*, p. 41.

57   *Globe*, March 30, 1861.

58   Creighton, *John A. Macdonald*. Vol. 1, p. 309.

59   Macdonald to Ryerson, March 18, 1861. LAC. *Macdonald Papers*. MG26-A. Vol. 51.

60   *Letter to the Electors of the City of Kingston*, June 10, 1861. LAC. *Macdonald Papers*. MG26-A. Vol. 546.

61   *New York Herald*, July 13, 1861.

62   *London Free Press*, September 11, 1861.

63   Ibid.

64   Galt to Amy Galt, December 6, 1861. LAC. *Galt Papers*. MG27. ID8. Vol. 2.

65   Winks, *The Civil War Years*, p. 65.

66   *New York Times*, November 17, 1861.

67   *New York Herald*, November 18, 1861.

68   *Philadelphia Sunday Transcript*, November 27, 1861. Cited in Foreman, *A World on Fire*, pp. 177–78.

69   Victor Cohen, "Charles Sumner and the Trent Affair," p. 206.

70 Doris Kearns Goodwin, *Team of Rivals*, p. 397.

71 Sandburg, *Abraham Lincoln*, p. 268.

72 Mahin, *One War at a Time*, p. 66.

73 Van Deusen, *William Henry Seward*, p. 309.

74 Norman Ferris, *The Trent Affair*, p. 29.

75 James McPherson, *Battle Cry of Freedom*, p. 390.

76 Ibid., p. 310.

77 Benjamin Moran: Personal Journal, November 27, 1861. See Simpson et al. (ed.), *The Civil War*, p. 645.

78 Charles Adams to Henry Adams November 30, 1861. See Ibid., p. 652.

79 Goodwin, *Team of Rivals*, p. 397.

80 Bourne, "British Preparations for War with the North 1861–1862," p. 609.

81 Macdonald to Monck, December 17, 1861. LAC. *Monck Papers*. MG27. IB2. Vol. 1.

82 *Globe*, November 23, 1861.

83 *Toronto Leader*, December 7, 1861.

84 *Globe*, December 18, 1861.

85 *New York Herald*, December 13, 1861.

86 *New York Herald*, December 24, 1861.

87 *Buffalo Express*, December 30, 1861. Cited in Winks, *The Civil War Years*, p. 100.

88 Macdonald to Sidney Smith, December 23, 1861. LAC. Macdonald Papers. MG26-A. Vol. 508.

89 Macdonald to Monck, December 26, 1861. LAC. *Monck Papers*. MG27. IB2. Vol. 1.

90 Galt to Amy Galt, December 5, 1861. LAC. *Galt Papers*. MG27. ID8. Vol. 2.

91 Galt to Macdonald, December 5, 1861. LAC. *Galt Papers*. MG27. ID8. Vol. 7.

92 Sandburg, *Abraham Lincoln*, p. 269.

93 Ibid.

94 Galt to Amy Galt, December 5, 1861. LAC. *Galt Papers*. MG27. ID8. Vol. 7.

95 Galt to Macdonald, December 5, 1861. LAC. *Galt Papers*. MG27. ID8. Vol. 7.

96 Lyons to Monck, December 9, 1861. LAC. *Monck Papers*. Reel A-756.

97 Monck to Newcastle, December 20, 1861. LAC. *Monck Papers*. Reel A-756.

98 Ibid.

99 Davis Message to Confederate Congress, November 18, 1861. Cited in Simpson, et. al. (ed.), *The Civil War*, p. 633.

100 Crook, *Diplomacy During the American Civil War*, p. 51.

101 Sandburg, *Abraham Lincoln*, pp. 268–69.

102 Stahr, *Seward*, pp. 314–15.

103 Winks, *The Civil War Years*, p. 76.

104 Wilmott to Williams, December 26, 1861. LAC. *Letters of William Fenwick Williams*. MG24-A. Vol. 67.

105 Ibid.

106 Burgoyne to Williams, December ?, 1861. LAC. *Letters of William Fenwick Williams* MG24-A. Vol. 67.

107 Ibid.

108 McPherson, *Battle Cry of Freedom*, p. 390.

109 Goodwin, *Team of Rivals*, p. 400.

110 Bourne, "British Preparations for War with the North," p. 606.

111 Sandburg, *Abraham Lincoln*, pp. 269–70.

CHAPTER THREE: SARAH EMMA EDMONDS: DONNING THE BLUE AND GREY

1 Larry Eggleston, *Women in the Civil War*, p. 2.

2 Elizabeth Leonard, *All the Daring of the Soldier*, p. 229; see also James McPherson, *For Cause and Comrades*, pp. 5–7.

3 Eggleston, *Women in the Civil* War, p. 2.

4 Sarah Emma Edmonds, *Nurse and Spy in the Union Army*, p. 247.

5 Ibid., p. 18.

6 DeAnne Blanton and Lauren Cook, *They Fought Like Demons*, p. 27.

7 Louise Chipley Slavicek, *Women and the Civil War*, p. 27.

8 Jasper Wolverton to Roseltha Wolverton, July 21, 1861. AO. Wolverton Family fonds. Series F4345-6.

9 Morley S. Wickett, "Canadians in the United States," p. 86.

10 Ibid., pp. 86, 91.

11 Riggins to brother, March 12, 1862. LAC. *Riggins Letters*. MG24. F98.

12 Ibid.

13 Fred Gaffen, *Cross-Border Warriors*, p. 10.

14 Mackenzie to "James," June 22, 1861. LAC. *Mackenzie Papers*. MG24. B18. 1666.

15 Winks, *The Civil War Years*, p. 135.

16 In 1869 Benjamin Gould cited the number of British North Americans having served in the war was 53,532. Scholars have been arguing about the number ever since. Despite Gould's certainty, the exact number is, in fact, impossible to ascertain.

Record keeping at the time was often shoddy, Canadian recruits often lied to avoid breaking the law forbidding them to enlist in a foreign army and recruiters often recorded recruits' place of birth as the county in which they needed to meet their quota. By the 1990s, a consensus formed among scholars that the number of Canadians and Maritimers serving was between 35,000 and 50,000, so to estimate that about 40,000 served is probably as close as we will ever get. See Benjamin Gould, *Investigations in the Military and Anthropological Statistics of American Soldiers*, p. 27; Lois Darroch, "Canadians in the American Civil War," p. 55; and Andrew Moxley and Tom Brooks, "Drums Across the Border: Canadians in the Civil War," p. 59.

17   D.C. Bélanger, *French Canadians and the Franco-Americans in the Civil War Era*, p. 42.

18   Cameron to Giddings, April 30, 1861. *The War of the Rebellion*. Series 1. Vol. 43. Part II, p. 137.

19   *Toronto Leader*, April 29, 1861.

20   Ibid., May 2, 1861.

21   *Globe*, May 19, 1861.

22   *Toronto Leader*, July 12, 1861.

23   *New York Tribune*, September 11, 1861.

24   Winks, *The Civil War Years*, p. 189.

25   *Globe*, October 15, 1861.

26   Head to Lyons, October 8, 1861. LAC. *Head Papers*. Reel M-194.

27   Cameron to Seward, October 10, 1861. Copy to Lyons to Head, October 25, 1861. LAC. *Head Papers*. Reel M-194.

28   Ella Lonn, *Foreigners in the Union Army and Navy*, p. 68.

29   Williams to Head, April 29, 1861. LAC. *Head Papers*. Reel M-194.

30   Marguerite Hamer, "Luring Canadian Soldiers into Union Lines During the War Between the States," p. 152.

31   Gordon to Newcastle, March 17, 1862. Copy to Monck. LAC. *Monck Papers*. RG7. G6. Vol. 9.

32   *Toronto Leader*, August 7, 1862.

33   *Windsor Star*, October 7, 1861.

34   Head to Lyons, October 1, 1861. LAC. *Head Papers*. Reel M-194.

35   Newcastle to Monck, November 10, 1861. LAC. *Monck Papers*. RG7. G6. Vol. 9.

36   Wade to parents, September 20, 1861. Cited in Cousins, "Letters of Norman Wade," p. 126.

37   Wade to sister, December 29, 1861. Cited in Cousins, "Letters of Norman Wade," p. 130.

38   Lois Darroch, *Four Who Went to the Civil War*, p. 123.

39   Lyons to Head, August 2, 1861. LAC. *Head Papers*. Reel M-194.

40   Lyons to Monck, December 11, 1861. LAC. *Monck Papers*. Reel A-756.

41 Stuart to Monck, September 14, 1862. LAC. *Monck Papers*. RG7. G6. Vol. 9.

42 Riggins to sister, July 27, 1862. LAC. *Riggins Letters*. MG24. F98.

43 Riggins to sister, August 9, 1862. LAC. *Riggins Letters*. MG24. F98.

44 Edmonds, *Nurse and Spy in the Union Army*, p. 58.

45 McPherson, *Battle Cry of Freedom*, p. 359.

46 Ibid., p. 73.

47 Ibid., p. 98.

48 Leonard, *All the Daring of the Soldiers*, p. 174.

49 Edmonds, *Nurse and Spy in the Union Army*, p. 120.

50 Ibid., p. 118.

51 Ibid., p. 220.

52 Goodwin, *Team of Rivals*, p. 444.

53 Joseph B. Mitchell, *Decisive Battles of the Civil War*, p. 56.

54 *Detroit Free Press*, August 1, 1862.

55 Ibid., August 16, 1862.

56 *Globe*, August 22, 1862.

57 Ibid., August 11, 1862.

58 Ella Lonn, *Desertion During the Civil War*, p. 201.

59 *Globe*, August 9, 1863.

60 William Fox, *Regimental Losses in the American Civil War*, pp. 48–49.

61 Riggins to sister, June 22, 1862. LAC. *Riggins Letters*. MG24. F98.

62 Riggins to sister, August 9, 1862. LAC. *Riggins Letters*. MG24. F98.

63 Anderson to Amie, September 12, 1863. LAC. *Civil Secretary's Correspondence*. Vol. 97-98, #10948.

64 Riggins to sister, March 19, 1862. LAC. *Riggins Letters*. MG24. F98.

65 Jasper Wolverton to Reeltha Wolverton, July 23, 1861. AO. Wolverton Family fonds. Series F4354-6.

66 Riggins to sister, July 22, 1862. LAC. *Riggins Letters*. MG24. F98.

67 Mitchell, *Decisive Battles of the Civil War*, p. 87.

68 Edmonds, *Nurse and Spy in the Union Army*, p. 278.

69 Riggins to mother, September 28, 1862. LAC. *Riggins Letters*. MG24. F98.

70 Goodwin, *Team of Rivals*, p. 485.

71 Edmonds, *Nurse and Spy in the Union Army*, p. 299.

72 Ibid., p. 359.

73 Francis M. Wafer, *A Surgeon in the Army of the Potomac*. Cheryl Wells (ed.), p. 50.

74 L.D. Milani, "Four Who Went to the Civil War," p. 269.

75 Jim Cougle, *Canadian Blood, American Soil*, pp. 7–10.

76 Collins to Gray, September 24, 1864. LAC. *Monck Papers*. MG24. B156. Vol. 1.

77 Lyons to British Consuls. Copy to Monck. May 3, 1862. LAC. *Monck Papers*. Reel A-756.

78 Russell to Lyons. Copy to Monck. August 14, 1862. LAC. *Monck Papers*. Reel A-756.

79 Lyons to Seward, March 19, 1863. Copy to Lyons to Monck, March 21, 1863. LAC. *Monck Papers*. RG7. G6. Vol. 9.

80 Seward to Lyons, April 15, 1863. Copy to Lyons to Monck. April 25, 1863. LAC. *Monck Papers*. RG7. G6. Vol. 9.

81 Ibid.

82 Eugene C. Murdock, "New York's Civil War Bounty Hunters," p. 259.

83 *New York Times*, August 25, 1864.

84 Murdock, "New York's Civil War Bounty Hunters," p. 261.

85 Ibid.

86 Ibid., p. 271.

87 Ibid., p. 274.

88 *New York Times*, July 26, 1864.

89 Lyons to Monck, December 8, 1863. LAC. *Monck Papers*. RG7. G6. Vol. 2.

90 Monck to Lyons, July 26, 1864. LAC. *Monck Papers*. RG7. G1. Vol. 23.

91 Raney, "Recruiting and Crimping in Canada for the Northern Forces," p. 29.

92 Donahue to Lyons, June 14, 1864. Copy to Monck. LAC. *Monck Papers*. RG7. G1. Vol. 23.

93 Bill Twatio, "The Freedom Fighters," *National Post*, February 14, 2012.

94 Daly to Monck, April 25, 1864. LAC. *Civil Secretary's Correspondence*. RG7. G20. Vol. 99–100, #11217.

95 LAC. *Civil Secretary's Letterbook*. RG7. G17. Vol. 20.

96 Eugene C. Murdock, *Patriotism Limited*, p. 114.

97 Raney, "Recruiting and Crimping in Canada for the Northern Forces," p. 27.

98 Monck to Cardwell, August 8, 1864. LAC. *Monck Papers*. RG7. G6. Vol. 13.

99 Lyons to Monck, August 17, 1864. LAC. *Monck Papers*. RG7. G6. Vol. 13.

100 *The War of Rebellion*. Series 1. Vol. 43. Part II, p. 455.

101 *Report of a Committee of the Honourable the Executive Council*. May 10, 1864. LAC. Ministry of Militia fonds. RG9. ID1. Vol. 1.

102 *Globe*, July 20, 1864.

CHAPTER FOUR: JACOB THOMPSON AND THE CONFEDERATES IN THE ATTIC

1 Freeman, *Lee*, p. 312.

2 Ibid., p. 320.

3 Shelby Foote, *The Civil War*, p. 530.

4 Freeman, *Lee*, p, 340.

5 William Davis, *Jefferson Davis*, p. 506.

6 Foreman, *A World on Fire*, p. 723.

7 Ibid., p. 769.

8 Seward to Lyons, August 31, 1861. Copy to Head, September 30, 1861. LAC. *Head Papers*. Reel M-194.

9 *New York Herald*, May 18, 1863.

10 Lyons to Monck, December 22, 1863. LAC. *Monck Papers*. RG7. G6. Vol. 11.

11 *Toronto Leader*, November 18, 1863.

12 *New York Times*. Reprinted in *Globe*, November 20, 1863.

13 *New York Herald*, November 15, 1863. Reprinted in the *Globe*, November 19, 1863.

14 Ibid., Reprinted in the *Globe*, November 20, 1863.

15 Lyons to Monck, December 9, 1863. LAC. *Monck Papers*. RG7. G6. Vol. 11.

16 *New York Herald*, December 16, 1863. Reprinted in *Globe*, November 17, 1863.

17 E.M. Saunders, *The Life and Letters of the Right Honorable Sir Charles Tupper*, pp. 90–91.

18 *New York Herald*, December 21, 1863.

19 Lyons to Russell. Copy to Monck, December 29, 1863. LAC. *Monck Papers*. RG7. G1. Vol. 159.

20 Howard to Seward, December 9, 1863. Cited in Winks, *The Civil War Years*, p. 257.

21 Russell to Adams. Copy to Newcastle to Monck, February 23, 1864. LAC. *Monck Papers*. RG7. G1. Vol. 159.

22 Adams to Russell. Copy to Newcastle to Monck, February 12, 1864. LAC. *Monck Papers*. RG7. G1. Vol. 159.

23 McPherson, *Battle Cry of Freedom*, p. 591.

24 Goodwin, *Team of Rivals*, p. 523.

25 *Montreal Gazette*, July 21, 1863.

26 *Toronto Leader*, July 17, 1863.

27 Ibid., July 25, 1863.

28 *Globe*, July 21, 1863, and July 28, 1863.

29 David A. Wilson, *Thomas D'Arcy McGee*. Vol. 2, p. 171.

30 *Globe*, August 19, 1863.

31 White, *A. Lincoln*, p. 601.

32 G.P. de T. Glazebrook, *A History of Canadian External Relations*, p. 76.

33 Davis, *Jefferson Davis*, p. 544.

34 Michael Ballard, *Vicksburg*, p. 198.

35 Monck to Holcombe, May 14, 1864. LAC. *Monck Papers*. RG7. G1. Vol. 159.

36 John William Headley, *Confederate Operations in Canada and New York*, pp. 220–21.

37 Newcastle to Head, June 1, 1861. LAC. *Head Papers*. Reel M-194.

38 Lyons to Monck, November 14, 1861. LAC. *Monck Papers*. Reel A-757.

39 *New York Times*, December 5, 1864.

40 Monck to Cardwell, February 8, 1865. LAC. *Monck Papers*. RG7. G1. Vol. 161.

41 Monck to Cardwell, December 15, 1864. LAC. *Monck Papers*. RG7. G1. Vol. 161.

42 Lt. Col. George T. Denison, *Soldiering in Canada*, p. 59.

43 Ibid.

44 *Toronto Leader*, October 6, 1863.

45 Robert Chadwell Williams, *Horace Greeley*, p. 250.

46 Ibid., p. 255.

47 Greeley to Lincoln, July 7, 1864. Cited in William Jewett Tenney, *The Military and Naval History of the Rebellion in the United States*, p. 660.

48 Ibid.

49 Lincoln to Greeley, July 9, 1864. Ibid.

50 Greeley to Lincoln, July 12, 1864. Ibid.

51 Lincoln, "To Whom It May Concern," July 18, 1864. Cited in Tenney. *The Military and Naval History of the Rebellion in the United States*, p. 1867.

52 *New York Tribune*, July 22, 1864.

53 Ralph Fahrney, *Horace Greeley and the Tribune in the Civil War*, p. 167.

54 McPherson, *Battle Cry of Freedom*, p. 769.

55 Ibid.

56 *New York Herald*, August 22, 1864.

57 Chauncey M. Depew, *My Memories of Eighty Years*, pp. 62–63.

58 Williams, *Horace Greeley*, p. 251.

59 Charles Frohman, *Rebels on Lake Erie*, p. 98.

60 Wilfrid Bovey, "Confederate Agents in Canada During the American Civil War," p. 49.

61 Foreman, *A World on Fire*, p. 716.

62 Thompson to Hill, September 22, 1864. Ibid., p. 236.

63 *Toronto Leader,* September 30, 1864.

64 *Globe,* September 29, 1864.

65 Dix to Stanton, September 30, 1864. *The War of the Rebellion.* Series 1. Vol. 43. Part II, pp. 255–33.

66 Foreman, *A World on Fire,* p. 683.

67 Burnley to Russell, October 14, 1864. LAC. *Monck Papers.* CIHM no. 51406.

68 Seward to Burnley, September 26, 1864. LAC. *Monck Papers.* CIHM no. 51406.

69 Hiscock to Stanton, September 23, 1864. LAC. *Monck Papers.* CIHM no. 51406

70 Seward to Burnley, October 1, 1864. LAC. *Monck Papers.* CIHM no. 51406.

71 Frank Klement, *The Limits of Dissent,* p. 253.

72 Headley, *Confederate Operations in Canada and New York,* p. 219.

73 Wood Gray, *The Hidden War,* p. 168.

74 Ibid.

75 Headley, *Confederate Operations in Canada and New York,* p. 224.

76 Hines to Sedden, July 1, 1864. Cited in Bethania Meradith Smith, "Civil War Subversives," p. 233.

77 Headley, *Confederate Operations in Canada and New York,* p. 226.

78 Ibid., p. 221.

79 McPherson, *Battle Cry of Freedom,* p. 591.

80 Dix to Stanton, September 30, 1864. Hill to Potter, September 21, 1864. *The War of the Rebellion.* Series 1. Vol. 43. Part II, pp. 229, 234.

81 Smith to Monck, October 18, 1864. LAC. Officer of the Governor General fonds. RG7. G6. Vol. 1, p. 118.

82 Winks, *The Civil War Years,* p. 303.

83 Seward to Lyons, October 29, 1864. LAC. *Monck Papers.* CIHM no. 51406.

84 Seward to Lyons, November 1, 1864. LAC. *Monck Papers.* CIHM no. 51406.

85 Seward to Russell, October 24, 1864. Copy to Monck. LAC. *Monck Papers.* CIHM no. 51406.

86 Winks, *The Civil War Years,* p. 307.

87 *New York Times,* October 20, 1864. *New York Herald,* October 24, 1864.

88 *Montreal Gazette,* October 26, 1864. *Toronto Leader,* October 25, 1864. *Saint John Morning Telegraph,* October 27, 1864.

89 *Globe,* October 24, 1864.

90 *Toronto Leader,* November 9, 1864.

91   *Globe*, October 27, 1864.

92   Burnley to Monck, October 23, 1864. Office of the Governor General fonds. RG7. G6. Vol. 1, p. 136.

93   Seward to Lyons, November 3, 1864, Copy Burnley to Monck. November 7, 1864. Officer of the Governor General fonds. RG7. G6. Vol. 1, p. 138.

94   Gregory to Stanton, October 22, 1864; and Stanton to Gregory, October 22, 1864. *The War of the Rebellion*. Series 1. Vol. 43. Part II, p. 452.

95   Stanton to Grant, October 23, 1864. Grant to Stanton. October 24, 1864. *The War of the Rebellion*. Series 1. Vol. 43. Part II, pp. 452–53, 456.

96   *Richmond Whig*, October 16, 1864. Cited in Foreman. *A World on Fire*, p. 697.

97   Headley, *Confederate Operations in Canada and New York*, p. 265.

98   Ibid.

99   Foreman, *A World on Fire*, p. 701.

100 Smith, "Civil War Subversives," p. 239.

101 Headley, *Confederate Operations in Canada and New York*, p. 267.

102 *New York Times*, November 7, 1864.

103 Headley, *Confederate Operations in Canada and New York*, p. 271.

104 Ibid.

105 *New York Times*, November 26, 1864.

106 Foreman, *A World on Fire*, p. 702.

107 Ibid., p. 254.

108 Burnley to Monck, November 12, 1864. LAC. *Monck Papers*. CIHM no. 51406.

109 Grant to Dix, November 6, 1864. Cited in Bovey, "Confederate Agents in Canada During the American Civil War," p. 50.

110 Seward to Monck, November 7, 1864. LAC. *Monck Papers*. RG7. G5. Vol. 69.

111 Monck to Cardwell. November 25, 1864. LAC. *Monck Papers*. RG7. G5. Vol. 69.

112 *Globe*, December 5, 1864.

113 Kingsmill to Macdonald, November 19, 1864. LAC. *Macdonald Papers*. CIHM no. 51406.

114 *Globe*, December 15, 1864.

115 *New York Times*, December 29, 1864.

116 *New York Herald*, December 17, 1864.

117 *London Times*, December 29, 1864.

118 Winks, *The Civil War Years*, p. 319.

119 Ibid., p. 345.

120 Seward to Russell, October 24, 1864. Copy to Monck. LAC. *Monck Papers*. RG7. G5. Vol. 69.

121 Seward to Burnley, January 10, 1865. LAC. *Monck Papers.* CIHM no. 51406.

122 *Toronto Leader,* January 5, 1864.

123 Swinyard to Macdonald, December 31, 1864. LAC. *Macdonald Papers.* MG26-A. Vol. 56.

CHAPTER FIVE: GEORGE BROWN AND THE IMPROBABLE NATION

1   J.M.S. Careless, *Brown of the Globe.* Vol. 2, p. 127.

2   Oscar D. Skelton, *Life and Times of Sir Alexander Tilloch Galt,* pp. 79–82.

3   Bruce Knox, "Conservative Imperialism," p. 334.

4   Ged Martin, "Launching Canadian Confederation: Means to Ends," p. 586.

5   Donald Creighton, "The United States and Canadian Confederation," p. 210.

6   Knox, "Conservative Imperialism," p. 334.

7   Ibid.

8   Lytton to Head, December 12, 1858. LAC. *Head Papers.* Reel M-194.

9   Knox, "Conservative Imperialism," p. 341.

10   J.M.S. Careless, *Brown of the Globe.* Vol. 1, p. 253.

11   Ibid., p. 320.

12   Ibid., p. 321.

13   J.A. Gibson, "The Colonial Office View of Canadian Federation," p. 296.

14   Creighton, *John A. Macdonald.* Vol. 1, pp. 291–93.

15   Monck to Newcastle, August 4, 1862. LAC. *Monck Papers.* RG7. G6. Vol. 9.

16   *London Times,* June 6, 1862. *New York Tribune,* May 29, 1862.

17   D.M.L. Farr, *The Colonial Office and Canada,* p. 9.

18   Newcastle to Monck, July 22, 1862. LAC. *Monck Papers.* RG7. G6. Vol. 9.

19   Lyons to Monck, February 25, 1862. LAC. *Monck Papers.* Reel A-756; and Lyons to Monck, February 27, 1862. LAC. *Monck Papers.* Reel A-756.

20   Lyons to Monck, February 27, 1862. LAC. *Monck Papers.* Reel A-756.

21   *Globe,* January 27, 1864.

22   Careless, *Brown of the Globe.* Vol. 2, p. 120.

23   Ibid., p. 122.

24   C.P. Stacey, "Britain's Withdrawal from North America."

25   Kenneth Bourne, *Britain and the Balance of Power in North America,* p. 256.

26   *Toronto Leader,* June 18, 1864.

27 Gettysburg Address. Cited in White, *A. Lincoln*, p. 605.

28 Rod Preece, "The Political Wisdom of Sir John A. Macdonald," p. 460.

29 Edmund Burke, *Reflections on the Revolution in France*, p. 19.

30 Preece, "The Political Wisdom of Sir John A. Macdonald," p. 468.

31 P.B. Waite, *The Confederation Debates in the Province of Canada*, p. 155.

32 Joseph Pope, *Documents on the Confederation of British North America*, p. 57.

33 Christopher Moore, *1867*, p. 41.

34 Edmund Burke, speech to the voters of Bristol. Connor Cruise O'Brien, *The Great Melody*, p. 75.

35 Waite, *Confederation Debates in the Province of Canada*, p. 59.

36 Ibid., p. 60.

37 Ibid., p. 131.

38 Ibid., p. 86.

39 Ibid., p. 60.

40 Brown to Anne Brown, September 13, 1864. LAC. *Brown Papers*. MG27. ID8. Vol. 2.

41 *Globe*, September 21, 1864.

42 Ibid.

43 *Globe*, November 3, 1864.

44 C.P. Stacey, *Canada and the British Army*, p. 158.

45 Ibid., p. 167.

46 Cardwell to Monck, October 30, 1864. LAC. *Monck Papers*. MG27. IB2. Vol. 1.

47 Bourne, *Britain and the Balance of Power in North America, 1815–1908*, p. 265.

48 Monck to Cardwell, November 7, 1864. LAC. *Monck Papers*. MG27. IB2. Vol. 1.

49 Cardwell to Monck, December 3, 1864. LAC. *Monck Papers*. MG27. IB2. Vol. 1.

50 Brown to Anne Brown, December 5, 1864. LAC. *Brown Papers*. MG27. ID8. Vol. 2.

51 Brown to Macdonald, December 22, 1864. LAC. *Macdonald Papers*. MG26-A. Vol. 188.

52 *New York Times*, December 19, 1864.

53 *Chicago Tribune*, December 17, 1864. Cited in Winks, *The Civil War Years*, p. 138.

54 Macdonald to Swinyard, December 19, 1864. Joseph Pope, *The Correspondence of Sir John A. Macdonald*, p. 19.

55 Ibid.

56 Ibid.

57 Winks, *The Civil War Years*, p. 322.

58 Monck to Cardwell, November 25, 1864. LAC. *Monck Papers*. RG7. G5. Vol. 69.

59   Adams to Seward, February 9, 1865. Cited in Foreman, *A World on Fire*, p. 740.

60   Russell to Bruce, February 13, 1865. Copy to Monck. LAC. *Monck Papers*. RG7. G5. Vol. 69.

61   Thompson to Benjamin, December 3, 1864. Wink, *The War of the Rebellion*, p. 200.

62   Ibid.

63   Benjamin to Thompson, December ?, 1864. Cited in William Tidwell, James Hall and David Winfred Gaddy, *Come Retribution*, p. 203.

64   Ibid., p. 204.

65   Mallory to Thompson, December 19, 1864. Cited in Headley, *Confederate Operations in Canada and New York*, p. 310.

66   Denison, *Soldiering in Canada*, p. 61.

67   Thompson to Lincoln, February 2, 1865. Cited in Headley, *Confederate Operations in Canada and New York*, p. 325.

68   Thompson to Mason, January 21, 1865. Ibid.

69   December 24, 1864. Exhibit F. Ibid., p. 346.

70   Ibid.

71   Headley, *Confederate Operations in Canada and New York*, p. 354.

72   Waite, *Confederation Debates in the Province of Canada, 1865*, p. 132.

73   George Brown, speech to the Legislature, February 8, 1865. LAC. *Brown Papers*. Reel-1605.

74   Tupper to Macdonald, January 4, 1865. LAC. *Macdonald Papers*. MG24-A. Vol. 2.

75   Macdonald to Gray, March 24, 1865. LAC. *Macdonald Papers*. MG24-A. Vol. 510.

76   *Morning News*, March 10, 1865. Cited in P.B. Waite, *The Life and Times of Confederation*, pp. 245–46.

77   Whelan to Galt, December 17, 1864. Cited in W.G. Ormsby, "Letters to Galt concerning the Maritime Provinces and Confederation," p. 167.

78   Winks, *The Civil War Years*, p. 362.

CHAPTER SIX: JOHN A. MACDONALD: THE INDISPENSABLE MAN

1   Potter to Seward, April 24, 1865. Cited in Anthony S. Pitch, *They Have Killed Papa Dead!*, pp. 171–72.

2   Michael W. Kauffman, *American Brutus*, p. 263.

3   Potter to Seward, April 27, 1865. Cited in Pitch, *They Have Killed Papa Dead!*, p. 172.

4   Graf P. LeRoy (ed.), *The Papers of Andrew Johnson*. Vol. 7, p. 544.

5   John Surratt lecture in Rockville Maryland. *Washington Evening Star*, December 7, 1870.

6   Booth diary. Cited in Kauffman, *American Brutus*, pp. 399–400.

7   Kauffman, *American Brutus*, pp. 310, 320.

8   Albert Castel, *The Presidency of Andrew Johnson*, p. 24.

9   *Globe*, May 3, 1865.

10   *Montreal Gazette*, May 6, 1865; and *Montreal Evening Telegraph* and *Daily Commercial Advertiser*, May 5, 1865.

11   *New York Tribune*, May 22, 1865; and *Globe*, May 20, 1865.

12   *New York Tribune*, May 22, 1865.

13   Cardwell to Monck, April 15, 1865. LAC. *Monck Papers*. RG7. G1. Vol.161.

14   T.P. Slattery, *The Assassination of Thomas D'Arcy McGee*, p. 337.

15   Palmerston to Queen Victoria, January 20, 1865. Cited in Brian Jenkins, *Fenians and the Anglo-American Relations during Reconstruction*, pp. 41–42.

16   Queen Victoria, Journal. February 12, 1865. Ibid.

17   Cardwell to Arthur, April 12, 1865. LAC. *Monck Papers*. Reel A-756.

18   Alexander Galt to Anne Galt, May 17, 1865. LAC. *Galt Papers*. MG27. ID8. Vol. 3.

19   Cardwell to Monck, May 22, 1865. LAC. *Monck Papers*. Reel A-756.

20   Alexander Galt to Anne Galt, January 14, 1867. LAC. *Galt Papers*. MG27. ID8. Vol. 3.

21   Macdonald, Cartier, Galt, Brown to Monck, July 12, 1865. LAC. *Monck Papers*. RG7. G1. Vol. 161.

22   Benn Pitman, *The Assassination of President Lincoln and the Trial of the Conspirators*, p. 26.

23   Ibid., p. 27.

24   Ibid.

25   Ibid., pp. 26–28.

26   Ibid., p. 28.

27   Ibid., p. 32.

28   *Montreal Evening Telegraph*, June 8, 1864.

29   Holt to Stanton, December 15, 1866. Cited in Pitman, *The Assassination of President Lincoln and the Trial of the Conspirators*, p. 302.

30   *New York Herald*, August 12, 1866.

31   *New York Herald*, April 16, 1867.

32   Pitman, *The Assassination of President Lincoln and the Trial of the Conspirators*, p. 402.

33   Charles Creighton Hazewell, "Assassination," July 1865. *The Atlantic Monthly Presents, Special Commemorative Issue*, March, 2012, p. 112.

34   Florence Elizabeth Gibson, *The Attitudes of the New York Irish Toward State and National Affairs*, p. 186.

35 *Irish Canadian*, April 17, 1864.

36 Ibid., November 2, 1864.

37 *Globe*, November 8, 1864.

38 Wilson, *Thomas D'Arcy McGee*. Vol. 2, p. 285.

39 Ibid., p. 251.

40 Peter Edwards, *Delusion*, p. 46.

41 McMicken to Macdonald, December 28, 1864. LAC. *Macdonald Papers*. MG26-A. Vol. 236.

42 Jenkins, *Fenians and the Anglo-American Relations during Reconstruction*, p. 34.

43 Russell to Monck, December 23, 1864. LAC. *Monck Papers*. RG7. G1. Vol. 161.

44 Seward to Burnley, March 20, 1865. Cited in Jenkins, *Fenians and the Anglo-American Relations during Reconstruction*, p. 39.

45 Edwards, *Delusion*, p. 248.

46 W.C. Chewett, *The Fenian Raid into Canada*, pp. 17–18.

47 Sir Arthur Doughty (ed.), *The Elgin-Grey Papers*, p. 150.

48 Potter to Seward, January 6, 1865. Cited in J.G. Snell, "John F. Potter, Consul General to British North America," p. 110.

49 Potter to Seward, June 26, 1865; and Seward to Potter, July 5, 1865. Cited in Snell, "John F. Potter," p. 112.

50 *Globe*, July 14, 1865.

51 *Montreal Gazette*, July 15, 1865. *Halifax Morning Chronicle*, August 1, 1865.

52 *Montreal Gazette*, July 19, 1865.

53 W.D. Overman (ed.), "Some Letters of Joshua R. Giddings on Reciprocity," p. 292.

54 Winks, *The Civil War Years*, p. 166.

55 W.L. Morton. *The Critical Years*, p. 184.

56 McMicken to Macdonald, September 25, 1865. LAC. *Macdonald Papers*. MG26-A. Vol. 236.

57 *New York Herald*, October 24, 1865.

58 Tilley to Macdonald, September 13, 1965. LAC. *Macdonald Papers*. MG26-A. Vol. 51.

59 Creighton, *John A. Macdonald*. Vol. 1, p. 425.

60 Moore, *1867*, p. 184.

61 *London Free Press*, November 9, 1965.

62 Macdonald to Brydges, November 14, 1865. LAC. *Macdonald Papers*. MG26-A. Vol. 512.

63 Edwards, *Delusion*, p. 249.

64 *Globe*, January 29, 1866.

65   *New York Times*, February 27, 1866.

66   Bruce to Clarendon, April 17, 1866. Cited in Jenkins, *Fenians and the Anglo-American Relations during Reconstruction*, p. 129.

67   Elisabeth Batt, *Monck*, p. 133.

68   Adams to Seward, February 22, 1866. Cited in Jenkins, *Fenians and the Anglo-American Relations during Reconstruction*, p. 90.

69   Seward to Adams, March 22, 1866. Cited in Jenkins, *Fenians and the Anglo-American Relations during Reconstruction*, p. 101.

70   McMicken to Macdonald, March 12, 1866. LAC. *Macdonald Papers*. MG26-A. Vol. 237.

71   Monck to Cardwell, March 9. 1866. LAC. *Monck Papers*. MG7. IB2. Vol. 1.

72   Monck to Cardwell, March 15, 1866. LAC. *Monck Papers*. MG27. IB2. Vol. 1.

73   Slattery, *The Assassination of Thomas D'Arcy McGee*, p. 300.

74   *Globe*, March 30, 1866.

75   W.S. Neidhardt, *Fenianism in North America*, p. 43.

76   Ibid., p. 44.

77   *New York Times*, May 30, 1866.

78   Monck to Williams, April 4, 1866. LAC. *Monck Papers*. MG27. IB2. Vol. 1.

79   *Halifax Evening Express*, April 16, 1866.

80   Cited in Waite, *The Life and Times of Confederation*, p. 271.

81   Tilley to Macdonald. April 20, 1866. LAC. *Macdonald Papers*. MG26-A. Vol. 51.

82   Tilley to Macdonald. April 21, 1866. LAC. *Macdonald Papers*. MG26-A. Vol. 51.

83   *New York Times*, May 5, 1866.

84   Neidhardt, *Fenianism in North America*, p. 55.

85   Elwood Jones, "Civil War Veteran, POW," *Peterborough Examiner*, February 23, 2008; and Howard Pammett, "Counties Grow," *Peterborough Examiner*, March 6, 1952.

86   F.W. Campbell, *Fenian Invasions of Canada of 1866 and 1870*, p. 44.

87   Monck to Cardwell, June 7, 1866. LAC. *Monck Papers*. MG27. IB2. Vol. 1.

88   Jenkins, *Fenians and the Anglo-American Relations during Reconstruction*, p. 150.

89   *Globe*, June 6, 1866.

90   Seward to Bruce, June 11, 1866. Cited in Jenkins, *Fenians and the Anglo-American Relations during Reconstruction*, p. 156.

91   Bruce to Monck, June 11, 1866. LAC. *Monck Papers*. Reel A-757.

92   Monck to Bruce, June 14, 1866. LAC. *Monck Papers*. Reel A-757.

93   Monck to Carnarvon, July 21, 1866. LAC. *Monck Papers*. Reel A-757.

94   *London Times*, August 11, 1866.

95 *Toronto Daily Telegraph*, July 11, 1866.

96 McGee to Monck, June 4, 1866. LAC. *Monck Papers*. MG27. IB2. Vol. 1.

97 *Globe*, June 12, 1866.

98 *New York Tribune*, August 21, 1866.

99 Dixon to Monck, August 23, 1866; and Monck to Carnarvon, August 27, 1866. LAC. *Monck Papers*. MG27. IB2, Vol. 1.

100 Disraeli to Derby, September 30, 1866. Cited in Jenkins, *Fenians and the Anglo-American Relations during Reconstruction*, p. 191.

101 *New York Tribune*, October 29, 1866.

102 Helen MacDonald, *Canadian Public Opinion in the American Civil War*, p. 118.

103 Seward to Bruce, October 26, 1866. Cited in Jenkins, *Fenians and the Anglo-American Relations during Reconstruction*, p. 205; and Carnarvon to Monck, November 12, 1866. LAC. *Monck Papers*. Reel A-757.

104 *St. John Morning Telegraph*, November 3, 1866.

105 President Andrew Johnson, State of the Union Address, December 3, 1866.

106 Carnarvon to Derby, October 11, 1866. Cited in Knox, "Conservative Imperialism," p. 347.

107 Knox, "Conservative Imperialism," p. 346.

108 Monck to Macdonald; Macdonald to Monck. LAC. *Monck Papers*. Reel A-757.

109 Brown to Anne Brown, August 6, 1866. LAC. *Brown Papers*. MG27. ID8. Vol. 3; and *Globe*, August 8, 1866.

110 Batt, *Monck*, p. 34.

111 Galt to Anne Galt, June 23, 1867. LAC. *Galt Papers*. MG27. ID8. Vol. 3.

112 Gwyn, *John A*, p. 266.

113 Macdonald to Tilley, October 8, 1866. LAC. *Macdonald Papers*. MG26-A. Vol. 513.

114 Edwards to Monck, November 15, 1866. LAC. *Monck Papers*. Reel A-757.

115 Gwyn, *John A*, p. 390.

116 Ibid., p. 413.

EPILOGUE: DANGER IN THE WAR'S SHADOW

1 *Halifax Morning Chronicle*, July 1, 1867.

2 Bovey, "Confederate Agents in Canada During the American Civil War," p. 139.

3 Ibid., p. 140.

4 Denison, *Soldiering in Canada*, p. 67.

5 Jubal Early, *A Memoir of the Last Year of the War for Independence in the Confederate States of America*, p., xiii.

6   Thomas A. Desjardin, *These Honored Dead*, p. 124.

7   *New York Times*, June 13, 1867.

8   Denison, *Soldiering in Canada*, p. 69.

9   *New York Times*, June 13, 1867.

10   Varina Davis, *Jefferson Davis*, p. 799.

11   Jefferson Davis, *Private Letters*, p. 282.

12   Alexander Galt to Amy Galt, December 28, 1866. LAC. *Galt Papers*. MG27. ID8. Vol. 3.

13   Macdonald to Brown, April 11, 1865. LAC. *Macdonald Papers*. MG26-A. Vol. 146.

14   W.F. Spencer, *The Confederate Navy in Europe*, p. 2.

15   James T. DeKay, *The Rebel Raiders*, p. 26

16   Theodore Clarke Smith, "Expansion After the Civil War," p. 2.

17   David Shi, "Seward's Attempt to Annex British Columbia," p. 222.

18   Paolino, *The Foundations of the American Empire*, p. 12.

19   *London Times*, May 11, 1867. Reprinted *New York Times*, *Montreal Gazette*, May 24, 1867.

20   Richard Neunherz, "Hemmed In: Reactions in British Columbia to the Purchase of Russian America." p. 101.

21   Ibid., p. 103

22   *New York Tribune*. Cited in Lester B. Shippee, *Canadian-American Relations*, p. 198.

23   Shippee, *Canadian-American Relations*, p. 198.

24   Shi, "Seward's Attempt to Annex British Columbia," p. 224.

25   Seymour to Buckingham, June 26, 1867. Cited in Neunherz, "Hemmed In," p. 101.

26   Geoffrey Perret, *Ullysses S. Grant*, p. 405.

27   Maureen M. Robson, "The Alabama Claims and the Anglo-American Reconciliation," p. 3.

28   Perret, *Ullysses S. Grant*, p. 407.

29   Ibid., p. 408.

30   Allan Nevins, *Hamilton Fish*, p. 397.

31   Thornton to Macdonald, February 15, 1870. LAC. *Macdonald Papers*. MG26-A. Vol. 516.

32   Fish diary, April 15, 1870. Cited in Jenkins, *Fenians and the Anglo-American Relations during Reconstruction*, p. 303.

33   Ibid.

34   Ibid., November 9, 1869.

35   Goldwin Smith, *The Treaty of Washington, 1871*, p. 25.

36   Fish diary, September 26, 1870.

37   Nevins, *Hamilton Fish*, p. 426.

38   Ibid., p. 441.

39   Ibid., p. 412.

40   Adrian Cook, *The Alabama Claims*, p. 133.

41   Fish diary, September 18, 1870.

42   Ibid.

43   Richard Gwyn, *Nation Maker*, p. 97.

44   Ibid., p. 141.

45   Foreman, *A World on Fire*, p. 802.

46   Nevins, *Hamilton Fish*, p. 414.

47   Macdonald to Rose, January 21, 1870. LAC. *Macdonald Papers*. MG26-A. Vol. 516.

48   Macdonald to Campbell, November 1, 1870. LAC. *Macdonald Papers*. MG26-A. Vol. 342.

49   Macdonald to Tupper, March 21, 1871. LAC. *Macdonald Papers*. MG26-A. Vol. 4.

50   Gwyn, *Nation Maker*, p. 167.

51   Donald Creighton, *John A. Macdonald*. Vol. 2, p. 94.

52   Cook, *The Alabama Claims*, p. 175.

53   Macdonald to Tupper, April 29, 1871. LAC. *Macdonald Papers*. MG26-F. Vol. 4.

54   Speech of Sir John A. Macdonald on introducing the bill to give effect to the Treaty of Washington as regards Canada: Delivered in the House of Common of Canada, on Friday the 3rd of May 1872. Joseph Edmund Collins, *Life and Times of the Right Honourable Sir John A. Macdonald*, p. 533.

55   Ibid., p. 572.

56   *List of Pensioners on the Roll*, January 1, 1883. Washington D.C.: U.S. Government Printing Office, 1883, pp. 617–26.

BIBLIOGRAPHY

ARCHIVAL SOURCES

Library and Archives of Canada (LAC)

4th Viscount Lord Charles Stanley Monck Papers

Alexander Tilloch Galt Papers

British Military Records

Charles Riggins Letters

Civil Secretary's Correspondence, Governor General's Office Record Group

Civil Secretary's Letterbook, Governor General's Office Record Group

Correspondence Respecting the Attack on St. Albans Vermont and Naval Forces on the North American Lakes

Dispatches from British Minister in Washington, Governor General's Office Record Group

Dispatches from the United States Consul in Montreal 1850–1906

Dispatches Received by Lieutenants Governor of Nova Scotia and New Brunswick, Governor General's Office Record Group

George Brown Papers

Joseph Howe Papers

Ministry of Militia fonds

Office of the Governor General fonds

Sir Edmund Walker Head Papers

Sir John A. Macdonald Papers

William Fenwick Williams Letters

William Lyon MacKenzie Papers

Archives of Ontario (AO)

Province of Canada Sessional Papers
Wolverton Family fonds

NEWSPAPERS

Detroit Free Press

Globe (Toronto)

Halifax Evening Express

Halifax Morning Chronicle

Hamilton Daily Spectator

Hamilton Times

Irish Canadian (Toronto)

London Free Press (Canada West)

London Times (Britain)

Montreal Evening Telegraph

Montreal Gazette

New York Herald

New York Times

Peterborough Examiner

St. John Morning Telegraph

Toronto Daily Telegraph

Toronto Leader

Windsor Star

SECONDARY SOURCES

Allen, Felicity. *Jefferson Davis: Unconquerable Heart*. Shades of Blue and Gray Series. Columbia: University of Missouri, 2000.

Ballard, Michael. *Vicksburg: The Campaign That Opened the Mississippi*. Chapel Hill: University of North Carolina Press, 2004.

Batt, Elisabeth. *Monck: Governor General, 1861–1868*. Toronto: McClelland & Stewart, 1976.

Bélanger, D.C. *French Canadians and the Franco-Americans in the Civil War Era*. Montreal: Marianopolis College, 2001.

Blanton, DeAnne and Cook, Lauren. *They Fought Like Demons: Women Soldiers in the American Cival War*. Baton Rouge: Louisiana State University Press, 2002.

Blight, David W. (ed.). *The Underground Railroad in History and Memory: Passages to Freedom*. New York: HarperCollins, 2004.

Blumenthal, Henry. "Confederate Diplomacy: Popular Notions and International Realities." *Journal of Southern History*. Vol 32, no. 2 (May 1966).

Bordewich, Fergus M. *Bound For Canaan: The Epic Story of the Underground Railroad, America's First Civil Rights Movement*. New York: Amistad Press, 2006.

Bourne, Kenneth. *Britain and the Balance of Power in North America, 1815–1908*. Berkley: University of California Press, 1967.

———. "British Preparations for War with the North, 1861–1862." *The English Historical Review*. Vol. 76, no. 301 (October 1961).

Bovey, Wilfrid. "Confederate Agents in Canada During the American Civil War." *Canadian Historical Review*. Vol. 2, no. 1 (1921).

Brands, H.W. *The Man Who Saved the Union: Ulysses S. Grant in War and Peace*. New York: Doubleday Press, 2012.

Brodie, Patrick. *The Odyssey of John Anderson*. Toronto: University of Toronto Press, 1989.

Burke, Edmund. *Reflections on the Revolution in France*. 1790. London: J.M. Dent and Sons, 1910.

Burton, Anthony. *The Rise and Fall of King Cotton*. London: BBC, 1984.

Campbell, F.W. *Fenian Invasions of Canada of 1866 and 1870*. 1904. Montreal: J. Lovell & Son, 1989.

Careless, J.M.S. *Brown of the Globe*. Vol. 1, *Voice of Upper Canada, 1818–1859*. Toronto and Oxford: Dundurn Press, 1989.

———. *Brown of the Globe*. Vol. 2, *Statesman of Confederation 1860–1880*. Toronto and Oxford: Dundurn Press, 1989.

Castel, Albert. *The Presidency of Andrew Johnson*. Lawrence, Kansas: Regents Press of Kansas, 1979.

Catton, Bruce. *The Army of the Potomac: Mr. Lincoln's Army*. New York: Doubleday and Company, 1951.

Chewett, W.C. *The Fenian Raid into Canada*. Toronto: W.C. Chewett & Company, 1866.

Cohen, Victor. "Charles Sumner and the Trent Affair." *Journal of Southern History*. Vol. 22, no. 2 (May 1956).

Collins, Joseph Edmund. *Life and Times of the Right Honourable Sir John A. Macdonald: Premier of the Dominion of Canada*. 1883. Toronto: Rose Publishing, 1940.

Cook, Adrian. *The Alabama Claims: American Politics and Anglo-American Relations, 1865–1872*. Ithaca: Cornell University Press, 1975.

Cougle, Jim. *Canadian Blood, American Soil: The Story of Canada's Contribution to the American Civil War*. Fredericton: Civil War Heritage Society of Canada, 1994.

Cousins, Leone. "Letters of Norman Wade." *Nova Scotia Historical Quarterly*. Vol. 4, no. 2 (1974).

Creighton, Donald. *John A. Macdonald*. Vol. 1, *The Young Politician*. Toronto: MacMillan of Canada, 1952.

———. *John A. Macdonald*. Vol. 2, *The Old Chieftan*. Toronto: Macmillan of Canada, 1952.

———. "The United States and Canadian Confederation." *Canadian Historical Review*. Vol. 39, no. 3 (1958).

———. *The Road to Confederation*. Toronto: Macmillan of Canada, 1964.

Crook, D.P. *Diplomacy During the American Civil War*. New York: John Wiley and Sons, 1975.

Darroch, Lois. *Four Who Went to the Civil War*. Willowdale: Ampersand Press, 1985.

———. "Canadians in the American Civil War." *Ontario History*. Vol. 83, no. 1 (March 1991).

Davis, Jefferson. *Private Letters, 1823–1889*. Hudson Stode (ed.). New York: Harcourt Brace and World, 1966.

Davis, Varina. *Jefferson Davis: Ex-President of the Confederate States of America; A Memoir by his Wife*. Vol. 2. New York: Belford Company Publishers, 1890.

Davis, William. *Jefferson Davis: The Man and His Hour*. New York: HarperCollins, 1991.

De Kay, James T. *The Rebel Raiders*. New York: Ballantine, 2002.

Denison, Lt. Col. George T. *Soldiering in Canada: Recollections and Experiences*. Toronto: George N. Morang and Company, 1900.

Depew, Chauncey M. *My Memories of Eighty Years*. New York: Charles Scribner and Sons, 1924.

Desjardin, Thomas. *These Honored Dead: How the Story of Gettysburg Shaped American Memory*. Cambridge: Da Capo Press, 1993.

Doughty, Sir Arthur (ed.). *The Elgin-Grey Papers, 1846–1852*. Ottawa: King's Printer, 1957.

Early, Jubal. *A Memoir of the Last Year of the War for Independence in the Confederate States of America*. 1866. Columbia: University of South Carolina, 2001.

Edmonds, Sarah Emma. *Nurse and Spy in the Union Army: The Adventures and Experiences of a Woman in Hospitals, Camps and Battle-Fields*. Chicago: W.S. Williams & Co., 1865.

Edwards, Peter. *Delusion: The True Story of Victorian Superspy Henri Le Caron*. Toronto: Key Porter Books, 2008.

Eggleston, Larry. *Women in the Civil War: Extraordinary Stories of Soldiers, Spies, Nurses, Doctors, Crusaders, and Others*. Jefferson: McFarland and Company, 2003.

Errington, Jane. *The Lion, the Eagle, and Upper Canada: A Developing Colonial Ideology*. 2nd ed. Montreal and Kingston: McGill-Queen's University Press, 2012.

Fahs, Alice. "The Feminized Civil War: Gender, Northern Popular Literature, and the Memory of the War, 1861–1900." *Journal of American History*. Vol. 85, no. 4 (March 1999).

Fahrney, Ralph. *Horace Greeley and the Tribune in the Civil War*. Cambridge, Massachusetts: Da Capo Press, 1970.

Farr, D.M.L. *The Colonial Office and Canada, 1867–1887.* Toronto: University of Toronto Press, 1955.

Fehrenbacher, Don E. "The Anti-Lincoln Tradition." *Papers of the Abraham Lincoln Association.* Vol. 4 (1982).

Ferris, Norman. *Desperate Diplomacy: William H. Seward's Foreign Policy, 1861.* Knoxville: University of Tennessee Press, 1976.

———. *The Trent Affair: A Diplomatic Crisis.* Knoxville: University of Tennessee Press, 1977.

Foster, Frances Smith. *Witnessing Slavery: The Development of Anti-Bellum Slave Narratives.* Madison: University of Wisconsin Press, 1994.

Fox, William. *Regimental Losses in the American Civil War, 1861–1865. 1898.* Albany: Morningside Bookshop, 1974.

Foote, Shelby. *The Civil War: A Narrative.* 3 vols. New York: Vintage Books, 1986.

Foreman, Amanda. *A World on Fire: Britain's Crucial Role in the American Civil War.* New York: Random House, 2011.

Franklin, John Hope and Loren Schweninger. *Runaway Slaves: Rebels on the Plantation.* New York: Oxford University Press, 1999.

Freeman, Douglas Southall. *Lee: An Abridgement in One Volume.* New York: Touchstone Books, 1997.

Frohman, Charles. *Rebels on Lake Erie.* Columbus: Ohio Historical Society, 1965.

Frost, Karolyn Smardz. *I've Got a Home in Glory Land: A Lost Tale of the Underground Railroad.* Toronto: Thomas Allen Publishers, 2007.

Gaffen, Fred. *Cross-Border Warriors: Canadians in American Forces from the American Civil War until the Gulf.* Toronto: Dundurn Press, 1996.

Gansler, Laura Leedy. *The Mysterious Private Thompson: The Double Life of Sarah Emma Edmonds.* Lincoln: University of Nebraska Press, 2005.

Gara, Larry. *The Liberty Line: The Legend of the Underground Railroad.* Lexington: University Press of Kentucky, 1996.

Gates, Henry Louis, Jr. (ed.). *The Classic Slave Narratives.* New York: Penguin Books, 1987.

Gibson, Florence Elizabeth. *The Attitudes of the New York Irish Toward State and National Affairs, 1848–1892.* New York: Columbia University Press, 1951.

Gibson, J.A. "The Colonial Office View of Canadian Federation, 1856–1868." *Canadian Historical Review.* Vol. 35 (December 1954).

Glazebrook, G.P. de T. *A History of Canadian External Relations.* London: Oxford University Press, 1942.

Goodwin, Doris Kearns. *Team of Rivals: The Political Genius of Abraham Lincoln.* New York: Simon & Shuster, 2005.

Gould, Benjamin. *Investigations in the Military and Anthropological Statistics of American Soldiers.* 1869. New York: Arno Press, 1979.

Geary, James. *We Need Men: The Union Draft in the Civil War.* Dekalb: Northern Illinois University Press, 1991.

Gray, Wood. *The Hidden War: The Story of the Copperheads.* 1942. New York: Viking Press, 1964.

Gwyn, Richard, *John A: The Man Who Made Us.* Toronto: Vintage Books, 2007.

———. *Nation Maker: Sir John A. Macdonald; His Life, Our Times.* Vol. 2, *1867–1891.* Toronto: Random House Canada, 2011.

Hamer, Marguerite. "Luring Canadian Soldiers into Union Lines During the War Between the States." *Canadian Historical Review.* Vol. 27, no. 1 (March 1946).

Haviland, Laura. *A Woman's Life-work.* Cincinnati: L.S. Haviland, 1881.

Hazewell, Charles Creighton. "Assassination." July 1865. *The Atlantic Monthly Presents, Special Commemorative Issue.* (March 2012).

Headley, John William. *Confederate Operations in Canada and New York.* New York and Washington: Neale Publishing Company, 1906.

Hitsman, J.M. "Winter Troop Movements to Canada, 1862." *Canadian Historical Review.* Vol. 43, no. 2 (1962).

Horan, James D. *Confederate Agent: A Dictionary in History.* New York: Crown, 1954.

Hoy, Claire. *Canadians in the Civil War.* Toronto: McArthur & Company, 2004.

Hummel, Jeffrey Rogers. *Emancipating Slaves, Enslaving Free Men: A History of the American Civil War.* Chicago: Carus Publishing, 1996.

Jenkins, Brian. *Fenians and Anglo-American Relations during Reconstruction.* Ithaca and London: Cornell University Press, 1969.

Jones, Preston. "Civil War, Culture War: French Quebec and the American War Between the States." *Catholic Historical Review.* Vol. 87, no. 1 (January 2001).

Kauffman, Michael W. *American Brutus: John Wilkes Booth and the Lincoln Conspiracies.* New York: Random House, 2004.

Kendall, John C. "The New York City Press and Anti-Canadianism: A New Perspective on the Civil War Years." *Journalism Quarterly.* Vol. 52 (1975).

Klement, Frank. *The Limits of Dissent: Clement L. Vallandigham and the Civil War.* Lexington: University Press of Kentucky, 1970.

Knox, Bruce. "The Rise of Colonial Federation as an Object of British Policy." *Journal of British Studies.* Vol. 2, no. 1 (November 1971).

———. "Conservative Imperialism, 1858–1874: Bulwer-Lytton, Lord Carnarvon and Canadian Confederation." *International History Review.* Vol. 6, no. 3 (August 1984).

Lamontagne, Léopold, "The Ninth Crusade." *Canadian Historical Review.* Vol. 32 (September 1951).

Landon, Fred. "The Trent Affair of 1861." *Canadian Historical Review.* Vol. 3 (March 1922).

———. "The Negro Migration to Canada after the Passing of the Fugitive Slave Act." *Journal of Negro History.* Vol. 5, no. 1 (1920).

———. "Canadian Opinion of Southern Secession, 1860–1861." *Canadian Historical Review.* Vol.1, no. 3 (1920).

———. "Canadian Negroes and the John Brown Raid." *The Journal of Negro History.* Vol. 6, no. 2 (April 1921).

———. "The Anderson Fugitive Case." *The Journal of Negro History.* Vol. 7, no. 3 (July 1922).

Lawless, J.M.S. *Canada: A Story of Challenge.* 1953. Toronto: Macmillan of Canada,1970.

Lawson, Murray. "Canada and the Articles of Confederation." *American Historical Review.* Vol. 58, no. 1 (October 1952).

Leonard, Elizabeth. *All the Daring of the Soldier: Women of the Civil War Armies.* New York: W.W. Norton, 1999.

LeRoy, Graf P. (ed.). *The Papers of Andrew Johnson.* Vol. 7, *1864–1865.* Knoxville: University of Tennessee Press, 1986.

Lonn, Ella. *Desertions During the Civil War.* New York: Greenwood Press, 1928.

———. *Foreigners in the Union Army and Navy.* New York: Greenwood Press, 1969.

Macdonald, J.A. *Troublous Times in Canada.* Toronto: Johnston, 1910.

MacDonald, Helen. *Canadian Public Opinion in the American Civil War.* 1926. New York: Columbia University Press, 1974.

Mahin, Dean B. *One War at a Time: The International Dimensions of the American Civil War.* Washington: Brassey's, 2000.

Martin, Ged. "Launching Canadian Confederation: Means to Ends, 1836–1864." *Historical Journal.* Vol. 27, no. 3 (September 1984).

Marquis, Greg. *In Armageddon's Shadow: The Civil War and Canada's Maritime Provinces.* Montreal-Kingston: McGill-Queen's University Press, 2000.

McPherson, James. *Battle Cry of Freedom.* New York: Oxford University Press. 1988.

———. *What They Fought For, 1861–1865.* Baton Rouge: Louisiana State University Press, 1994.

———. *Tried by War: Abraham Lincoln as Commander in Chief.* New York: Penguin Press, 2008.

———. *For Cause and Comrades: Why Men Fought in the Civil War.* New York: Oxford University Press, 1997.

Milani, L.D. "Four Who Went to the Civil War." *Ontario History.* Vol. 51, no . 4 (1959).

Mitchell, Joseph B. *Decisive Battles of the Civil War.* New York: Fawcett Books, 1955.

Mitchell, Reid. *Civil War Soldiers.* Markham: Viking Penguin, 1988.

Moore, Christopher. *1867: How the Fathers Made a Deal.* Toronto: McClelland & Stewart, 1997.

Morton, W.L. *The Critical Years: The Union of British North America, 1857–1873.* Toronto: Oxford University Press, 1964.

Moxley, Andrew, and Tom Brooks. "Drums Across the Border: Canadians in the Civil War." *Canadian Military Then and Now.* Vol 1, no. 6 (November 1991).

Murdock, Eugene C. "New York's Civil War Bounty Hunters." *The Journal of American History*. Vol. 53, no. 2 (September 1966).

———. *Patriotism Limited, 1861–1865: The Civil War Draft and the Bounty System*. Kent, Ohio: Kent State University Press, 1967.

Myers, Phillip. *Caution and Cooperation: The American Civil War in British-American Relations*. Kent, Ohio: Kent State University Press, 2008.

Neidhardt, W.S. "The Fenian Brotherhood and Western Ontario." *Ontario History*. Vol. 60 (1968).

———. "The Fenian Trials in the Province of Canada, 1866–1867." *Ontario History*. Vol. 66 (1974).

———. *Fenianism in North America*. University Park: Pennsylvania State University, 1975.

Neunherz, Richard. "Hemmed In: Reactions in British Columbia to the Purchase of Russian America." *Pacific Northwest Quarterly*. Vol. 8, no. 3 (July, 1989).

Nevins, Allan. *Hamilton Fish: The Inner History of the Grant Administration*. 1936. New York: Dodd, Mead & Company, 1957.

O 'Brien, Connor Cruise. *The Great Melody*. Chicago: University of Chicago Press, 1992.

Oates, Stephen. *With Malice Toward None: The Life of Abraham Lincoln*. New York: Mentor, 1977.

Ormsby, W.G. "Letters to Galt concerning the Maritime Provinces and Confederation." *Canadian Historical Review*. Vol. 24, no. 2 (June 1953).

Overman, W.D. (ed.). "Some Letters of Joshua R. Giddings on Reciprocity." *Canadian Historical Review*. Vol. 16 (September 1935).

Paolino, Ernest. *The Foundations of the American Empire: William Henry Seward and United States Foreign Policy*. Ithaca: Cornell University Press, 1972.

Perret, Geoffrey. *Ullysses S. Grant: Soldier and President*. New York: Random House, 1997.

Peterson, Robert, and John Hudson. "Foreign Recruitment for Union Forces." *Civil War History*. Vol. 7 (1961).

Pierce, E.L. *Memoir and Letters of Charles Sumner*, Vol. 4. 1893. Charleston: Nabu Press, 2011.

Pitch, Anthony S. *They Have Killed Papa Dead! The Road to Ford's Theatre, Abraham Lincoln's Murder and the Rage for Vengeance*. Hanover: Steerforth Press, 2008.

Pitman, Benn. *The Assassination of President Lincoln and the Trial of the Conspirators*. 1865. Clark, New Jersey: Law Book Exchange Ltd., 2006.

Porter, Kenneth W. *The Black Seminoles: History of a Freedom-Seeking People*. Gainesville: University of Florida Press, 1996.

Pope, Joseph. *Documents on the Confederation of British North America: A Compilation based on Joseph Pope's Confederation Documents Supplemented by Other Official Material*. Toronto: McClelland and Stewart, 1969.

Preece, Rod. "The Political Wisdom of Sir John A. Macdonald." *Canadian Journal of Political Science*. Vol. 17, no. 3 (September 1984).

Raddall, Thomas. *Halifax: Warden of the North*. Garden City: Doubleday & Company, 1965.

Raney, William F. "Recruiting and Crimping in Canada for the Northern Forces, 1861–1865." *Mississippi Valley Historical Review*. Vol. 10, no. 1 (June 1923).

Rasmussen, Daniel. *American Uprising: The Untold Story of America's Largest Slave Revolt*. New York: HarperCollins, 2011.

Reinders, Robert C. "The John Anderson Case, 1860-1: A Study in Anglo-Canadian Imperial Relations." *Canadian Historical Review*. Vol. 57, no. 4 (December 1975).

Riddell, William Renwick. "The Fugitive Slave in Upper Canada." *Journal of Negro History*. Vol. 5, no. 3 (July 1920).

———. *Benjamin Franklin and Canada: Benjamin Franklin's Mission to Canada and the Causes of Its Failure*. Toronto: University of Toronto Press, 1923.

Ridley, Jasper. *Lord Palmerston*. London: Constable Press, 1970.

Robson, Maureen M. "The 'Alabama' Claims and Anglo-American Reconciliation, 1865–71." *Canadian Historical Review*. Vol. 42, no. 4 (1961).

Robertson, James. *Soldiers Blue and Gray*. Boston: Warner Books, 1991.

Rorabaugh, W.J. "Who Fought for the North in the Civil War? Concord, Massachusetts, Enlistments." *Journal of American History*. Vol. 73, no. 3 (December 1986).

Rozwene, Edwin (ed.). *Causes of the Civil War*. Boston: D.C. Heath and Company, 1963.

Sandburg, Carl. *Abraham Lincoln: The Prairie Years and the War Years*. New York: Harcourt, Brace and Company, 1954.

Saunders, E.M. *The Life and Letters of the Right Honorable Sir Charles Tupper*. London: Cassell and Company, 1916.

Shi, David. "Seward's Attempt to Annex British Columbia, 1865–1869." *Pacific Historical Review*. Vol. 47, no. 2 (May 1978).

Shippee, Lester B. *Canadian-American Relations*. New Haven: Yale University Press, 1939.

Singleton, Robard. "Resistance to Black Republican Domination." Edwin Rozwene (ed.). *Causes of the Civil War*. Boston: D.C. Heath and Company, 1963.

Simpson, Brooks et al. (eds.). *The Civil War: The First Year by Those Who Lived It*. New York: Library of America, 2011.

Skelton, Oscar D. *The Life and Times of Alexander Galt*. Toronto: Oxford University Press, 1920.

Slattery, T.P. *The Assassination of Thomas D'Arcy McGee*. Toronto: Doubleday Canada, 1968.

Slavicek, Louise Chipley. *Women and the Civil War*. New York: Chelsea House, 2009.

Smith, Goldwyn. *The Treaty of Washington, 1871: A Study in Imperial History*. Ithaca: Cornell University Press, 1941.

Smith, Bethania Meradith. "Civil War Subversives." *Journal of the Illinois State Historical Society*. Vol. 45, no. 3 (Autumn 1952).

Smith, Theodore Clark. "Expansion After the Civil War, 1865–1871." *Political Science Quarterly*. Vol. 16, no. 3 (September 1901).

Snell, J.G. "John F. Potter, Consul General to British North America, 1864–1865" *Wisconsin Magazine of History*. Vol. 55, no. 2 (Winter 1971–72).

Spencer, W.F. *The Confederate Navy in Europe*. Tuscaloosa: University of Alabama, 1983.

Stacey, C.P. "Fenianism and the Rise of National Feeling in Canada at the Time of Confederation." *Canadian Historical Review*. Vol. 12 (September 1931).

———. "Britain's Withdrawal from North America 1864–1871." *Canadian Historical Review*. Vol. 36, no. 3 (September 1955).

———. *Canada and the British Army, 1846–1871*. Toronto: University of Toronto Press, 1963.

Stahr, Walter. *Seward: Lincoln's Indispensable Man*. New York: Simon & Shuster, 2012.

Stampp, Kenneth *Peculiar Institution: Slavery in the Ante-Bellum South*. New York: Alfred A. Knopf, 1956.

Stewart, James Brewer. "From Moral Suasion to Political Confrontation." David W. Blight (ed.). *The Underground Railroad in History and Memory: Passages to Freedom*. New York: HarperCollins, 2004.

Surdam, David George. *Northern Naval Superiority and the Economics of the American Civil War*. Columbia: University of South Carolina Press, 2001.

Sweet, H. (ed.). *The Jurist*. January 19, 1861. Vol. 7, pt. 2. London: Hodges and Smith and Company, 1862.

Taylor, Alan. *The Civil War of 1812: American Citizens, British Subjects, Irish Rebels, and Indian Allies*. New York: Alfred A. Knopf, 2010.

Taylor, John M. *William Henry Seward: Lincoln's Right Hand Man*. New York: HarperCollins, 1991.

Teatero, William. *John Anderson Fugitive Slave*. Toronto: Slave Treasure Island Books Publication, 1986.

Tenney, William Jewett. *The Military and Naval History of the Rebellion in the United States*. New York: D. Appleton & Company, 1867.

Tidwell, William, James Hall, and David Winfred Gaddy. *Come Retribution: The Confederate Secret Service and the Assassination of Lincoln*. Ann Arbor: University of Michigan Press, 1988.

Trevelyan, G.M. *British History in the Nineteenth Century, 1815–1914*. London: 1950.

Twatio, Bill. "The Freedom Fighters." *National Post*. February 14, 2012.

Twelvetrees, Harper (ed.). *The Story of the Life of John Anderson: The Fugitive Slave*. London: W. Tweedie, 1863.

United States War Department. *The War of Rebellion: A Compilation of the Official Records of the Union and Confederate Armies*. Washington, D.C.: U.S. Government Printing Office, 1880–1901.

———. *List of Pensioners on the Roll*. January 1, 1883. Washington, D.C.: U.S. Government Printing Office, 1883.

Van Deusen, Glyndon G. *William Henry Seward*. New York: Oxford University Press, 1967.

Wade, Norman. "Letters of Norman Wade." Leone Cousins (ed.). *Nova Scotia Historical Quarterly*. Vol. 4, no. 2 (1974).

Wafer, Francis. M. *A Surgeon in the Army of the Potomac*. Cheryl Wells (ed.). Montreal and Kingston: McGill-Queen's University Press, 2008

Waite, P.B. *The Life and Times of Confederation, 1864–1867: Politics, Newspapers, and the Union of British North America*. Toronto: University of Toronto Press, 1962.

———. *Confederation Debates in the Province of Canada, 1865*. Toronto: McClelland & Stewart, 1963.

Walker, James. *A History of Blacks in Canada*. Ottawa: Ministry of State and Multiculturalism, 1980.

Walrond, Theodore (ed.). *Earl of Elgin: Letters and Journals of James, Eighth Earl of Elgin*. London: John Murray Press, 1872.

Warren, Donald. *The Idea of Continental Union: Agitation for the Annexation of Canada to the United States, 1849–1893*. Lexington: University of Kentucky Press, 1960.

Warren, Gordon. *Fountain of Discontent: The Trent Affair and Freedom of the Seas*. Boston: Northeastern University Press, 1981.

Warren, Robert Penn. *Jefferson Davis Gets His Citizenship Back*. Lexington: University Press of Kentucky, 1980.

Wayne, Michael. "The Black Population of Canada West on the Eve of the American Civil War: A Reassessment Based on the Manuscript Census of 1861." *Histoire sociale / Social History*. Vol. 28, no. 56 (1995).

Weber, Jennifer. *The Rise and Fall of Lincoln's Opponents in the North*. New York: Oxford University Press, 2006.

White, Ronald. *A. Lincoln: A Biography*. New York: Random House, 2009.

Wickett, S. Morely. "Canadians in the United States." *Annals of the American Academy of Political and Social Science*. Vol. 45, *Canadian National Problems*. January 1913.

Wilgus, William, *The Railway Interrelations of the United States and Canada*. New Haven: Yale Press, 1937.

Williams, David. *A People's History of the Civil War: Struggles for the Meaning of Freedom*. New York: The New Press, 2006.

Williams, Robert Chadwell. *Horace Greeley: Champion of American Freedom*. New York: New York University Press, 2006.

Wilson, David A. *Thomas D'Arcy McGee*. Vol. 2, *The Extreme Moderate, 1857–1868*. Montreal and Kingston: McGill-Queen's University Press, 2011.

Winks, Robin. *The Civil War Years: Canada and the United States*. 1960. Montreal: Harvest House, 1998.

———. *The Blacks in Canada*. Montreal and Kingston: McGill-Queen's University Press, 1997.

ACKNOWLEDGEMENTS

My mother's voracious reading and her fascination with documentaries and current events stirred my interest in politics and the past. Later, historians Donald Creighton and J.M.S. Careless turned that interest to passion, convincing me that Canada's story was fun and rich with fascinating characters. Bruce Catton introduced me to the Civil War, and then, on so many of my visits to Gettysburg, the encyclopedic knowledge of battlefield guide Ed Guy inspired me to learn more. Shelby Foote, Ken Burns and James McPherson took me deeper into the war's beguiling world. The overarching lesson I have learned is not just that history is interesting but that it's important. I have come to believe that the only way we can understand where we are, and have any sense of where we should go is to know where we have been. Otherwise we are condemned to stumble along as amnesiacs, constantly confused, surprised and gullible. To all who encouraged, instructed and provoked new questions, I am grateful.

I owe a debt to many talented people at the Trent University and Queen's University libraries, the Archives of Ontario in Toronto and Library and Archives Canada in Ottawa. Their professionalism and skill at helping me access their materials, and their willingness to bring more from elsewhere, were invaluable. Thank you to Ken Armstrong, Pete O'Grady and James Arnett, who volunteered source material.

I am indebted to Princeton's James McPherson, University of Waterloo's Debra Nash-Chambers and Jane Errington of Queen's University. Each combed an early draft for factual errors and made helpful suggestions. The editing skills of Lisa Clark, Linda Pruessen, Caleb Snider, Jane McWhinney and Craig Pyette all improved my often sloppy prose.

Daphne Hart of the Helen Heller Agency is my hard-working literary agent and I am grateful for her ongoing support and encouragement. I am grateful as well to Knopf Canada publisher Anne Collins for seeing merit in the book and to Craig Pyette who, with Amanda Betts, shepherded it through its many stages. I thank everyone involved at Random House of Canada Ltd. and Random House Inc. in the United States, as well.

Partners of authors all agree that living with a writer is not easy. My greatest debt is owed to my dear wife, Sue, who lost me for hours and sometimes days when I time-travelled back to the nineteenth century and occasionally had trouble getting all the way home. To Sue I owe everything.

PHOTO CREDITS

John Anderson, The Story of the Life of John Anderson, the Fugitive Slave, ed. Harper Twelvetrees, London 1865; *William Henry Seward*, Prints and Photographs Division, Library of Congress, LC-USZ62-21907; *Sarah Emma Edmonds*, Library and Archives Canada, Frank Thompson: Her Civil War Story, AMICUS 11061614 nlc-10242; *Hon. Jacob Thompson of Miss.* from the Brady-Handy Collection, Prints and Photographs Division, Library of Congress, LC-DIG-cwpbh-02851; *George Brown*, Library and Archives Canada, Hunter & Co., Canadian Intellectual Property Office fonds C-009553; *Sir John A. Macdonald* from the Brady-Handy Collection, Prints and Photographs Division, Library of Congress, LC-USZ62-122757

INDEX

Abbott, Anderson, 26
Abbott, John C., 184, 192
Abbott, Wilson, 26
abolitionists
    disappointed by Lincoln, 8, 166
    increasing activity by, 18, 20–25, 27–29,
        37, 50, 56–57
    Southern resentment of, 6, 10, 17, 33,
        39, 54, 91, 177
Adams, Charles Francis Jr., 78, 81, 93–94,
    156, 226, 266, 290–91, 303
Adams, Henry, 81
Adams, John, 3
Alabama (Confederate warship), claims
    surrounding, 290–92, 294–304
Alaska, 292–93
Alien Act (1865; Canada), 226, 285
Anderson, John, 10, 204, 304
    biography of, 19–23, 31–33
    described, 14–15
    extradition trial, 16–17, 35–44, 54–56,
        58
    historical importance, 44–54
    life after being cleared, 56–58
Anderson, Marie (wife of John), 20, 32, 58
Anderson, Osborne, 30
Anderson, Peter, 130–31
Anderson, Robert, 67–68, 70
Andrew, John, 80
Andrews, Israel, 76
anti-slavery societies, 28
Archibald, Adams George, 232
Arnold, Benedict, 3
Arnold, Samuel, 242, 254

Ashmun, George, 75–76, 89, 98, 162, 235
Atzerodt, George, 242–43, 254

Baker, Lafayette, 242
Baker, Luther, 244
Banks, Nathaniel, 275–76
Baring, Alexander, 35
Barton, Clara, 110
Bates, James, 189–91, 286
battles, Civil War (U.S.). *See also* the Civil
        War (U.S.)
    Antietam, 130–31, 259
    Bull Run. *See* Manassas *below*
    Cold Harbor, 174, 209
    Fredericksburg, 131–32, 149, 259
    Gettysburg, 2, 133–35, 148–51, 206,
        211, 271, 286–87, 291
    Manassas (First and Second), 81–84, 97,
        107, 110, 122, 126, 130–31, 165, 235
    New Orleans, 130, 187
    Petersburg, 135, 185, 233, 287
    Vicksburg, 133, 150–51, 161, 206, 291
    the Wilderness, 135, 174, 209
    Williamsburg, 125, 135
Beall, John, 170–72, 189, 193, 228, 230,
        252–53,
Beatty, James, 97
Beauregard, P.G.T., 82, 126, 161
Belleau, Narcisse, 256
Benjamin, Judah, 160–61, 227
Bernard, Susan Agnes, 284
Bibb, Henry, 22, 29
Bismarck, Otto von, 66, 209, 249
Black, Jeremiah, 169

JOHN BOYKO is the author of four previous books, including the critically acclaimed *Bennett: The Rebel Who Challenged and Changed a Nation* and *Last Steps to Freedom: The Evolution of Canadian Racism*. Called by the *Globe and Mail* "a distinguished scholar of Canadian political history" and praised by the *Winnipeg Free Press* for his "encyclopedic knowledge of Canadian history," John Boyko has earned degrees from Queen's, Trent and McMaster universities. He is a former dean of history and currently an administrator at Lakefield College School, and an op-ed contributor to newspapers across Canada. He lives in Lakefield, Ontario.